# QUAKERS, POLITICS, AND ECONOMICS

Quakers and the Disciplines:
Volume 5

Edited by:
David R. Ross and Michael T. Snarr

# Quakers
## *and the*
# Disciplines

**Full Media Services**
http://www.fullmediaservices.com

**Friends Association for Higher Education**
http://www.quakerfahe.org

**Volume 1.**
Quaker Perspectives in Higher Education
May 2014

**Volume 2.**
Befriending Truth: Quaker Perspectives
June 2015

**Volume 3.**
Quakers and Literature
June 2016

**Volume 4.**
Quakers, Business, and Industry
June 2017

**Volume 5.**
Quakers, Politics, and Economics
June 2018

Longmeadow, MA | Philadelphia, PA | Windsor, CT

**Quakers and the Disciplines Editorial Committee:**

Paul Anderson
(Series Editor, 2014-Present)

Donn Weinholtz
Abigail E. Adams
Ben Pink Dandelion
Barbara Addison
Don Smith
Jean Mulhern
Stephen W. Angell

As a venture of the Friends Association for Higher Education, the Quakers and the Disciplines series gathers collections of essays featuring the contributions of Quakers to one or more of the academic disciplines. Noting historic values embraced within the Religious Society of Friends regarding particular fields of inquiry, each volume includes essays highlighting contributions by Quakers as means of addressing the needs of contemporary society. Each volume is designed to be serviceable within classroom and other discussion settings, fostering explorations of how pressing issues of the day might be addressed with creativity and passionate concern, informed by a rich heritage of faith, discovery, and action.

## ACKNOWLEDGMENTS

We wish to thank several people who made possible this volume about Quakers and their involvement in politics and economics. Our sincere gratitude goes to all the contributors whose hard work and keen research skills make this valuable information available to the public. We are also extremely grateful to Emma Marks for reading and commenting on every aspect of this book; and Keni Brown for copyediting suggestions on multiple chapters.

# CONTENTS

i. List of Contributors.................................................................xi
ii. Introduction, **Tom Head**.................................................1

## Part I: Theorising Quakers and Enterprise
1. Quakers and Capitalism: A History of Paradoxes,
   **Steve Dale Davison**.................................................10
2. Thomas Kelly on "The Eternal Now and Social Concern,"
   **Ron Rembert**.................................................37

   Discussion Questions.................................................51

## Part II: Perspectives on Contemporary Economic Issues
3. How the Nordics' Experience with Economics Affirms and Challenges
   Friends, **George Lakey**.................................................53
4. Governing the World from the Ground Up Through Power Grounded
   in the Light: A Proposal for Action Research on Quaker and Gandhian
   Responses to our Global Crises, **Gray Cox**.................................................71
5. Responsibility in Business: What Can We Learn from the Quakers?
   **Nicholas Burton** and **Alex Hope** .................................................91

   Discussion Questions.................................................117

## Part III: Contributions and Challenges of Quaker Organizations
6. Quakers in the Coalfields: Economic Justice and the American Friends
   Committee, 1920-Present, **Paul Moke**.................................................120
7. Working in Congress to End Poverty: Looking for Answers in All the
   Wrong Places, **Ruth Flower**.................................................144
8. Linking Politics, Economics and Friends Around the World: The Work
   of Quakers at the United Nations,
   **Lori Heninger** and **David Atwood**.................................................168
9. Fifty Years of Right Sharing: A Brief History of the Right Sharing of
   World Resources Program, **Steve Dale Davison**.................................................189

   Discussion Questions.................................................212

## Part IV: Historical Engagement by Friends

10. The Radical Hicksite Critique of the Emerging Capitalist Order: Cornelius C. Blatchly, Benjamin Webb, and Friends, 1827-1833, **Tom Hamm**............................................................214

11. Conflict between Friends: Southern African Quakers' Critique of AFSC's Approach to End Apartheid, **Robynne Rogers Healey**......235

    Discussion Questions.................................................261

## Part V: Contributions by Prominent Quakers

12. John Bellers and the Evolutionary Potential of Quakerism, **Keith Helmuth**.............................................................263

13. John Woolman and Economics: "A Feeling Knowledge" of "the Connection of Things," **Mike Heller**.....................................283

14. John Wooman and Land, **Geoffrey Plank**.........................304

15. Lucretia Coffin Mott: A Rebel for Social Change, **Jean Mulhern** and **Cathy Pitzer**.................................322

16. Kenneth and Elise Boulding: Friends for Peace and Betterment, **Robert Scott** and **Russell Boulding**.............................344

    Discussion Questions.................................................373

Index.....................................................................374

## LIST OF CONTRIBUTORS

**David Atwood** was the Representative for Disarmament and Peace at the Quaker United Nations Office in Geneva from 1995 to 2011. He also served as QUNO's director from 2004 to 2011. He is retired but continues to work as a consultant on peace and security concerns, principally with the Small Arms Survey (Geneva). He is a native of North Carolina and received a Ph.D. in Political Science from the University of North Carolina-Chapel Hill in 1982. He has lived in Europe since 1978. Prior to moving to Geneva, he was Tutor in Peace Studies at Woodbrooke in Birmingham (UK) from 1978 to 1988 and General Secretary of the International Fellowship of Reconciliation from 1988 to 1994. He currently lives in Paris.

**J. Russell Boulding,** the oldest son of Kenneth and Elise Boulding, is a retired environmental consultant who specialized in soil and groundwater contamination assessment and prevention, and is the author of more than 200 books, chapters, articles, and consultant reports. In 1973 he assisted Kenneth and Elise in the development of their jointly taught course The Global System of the Planet Earth. In the late 1980s he assisted in organizing and editing Elise's One Small Plot of Heaven. In retirement he enjoys living on a 36-acre homestead near Bloomington, Indiana, that includes his wife, daughter, and three grandchildren, and activities as an independent scholar pursuing geologic research and projects that help make his parent's work available to a new generation of scholars and activists.

**Nicholas Burton, Ph.D.** is a Senior Lecturer in Strategic Management and Corporate Responsibility at Northumbria University. Nicholas is a member of Pickering & Hull Area Meeting, and publishes in the area of Quakers & Business. Nicholas is a Director and Trustee of Bootham School in York, and is a member of Quakers & Business, convening the Academic Research Working Group. Currently working on a number of projects funded by the Quaker community investigating Quaker practices and business, and the Quaker Business Method, Nicholas is also an associate tutor at Woodbrooke Quaker Study Centre. In a broader management perspective, Nicholas co-chairs the British Academy of Management Strategy group.

**Gray Cox** is a professor of philosophy, peace studies, and language learning at College of the Atlantic, a school for human ecology in Bar Harbor, Maine. His works include articles on artificial intelligence, Gandhi, and ethics, and three books: *The Ways of Peace: A Philosophy of Peace as Action*; *The Will at the Crossroads: A Reconstruction of Kant's Moral Philosophy*; and *A Quaker Approach to Research: Collaborative Practice and Communal Discernment*. He is a founding member and current Clerk of the Quaker Institute for the Future. He is a singer/songwriter with albums in English, Spanish, and French. He is currently writing a musical for spirit-led social change, "Fire in the Commons," which draws on thirty years of experience leading Imaging a World Without Weapons Workshops.

**Steven Dale Davison** is the author of The Gathered Meeting, Pendle Hill Pamphlet #444, and of two blogs, Through the Flaming Sword: Exploring Quaker Spirituality, Faith & Practice (throughtheflamingsword.wordpress.com), and BibleMonster: Contemporary issues under the light of a radical Bible (biblemonster.com), now suspended. He was Rutgers University's first Studies in Religion BA graduate and is a recipient of Earlham School of Religion's Patrick D. Henry Scholarship for Christian Writers. He is currently working on a book on Quakers and Capitalism: Being a reflective history of Quaker contributions to capitalist culture and of Friends' critique of its social consequences through the twentieth century and some proposals for a living testimony on economic justice. He recently retired as New York Yearly Meeting's communications director.

**Ruth Flower** recently retired from the Friends Committee on National Legislation (FCNL), and is continuing as a consultant on Native American policy. Ruth joined FCNL's staff in 1981 and served until 1996 as the lobbyist on domestic policy (poverty, federal budget, immigration, criminal justice, Native American issues, civil rights, and campaign finance issues). After heading the Government Relations Office of the American Association of University Professors for ten years, she returned to FCNL as Legislative Director in 2006 until her retirement in 2016. Ruth received her bachelors and juris doctor degrees from the University of California. She is a member of Adelphi Friends Meeting in Maryland, and has been active on committees in Baltimore Yearly Meeting, and on the board of Friends House Retirement Community in Sandy Spring, Maryland.

**Thomas D. Hamm** is professor of history and director of special collections at Earlham College, where he has taught since 1987. He received his Ph.D. in history from Indiana University in 1985. He is a member of West Richmond Meeting in the New Association of Friends. He is the author of numerous books and articles on aspects of Quaker history. This essay is part of a book-length work on Hicksite Friends in the nineteenth century.

**Tom Head** is Professor of Economics at George Fox University in Newberg, Oregon, where he has taught for over forty years. His Quaker journey began at the time of the Vietnam War when he sought and received a discharge from the military as a conscientious objector. He is a member of Bridge City Friends Meeting in Portland, Oregon and has been actively involved with a number of Quaker organizations including the Friends Association for Higher Education, the American Friends Service Committee, the Quaker United Nations Offices in both New York and Geneva, and the Quaker Institute for the Future. His current research and writing focuses on the broad theme of world religions and the global economy.

**Robynne Rogers Healey** (PhD, University of Alberta) is professor of history and co-director of the Gender Studies Institute at Trinity Western University in Langley, British Columbia. She convenes the Conference of Quaker Historians and Archivists and is publications chair for the Canadian Friends Historical Association. Her publications include chapters in *The Cambridge Companion of Quakerism* (CUP, 2018), *Early Quakers and Their Theology* (CUP, 2015), *The Oxford Handbook of Quaker Studies* (OUP, 2013), *American Churches and the First World War* (Pickwick, 2016), *Canadian Churches and the First World War* (Pickwick, 2014), and the book *From Quaker to Upper Canadian: Faith and Community Among Yonge Street Friends, 1801-1850* (MQUP, 2006).

**Mike Heller** is a Professor of English at Roanoke College, Salem, VA, where he teaches courses in Peace and Justice Studies as well as spiritual autobiography and American Literature. He is a member of the Roanoke Quaker Meeting. He has edited or co-edited books on Mahatma Gandhi and John Woolman, including *The Tendering Presence: Essays on John Woolman* (Pendle Hill Publications, 2003), and Pendle Hill Pamphlet 389, "From West Point to Quakerism." He and his wife Rebecca A. Heller live in Roanoke, Virginia, not far from their two children, their spouses, and six grandchildren.

**Keith Helmuth** is a founding trustee of Quaker Institute for the Future, serving as its first Board Secretary and Coordinator of Publications. He is the author of *Tracking Down Ecological Guidance* and the co-author of *Paths of Faith in the Landscape of Science* and *Right Relationship: Building a Whole Earth Economy*. He taught environmental studies and community economic development at Friends World College in the 1960s. He operated a small farm and market garden business in the St. John Valley of New Brunswick for almost three decades. He lives in Woodstock, NB and is currently the Publisher and Managing Editor of Chapel Street Editions. He is a member of New Brunswick Friends Meeting (Canadian Yearly Meeting).

**Lori Heninger**, Ph.D., is the Executive Director of the Montclair Fund for Women. Lori has decades-long experience working in and leading nonprofits in the U.S. and internationally, and is passionate about the creation of a better world through excellence in organizational structure, planning and managing. Her recent book, *Managing As Mission: Nonprofit Managing For Sustainable Change*, is published by CRC Press. Dr. Heninger has worked in over 30 countries in both humanitarian and development contexts, and was Co-Director of the Quaker UN Office. She is a member of Shrewsbury Meeting in New Jersey. Lori received her BA in Education from Kean University, her Masters in Social Work from Columbia University and her Ph.D. in Social Welfare from New York's City University Graduate Center. Lori is happily married, has one child (of whom she is very proud), two dogs and two cats. She lives in New Jersey.

**Alex Hope**, Ph.D., is Associate Professor of Business Ethics at Newcastle Business School, Northumbria University. He undertakes teaching, research, and consultancy across topics such as responsible business, sustainable development, corporate social responsibility, energy policy, and business ethics. He is currently Director of Student Satisfaction and Engagement and leads the school's Responsible Management Education project. Alongside his work at Newcastle Business School, Alex is an Associate Lecturer at the Open University tutoring Environmental Management modules, is Vice-Chair of the United Nations Principles of Responsible Management Education (UN PRME) steering group, and Co-Chair of the UN PRME Climate Change and Environment working group. He holds a Ph.D. in Sustainable Development and BSc (Hons) in Environmental Management. Prior to his academic career, Alex worked in retail management, local government and as a sustainability consultant.

**George Lakey** is an activist-sociologist, writer, and trainer who has taught at Woodbrooke and Pendle Hill, Haverford College, the University of Pennsylvania, and most recently served as Eugene M. Lang Professor for Issues of Social Change at Swarthmore College. In 2010 he was named "Peace Educator of the Year" by the Peace and Justice Studies Association. His nine books have all been about change and how to achieve it. His first arrest was for a sit-in during the civil rights movement; more recently he was arrested in the successful Quaker campaign to stop PNC Bank from financing mountaintop-removal coal mining. He has co-founded and led a number of organizations, both Quaker and non-Quaker, and led over 1500 workshops on five continents. His home Meeting is Central Philadelphia.

**Jean Mulhern** recently retired from the S. Arthur Watson Library, Wilmington College (Ohio), where she was the director after previously serving for 23 years as the library director at Wilberforce University. At Wilmington she worked with Dr. T. Canby Jones to organize and preserve his papers and with Dr. D. Neil Snarr to digitally preserve Quaker historical documents held in private collections. She earned her Ph.D. in leadership in Higher Education from the University of Dayton with previous degrees from Kent State University and Heidelberg University (Ohio). She continues to be active in historical and genealogical research and as a library consultant.

**Paul Moke** is Professor of Political Science and Criminal Justice at Wilmington College in Wilmington, Ohio. His educational background includes an M.A. in social science from the University of Chicago, a J.D. from the Ohio State University College of Law, and a Ph.D. in political science from the University of Cincinnati. He is the author of *Earl Warren and the Struggle for Justice* as well as several law review articles on voting rights and judicial selection. His interest in Appalachian history arises from his family roots in the region as well as field research he conducted in McDowell County West Virginia in 2014.

**Cathy Pitzer** recently retired from Wilmington College (Ohio) where she taught sociology. During her eighteen years of teaching she designed many innovative projects to encourage students to engage with their local communities in courses such as Society and Business and Rural Sociology. She holds degrees from the University of Pennsylvania and Emory University and is on the Executive Board of the Friends Association for Higher Education. She is currently an agricultural researcher for the U.S Department of Agriculture in southern Ohio. She is an avid golfer and reader of mystery novels.

**Geoffrey Plank** is Professor of Early Modern History at the University of East Anglia. He is the author of *John Woolman's Path to the Peaceable Kingdom: A Quaker in the British Empire* (University of Pennsylvania Press, 2012), and co-editor, with Brycchan Carey, of *Quakers and Abolition* (University of Illinois Press, 2014). He is currently studying the role of warfare in shaping the early modern Atlantic World.

**Ron Rembert** serves as Professor of Religion/Philosophy at Wilmington College where he has been teaching since 1989. Arriving at Wilmington, he grew interested in Thomas Kelly from hearing the college's institutional history and memorable stories shared by T. Canby Jones, one of Thomas Kelly's students at Haverford College, and engaging in lively discussions with Sterling Olmsted, a Woolman and Gandhi scholar who taught and served as an administrator at the college. With gratitude, he recalls these two guiding lights of Wilmington College and FAHE. Ron lives in Wilmington with his wife, Theresa.

**David R. Ross** is Associate Professor of Economics Bryn Mawr College, focusing on industrial organization, quantitative methods, and the environmental economics as applied to the challenges facing ex-urban communities. He holds degrees from Williams College and Northwestern University and is the co-author of the classic text, *Industrial Market Structure and Economic Performance*. Within FAHE, he has served as Presiding Clerk (2001-2003) and on the Executive Committee (1999-2004 and 2009-2011).

**Robert H. Scott, III** is Professor of Economics and Finance at Monmouth University. He has published articles on credit cards, consumer debt, financial literacy, inequality, startup business financing, South American development, and ecological economics. His biography *Kenneth Boulding: A Voice Crying in the Wilderness* (2015) is included in Palgrave's Great Thinkers in Economics book series.

**Michael T. Snarr** is Professor of Political Science at Wilmington College where he teaches Introduction to Global Issues, Global Politics, Case Studies in Nonviolence, and the Global Politics of Food. Over the past several years he has taken hundreds of students to Washington, DC for FCNL's Spring Lobby Weekend. He has also led student trips to Central Mexico, the US-Mexican border, the United Nations, Costa Rica, Europe, and China. He is co-editor of *Foreign Policy in Comparative Perspective: Domestic and International Influences on State Behavior* and *Introducing Global Issues*, now in its 6th edition. Michael has served on the Policy Committee at FCNL, the Quaker United Nations Organization Committee, and the board of the Christian Peacemaker Teams.

# Introduction

**By Tom Head**

This fifth volume in the *Quakers and the Disciplines* series brings together a collection of essays by Quaker scholars and practitioners in the fields of Economics and Politics. To some degree *Quakers, Politics, and Economics* constitutes a second or companion volume on the topic of Quakers in business, following directly after last year's *Volume 4–Quakers, Business, and Industry.* However, this new collection widens considerably the scope of inquiry with topics ranging all the way from personal devotion to global governance. The thought and practice of Quakers in the realms of both politics and economics is explored philosophically, organizationally, historically, and biographically.

Woven throughout the chapters of this book are many themes of interest with respect to the integration of faith, politics and economics. These include:

- Religion as not just a private commitment but also a public witness.
- Explorations of the moral dimensions of economic and political life.
- Exemplary thought and practice in the lives of individual Quakers.
- The blend of service, advocacy, and activism experienced by Friends.
- The role of faith in defining and building a just social order.
- The efforts of Quaker organizations and movements to bring about political and economic reforms.
- Visions of constructive and compassionate ways to address global challenges and crises.

This volume begins with Steven Dale Davison's comprehensive economic history of Friends from the 1650s through the 20th Century. Davison details the ways in which Quakers over the centuries have related to the economic sphere, to wealth and poverty, and to markets, government, and social programs. Over time the private and public manifestations of the Quaker faith have changed considerably, and this first chapter offers a sketch of the history, ideas, and personalities characterizing each era in the evolution of Friends engagement with politics and economics. Following this history, Ron Rembert's chapter examines our varieties of Quaker thought with respect to both public and private life by drawing upon the works of Thomas Kelly to explore philosophically the interplay of contemplation and activism. Rembert draws particularly on Kelly's essay, "The Eternal Now and Social Concern," and in so doing, offers a chapter that is both informative and inspirational. How are we to be open to empowerment by the "Eternal Now" as we grapple with the demands and challenges of politics and economics?

The second part of the book explores perspectives on contemporary economic issues. Drawing upon his research in the book *Viking Economics*, scholar and activist George Lakey analyzes how the economic experiences in the Nordic countries of Denmark, Norway, Sweden, and Iceland both affirm and challenge Friends. He finds these societies in alignment with the Society of Friends in the sense that the Nordics have been value-driven, have produced outcomes consistent with Quaker testimonies, and have challenged dominant paradigms. Lakey argues that the *ethical* and the *practical* are not opposed realities. Nor must there be a trade-off between *equality* and *individual freedom*. Lakey builds the case that it is quite possible to move in the direction of both more equality and more freedom, a conclusion with significant appeal to Quakers and all others who proceed with the outlook that faith can constructively and abundantly shape our lives and our communities for the better.

Drawing upon Quaker and Gandhian traditions, philosopher and peace scholar Gray Cox proposes an ambitious research agenda to be carried on in a spirit-led manner. Through a multicultural lens, he outlines four global and inter-related threats we face today: the economic/ecological, the military/governance, the technological, and the moral/spiritual. In his search for a response to these threats, Cox draws upon the work and methodology of the Quaker Institute for the Future and its practice of holding a "meeting for worship for the conduct of research." In this context, truth can and does prosper; a living Presence is here to teach, to heal, and to transform the way we go about governing, communicating, and managing.

Focusing specifically on the commercial experience of Friends, management scholars Nicholas Burton and Alex Hope write about what we can learn from the Society of Friends with respect to responsibility in business. Burton and Hope review the scholarly work on the role of Quakers in business and the distinctives of Quaker business practice. They conclude with a significant discussion of lessons for contemporary business practice in which they treat corporate governance, networks and movements, and business models in both faith-based and secular contexts. This chapter is likely to be of particular interest to management scholars, business schools, and those working in corporate settings.

Following the chapters on contemporary economic issues, the third section of the book gives direct attention to reviewing the work of various Quaker organizations engaged in economic and political affairs. Paul Moke begins this section with a history of the American Friends Service Committee's (AFSC's) engagements in the coalfields of Appalachia, stretching across nearly a century beginning with the period of severe recession in the late 1920s and continuing into the present day. In doing so, Moke's history of the AFSC in this region offers a case study of Quaker engagement with issues of economic justice, political reform, as well as relief, reconstruction, and social service. The story is not a simple one, in part because the liberalism of those offering help and service was not always fully in tune with those being served and with other stakeholders, such as government officials.

In the next chapter, Ruth Flower offers a history of the work of the Friends Committee on National Legislation (FCNL) with respect to poverty policy in the United States spanning from the 1940s and 50s to the present day. Flower served on the FCNL staff from 1981 to 1996 and again from 2006 until her retirement in 2016, and she continues to work with FCNL as a consultant on Native American policy. Thus, she is drawing upon a great deal of personal experience and engagement as she writes about the evolution of poverty policy in the work of FCNL, offering an insider's view of this Quaker work. Importantly, the chapter gives significant attention to the labyrinth of issues to which poverty is linked and intertwined, particularly civil rights, discrimination, racism, exploitation, health care, and education and budget priorities.

Moving to the international arena, Lori Heninger and David Atwood chronicle the work of Friends at the United Nations. The Quaker United Nations Office (QUNO) was one of the first NGOs to be credentialed in the UN system; it was in 1948 that the Friends World Committee for Consultation (FWCC) was granted consultative status at the United Nations. While one 'office' in name and purpose, QUNO has two physical locations, one in New York where the headquarters and general assembly are located and another in Geneva, Switzerland the UN Headquarters and UN General Assembly are located.

Heninger and Atwood are writing as those whose have had considerable experience working within QUNO; Lori Heninger served as Co-Director of

QUNO-New York from 1998 to 2004, and David Atwood joined the QUNO-Geneva staff starting in 1995, serving as Director from 2004-2011. Both Heninger and Atwood have also had significant experience with other NGOs. After a general introduction to the origins, history, and methodology of the Quaker United Nations Office, the bulk of the chapter reviews two case studies of the work of Friends at the international policy level: disarmament with respect to small arms and light weapons and the UN work on financing for development. Both topics involve a form of peacemaking, the first addressing weaponry and the second addressing the structural violence of extreme poverty and inequality.

In his second contribution to this volume, Steven Davison brings this section on Quaker NGOs to a close with a history of Right Sharing of World Resources (RSWR), a Quaker effort addressing economic justice, particularly in the developing world where extremes of economic suffering are so prevalent. Davison details the origins of RSWR within the context of the Friends World Committee for Consultation and the eventual spinning off of RSWR as an independent organization. As has been the case with other Quaker efforts focused on political and economic testimonies, the work emerges as both service and advocacy.

While all of the preceding chapters on Quaker service and advocacy bodies—AFSC, FCNL, QUNO, and RSWR—of necessity involve a measure of historical narrative, the next section on historical engagement of Friends offers two essays which focus in detail on specific historical episodes in which Quakers, in one way or another (*and* for better or worse) have engaged with political and economic issues.

Historian Thomas Hamm examines Quaker responses to economic liberalism, capitalism, and laissez faire economics at the time of and immediately following the Hicksite Separation of 1827-1828. While some Friends were clearly skeptical about capitalism and deeply concerned with the potential for injustice in unrestricted free markets, others clearly embraced free-market ideologies. On the socio-economic tenets, Friends in 1827-1833, even those who were unified with respect to theological liberalism, were not of one mind with respect to the emerging capitalist market economy of their day. While I do not observe configurations among 21st Century Friends that are as extreme as those Hamm portrays among 19th Century Friends, his case study does offer insight into the varieties of thought existing today. While Quakers broadly embrace economic justice, equity, and fairness, we still find, even within unified branches of Friends, a broad array of ideas about how things might best unfold in social and economic spheres. Friends are not always of one mind with regard to economic and political affairs.

Similarly, although in a very different time and place, the late 20th Century period of South African apartheid, we find Friends once again not being of one mind. Historian Robynne Rogers Healey writes about conflict between South African Quakers and the efforts of the American Friends Service Committee staff and volunteers. It is not always a comfortable story, and it may very well be the case that various participants have seen it through a variety of lenses and have accordingly come to somewhat different conclusions. It is likely that most or all of those involved shared the same ultimate goals, but disharmony, tension, and conflict still emerged and complicated the effort. A devotion to peace, justice, and building good order does not necessarily guarantee unity about priorities and strategies, and an examination of an uncomfortable case study such as this one offers us opportunity for reflection and the development of insight with respect to how spiritual beliefs shape political and economic strategies *and* how we handle our own internal conflicts.

The fifth and concluding section richly documents the contributions of five prominent Friends—John Bellers, John Woolman, Lucretia Mott, Elise Boulding, and Kenneth Boulding—to a Quaker understanding of economics, politics, and the larger human story. It seems fitting that references to Quaker economist Kenneth Boulding bookend this entire section. As you will read, in the first chapter of this section Keith Helmuth begins his writing on John Bellers by referencing the thought and work of Kenneth Boulding, and then at the very end of the section, the final chapter is devoted to an exploration the lives and contributions of both Elise and Kenneth Boulding.

On a personal note, I would observe that to have my mentor Kenneth Boulding show up in this prominent way is neither a surprise nor a coincidence. He was a remarkable scholar. While he was nominated for both the Nobel Peace Prize and the Nobel Prize in Economics, he received neither. For many of us in the economics profession, it is disappointing that he did not at least receive the prize in Economics; his contributions as an economist certainly merited such an honor. My own hypothesis as to why he did not receive the Economics prize is that he never promoted himself or his ideas. He approached scholarship in the same way as he approached rising to minister in a meeting for worship. He quietly and humbly drew upon the Source of Truth, never building his own academic empire but instead consistently seeking the Light and freely sharing his *ministry of scholarship* with all. This quality was, of course, not Kenneth's alone; it can be seen in significant measure in each of the Friends presented in this section. They *all* deserve a Nobel prize, and I would speculate that not a single one of them would have ultimately considered such an accolade to be the important outcome of their life and work.

Keith Helmuth begins this last section with a piece that I would characterize as one exploring nothing less than *truth seeking*. What does it mean to search for truth? Helmuth uses as his point of departure the posture that Kenneth Boulding took, but he then carries us back three centuries to exemplar John Bellers, a person who foreshadows much of what unfolds in subsequent centuries with respect to understanding human betterment and the common good. Bellers' vision is holistic and reaches beyond the confines of any one religion, culture or moment in time. At one point, Helmuth suggests that many figures beyond Friends–Confucius, Bodidharma, Thich Nhat Han, and modern poet Mary Oliver–would salute Bellers' witness. While this suggestion is perhaps a stretch for some readers, it does take us to the Source in a way that appeals to many Friends. Should not the best, clearest, and deepest understanding of right relationship ring true for all those truly seeking the Light, in whatever time and place that may occur? Ultimately, best practices with respect to human wellbeing and the commonwealth of life on this Earth are not culture bound. Helmuth's essay brings to our attention an early Friend who can and will connect with political and economic wisdom across the centuries and the oceans.

In this collection of Quaker biographies we find not one, but two essays on John Woolman. In the first of these chapters, Mike Heller brings us a portrait, as he says, of "one of the most fascinating Quakers to have written about economic issues, poverty, and wealth." Heller draws particularly on Woolman's essay "A Plea for the Poor," a classic piece of the literature of Quaker economics. He also, fittingly, circles around to Kenneth Boulding's *The Organizational Revolution: A Study in the Ethics of Economic Organization* in which Boulding explores how wrongs are righted: in brief, scientists show us where we are, and saints point to where we ought to go. And not surprisingly, Boulding's quintessential example of a saint is John Woolman, a prophetic, truth-seeking voice, discerning with clarity what the economy can and should be doing *for all.*

In the second chapter on John Woolman, Geoffrey Plank plows new ground with respect to Woolman scholarship, focusing very specifically on Woolman's relationship to the land, to ownership, and to the authority and responsibilities of estate holders. In Plank's portrait, Woolman does not come across quite as modern and universal as we might wish him to do so. Woolman is, at least in some respects, a man of his times, and his attitudes toward ownership and the gender-related aspects of ownership are at least in part a product of those times. Nonetheless, we still see in Woolman a faithful Friend seeking and affirming moral clarity. The emerging portrait is a human one, a person of his times but also a person paying attention to economic morality and striving to avoid bad and damaging practices. In this sense, Woolman appears perhaps a bit less saintly but also human, approachable, and real and thus an example that we ordinary human beings can identify with even more closely. Perhaps a lesson here is that he was one of us, and we *can* do what he did.

Next in this series of biographies is Jean Mulhern and Cathy Pitzer's chapter on Lucretia Coffin Mott. Significantly, Mulhern and Pitzer note how Mott's acceptance of those from other faiths put her at odds with her Quaker community. Just as Bellers' perspectives transcended culture, gender, geography, race, religion, and politics, so did Mott's. In Lucretia Mott's case, the emphasis was on confronting injustice and pursuing human rights through nonviolent change, a mission originating in her life as a Friend but certainly in tune with the witness that emerges from truth seekers of many faiths. As Mulhern and Pitzer note, "Her objective was always to align the moral compass of the country against injustice, a long-term project." And the work continues, much accomplished and much yet to be achieved.

Fittingly, this section, and the book as a whole, concludes with a piece on the spiritual foundations of Kenneth & Elise Boulding's contributions as social scientists. The chapter is a collaboration between economist Robert Scott and J. Russell Boulding, a son of Elise and Kenneth with a particular interest in carrying on the work of his parents. The combined efforts of Robert Scott and Russell Boulding result in a delightful portrait of these two remarkable Friends. Their story is a rich and special one. They did not always agree. They certainly had different personal histories, as well as different impulses and perspectives about some social issues and even about their own values and beliefs. But their mutual respect was deep and real, and they together–sometimes close, sometimes distant–accomplished much. Their devotion to values that Quakers hold dear was apparent in their individual lives, their life as a couple, their scholarship, and their work for peace and justice in the wider world. Theirs were lives that flowed out of spiritual centeredness, and perhaps therein lies the most important lesson that this essay, and this volume as a whole, has to offer.

Throughout this collection of essays, the stories we encounter invite us to center down and to discern what *speaking truth* to both wealth and power has meant and will mean. In whatever ways we might frame our terminology–Truth-seeking, Mindfulness, Christ-likeness, the Eternal Now, the Light–spiritual centeredness is the fount from which our politics and economics must flow if we are to shape our lives and our communities for the betterment of all.

# <u>PART I</u>
## *Perspectives on Political Economy*

# 1| Quakers and Capitalism: A History of Paradoxes

**By Steven Dale Davison**

Quaker economic history–the history of Quaker fortunes, of Quaker contributions to capitalist culture, and of Quaker consciousness regarding the social and economic order–is rife with paradoxes.

First, much of this history is virtually unknown among Friends. To my knowledge no one has ever written an economic history of Friends, despite its obvious and enormous importance to both the Quaker movement and modern world history, though there have been some treatments of specific people and topics.[1] This in spite of the fact that Friends are obsessed with their own history.

Second, Friends have ridden a social status roller coaster, starting off as yeoman farmers and small town trades people, then becoming business entrepreneurs and one of the wealthiest communities in the English speaking world, and now Friends are mostly middle class. What has driven these extraordinary swings in Quaker fortunes?

Third, Friends are nowadays a bit nervous about both money and business, even though, for more than two hundred years, Friends were better with money and business than just about anybody. Meetings are often reticent about asking for financial support. Both monthly meetings and yearly meetings often find drafting and approving budgets difficult and the resulting budgets often do not fully reflect the communities' financial realities. Employees of Quaker institutions sometimes find their experience does not match their expectations of a religious body dedicated to equality, integrity, and good treatment of others.

---

[1] These include Benjamin (1976), Emden, (1939), Grubb (1930), Gwyn (1995), Raistrick (1950), Tolles (1948), and Walvin (1997).

Moreover, some Friends these days are sometimes actually hostile to the business people and the corporate executives in their midst.[2]

Where did the wisdom and experience that Friends once had about money, business, and management go? Why this profound shift in attitude toward business and people in business?

Finally, while Quakers from their earliest days have had a disproportionate influence on capitalist culture, especially in the beginning in Great Britain, Friends are only now beginning to develop a coherent, comprehensive testimony on economics. I don't mean a testimony on money and its stewardship in their personal lives, but on capitalism as a system. Why, when Friends have been in the forefront of so many other reform efforts, have they been so tardy in articulating a clear vision of a just and equitable economic system?

This essay paints in broad strokes a brief economic history of Friends in an attempt to stimulate interest in these areas. It is exploratory, just brushing the surface of issues for other historians and economists to address more fully. It is more a presentation of evidence in support of a set of observations than a comprehensive ordering of historical facts.

And it's somewhat schematic. For the history of Quaker fortunes, of Quaker contributions to capitalist culture, and of Quaker consciousness regarding economics and the social order has passed through four phases. These have been punctuated by transition periods in which external forces driving changes in the economic life of Friends collided with corresponding internal forces driving change inside Quaker culture. Here is a brief outline of this history:

## A Schematic Outline of Quaker Economic History

Phase I: *The Lamb's War (the 1650s)*: Early Quakers ground their stance toward the social order in what they called the Lamb's War (Revelation 17:14), a religious apocalyptic faith in its transformation, while their everyday encounters with others challenge accepted social norms regarding social class (Gwyn, 1986). Early Friends are predominantly yeoman farmers and small town trades people.

Transition: *The persecutions (1661-1689)*: A major transition period begins with the Restoration of the monarchy in 1661 and the passage of the Clarendon Acts. It is characterized by the paradox of intense economic persecution on the one hand and incredible financial success notwithstanding. In the end, Quakers "cut a deal" with the state, accepting religious tolerance in return for abandoning their assault on the social order. Friends are driven from the land into business.

---

[2] These observations are anecdotal and come from the author's own experience rather than from in-depth study.

Phase II: *The "Double Culture" period (18ᵗʰ Century)*: Quaker culture is characterized by the paradox of radical withdrawal from society on every front except those of commerce, the sciences, and the applied arts. In these areas Friends' engagement is intense and of world-changing significance. Friends in Great Britain drive the emergence of industrial capitalism and become extremely wealthy.

Transition: *The rise of evangelicalism (1795-1828)*: A minor transition period begins when the just-emerging evangelical movement shapes and, for much of the next century, dominates both the culture of Friends and the simultaneously emerging discipline of political economy.

Phase III: *Partial reengagement (19ᵗʰ Century)*: Friends continue to dominate aspects of industrial capitalism's growth, while their evangelicalism calls them out in limited ways from their withdrawal from wider society. They become reformers in some areas and drive the rise of the philanthropic movement in Britain. Always more diverse, American Quakerism fragments not just around religious conflict, but also along fault lines between the classes.

Transition: *The rise of liberalism (1895-1920)*: Another major transition period occurs when the rise of a new liberal spirit in Quakerism awakens an all-new consciousness of capitalism as a system. The passage of the final, decisive elements of limited liability law in both the UK and the US begins to deconstruct the fabulous wealth of British Quaker families.

Phase IV: *Liberal reengagement (20ᵗʰ Century)*: Friends break with their two-hundred-year-old tradition of leaving the "system" more or less alone. They shift socially from the business upper classes toward the middle class as they leave self-employment and business ownership. Quakers not only lose their leadership role in the wider economic culture, they actually become somewhat hostile toward business and business people in their own ranks. Notwithstanding their new awareness of capitalism's structural flaws, they are late in developing a clear testimony regarding the capitalist system they helped create.

## Phase I: The Lamb's War and the World Order–the 1650s

The Children of Truth, as Friends called themselves at first, preached and lived a vision of a radically reconstructed economy as a natural outgrowth of the "Lamb's War" waged on behalf of Christ's active return. Friends in the 1650s expected the ensuing second coming of Christ to make all things new, including the social-economic order, but they weren't focused on the social-economic order itself (Gwyn, 1986; Gwyn, 1995).

They were mostly attacking the Church of England, and their critique was grounded in their experience of the Light and in their distinctive reading of

Scripture rather than any political or economic ideology. Theirs was a moral and religious "war" fought with the Word, the gospel of Christ preached in the spirit of Christ, and with lives that testified to their Truth. The economic dimensions of the anticipated renewal of the world order remained only partially and vaguely articulated.

The testimonial aspect of their lives, on the other hand, included practices that did assault the social order in dramatic ways, in the most commonplace everyday encounters with others. Their refusal to give "hat honour" to people of higher social class and their insistence on addressing everyone as equals in what came to be called plain speech was a direct affront to the social class standing of their "superiors." Thus their contemporaries in the 1650s saw Friends as dangerous destabilizers of the social order.

This raises the question of what social classes were these Children of Truth. Most of them were yeoman farmers and husbandmen or small-town trades people (Braithwaite, 1981, p. 512; Braithwaite, 1979, pp. 460-461; Raistrick, 1950, pp. 28-32). The yeoman and husbandman classes were descendents of the feudal villein class. Villeins were peasants who enjoyed no privileges in the manorial system and had no responsibilities that bound them economically, socially, or politically to their superiors, and they owned their land in their own right. Our word villain derives from the name for this social class. This says something about the tensions already inherent in the system.

## Transition: Persecutions and Incipient Capitalism

The crucial turning point in Quaker economic history was the Restoration of King Charles II in 1661, which ended the great Puritan experiment in government and brought on persecutions that tried to wipe out the Quaker movement and empty Quaker purses into the state treasuries. These forces redefined Quaker economic life, both in its inward and testimonial dimensions and in its outward expressions and circumstances in the world.

The great paradox of this period, and perhaps the greatest paradox in the whole history of Friends, was that, despite the decades-long, deliberate assault on Quaker wealth at an almost unimaginable scale, Friends emerged as one of the wealthiest communities in the world.

All the acts of persecution against Friends carried financial penalties or had indirect economic consequences. Some were primarily financial in their effect. The persecutions represented a financial feeding frenzy that unleashed local authorities upon Quaker property and assets. They took the form of fines and of distraints, the seizure of goods, tools, and other property in lieu of fines when Friends couldn't or wouldn't pay them. In addition to the fines and distraints, most of the movement's leaders were thrown in gaol during this period, especially in the 1660s, and very many of them died in those gaols, including most of the movement's leadership (Braithwaite, 1979, pp. 21-115).

The economic toll staggers the imagination. Between 1670 and 1685, Friends suffered £48,000 in fines at a time when ten pounds was a considered a good annual wage (Barbour and Frost, 1988, p. 64). The state seized an estimated £1.125 million over 175 years in tithe fines alone (Raistrick, 1950, pp. 39-40). A fairly careful audit of Quaker losses made in 1833 for the period between 1700 and 1829 came to £903,625 in tithe fines, and this was *after* the persecutions officially ended (Raistrick 1950, p. 39). Distraints for ecclesiastical tithes continued into the nineteenth century, averaging £5,000 a year in the early 1700s and actually rising to £8,000 a year by 1800 (Raistrick, 1950, 39).

As we said earlier, the majority of early Friends, especially in the North of England where the movement was born, were farmers, and most raised dairy cattle and sheep as a secondary investment. Some were actually pastoralists primarily.

The fines, distraints, and imprisonments hit these folk very hard. Fines wiped out their cash reserves, making it hard to buy seed for the next season or make it through the lean times just before harvests or shearings. Distraints took away their tools. Imprisonment removed farmers from their holdings over the narrow time-windows that were crucial for agricultural work.

Thus, the persecutions systematically drove these folk off their farms. Many turned to the wool-related trades. They already knew the industry, its economy, its technologies, and its people, at least locally, because they had been wool suppliers (Raistrick, 1950, pp. 53-54, 69-85).

This movement of Quaker farmers into the wool trade helped to shape the industry for several generations (Raistrick, 1950, p. 70). Furthermore, many of these Friends moved on from the wool industries to other ventures. John Gurney moved from wool stapling to banking, as one example.

By the end of this transition period, Quakers had become a movement of trades people and merchants in the midst of an expanding and increasingly international economy. Soon they would help lead the transition from mercantile capitalism to industrial capitalism.

## Phase II: The "Double Culture" Period

Officially, the persecutions ended in 1689 with the passage of the Toleration Act, which allowed freedom of worship to nonconformists as long as they accepted certain oaths of allegiance to the crown—which Friends were loathe to give. And Friends still owed tithes to support the Church of England, which they were loathe to pay. However, as Doug Gwyn (1995) describes in *The Covenant Crucified*, Quakers were offered a deal: stop invading churches and preaching apocalyptic change and we will stop persecuting you—more or less. Make religion a private affair and cede the public sphere to the state.

Quakers accepted the deal. They withdrew from almost every social sphere. But not from the sphere of business into which they had been thrown. Here, and in the related fields of science and what we now call technology, they could not have been more engaged. Quakers became a people with a double culture.

By this I mean that they lived in two cultures at once. One was a walled garden. It was inward-looking, closed and insulated from the wider society, and full of distinctive social norms and behaviors that served as walls against the wider society's influences. In some cases, like endogamous marriage and an asceticism that denied them many forms of social discourse, these behaviors were *designed* as walls. Into this garden they withdrew much of their energy, attention, and social engagement.

But they did not withdraw *all* of their energies and attention. Their social economic circumstances had driven them out of the agrarian and village life that, to some degree, at least, could have sustained a complete withdrawal from society, and into commerce, where they were forced, instead, to stay engaged in the wider world. Here, the ethos that Max Weber (1905) describes in *The Protestant Ethic and the Spirit of Capitalism* served them well: the very asceticism that prohibited joining social clubs, or going to the theater and to dinner parties with their new social peers, turned their livelihoods into religious callings. Weber actually mentions Friends specifically quite often in his book and in many ways Quakers exemplified his thesis better than other Protestant groups.

So their economic lives did call Quakers back into the world, but they brought some of their walls with them. Their plain speech and plain dress still set them apart. Through their intense culture of eldership, their meetings kept a close eye on their behavior in the world. Their intermarriage, their apprentice system, their internal networks of travel and communication, and their preference for doing business with other Friends, all narrowly channeled the flow of their energies into their business ventures while at the same time walling them off in other ways.

Yet, these two cultures were intimately related. This was one people, after all. Individual Quakers, their families and meetings, lived these two cultures as one life. They were living in the garden and at the same time living in the world around them, living in a culture they had created for themselves and also living in the wider culture. They fused the two cultures without apparent contradiction and with phenomenal success.

## Quaker Success

By inculcating the spiritual values that drew them inward toward each other and toward their Inner Teacher, Quaker culture encouraged their creative, successful economic engagement in the world.[3] In the first place, Quaker culture helped shape *Quaker character* so as to make Friends successful business people. Quakers also adopted *corporate practices* that fostered economic and financial success. It's hard to exaggerate the importance of these corporate Quaker practices in building their personal fortunes.

The third and perhaps most important factor in fostering Quaker wealth in this period was *Quaker intervisitation* and the traveling ministry and its parallel networks of written correspondence. These communication and visitation networks soon became so active and so fully developed that only one or two degrees of separation stood between a given Quaker and a prospective business partner across the country or even across the ocean.

Finally, we must credit *sublimation*. All the energy (and money) that Quaker character and culture repressed had to go somewhere. If you couldn't buy a piano or join a social club, you could plow your money back into the business or experiment with a new casting technique.

Thus, when Quaker character, with the indispensable support of Quaker culture, tackled a worldly problem, it tended to generate creativity and innovation, a freedom of modes of thinking paradoxically opposite to the gradually solidifying and ultimately ossifying modes of religious thinking that took hold in Quaker culture over the next century and a half. It would barely stretch the truth of the matter to say that Quakers were the wellspring from which gushed many of the main streams of industrial capitalist development. I like to say that the industrial revolution would have taken place in England eventually without Friends—but it didn't. Here are the key areas in which Quakers helped jumpstart industrial capitalism.[4]

## Technological Innovation

A full discussion of significant, and even essential, technical breakthroughs engineered by Quakers is beyond the scope of this chapter. But we can list some of them to give a sense of the movement's impact on industrial capitalism.

---

[3] See Braithwaite (1979), Punshon (1984); Raistrick (1950) and Walvern 1997 for a general discussion of the factors behind Quaker business suceess.

[4] Several books have been written on this subject. See Benjamin (1976), Emden (1939), Grubb (1930), Raistrick (1950), Tolles (1948). Here I only summarize as concisely as possible how Quakers were virtually indispensable to the industrial revolution.

- *The price tag.* Most famous, probably, is the invention of the price tag, which totally transformed the nature of retail market competition.
- *Industrial tooling materials.* Friends revived the British iron industry, developed improvements in cast iron, and most importantly, they developed cast steel, which made it possible to mass-produce goods that were more durable than those made with iron and, at least as important, to mass-produce durable machine parts. Machines could mass-produce goods; now you could mass-produce machines.
- *Mining and smelting.* Friends either developed or revived several mining and metal industries besides iron and steel, including copper, lead, zinc, tin, and silver. For at least the first 75 years of the eighteenth century, they provided the silver that backed up the Bank of England (Raistrick, 1950, pp. 180-182).
- *Industrial strength transport.* Friends built the first railroad and developed the technologies essential for its expansion: iron bridges and iron rails. Quakers invented the passenger train and helped build England's canals, as well (Raistrick, 1950, pp. 216-217).
- *Finance.* Friends formed a number of banks, including Lloyds, the Barclay, the Gurney Bank of Norwich, and Overend, Gurney and Company, which was for forty years the greatest discount house in the world. Lloyds was the first bank to diversify its operations and serve more than one industry. Private banks had originally grown up from the need for transaction clearinghouses within a given industry.
- *Energy.* It was shortage of fuel (wood) that had stalled the British iron industry. British Quaker iron magnates developed rotated crop coppice farming to solve this problem of dwindling timber supplies. But their real breakthrough was coke: a fuel that burned hot enough to make quality steel possible. They also invented the safety match; for the first time in human history, you could afford to let the fire go out because you could restart it easily any time you wanted.
- *The industrial business model.* Friends were among the very first to develop an industrial production model that capitalized on the material potential of quality iron and cast steel, including the first use of interchangeable parts. They also developed the first conglomerates and some business associations.

Friends developed whole new industries and revived a number of others, as well. To the iron industry and the others we've mentioned we could add brass and zinc production, lead mining, silver mining, porcelain, chocolate, clockworks, and English cutlery, just to name a few.

Some Friends were venture capitalists, also. Sampson Lloyd saw the capital-starved Boulton and Watt company through Watt's completion of their steam engine prototype. Other firms that Boulton and Watt had approached had failed to see the potential and couldn't deal with the risk. Thus Quakers ended up financing the development of the steam engine.

### The Consumer Economy

Once the industrial model had been conceived and equipped, the explosive growth of some of these industries transformed the wider economy's very structure in the most profound way. An all-new economic sector shoved its way between the existing economies of church, state, agriculture (the landed gentry), and the guilded trades. This new economic activity was the *consumer economy*–the mass production of commodities designed for household consumption by a new middle class.

Quakers played a key role in both the creation of the consumer and the building of the consumer economy. They did this by being the first to develop product lines that were attractive to the emerging bourgeoisie, beginning with the Sheffield steel cutlery just mentioned and expanding this market base with more and more new products for household consumption. William Cookworthy discovered Britain's first clay deposits suitable for porcelain and soon Quakers were making true porcelain goods that compared to those from China itself (Raistrick, 1950, p. 208). Robert Ransome developed a tempered cast iron plough share that was far superior to hammered iron plough shares, then patented a new tempering technique that lasted much longer yet. Then in 1808, he invented the interchangeable part, which eliminated the need to disassemble the plough to replace the share. As Raistrick (1950) puts it, "It is difficult to over-estimate the importance of this introduction" (p. 212).

Joseph Fry got into soap and this firm eventually became Lever Brothers. Benjamin Huntsman developed new ways to temper steel and this revolutionized cutlery production, greatly accelerating the Sheffield steel and cutlery industries. It also transformed everyday household life by putting knives and forks on the table for the first time, replacing bread and the spoon (Walvern, 1997, p. 116). Friends became important producers in clock and watch making. We could go on.

## Business, Workers, and John Bellers

Meanwhile, emerging industrial capitalism was creating massive social dislocation, as the serf classes became the working classes. Widespread poverty in urban concentrations and a whole new panoply of social ills called for attention. Friends did better than most to meet these challenges. Just as they experimented with new methods of production and distribution, so some Friends experimented with new approaches to worker relations, trying innovative approaches to housing, education, and social welfare for their workers, and looking for ways to cushion the shock of unemployment and disability. But, with one notable exception, they limited their efforts to their own businesses.

The exception to this pattern of paternalistic in-house social reform was John Bellers (1654-1725). John Bellers saw the socio-economic ills of emerging industrial capitalism as a *systemic* problem that required a systemic solution. He was virtually the first person to do so and, among Friends, the last, until Seebohm Rowntree two hundred years later.

Bellers's great life work was a continuing effort to "raise a colledge of industry," a workers community that would not only provide work for those who were out of work, but also provide them with a community, including housing, with technical training and general education, and also function as a research institute that could experiment with new modes of production. He tried to convert London Yearly Meeting to his cause. The farthest he got was the founding of Clerkwell School. He wrote to Parliament several times to no avail. He also wrote several essays on the causes and cures for poverty (Clarke, 1987).

Bellers was the first person to call for a European state as a solution for constant warfare on the continent, to call for the certification of doctors and of medicines to protect patients, to call for medical journals to keep doctors informed of the latest methods. He was the first person in the English-speaking world to call for the abolition of the death penalty.

But it was his compassion for the poor and the working class and his ideas for addressing these social ills that attracted the attention of Karl Marx and Friedrich Engels, who mention him by name in *Das Kapital*, and which made him required reading in Soviet schools during the Soviet period. As a result, he is perhaps the second most famous Quaker in world history, assuming that William Penn is the first most famous and that Richard Nixon doesn't count. And yet he is almost totally forgotten by his own community (Clarke, 1987, pp. 26-28). In all my presentations about this material, to perhaps one hundred Friends, only a handful have heard of John Bellers. Bellers's failure to convince Friends of the value of his ideas and his subsequent anonymity among Friends, coupled with his success in convincing Marx and Engels and his fame among communists, stands as one of the most telling paradoxes in Quaker economic history.

### John Woolman

Bellers was not alone in his concern for the poor. John Woolman also wrote quite a bit about the causes of poverty and the plight of the poor. His *A Plea for the Poor: A Word of Remembrance & Caution to the Rich* is fairly well known. But he also wrote "Considerations on Pure Wisdom, and Human Policy; on Labor; on Schools; and on the Right Use of the Lord's Outward Gifts," and "Serious Considerations on Trade."

However, Woolman addressed individuals with his work, not the economic system. He saw clearly a connection between the lives of the rich and the plight of the poor, but his solution was to appeal to individual conscience. He returned over and again in his essays to the idea that if everyone were to be satisfied with a modest lifestyle and give over desires for more than what they really needed to be secure from want, then no one would want. Selfishness on the part of the rich and of society in general and lack of consciousness of the travails of the worker were the problem.

In this way, John Woolman was a child of the double culture period in that he saw economic life as an aspect of one's private religious life, rather than as an aspect of the social order that required collective, public, or systemic or structural attention and remedies. He took for granted the trade that Friends had made by the end of the persecutions, of toleration of belief for withdrawal from revolutionary action.

### Transition: The Coevolution of Evangelicalism and Political Economy

After a century of energetic business engagement combined with withdrawal into Quaker peculiarity, two new intellectual movements emerged simultaneously from the same environment in late eighteenth-century Britain to transform both Quaker culture and capitalist culture. These two movements then co-evolved through their early formation in dynamic interdependence with each other, passing genetic material back and forth as they matured. These movements were the new discipline of political economy and Christian evangelicalism. Evangelicalism soon came to dominate not only much of Quaker culture but also much of political economic thinking as the nineteenth century progressed. For Friends, evangelicalism also opened new doors out of their walled garden into the world, as evangelists and as reformers.

The earliest political economists were moral philosophers, so their economic thinking was of a piece with their moral worldviews. Adam Smith's first book was *The Theory of Moral Sentiments*. But he is better known for *An Inquiry into the Nature and Causes of the Wealth of Nations*, which was published in 1776. In this second book, something new was born: Adam Smith applied scientific thinking to the dynamics of commerce for the first time and gave birth to the discipline of political economy.

The classical school begun by Smith and continued by David Ricardo (who married a Quaker), Jeremy Bentham, James Mill, and his son John Stuart Mill became increasingly secular and scientific in its approach.

But the next figure after Smith to contribute to the new discipline was an evangelical minister–Thomas Robert Malthus. Malthus's economic thinking was heavily influenced by his theology, and his work gave rise to a new evangelical branch of the discipline.[5] This evangelical branch remained as much a moral philosophy as it was economic. Through Malthus and those who followed him, evangelical Christianity gave a moral-religious shape to the "dismal science," a term coined to express the pessimism of Malthus's political economic theories. His version of the "dismal science" came to dominate both the development of the discipline and its application in public policy through much of the first half of the nineteenth century in Britain, especially concerning the welfare of the poor. Some aspects of evangelical political economy remain influential in the thinking of some conservatives even today.

An evangelical minister named Thomas Chalmers continued Malthus's work and had an oversized influence on the thinking of the time, not just because of his popular writings, but also because he was able to test his ideas in the field. On the strength of his ideas, he was given charge of parish poor relief in the poorest parish of Glasgow, Scotland, where he had earned his degree. His efforts were quite successful on paper, but were so exhausting that he soon left the position (Hilton, 1988). Chalmers was close enough to Joseph John Gurney for Gurney to write a memoir of their relationship (Gurney, 1853).

Political economists like Malthus and Chalmers saw the economy as a moral system because it was driven by human decisions. For them, Adam Smith's "invisible hand" in the market was the hand of a God who watched and intervened in human affairs. Market policy therefore required a moral philosophy in which you did not presume to meddle in God's mechanisms. This was a moral argument for *laissez faire*. You likewise left individuals to choose their actions– and suffer the consequences. Thus, economic downturns, bankruptcy, and social

---

[5] This story is covered in detail by Hilton (1988).

ruin were viewed as divine judgment for the sins of greed and pride (Hilton, 1988).

These economists felt that poverty was due to improvidence and licentious habits–laziness, gambling, drinking, wantonness of all kinds, and, of course, sex. Sex led to overpopulation among the working classes, which led to poverty. This was the linchpin of the Malthusian theory that population would outstrip food supplies unless checked by moral restraints–or, lacking moral restraints, by God's judgment through catastrophes like wars, plagues, and famine. Sex was the great temptation of the poor, just as speculation was the great temptation of the rich.

However, the same evangelical spirit that warned these thinkers and their policy-making disciples off of economic intervention also called Friends to address the evils they saw in the society around them.

## Phase III: Partial reengagement (19th Century)

The Quaker economic engine gained momentum through the nineteenth century. New industries, new businesses, new technologies and industrial techniques, new infrastructures–Friends just kept innovating and prospering. Meanwhile, however, new and old social ills called for more concerted attention.

Friends and the wider evangelical movement played a key role in the abolition of the slave trade in Britain in 1833, even though that trade had been a key driver of capitalism's rise. In response to the world that Charles Dickens portrayed in his novels, Quakers helped to establish private philanthropy as a signature aspect of middle and upper class piety in the Victorian age. The evangelical spirit of the time helped foster this approach (Hilton, 1988).

On the other hand, evangelical political economy tended to forestall more systemic thinking about business cycles and other economic phenomena and issues, and it tended to prevent systemic solutions and state interventions designed to ameliorate poverty and economic suffering. Instead it encouraged moral solutions and efforts aimed at individuals.

Eventually, though, failures on several fronts began to weaken evangelical influence on political economy (Hilton, 1988).

- As economic theory, evangelical political economy failed to keep up with the more effective economic tools of classical economics, as represented especially by the genius of John Stuart Mill, who published his masterpiece, *Principles of Political Economy*, in 1848.
- As public policy, it failed to deal effectively with the intensifying problems of industrial capitalism and eventually gave way to organized

philanthropy in the private sector and more liberal policies in British government.

- As moral philosophy, it collapsed in the face of a moral calamity—the Irish famine of 1845-1847—in which the harsh *laissez faire* policies it generated actually intensified the suffering until they were abandoned, and the harsh moral tone of English policy makers caused a social backlash. Meanwhile, however, Quakers provided practically the only effective famine relief during the crisis (Hilton, 1988).

- One more factor turned the tide against evangelical political economy in the mid-to-late-19th century—in a word, optimism. Evangelical political economy was in its essence pessimistic because the human battle against sin was a losing battle. One looked to the divine battle on the cross for victory, not to markets, the government, or social programs. Eventually, those whose hopes were rising on the new economy with its new technologies chose the optimism of the classical economists over the ineffectual moralizings of the evangelicals.

Meanwhile, as H. Larry Ingle (1998) has argued in *Quakers in Conflict*, social class played a role in the great separations of 1828, especially in Philadelphia Yearly Meeting. There the divisions were not only between Hicksite and Orthodox but between the mostly Orthodox business class in Philadelphia and the mostly Hicksite farmers in the outer counties, whose ties to the land made it hard to participate in yearly meeting life to the same degree. Issues of power, class, and governance played a significant role in the conflict alongside theology.

## Transition: The Liberalization of Quaker Engagement

The second major transition period in Quaker economic history began with the Friends conferences held in the late nineteenth century. The Richmond Conference, held in Richmond, Indiana, in 1887, and the Richmond Declaration of faith that it produced evinced a reaction in some parts of Quakerism against its staunch evangelicalism and especially against the way it leaned toward a rigid and virtually creedal authority for a conservative reading of scripture and away from the authority of the Inner Light. London Yearly Meeting, though strongly Orthodox/evangelical up to that time, could not endorse the Richmond Declaration. Then the Manchester Conference, held in Manchester, England, in

1895 released a new liberalizing energy in that yearly meeting, which soon spread to America under the influence of Rufus Jones.[6]

## Quaker Demographics, Quaker Businesses, and Limited Liability Law

American Quakers had always been a very diverse lot economically, with wealthy families in Philadelphia, but also small farm owners in Iowa, and lots of people in between. Thus, it is difficult to write a concise, coherent economic history of American Friends. Friends in Great Britain, however, were a bit more homogenous; for two centuries, most were business people and many were upper class or upper middle class.

In both Great Britain and the United States, however, a powerful new development began to utterly transform the Quaker business classes and through them the wider Quaker culture: the final clarification and cementing of limited liability law.

Throughout the double culture period, Quakers families had owned their own businesses. In the 1860s, however, both Britain and the US passed laws that limited an investor's liability for a business's debts to the value of their investment and both countries expanded these limited liability protections over time. This greatly expanded the opportunities to form corporations owned by otherwise unrelated shareholders, and corporate capitalism was born.

The final step to open the floodgates of shareholder-owned corporate capitalism came with a ruling by the House of Lords (equivalent to the Supreme Court in US law) in the case of Salomon v A Salomon & Co Ltd in 1897. This ruling solidified the doctrine that a corporation was legally speaking a "fictitious person," and definitively established that a company's creditors could not sue the shareholders to pay the company's debts. Since corporate law in the United States was centered in the states, these changes took place in a more piecemeal fashion as one state after another expanded and defined its limited liability statutes, but the effect on Quaker business owners was the same.

These final protections for shareholders released tremendous amounts of economic energy. It also ultimately deconstructed the great Quaker family businesses and the wealth base of the families that owned them. One by one beginning in the early twentieth century, Quaker family-owned businesses went public and the members of these families ended up managers in companies they had previously owned or they left business altogether. Barclay's Bank, Lever, Brothers, Cadbury Chocolate—dozens of Quaker businesses became shareholder

---

[6] See Punshon (1984, pp. 203, 209-215) for a discussion of the importance in Quaker history of these two conferences.

owned. As the twentieth century progressed, Friends largely lost their controlling role in the companies they had founded and a two-centuries-long era of Quaker business-based wealth gradually came to an end.

## The Liberalization of Quaker Witness

The new liberal spirit that was released by the Richmond Conference and especially by the Manchester Conference in the 1890s gave a new shape not just to Quaker theology but to Quaker social witness, as well. In this, Friends were not alone. Similar movements toward greater engagement with the world's problems were also happening in the wider culture, both secular and religious. Both the social gospel movement and the Pentecostal movements were born in this time. In the beginning, the latter had a strong social witness focus, notably regarding racial integration (Briggs, 1961, p. 20).

Along parallel lines, the progressive movement also emerged, focused on eliminating problems caused by industrialization, urbanization, immigration, and corruption in government, and on efficiency and scientific management in both government and business (Wilson, 1992). Science and what we now call technology were also on the march, affecting every aspect of life, including religion. Liberal Friends eagerly embraced the new scientific methods being used to understand the Bible, while the advances in science, especially the theory of evolution, worked to undermine the ultimate authority that the evangelical age had conferred on the literal reading of Scripture. It was Seebohm Rowntree who brought this spirit to Quaker economic consciousness.

## Seebohm Rowntree

For two hundred years after John Bellers published his "Proposals for a Colledge of Industry," Friends abided by the bargain they'd struck with the state and with the demands of the emerging capitalist system. They stayed away from systemic—let alone radical—efforts to restructure the social order; and by "radical" I mean efforts aimed at the *roots* of economic oppression, injustice, and poverty. Keeping to themselves, they confined religion, morality, and ethics within the walls of Quaker peculiarity. Following Woolman's lead, they appealed to individual conscience as their strategy for social change, and strove themselves for the highest standards of personal conduct in business.

Then came Seebohm Rowntree, scion of the British family of chocolatiers. Throughout his life, this extraordinary man worked to articulate and activate a new liberal engagement with the social order and helped to define the structural character of socio-economic problems like poverty. He helped establish public–

that is to say, governmental–responsibility for these problems. And he threw himself into the struggle for change.

His first and most important contribution was a book, *Poverty: A Study in Town Life*, published in 1901. *Poverty* was a thorough sociological statistical study of poverty in Rowntree's town of York, where his chocolate factory and the railroad were the only major employers. It was modeled on the first statistical sociological study in history done by Charles Booth and published in 17 volumes between 1889 and 1893.

Booth's *The Life and Labour of the People of London* had demonstrated that one third of London's population lived below "the poverty line," a concept he created, expressed as the income needed to cover the basic necessities of life. And his graphic descriptions of their circumstances were truly disturbing. Booth's study demonstrated that poverty and its ills were inherent in the character of capitalism itself, not in the character of its workers. The poor were victims, not causes, of their suffering. And paternalistic attempts to solve the problem by morally elevating the poor were ill-conceived and failed to address the real causes of their suffering, which was that, while most poor people worked, they simply weren't being paid enough.

But Booth's work was too massive and dense to attract widespread attention. Rowntree saw the problem and he resolved to recreate Booth's methods on a smaller scale in York. His resulting book was well organized and well written, it was short and accessible, and it struck a chord. It spoke to the liberal-scientific worldview that was emerging at the time and it resonated with other reformist forces at work in English and American society. And Rowntree came to the same conclusions as Booth, that poverty was structural, not moral, in its origins (Rowntree, 1901).

It had a tremendous impact and became a bestseller. Someone recommended it to Winston Churchill, then a young Conservative Member of Parliament, who couldn't get it out of his consciousness, calling it "a book which has fairly made my hair stand on end" (Walvin, 1997, p. 199). Churchill's fellow MP Lloyd George would brandish *Poverty* as he spoke to large crowds all over Great Britain campaigning for the New Liberalism that he, Churchill, and others had inaugurated in 1906. In 1911 Parliament passed the National Insurance Act, providing for state-funded insurance for unemployment, sickness, and old age. The modern welfare state had been born and *Poverty: A Study in Town Life* had provided much of the prevailing argument for the change, with its clear exposition, demonstrable evidence, and straightforward, scientific approach.

The book even influenced American economic policy. Mollie Orshansky, an economist working in President Johnson's Social Security Administration, borrowed the formula for calculating the poverty line that Rowntree had modified from Booth's work and used it as the basis for the "Orshansky Poverty Thresholds," which are in turn the basis for the US government's measure of poverty today (Cassidy, 2016, p. 42).

In this and in his other books and in his long and distinguished career as a public servant, Seebohm Rowntree helped to lead Friends through the transition into the twentieth century and a new liberal engagement with social problems. By "liberal" I mean an optimistic faith in the ability of society (meaning, mostly, government, but also civil society) to improve things by studying social problems, proposing solutions, developing programs, and creating institutions for implementing the programs.

This was a fundamental break from the double-culture compromise forged in the persecutions of the first transition period, in which Friends would leave the state and the foundations of the social order alone, as long as they were left alone in return. Under the leadership of Seebohm Rowntree and others in this new liberal movement, Quaker religion once again became a public, and not just a private, affair.

Then, just as the New Liberalism and the economic reforms of Churchill, George, Rowntree, and the Labour Party were hitting their stride, war exploded in Europe.

## The Great War and the Dawn of the Liberal Century

The final factor in this transition period was World War I. The ferment among Friends over the social order had been gaining mass and velocity when the Great War broke out, but the war gave it new momentum. Four notable things happened during the war to usher in a new age of Quaker witness.

- First, for the first time since the late seventeenth century, Quakers suffered persecution for their religious convictions. In the 1690s, with the Toleration Act, Friends had agreed to give up their claim on the social order in return for religious tolerance. During the war, the state reneged on its tolerance, so now the deal was off.
- Second, the War prompted deep Quaker soul searching about witness in general, and all the thinking and talking and writing revitalized Quaker testimonial life, beginning with the peace testimony, but not stopping there. Their new prophetic spirit found a prophetic voice, and that prophetic voice bespoke a momentous sea change in Friends engagement with the social order. The double-culture period had been faltering for decades. Now it was over.

27

- Third, with the formation of the ambulance teams and then of the service committees during and after the war, the prophetic spirit of Friends found its hands and feet. A new era of testimonial innovation and international action was born. Quakers invested hearts, minds, and bodies in trying to change the world again.
- Finally, because of the public controversies surrounding Quaker conscientious objectors and then the creation of the ambulance teams and the relief work after the war, many more people around the world knew who the Quakers were—or at least, that they existed. Friends were thrust out of their peculiar insulation onto the world stage.

## Phase IV: Liberal Reengagement in the Twentieth Century

Quakers became increasingly involved in efforts to "change the world" as the twentieth century progressed. Starting with the formation of the service committees during the Great War, they created one new witness-oriented organization after another. And, for the first time since John Bellers, and beginning with Seebohm Rowntree, individual Friends rose to prominence in the sphere of economics.[7]

### Quaker Economic Witness Organizations

There was very little organized Quaker witness focused directly on the economic sphere beyond private philanthropy until the twentieth century. However, the emergence of the liberal movement in Quakerism coincided with a new awareness of capitalism as a system to be understood, critiqued, and even challenged, and of economics as a discipline. Several Quaker organizations created in this period spoke with their mission to economic concerns in some degree: the American Friends Service Committee, Quaker United Nations Office, Friends Committee on National Legislation, Right Sharing of World Resources, and most recently, the Quaker Institute for the Future. Brief sketches of three of these suggest the nature of this engagement with political economy.

**American Friends Service Committee (AFSC).** The most famous expression of this new energy was the formation of the ambulance and relief services of Friends during and just after the First World War and the incorporation of the American Friends Service Committee and the other service committees. While at first AFSC did not challenge the economic system as such,

---

[7] The term "economics" began to replace "political economy" in the early decades of the twentieth century as mathematical modeling increasingly came to dominate the discipline.

its service work has always been at least partially economic in character. Rebuilding war-torn France, feeding ravaged post-war populations, working with the poor in Appalachia, its prison work today—all these efforts either directly or indirectly addressed economic suffering.

**Right Sharing of World Resources (RSWR).** Quaker concern for the right sharing of the world's resources was born during the Fourth World Conference of Friends held in 1967 under the auspices of Friends World Committee for Consultation (FWCC) in Greensboro, North Carolina, on the campus of Guilford College. FWCC's efforts to implement this new concern passed through several stages as the organization adapted to the reality of limited resources and the difficulties of organizing internationally. Eventually, however, FWCC formed a World Resources Committee, hired a staff person, and launched a program—the One Percent More Program. This called for individual Friends to commit one percent of their after-taxes income to international development projects beyond what they already gave in charitable contributions. The program also sought to influence governments to commit one percent more of gross domestic product in development aid in the developing world. And it sought to influence Friends to consume less, since the over-developed countries were (and are) consuming far more than their share of the world's resources. The one percent formula did not take hold to any significant degree among Friends and the program's name was soon changed to Right Sharing of World Resources.

In 1998, FWCC decided to get out of the business of running programs like RSWR in order to refocus on its core mission of gathering Friends together into a common fellowship across international borders and theological boundaries. After looking unsuccessfully for a new home with another Quaker organization, RSWR in 1999 became its own independent Quaker nonprofit, which it remains today.

For fifty years now, RSWR has provided grants to local social and economic development projects in developing countries, mostly in Africa and India, but also in Central and South America. Right Sharing led the way in this kind of micro-funding. It now provides grants to women's self-help groups in India, Kenya, and Sierra Leone. These groups then give loans to the women's entrepreneurial projects. While its government lobbying efforts never fully matured, Right Sharing has continued to educate Friends about international poverty and development issues and to urge Friends to simplify their own lifestyles.

**Quaker Institute for the Future.** One Quaker organization has focused directly on the economic system as such—the Quaker Institute for the Future (QIF). QIF developed out of a gathering of Quaker economists, ecologists, and public policy professionals held at Pendle Hill in 2003. QIF's mission is to "advance a global future of inclusion, social and economic justice, and ecological well being through participatory research and discernment" (QIF, n.d.).

Building directly on Kenneth Boulding's groundbreaking work integrating economics and ecology, "QIF envisions a global future in which humanity is in right relationship with the commonwealth of life." "Underpinned by coherent and systemic analysis that supports strategic intervention and social action," QIF is an active publisher of pamphlets, research papers, reports, and think pieces, a newsletter, and a website, and it conducts conferences, workshops, and research seminars (QIF, n.d.).

### Quaker Economists in the Twentieth Century

During the Double Culture period, there were no Quaker economists to speak of (Powelson, 1987, p. 134). But in the twentieth century the movement produced several significant figures and a couple of true giants in the field.

**Herbert Hoover (1874-1964).** Many Friends do not know that Herbert Hoover was a Quaker active in meeting life all his life, an important public figure before he was president, a leader of the Progressive movement in both business and politics with a genius for organization and logistics, and a significant actor in economic affairs long before he faced the Great Depression (Wilson, 1992). However, in his attempt to avoid government intervention during the early days of the Depression, by supporting businesses but resisting federal aid to individuals, and relying instead on local governments and private giving for relief efforts, he represented aspects of the evangelical political economy of the previous century. His approach was, of course, decisively rejected in 1932 with the election of Franklin D. Roosevelt. Hoover was an active critic of the New Deal and remained interested in political economics for the rest of his life.

**A. J. Muste (1885-1967).** Abraham Johannes (A. J.) Muste was a Dutch-born political activist who became a key figure in the American labor movement beginning in the early 1920s (Hentoff, 1963). A Dutch Reformed minister in early life, he was influenced by Thomas Dewey and the Social Gospel movement of the time and by socialism. In 1918, he became a Friend and was for a while pastor of a Quaker church in Providence, Rhode Island, holding political salons in the meetinghouse that were attended by local pacifists and other radicals. In 1919, he began a career in labor union activism, later becoming Secretary of the Amalgamated Textile Workers of America and going on to form the American Workers Party. In midlife, Muste refocused his energies on Christian pacifism and was executive director of the Fellowship of Reconciliation from 1940 into the 1950s. He was active in the civil rights movement and then the movement against the war in Vietnam, and he remained a socialist throughout his life.

**Kenneth Boulding (1910-1993)**. It's hard to overstate the impact of Kenneth Boulding, not just as an economist, but also on the social sciences more generally. His insistence on the integral character of all the social sciences and his pioneering work on General Systems Theory was one of his greatest contributions. He was also an early adherent of evolutionary economics, which saw economics as evolving in the context of the evolution of the universe, and he applied principles and ideas from biological evolution to economic theory. Most famous perhaps is his 1966 essay *The Economics of the Coming Spaceship Earth*, in which he placed economic activity in the context of the ecological systems within which it operates for the first time, thus creating a new economic discipline. With the spaceship metaphor, he alerted the world to the limits to economic growth imposed by our singular planetary home. He also wrote on the economics of peace, economic ethics, the economics of knowledge, conflict theory, and the world as a total system, plus various Quaker writings and a book of sonnets.

**Jack Powelson (1920-2009)**. Economist Jack Powelson had a long and distinguished career in international development, advising presidents, governors of central banks, and finance ministers in Africa, Latin America, and Asia, and especially in China at the beginning of China's economic rise. He is perhaps best known, however, for the tension between himself and the Quaker community he loved; he felt shunned and criticized by Friends for his views on both economics and Quakerism, both of which some Friends perceived to be too conservative. Powelson therefore became a critic of modern liberal Quaker culture, feeling that "unprogrammed Quakers had turned themselves from a *personal* religion to a *political* religion" (emphasis his) and that liberal Quakerism had become quite illiberal in its attitudes toward more "conservative" views (Powelson, n.d.). In essence, he hearkened back to the Double Culture period's agreement to keep religion private and leave the social order to the experts and he echoed in some ways Herbert Hoover's approach to economic reform. He wrote eighteen books, mostly works on international development, but several were addressed directly to Friends, including *The Moral Economy*, *Dialogue with Friends*, and *Facing Social Revolution: The Personal Journey of a Quaker Economist*. In 2001, Powelson started an electronic journal called *The Classic Liberal Quaker*, changing its name to *The Quaker Economist* (tqe.quaker.org) in 2002.

**George Lakey (1937-)**. George Lakey has been in the forefront of virtually all of America's social change movements since the ban-the-bomb movement in the 1950s, both as an activist and as a thought leader. In his long career, he has returned repeatedly to the struggle for economic justice and equality and for fundamental changes to the economic order. In 1971, he helped found the Movement for a New Society (MNS), a network of groups working toward nonviolent social revolution and organized in part as living collectives and cooperatives. He helped write MNS's manifesto *Moving Toward a New Society*. In the 1980s, he organized and for seven years directed the Pennsylvania section of a national labor/community coalition called "Jobs with Peace." In 2009 he co-founded Earth Quaker Action Team (EQAT), which seeks to build a sustainable economy through nonviolent direct action. In 2017, he published *Viking Economics: How the Scandinavians got it right and how we can, too*, which describes the social welfare systems and economic policies of the Scandinavian countries, the political processes that got them there, and how this vision of social equality and well-being could work in the United States. While Lakey is not a trained economist, *Viking Economics* is rich with economic insight and analysis, and with attention to the practical requirements for radical social economic reform. He has also led the way in developing social change strategies, tactics, and arguments, as a writer and as an academic.

### Conclusion

The forces at work during the first decades of the twentieth century had changed Quaker consciousness. The rise of liberal Quakerism, the war's activation of modern Quaker witness, and the embrace of scientific and technical approaches to solving social problems have dominated the Quaker way throughout the ensuing decades. Changes in corporate law permanently altered both Quaker demographics and the Quaker ethos regarding business.

New trends within Quakerism accelerated these changes. The increasing use of meeting committees and the rise of independent Quaker institutions like AFSC to structure witness efforts, replacing the traditional eldership structures for Quaker ministry; a steady stream of convinced Friends who were increasingly likely to be post-Christian in their religious temperament; the blooming of new, mostly "post-Hicksite" meetings in college towns after World War II; and the reunification of previously Orthodox and Hicksite yearly meetings in the mid-1950s—these internal shifts both drove and reflected a new Quaker consciousness about the social order.

Now, one hundred years have passed since London Yearly Meeting approved in 1918 a new vision for Quaker witness in the form of Eight Principles of a Just Social Order. However, the fire that drove that vision and the preoccupation with the peace testimony at the 1920 Conference of All Friends in London has banked considerably. The Great Depression, the Second World

War, the Cold War and its threat of nuclear annihilation, the Vietnam War, the globalization of the economy, the rise of global terrorism as a tool for radical social change, global warming and the immanent collapse of ecosystems around the world–all these forces have shown us how huge and interconnected our social problems are. It's intimidating.

Yet the vision of a remade world remains a vital concern among Friends. Where do we go from here?

History's purpose is remembrance, instruction, and at its best, inspiration. Quakers have an extraordinary economic history, one that to a large degree Friends have forgotten. But whenever I have done programs on this history, Friends have consistently responded with amazement and excitement. I have written this essay and the book in progress from which it draws in the hope that it will spread this excitement, encourage new research, and inspire Friends to action. I hope that more qualified economists and historians will fill out the story. I hope that Friends and their meetings will more clearly articulate a Quaker economic testimony, a Quaker stand in relation to our economic system. I hope that more Friends will feel led to engage in economic witness. I hope that this knowledge of Quaker economic history will help to create an intellectual and religious ecosystem from which could grow a new vision for how the laws of earth household–economics–should operate.

For this is another time of radical transition. Corporate capitalism is convulsing with change. Whole industries are being disintermediated by digital technology and the internet and new ones are being created, just as happened in the early eighteenth century. Block chain technologies like Bitcoin are reinventing money itself. Artificial intelligence is predicted to surpass human intelligence by the middle of the current century, and robots are already taking over professions like medicine and the law that were once thought immune. Society is only now beginning to consider the implications of these developments (Ford, 2015; Kurzweil, 2005). The changes being driven by technology may become more transforming and disrupting than even the industrial revolution that Quakers helped to build two centuries ago.

Only this time, Friends will not be the builders. This time Quakers will be subjects of these changes–even victims–rather than their movers and shapers. In this Friends will be in solidarity with much of the rest of the world. This time the branches of the movement living in the overdeveloped world will likely see their circumstances and their power in the system continue to erode, while the branches living in the underdeveloped world will face an even more uncertain future.

And this time it's obvious–at least to some people–how completely integral and interdependent are economic activity and the ecosystems in which economies operate, as Kenneth Boulding first articulated. And many of these ecosystems are headed toward catastrophic collapse. Spaceship Earth is in trouble.

Finally, as it was during the persecutions of the late seventeenth century, Quaker meetings and institutions are in financial distress, but not this time from persecutions. Dwindling membership, the erosion of the wealth base of the Quaker middle class, decreasing financial support for Quaker institutions, and increasing costs are converging to challenge the very existence of institutions and structures that Friends have long taken for granted. Friends are not likely to come out the other side of these changes with more resources than they had going in. This time Friends will need an as-yet-unforeseen form of radical adaptation in Quaker culture.

For this adaptation to take place and succeed, the movement will need Friends who are steeped in the disciplines of politics, economics, and sociology, who understand, to the degree that it's possible, how the system works and where it's going. It will also need Friends who are steeped in the Holy Spirit, who can drink from the well of Living Water and receive the visions that this challenging time requires.

And I think we will need to understand ourselves better. Why have we forgotten John Bellers, Seebohm Rowntree, and much of the rest of our economic history? Why are we failing to support our meetings and institutions financially? Why do we sometimes look down on the business people in our meetings?

To answer these questions, to face an uncertain economic future with knowledge and intelligence, and even to more deeply tap the wellspring of the Spirit, we need to more fully understand our economic history and what it offers as instruction and inspiration.

## References

*All Friends Conference: Official Report.* (All Friends) (1920). Conference Continuance Committee. London: The Friends Bookshop.

Barbour, H. and Frost, J. W. (1988). *The Quakers.* New York: Greenwood Press.

Benjamin, P. S. (1976). *The Philadelphia Quakers in the Industrial Age: 1865-1920.* Philadelphia, PA: Temple University Press.

Booth, C. (1902). *The Life and Labour of the People of London.* London: Macmillan.

Braithwaite, W. C. (1979). *The Second Period of Quakerism*. (2nd Ed.). York, England: William Sessions Limited.

Braithwaite, W. C. (1981). *The Beginnings of Quakerism to 1660*. (2nd Ed.). York, England: William Sessions Limited.

Briggs, A. (1961). *A Study of the Work of Seebohm Rowntree, 1871-1954*. London, England: Longmans, Green and Co Ltd.

Cassidy, J. (2006, April 6). Relatively Deprived: How poor is poor?, *The New Yorker*..

Clarke, G., (Ed.) (1987). *John Bellers 1654-1725*. York, England: Sessions Book Trust.

Emden, P. H. (1939). *Quakers in Commerce: A Record of Business Achievement*. London: Sampson Low, Marston & Co., Ltd.

Ford, M. (2015). *The Rise of the Robots: Technology and the Threat of a Jobless Future*. New York: Basic Books.

Grubb, I. (1930). *Quakerism and Industry Before 1800*. London: Williams & Norgate, Ltd.

Gurney, J. J. (1853). *Chalmeriana, or Colloquies with Dr. Chalmers*. London: Robert Bentley.

Gwyn, D. (1986). *The Apocalypse of the Word: The Life and Message of George Fox (1624-1691)*. Friends United Press.

Gwyn, D. (1995). *The Covenant Crucified: Quakers and the Rise of Capitalism*. Wallingford, PA: Pendle Hill Publications.

Hentoff, N. (1963). *Peace agitator: The story of A.J. Muste*. New York: Macmillan.

Hilton, B. (1988). *The Age of Atonement: The Influence of Evangelicalism on Social and Economic Thought, 1785-1865*. New York: Oxford University Press.

Ingle, H. L. (1998). *Quakers in Conflict: The Hicksite Reformation*. Wallingford, PA: Pendle Hill Publication.Kurzweil, R. (2005). *The Singularity Is Near: When Humans Transcend Biology*. New York: Penguin Books.

Powelson, J. (1987). *Facing Social Revolution: The Personal Journey of a Quaker Economist*. (Social Order Series of The Pacific Yearly Meeting of the Religious Society of Friends). Boulder, CO: Horizon Society Publications.

Powelson (n.d.). John P. Powelson, 1920-2009. *The Quaker Economist*, vol. 9(162). Retrieved from http://tqe.quaker.org/2009/TQE162-EN-Jack.htmlThe Proceedings of London Yearly Meeting (Proceedings) (1915). Friends Historical Library (Serial Group 2), Swarthmore College, Swarthmore, PA.

The Proceedings of London Yearly Meeting (Proceedings) (1916). Friends Historical Library (Serial Group 2), Swarthmore College, Swarthmore, PA.

The Proceedings of London Yearly Meeting (Proceedings) (1917). Friends Historical Library (Serial Group 2), Swarthmore College, Swarthmore, PA. Punshon, J. (1984). *Portrait in Grey: A short history of the Quakers*. London: Quaker Home Service.

QIF (Quaker Institute for the Future) (n.d.). Quaker Institute for the Future. Retrieved from http://www.quakerinstitute.org/?page_id=7

Raistrick, A. (1950). *Quakers In Science and Industry; being an account of the Quaker contribution to science and industry during the 17th and 18th centuries*. London: The Bannisdale Press.

Report of the Fourth World Conference of Friends (FWCC) (1967). Friends World Committee for Consultation, Philadelphia, PA.

Rowntree, S. B. (1901). *Poverty: A Study of Town Life*. London: Macmillan & Co.

Tolles, F. B. (1948). *Meeting House and Counting House: The Quaker Merchants in Colonial Philadelphia: 1682-1783*. Chapel Hill, NC: University of North Carolina Press.

Walvin, J. (1997). *The Quakers: Money and Morals*. London: John Murray.

Wilson, J.H. (1992). *Herbert Hoover: Forgotten Progressive*. Long Grove, IL: Waveland Press.

Weber, M. (1905). *The Protestant Ethic and the Spirit of Capitalism*. New York: Charles Scribner's Sons.

Woolman, J. (1971). "A Plea for the Poor," *The Journal and Major Essays of John Woolman*, Phillips P. Moulton, editor. New York: Oxford University Press.

# 2 | Thomas Kelly on "The Eternal Now and Social Concern"

**By Ron Rembert**

And he [St. Augustine] creates a language of longing for a unified self: "I will not turn away from You, my God, my mercy, until You gather all that I am from this dispersed and deformed state to reform and renew me in the eternal present."

–Andrea Nightingale, 2007

'Blessed are those,' wrote the author [Thomas 'a Kempis] of the *Imitation of Christ*, 'who are glad to have time to spare for God.' And in this pointed beatitude, he gave not only a diagnosis but a prescription to the fevered life of our time.

–Douglas Steere, 1949

The opposite of contemplation is not action; it is reaction.

–Richard Rohr, 2013

On a Friday in 2005, I participated with students in a weekend lobbying experience in Washington, D.C. which followed in the steps and inspiration of Neil Snarr and Michael Snarr of Wilmington College, who set this program in motion. Travelling to the nation's capital with others from across the country, the group met with members of the Friends Committee on National Legislation (FCNL) on Saturday to discuss the top social and political issues of the day. These discussions prepared us for our ultimate goal, meeting with our federal legislators and lobbying them regarding one of those timely issues–environmental protection, military expenditures, economic development, etc. Before leaving the capital that weekend, the entire group gathered for a debriefing session to report on our lobbying experiences in various legislative offices.

The report of two student participants from North Carolina stood out. This duo claimed that the greatest impact of their meeting with staff members on Capitol Hill may have occurred at the outset. These two students began their lobbying effort by declaring that they were members of the Religious Society of Friends, and, for that reason, requested that their meeting with legislative staffers begin with a period of silence. The staff members appeared baffled, not anticipating such a request. The silence that followed lasted longer than expected. It even seemed somewhat uncomfortable at points. Did it make any difference to start this lobbying meeting this way? The two lobbyists felt that this sharing of silence made a difference, maybe more than the many words they proceeded to speak. In this special request, they modeled deep listening.

Would their words be remembered? Every participant expressed wonderment about their verbal messages and messaging during visits to legislative offices. It is not always easy to discern when clear speaking matches true listening. In contrast, would the refreshment of the opening silence linger? The two participants initiating this practice hoped for that result. Even if their words faded over time, perhaps that moment of silence would remain memorable and meaningful. Their spontaneous opening to that meeting was a genuine gesture, not a guideline provided by program leaders or the FCNL staff during preparation sessions. Their request cast that civic encounter with public officials in a spiritual light. Realizing it or not, these two students exemplified insights about promoting social change offered by Thomas Kelly in his essay, "The Eternal Now and Social Concern" (1941).

This essay, part of the posthumously published collection of Kelly (1941) reflections, *A Testament of Devotion*, explores the age old debate about contemplation and action that remains very relevant today, maybe even more so than when Kelly revisited the topic. His writing explores the background, the eternal now, so captivating to contemplatives, and the foreground, so compelling to action-oriented workers engaged in social change. Reconciliation of these two perspectives finds expression in the Friends' notion of a "concern" which serves as the focus of the last section of Kelly's essay. Starting with that traditional notion and placing it against the background and foreground of the "Eternal Now and Social Concern," I hope to promote appreciation for Kelly's analysis that challenges both contemplatives and activists.

## Contemplation and Action

Kelly (1941) introduces the contemplation/action debate with terms which he claims to borrow from German theology–the distinction between "This-sidedness and Other-sidedness"–or from everyday discourse, the distinction between "Here and Yonder" (p. 90). Activists orient themselves around issues "here" in the concrete, contemporary world which root them in a "this-sided" perspective. Contemplatives yearn for the "yonder" in a more abstract, mystical vision of "other-sidedness." Of course, both perspectives are attainable, but most of us prefer one more than the other.

Kelly (1941) generalizes that the Church vacillates in its attention between the two outlooks, stating:

> The church used to be chiefly concerned with the Yonder, it was oriented toward the world beyond, and was little concerned with this world and its sorrows and hungers. … All this is now changed. We are in an era of This-sidedness, with a passionate anxiety about economics and political organization (p. 90).

Questioning the vacillating dynamic of moving back and forth from one outlook to the other, Kelly proposes a balancing of the two perspectives, while adding a little more emphasis to the Other-sided perspective as the prior of the two. This tilt toward that perspective is not surprising, considering Kelly's sensitivity to mystical experience. In his essay, however, he concludes during his own time that "the church itself has largely gone 'this-sided,' and large areas of the Society of Friends seem to be predominately concerned with this world, with time, and with the temporal order" (p. 90).

Along similar lines, Martin Luther King, Jr. (2010) in his sermon, "Transformed Nonconformist," distinguishes between the two perspectives identified by Kelly: "Every true Christian is a citizen of two worlds, the world of time and the world of Eternity. We are, paradoxically, in the world and yet not of the world. To the Philippian Christians, Paul wrote, 'We are a colony of heaven'" (p. 12).

King (2010) employs graphic images to describe the two outlooks. For example, regarding the "world of time" or this-sidedness, he highlights pressures of conformity which challenge Christians in their stance toward social change. Will such religious activists choose to be molded by society, acting as an "anvil," or to be molders of society, acting as a "hammer" (p. 14). The "hammer" image may appear somewhat startling as a possible tool for social change, especially against a background of Kingian non-violence, but it has biblical usage representing the Word of God and musical meaning in such famous folk songs as "If I Had a Hammer." Using another set of images, King re-describes preoccupation with the sounds and signs of the time as performing like a "thermometer" that monitors and measures public opinion. On the other hand, a change maker informed by the world of Eternity has the potential to perform like a "thermostat" which adjusts and changes the temperature of such opinion. A conformist will likely respond passively to change like an anvil receiving blows or a thermometer recording heated issues. By comparison, the transformed non-conformist actively, but spiritually, takes up the hammer and serves as a thermostat, raising or lowering the heat-igniting social change.

Working effectively as a hammer or a thermostat involves much more than merely taking a stand of non-conformity. A non-conformist may easily misuse these two tools through secular motivations, seeking change only for the sake of change, disrupting the status quo only for the sake of disruption, or resisting "the powers that be" only for the sake of resistance. Nonconformity for these reasons inevitably proves selfishly destructive and blindly uncreative in the end. In contrast, a transformed nonconformist, according to King (2010), understands that "nonconformity is creative when it is controlled and directed by a transformed life and is constructive when it embraces a whole new outlook," specifically, "a Christian mindset" (p. 17). A transformed outlook has spiritual roots that change the agent seeking change, helping an activist avoid "cold hardheartedness," "self-righteousness," and an "annoyingly rigid and unreasonably impatient" attitude that so often characterize superficial and ineffective non-conformity (pp. 17–18).

Unfortunately, the church does not always accomplish its mission of preparing transformed non-conformists. Even non-conformists may not emerge from church communities. As King (2010) sadly cites, "nowhere is the tragic tendency to conform more evident that in the church" (p. 15). Is this tendency toward conformity in the church, in general, shared by the Society of Friends, in particular? Or are both captivated by the lure and luster of "this-sided" agendas? "This-sidedness" may prove a disorienting and distracting option if we lose sight of its dependence on "other-sidedness" which Kelly envisions and King reinforces. Can we live out a commitment to blend both dimensions, "this-sidedness" with "other-sidedness," and to promote "non-conformity" as "transformed"? The traditional understanding of a 'concern' in Friends' faith and practice calls us to these prospects.

### The Concept of Concern

Today, it is not uncommon to hear those involved in Friends' meetings or secular, social action groups to speak about their "agendas" or "strategies" or "goals and objectives." The concept of agenda often suggests some ideological or political orientation for change. The concept of strategy implies a calculated or systematic approach. And the concept of goals and objectives provides a predetermined aim or endpoint for an effort. Generally speaking, none of these concepts necessarily assumes a spiritual or religious dimension informing them. For Friends over time, the concept of a "concern" assumed such formation, although through more contemporary overuse, even this concept has become somewhat secularized in psychological terms. According to Roger Wilson:

> "Concern" is a word which has tended to become debased by excessively common usage among Friends, so that too often it is used to cover merely a strong desire. The true "concern" [emerges] as a gift from God, a leading of his spirit which may not be denied. Its sanction is not that on investigation it proves to be the intelligent thing to do—though it usually is; it is that the individual knows, as matter of inward experience, that there is something that the Lord would have done, however obscure the way, however uncertain the means to human observation. Often proposals for action are made which have every appearance of good sense, but as the meeting waits before God it becomes clear that the proposition falls short of "concern" (Faith and Practice 2002, p. 146).

Wilson distinguishes between what I will call a 'practical concern'–strong desire, intelligent investigation, proposals for action, appearance of good sense–and a 'spiritual concern'–undeniable gift from God, leading of his spirit, inward experience, more obscure and uncertain. Both types of concern are important; both are necessary for social change. But while a practical concern may be limited by a "this-sided" perspective, a spiritual concern opens to an "other-sided" view, contributing to a more balanced approach to social change.

Like Wilson, Kelly (1949) affirms in his essay that an authentic "concern" is a gift from God and a leading of his spirit. In his trademark style of creating hyphenated terms, Kelly distinguishes a concern for Friends as "God-initiated" (p. 111). Notice that he doesn't push to terms such as, "God-mandated," "God-directed," or "God-controlled" in his hyphenations. These other possible views of God's involvement suggest a divine dictum that Kelly does not conceive. A person led by God-initiated insight retains power to choose or not to choose the appropriate action, "a particularization of one's own responsibility" in a given situation (p. 109). For Kelly, one choosing to act "particularizes the cosmic tenderness" of God (p. 108). Each concern specifies "the special task" which needs doing in view of "the universal concern for all the good things that need doing" (p. 109). Thus, a concern has two dimensions, a specific task in the foreground which fixes our attention, and a universal concern in the background which informs our conviction; and both need to be recognized. Too much attention to the foreground while neglecting the background can lead to burnout; too much attention to the background with no foreground can lead to passivity.

Similar to Wilson, Kelly (1949) also explores inward experience of a concern which correlates one's internal compass with one's outward oriented effort. He claims, "the concern-oriented life is ordered and organized from within" (p. 110). What ordering within does Kelly envision? It's not surprising that he turns to traditional Friend's testimonies, integrity and simplicity, as guides to such ordering. In regard to integrity, for instance, Kelly believes that "we learn to say *No* as well as *Yes* by attending to the guidance of inner responsibility" (p. 110). It's tempting, especially with all of the calls for social change one can hear, to say *No* as well as *Yes* to the loudest voice or neediest voice. External factors, such as political parties, social movements or peer pressures, often determine when we say *No* or *Yes* to perceived responsibilities. Such voices may amplify legitimate problems, serious injustices, and corrupt policies. But these external needs may not call forth a "concern" that one act. Reorienting oneself from without to within in response to external voices is a spiritual move of integrity which signifies a concern-oriented life.

In regard to simplicity, Kelly (1949) implies that we initially think of this testimony in terms of apparel or architectural styles, but it serves a much more important role as a principle of orderly living enabling social change. Simplicity provides "the structure of a relatively simplified and co-ordinated life-program of social responsibilities" (p.110). The testimony of simplicity reorders the "hurried, superficial tendencies of our ego" which works against spirit led change (p. 110). In his *The Confessions*, St. Augustine (2010) exposes his ego struggles in serving God, offering a firsthand account of an ego-centered life disordered and unorganized within:

> When I was making my mind up to serve the Lord my God at last, as I had long since purposed, I was the one who wanted to follow that course, and I was the one who wanted not to. I was the only one involved. I neither wanted it wholeheartedly nor turned from it wholeheartedly. I was at odds with myself, and fragmenting myself. This

disintegration was occurring without my consent, but what it indicated was not the presence in me of a mind belonging to some alien nature but the punishment undergone by my own (p. 152).

A life *without* simplicity can appear distracted and disoriented, lacking a guide for *Yes* or *No* decisions that leads to confusion and incoherence–I want to follow this course/I do not want to follow this course; I don't want to wholeheartedly do this; I don't want wholeheartedly to turn from doing this–which is self-defeating and fragmented. Augustine's "I," self-centered and ego-driven, on the one hand, yet self-blinded and self-destructive, on the other, does not demonstrate integrity or simplicity in his yearning to serve God. The revealing admission, "I was the only one involved," is a sure sign that Augustine was not in touch with God-initiated concerns. To be at "odds" with oneself and "fragmenting" into "disintegration" does not reflect the presence of integrity and simplicity in guiding a concern oriented life.

Kelly, like Wilson, also realizes that a path chosen in following a spiritual concern may remain obscure and uncertain. Neither the means one pursues nor the end one reaches may be very clear. These sobering realizations, however, run counter to more typical expectations behind activism, as Kelly notes (1949):

> Nothing was to be undertaken unless the calculations showed that success was to be expected. No blind living, no marching boldly into the dark, no noble but ungrounded ventures of faith. We must be rational, sensible, intelligent, shrewd. But then comes the reality of the Presence, and the Now-Eternal is found to underlie and generate all time-temporals. And a life of amazing, victorious faith-living sets in. Not with rattle and clatter of hammers, not with strained eyebrows and tense muscles but in peace and power and confidence we work on such apparently hopeless tasks as the elimination of war from society, and set out toward a world-brotherhood and interracial fraternity in a world where all the calculated chances of success are very meagre (p. 103).

In a "this-sided" approach to change in which we "think life out all by ourselves," most expectations for action are clear–being "rational," "sensible," intelligent," "shrewd." At the same time, other expectations are excluded– "no blind living," "no marching boldly in the dark," and "no noble but ungrounded ventures of faith"–which reflect an "other-sided" perspective.

Both sets of expectations are important, but in the face of some problems such as war or race relations, those relying solely on a "this-sided approach" may prove inadequate. Only with the addition of expectations from the "other-sided" perspective might effective action arise.

A strong example of balancing the two perspectives appears in an episode involving John Woolman in an encounter with another about the owning of slaves, recorded in his insightful *Journal* (1989):

> About this time a person at some distance lying sick, his brother came to me to write his will. I knew he had slaves, and asking his brother, was told he intended to leave the slaves to his children. As writing is a profitable employ, as offending sober people is disagreeable to my inclination, I was straitened in my mind; but as I looked to the Lord, he inclined my heart to his testimony, and I told the man that I believed that practice of continuing slavery to this people was not right and had a scruple in my mind against doing writings of that kind: that though many in our Society kept them as slaves, still I was not easy to be concerned in it and desired to be excused from going to write the will. I spake to him in the fear of the Lord, and he made no reply to what I said, but went away; he also had some concerns in the practice, and I thought he was displeased with me.

> In this case I had a fresh confirmation that acting contrary to present outward interest from a motive of divine love and in regard to truth and righteousness, and thereby incurring the resentments of people, opens a way to a treasure better than silver and to a friendship exceeding the friendship of man (p. 46).

Like most of us, Woolman considers at the outset some of the "this-sided" factors that so often affect our decision-making processes—economic consequences ("writing is a profitable employ") and sociability ("offending sober people is disagreeable"). But as he turned from these factors to "other-sided" ones ("looked to the Lord"), a concern not to act surfaced. Woolman appears to receive God's leading for appealing to integrity, "a scruple in my mind," or a *No* moment speaking "in the fear of the Lord." Likewise, Woolman testifies regarding equality, proclaiming "the practice of continuing slavery to this people was not right," nor was the writing of wills to perpetuate that practice. What action does Woolman take in the situation? His action is one of gentle, yet forceful, opposition in word and deed. Does he initiate change as a result? His potential customer leaves without offering any clear response to Woolman, other than appearing "displeased."

What resulted from this Woolman/customer exchange? The obvious results are that the will regarding the slave was not written and the customer left upset and silent, perhaps even feeling resentment regarding the outcome. The less obvious, that is, more obscure and uncertain, but significant result is the expression of "divine love" and "truth and righteousness" which "opens a way to a treasure better than silver and to a friendship exceeding the friendship of man," the kingdom of God. Does Woolman record attainment of that goal in his journal entry? No. Does he clearly anticipate achieving that objective in the future? No. However, Woolman notices how expression of his concern not to act in this incident "opens a way to a treasure" whose reach lies beyond human judgment. He accepts responsibility for not acting as a means to testify, but does not anticipate the end, a prospect which lies beyond him.

### The Eternal Now

What Woolman opens to the other in this exchange is what Kelly (1949) describes as a "sense of Presence," the "Divine presence" (p. 94). This spiritual landscape provides a new spatial and temporal dimension to active change efforts.

In spatial terms, Kelly (1949) conceives of an "energizing, dynamic center not in us, but in Divine Presence in which we share" (p. 96). That center serves as a "center of gravity" from which "two beings, joined in a single configuration," function in tandem. God's concern becomes our concern, a spiritual point of departure for social change. This spatial view shifts our focus from the foreground of change, the efforts of the change agent, to the background of change, the inspiration of God. As in Woolman's case, whatever change occurs is not determined ultimately by what he does or does not do, but by what God completes through working in more than one dimension. The spatial dimension in which change occurs, therefore, is infinitely greater than our limited human perspective conceives.

In temporal terms, Kelly (1949) emphasizes the "holy Now," as the time frame of Divine Presence (p. 95). Past and future time are contained in the present moment. According to Kelly, "we have not merely rediscovered time; we have found in this Holy immediacy of Now the root and source of time itself" (p. 96). Again, as part of his unending prayers to God offered throughout *The Confessions*, St. Augustine (2010) strives for words pushing beyond human comprehension in grasping God's view of time:

> You are supreme and you do not change, and in you there is no "today" that passes. Yet in you our "today" does pass, inasmuch as all things

exist in you, and would have no means even of passing away if you did not contain them. Because your years do not fail, your years are one "Today." How many of our days and our ancestors' days have come and gone in this "Today" of yours, have received from it their manner of being and have existed after their fashion, and how many others will likewise receive theirs, and exist in their own way? Yet you are the selfsame: all our tomorrows and beyond, all our yesterdays and further back, you will make in your Today, you have made in your Today (p.19).

Our human view of time, understood in terms of a linear progression from past to future, yesterday to tomorrow, collapses into one divine perspective of "Today," the ever-present Now. That perspective liberates us from what we perceive as limitations of time–we can't go back to yesterday and we can't leap forward to tomorrow. But don't we often try both options by holding onto anguish about the past and anxiety about the future as sources for motivating our actions? Efforts at change are framed by our preoccupations with time as a commodity–"There's not much time left" or "We have no time to waste" or "We're running out of time" or "We'll be saving time with this approach." How can we be freed from trying to possess time? Control time? By opening ourselves to a time frame in which God's view of time prevails, we can act with faith that change ultimately lies beyond us, but also involves us. It invites us into "Wisdom" which St. Augustine in *The Confessions* (2010) describes as follows: "Rather should we say that in her there is no 'has been' or 'will be,' but only being, for she is eternal, but past and future do not belong to eternity" (p. 173).

According to Kelly (1949), three signs indicate that we are living within the spatial and temporal dimensions of the "Eternal Now," genuine expressions of love, joy and peace (pp. 99, 101). Note what signs are not indications–expressions of power or intimidation or antagonism or victory. For Kelly, these three signs, love, joy and peace are significant signposts, distinctive gifts of the Spirit.

In First Corinthians 13, we are provided words to describe in concrete terms this kind of love. Imagine an approach to change which displays these positive features, such as "patient," "kind," and "rejoicing in the truth," while avoiding negative attitudes, such as "envious," "boastful," "arrogant," "rude," "insistent," "irritable," "resentful," and "rejoicing in wrongdoing" (First Corinthians 13: 4–7, The New Oxford Annotated Bible). What type of change do these positive features of love seek? It is more fundamental change than our strategies and agendas aim to reach, as Kelly (1949) notes:

But what is the content and aim of this yearning Love, which is Divine Love loving its way into and through us to others? It is that they too may make the great discovery, that they also may find God or, better, be found by Him, that they may know the Eternal breaking in upon them and making their lives moving images of the Eternal Life (p. 100).

John Woolman's journal account (1989) of his experience as a visitor to "an Indian town called Wyalusing" illustrates this type of infused love which guides one into an open, listening space:

Love was the first motion, and then a concern arose to spend some time with the Indians, that I might feel and understand their life and the spirit they live in, if haply I might receive some instruction from them, or they be in any degree helped forward by my following the leading of Truths amongst them. As it pleased the Lord to make way for my going at a time when the troubles of war were increasing, and when by reason of much wet weather travelling was more difficult than usual at that season, I looked upon it as a more favourable opportunity to season my mind and bring me into a nearer sympathy with them (pp. 127-128).

In this account, Woolman does not claim himself to be the source of motivation for this visit, but grants his inducement to "love," "the first motion" for his "concern" to visit the Wyalusing community. For what purpose? Sometimes we hear of good-hearted visitors like Woolman approaching alienated communities with assumptions about ways of helping or aiding the other, presuming a somewhat paternal attitude before arriving. In contrast, Woolman, guided by a loving motivation, reverses this presumptive approach by his spirit-filled attitude to be the one helped and aided by his hosts, the Native American community, "to feel and understand their life and the spirit they live in." He yearns to "receive some instruction from them." If he can help, Woolman is willing, but only by learning and following whatever Truth-filled way forward he realizes with the help and aid of the community. A shared realization, based on "a nearer sympathy with them," enables Woolman to serve the Wyalusing community in serving itself through inspired leadings. In this episode, Woolman models the power of listening and learning, before speaking and teaching, as expressions of love.

Ultimately, we cannot separate effective speaking from deep listening. The Vietnamese Buddhist monk, Thich Nhat Hanh (1999) helps us understand the dependence of speaking upon listening in his commentary on 'Right Speech', a part of Buddha's Eightfold Path. By the title, "Right Speech," we might expect to learn lessons from Buddha about speaking rather than listening. But, as Thich Nhat Hanh emphasizes,

> Deep listening is the foundation of Right Speech. If we cannot listen mindfully, we cannot practice Right Speech. No matter what we say, it will not be mindful, because we will be speaking only our own ideas and not in response to the other person. In the *Lotus Sutra*, we are advised to look and listen with the eyes of compassion. Compassionate listening brings about healing (p. 86).

How do we know if we are engaged in deep or compassionate listening? Again, according to Thich Nhat Hanh (1999), "listening like that is not to judge, criticize, condemn or evaluate, but to listen with the single purpose of helping the other person suffer less" (88). It also important to notice that deep or compassionate listening is very active, not passive. Consider that the power of listening itself brings about healing. Yet, how much time do we spend preparing ourselves for speaking compared to listening? Isn't it easier to speak than to listen? Is it typical for us to assume that speaking is more powerful than listening?

In his Swarthmore Lecture, "Where Words Come From," Douglas Steere (1955) explores the impact of a "genuine listener" on "the inward spectator listener in the speaker":

> We have still to look at this condition of openness in a genuine listener which the inward spectator listener in the speaker so swiftly recognizes and responds to, this condition that opens doors in the speaker, this condition that brings the climate for self-disclosure, this situation where the deepest longings in the heart of the speaker feel safe to reveal themselves, this atmosphere where nothing needs any longer to be concealed. This truth of the matter is that there are no perfectly open listeners. Yet in those who approach this degree of openness, it is clear at the outset that they are involved. In some way, I, the speaker, matter to them. Neither of us is a ventriloquist's dummy for the other. Both of us affect each other and cannot come out of this encounter unscathed (pp. 9-10).

When the two North Carolina students asked for a period of silence during their lobbying efforts in Washington, D.C., they signaled an openness to be "genuine listeners" and, at the same time," invited "the inward spectator listener" in their hosts, the legislative staff members, to join them in the time and space of the "Eternal Now." Without using words, their silence contained a potential message encouraging openness, safety, self-disclosure, and meaningful encounter which deep listening enables. In this moment, these practitioners of peace made contemplation their action. Was their message received? Offering the message is all we can know. More power to them!

Without perhaps realizing it, these two notable student lobbyists were embodying insights shared by Thomas Kelly, Andrea Nightingale, Douglas Steere, Richard Rohr, Roger Wilson, St. Augustine, John Woolman, and Thich Nhat Hanh. We may not usually think of such contemplatives as sources for action. After all, in tackling the social, economic, and political issues of our time, we more easily focus attention on gathering pertinent information, clarifying key issues for debate and anticipating potential points of resistance. We prepare ourselves to be informed, intentional and engaging in our activism, whether in a congressional lobby encounter or in our local town council meeting. Should we also seek to be inspired and inspiring in these efforts? In his essay, "Eternal Now and Social Change," Thomas Kelly, complemented by these various contributors' insights, answers *Yes* to this question. He challenges us to be activists, but even more, to be contemplative activists.

## Queries regarding "The Eternal Now and Social Concern"

1. Do I view contemplation and action as opposites or complements?
2. Do I wait and listen for a concern to arise before moving toward action?
3. Do I feel the need to control the means and demand the ends of actions?
4. Am I able to maintain faithful effort when no results of my actions are realized?
5. Do I believe that changes of heart are part of changes in behavior?
6. Do I act with conviction that love, joy and peace initiate social change?
7. Do I experience deep listening as a source of healing?
8. Am I open to being empowered by the Eternal Now in everyday life?
9. Do I find guidance in St. Francis' prayer request, "Lord, make me an instrument of thy peace"?
10. Do I prepare for the work of a contemplative activist beyond that of a political activist?
11. Do I accept that the results of my efforts are ultimately God-inspired?

## References

*Faith and Practice: Philadelphia Yearly Meeting of the Religious Society of Friends* (2002)

Hanh, Thich Nhat. (1999). *The Heart of Buddha's Teaching: Transforming Suffering Into Peace, Joy, and Liberation.* New York, NY: Broadway Books.

Kelly, T. (1941). *A Testament of Devotion.* New York, NY: Harper and Row.

King, Jr., Martin Luther. (2010) *Strength to Love.* Minneapolis, MN: Fortress Press.

Nightingale, A. (2011). *Once Out of Nature: Augustine on Time and the Body.* Chicago, IL: University of Chicago Press.

Rohr, R. (2013) *Yes, And…* Cincinnati, OH: Franciscan Media.

Saint Augustine (2010) *The Confessions.* (Maria Boulding, Trans.) Hyde Park, NY: New City Press.

Steere, D. (1949). *Time to Spare.* New York, NY: Harper and Brothers.

Steere, D. (1955). *Where Words Come From.* London: George Allen & Unwin Ltd.

Woolman, John (1989). *The Journal and Major Essays of John Woolman.* In Moulton, P. (Ed). Richmond, IN: Friends United Press.

# Discussion Questions

1. John Woolman and Martin Luther King, Jr. are highlighted as models of contemplation and action in Rembert's chapter. Can you think of other additional models, either current or historic?

2. To what degree do today's Quaker activists and organizations tend to incorporate the "yonder" or "other-sidedness" perspective? Is this approach still important? If so, how can it be encouraged?

3. Quaker engagement with economics and the social order is described as "Liberal reengagement." Is that description still accurate for the current century? Might Quakers be moving into a fifth phase? If so, how would you describe it?

4. Why does John Woolman receive much more attention than John Bellers among contemporary Quakers?

5. Muste, Wilson, and Boulding, among others, are described as significant Quaker historical figures in the economic realm. What other figures would you add to this list?

# PART II
## Perspectives on Contemporary Economic Issues

# 3 | How the Nordics' Experience with Economics Affirms and Challenges Friends[1]

## By George Lakey

As a young adult exploring Quakerism for the first time, I was intrigued by Friends' willingness to contradict Conventional Wisdom. I was startled to learn that in the seventeenth century Friends refused to do the obvious—take weapons with them to defend their families against "the savages." I was told they wound up the safest people on the American frontier.

Back in England, Friends starting the York Retreat in the 18th century treated "the insane" as if, in spite of alarming symptoms suggesting the contrary, they were still people. In so doing Friends advanced the treatment of people who were mentally ill.

Early Quaker retail merchants refused to haggle, choosing instead to fix prices on their goods. The new practice was contrary to conventional wisdom and profitable to the Quakers.

As I learned of these bold contradictions of mainstream assumptions, I found a deeper, philosophical belief of my own challenged. I thought humans lived in two worlds simultaneously, one containing the values and ideals to which we aspire, and the other governed by what is "practical," the stubborn realities that violate ethical ideals. I believed that the existential task for humans is to live as gracefully as possible balancing these two worlds, trying whenever possible to reconcile them while knowing that, when push comes to shove, action requires deferring to what is "practical."

Those boldly innovative Quakers, however, refused to make easy exceptions to their ethical views and simply take guns to Pennsylvania, haggle in their shops, and keep the mentally ill in chains. They acted as if they lived in one world, not

---

[1] Much of this chapter is based on material drawn from Lakey (2016).

two. Their trick lay in designing alternative behaviors while dropping the ethically-wrong practices that Convention dictated. Their experiential religious practice, it turned out, encouraged experimentation.

When I joined Friends, I hoped to learn this prophetic perspective, and I've been reaching for it ever since. During the Obama presidency, for example, I was not entirely surprised when the Pentagon initiated a meeting with me. Swarthmore students and I were researching non-military means of countering the threat of terrorism. A policy planning unit in the Department of Defense wanted to hear about it.

I surmised that the Pentagon knew, perhaps better than anyone, that the "war on terror" was failing, and that the path to more security would require a paradigm shift. At Swarthmore, we were exploring an alternative paradigm—the power of nonviolence.[2]

I found the Pentagon folks highly receptive to what I shared, although when I asked about next steps they said that their own interest in nonviolent alternatives would not lead further. Such a degree of innovation, they explained, would require a major structural change.

A similar structural change is needed to break the false dichotomy between the ethical and the practical in the economic paradigm that dominates the U.S. and most of the world economies. The book *Viking Economics* (Lakey, 2016) describes a part of the world where that structural change was made, where the Nordic countries invented an economic model that substantially resolves the contradiction between ethical and practical. The remainder of this chapter describes this model and makes the case that it aligns with the Quaker prophetic tradition because it was value-driven, produced outcomes emerging from Quaker testimonies, and challenged the dominant capital-centered paradigm.

Classical and neoclassical economics start with the presumption that work is an unavoidable burden we take on to achieve a certain standard of living, that is, to fuel consumption. In sharp contrast, the Nordics built a value-driven economy on the recognition that it is deeply human to want to work. Useful, purposeful work provides meaning.

---

[2] I gave the students a "toolkit" of 8 counter-terrorism methods that have been used previously in situations where terror was a threat. All were non-military. Each student needed to apply the toolkit to a specific country suffering terrorist threat and design a nonviolent defense strategy for that country. The 8 tools are described in my brief article (Lakey, 2015). The course syllabus is included in McElwee, *et al.* (2009).

A values-based economy responding to prophetic vision protects citizens from:
- financial crises that are the inevitable result of inadequately-regulated or immorally-guided capital markets;
- dislocations associated with economic reorganization springing from increased globalization and technological innovation;
- policy-making blinkered by a false sense of having to cave in to "practical stubborn realities."

A worker-centered economy
- results in a high degree of equality in standards of living while maximizing individual freedom;
- minimizes the need for charity within a web of universal services;
- fosters a citizenry that accepts taxation as "what we pay for civilized society."

A century ago Swedes, Norwegians, Danes, and Icelanders faced some conditions similar to those challenging the United States and other industrialized economies today. Their transformation to humane, values-centered economies was far from inevitable. It came as a result of the prophetic vision of a valiant few. Their witness serves as a reminder to today's Religious Society of Friends that God's Peaceable Kingdom is achievable today on this Earth.

## The Secular Nordics Join the Prophetic Tradition[3]

When it comes to economics, the Nordics in effect joined the Quaker role of questioning the existence of two opposed realities, the ethical and the practical. The modern Vikings, like Friends, were impelled by an ethical imperative, and then found that value-driven change turned out to be immensely practical. As with those English Quaker merchants, prosperity followed when they devised an alternative to free-market capitalism.

A century ago the Scandinavians experienced immense poverty and inequality. Riven by class distinctions, they had only a pretense of democracy. People formed movements sharing a vision: shared abundance could be structured into an economy. They fervently valued individual freedom, arguably the Norwegians most of all because they had a culture characterized by a

---

[3] I studied four countries, Norway, Sweden, Denmark, and Iceland, because these are the inheritors of the ancient Viking legacy of "going where no one had gone before." The Finns use the Nordic economic model, but ethnically are Magyar, sharing that history with the Hungarians. In the book, I of course acknowledge the violent side of the Viking past as well.

stubborn individualism. Among all the Nordic countries there was a growing minority of people who revered equality and longed for democracy and solidarity.

In each Nordic parliament, some reformers worked for amelioration by trying to reduce poverty, increase the chance of social mobility, and develop programs for the poor and disabled—but always within the framework of capitalism.

At the grassroots level, however, new initiatives developed that went far beyond the reformers, projecting an economic vision that would abolish poverty and replace class domination with real democracy. That vision attracted mass support.

No two countries followed exactly the same path—some differences among them are described in my book *Viking Economics*—but the outcome was similar. The mass movements pushed economic elites out of their historic dominance, thereby creating the space to invent what economists now call the Nordic model.

Enough decades have passed that it is possible to judge the results. The Nordic countries play tag with each other at the top of international indices of economic well-being. The typical Organisation for Economic Co-operation and Development (OECD) index shows the Nordics in the top tier, the UK ranked somewhat above the middle, and the U.S. substantially lower or in the bottom tier.

Compared with the U.S., Norway has more start-ups per capita, Sweden has more patents, and Denmark is racing ahead in its response to climate change. Iceland's response to its 2008 financial collapse increased its equality, while the American response to 2008 increased its inequality.[4] Even though inequality is again increasing overall in Europe, the Nordics remain in the top tier of the OECD nations.[5]

Few outsiders realize that the Nordics began their decisive innovative turn while they were poor countries compared with the United States. Norway was the one Nordic country with substantial oil and gas, but by the time it began to flow (the 1970s) Norway had virtually abolished poverty.[6]

---

[4] For example, according to OECD figures in 2017, the Gini index for the four nations studied shows Iceland the most equal at .244 and Sweden the least at .281. The U.S. is .394 (OECD 2017). This note updates the footnote in my book.

[5] The Gini scores among OECD nations for family income shows the Nordics in the top tier in this order: Finland, Sweden, Norway, Germany, Iceland, Denmark (CIA, 2017). This note updates the footnote in my book.

[6] Two very different definitions of poverty live side by side in this field: "relative" and "absolute." An example of relative poverty is a Norwegian family of three in which the mom can't work. For her and her two children social assistance covers the cost of rent, utilities, clothes, and food, but it does not leave much for recreation. Relative poverty is defined by

While the Danish innovators were strongly influenced by Lutheran Bishop N.F.S. Grundtvig, they weren't as a whole particularly religious, and the Norwegian pioneer leadership was openly Marxist.[7] All of them were influenced by a Swedish academic, Gunnar Myrdal, who gained his economics Ph.D. (and eventually the Nobel Memorial Prize in Economics) with his dissertation replacing classical economic theory with a view that undergirds the high-productivity Nordic model.

## For Productivity, Put the Worker First Instead of Capital

Briefly put, Myrdal asserted that the classical premise that humans don't want to work is mistaken. On the contrary, it is deeply human to want to work, to enjoy the satisfaction of a job well done and know that we have contributed concretely to society, realizing our nature as social beings.

How has that central assumption been realized in practice? A highly productive economy comes from (a) designing jobs so the workers can experience satisfaction, (b) generating full employment, (c) providing abundant rest and renewal opportunities (Norwegians work the fewest hours of any country in Europe, while enjoying high worker productivity), (d) providing free training and education so workers can do their jobs well, (e) providing management practices that encourage worker creativity and innovation, (f) making it easy for workers to change jobs when they no longer find their jobs challenging or satisfying, (g) keeping wage rates at a low ratio from top to bottom of a firm.[8]

---

identifying the median income, calculating what 50% (sometimes 60%) of what that would be, and considering the result the poverty line. Absolute poverty means that an individual or family cannot afford basic means of livelihood. These are people who, for example, must choose between buying their medicine or buying food, or must choose between paying the rent or the utilities. The Nordics comply with the international norm of using "relative poverty" as the definition. In my study, I use the U.S. definition—absolute poverty—since it is salient to our discussion.

[7] Grundtvig was a nineteenth century forerunner of liberation theology. He framed the gospel in a way that could speak to people whether or not they agreed with his theology. His influence extended to Sweden and Norway, not least through his invention of the folk high school movement and his inspiring farmers to organize cooperatives. The Norwegian Labor Party broke with the Communist International and, while remaining Marxist for many decades, departed from orthodoxy by allying with family farmers and refusing armed struggle.

[8] Lars Sørensen, the CEO of the Danish pharmaceutical company Novo Nordisk, commented "When we have too wide a disparity between executive compensation and workers' compensation, we create a barrier to the employee passion and engagement that all companies need to achieve their objective." He was named the world's "best-performing" top executive by the *Harvard Business Review* (HBR, 2016).

From a sociological point of view, centering an economy on the worker as a humane social being instead of on capital has enormous ramifications in society. By reducing alienation, it reduces crime and other anti-social behaviors as well as forms of oppression such as racism.[9] It promotes democracy (very high voter participation rates and lively informed debates), and openness to further innovation (LGBT liberation, women taking charge). The political parties that carry this theory most strongly, and historically are responsible for creating the Nordic model, are parties that today push hardest for carbon neutrality.

At least since the days of debtors' prisons, a society's treatment of offenders and its economic system have been linked. The reigning paradigm in the U.S. considers the control of criminality dependent on punishment. Free-market economics sees punishment as a potential source of profits, so in the U.S. the phenomenon of mass incarceration follows, reinforced as it is by racism. Friends, long concerned about prison reform, are beginning to see this bigger picture more clearly.

The worker-centered Nordic economic model sees offenders as workers who need assistance to get back to a steady job. When incarceration seems necessary, the offenders get short sentences where the emphasis is skill-building, morale development, and increasing connection to community.

The result: the lowest recidivism rates in Europe and such remarkably low crime rates that BBC sent a team to Iceland to try to understand the achievement.

### Iceland, Centering the Worker, Refuses Austerity

In the first decade of 2000 Iceland went on a neo-liberal fling, de-regulating its banks. The bankers, encouraged by the *Wall Street Journal* among others, created a bubble and generated in 2008 what was perhaps the worst economic collapse of any country in history. The crisis was monetary as well as financial;

---

[9] In August 2017, I went to Oslo's Anti-Racism Center to check back in on their progress. (See my book for a report on my interview in 2010, in the chapter on racism.) They reported major progress on integrating immigrants in general including people of color. Norwegian racists are aware that they are losing and making louder noise and more drama as a result, including a Nazi march in Kristiansand in the summer of 2017. Sweden also has had increased Nazi activity, while the majority of Swedes hold firmly to a pro-immigrant position. Because Sweden has been experiencing more push-back, it is now adopting one of Norway's best practices in settling immigrants. See my book's second chapter for a description of Norway's policy.

Regarding crime, the Swedish newspaper *Aftonbladet* (Schori 2017; Tronarp and Sundholm 2017) reports that although admittance of migrants has dramatically accelerated since 2011, the violent crime rate remains the same as it was in 2005 (much lower than that of the U.S.). Perhaps the Nordic model supports low violent crime rates even among people coming from non-Nordic cultures.

people couldn't even get their money out of the ATMs. Icelanders staged a nonviolent revolution, brought down their government, and began criminal proceedings against the bankers. (Nine bankers were convicted.) The Icelanders believe in accountability.

However, the new socialist-green government, turning to the International Monetary Fund for support in the crisis, faced the IMF's usual prescription of austerity. As David Ross points out, the IMF relies on "incentives-based, capital-centric principles of economic organization" as the basis for its belief in austerity (personal communication October 27, 2017). This was in clear collision with Icelanders' democratically-based worker-centric commitment to meeting basic human needs.

Backed by the people, the government defied the IMF, boosted the country's safety net, kept people in their homes even though they were unable to keep up mortgage payments, kept employment high, and stimulated the economy.

The result: the IMF reported Iceland to be in very good shape by 2015, acknowledging in a sub-headline "Recovery achieved without compromising welfare model" (Hammar, 2015).

The U.S. also faced a financial crisis in 2008. Its crisis was less profound than Iceland's, and there is of course no comparison between the immense resources of the U.S. and those of tiny Iceland. Nevertheless, the U.S. elite chose bailouts and austerity as its response to the crisis. As late as 2017 the country had still not recovered fully except for the considerable gains made by the elite.

Quakers concerned about the testimony of equality will note that Iceland's worker-centered response to crisis increased its degree of equality (Bergmann, 2014, p. 161). In its capital-centered response, the U.S. accelerated its own inequality, already out of control for decades.

### Globalization and Employment

Unemployment can be deadly. Health economists David Stuckler and Sanjay Basu (2013) have shown that rising unemployment is accompanied by increased heart attacks, suicides, and death. Epidemiologists Richard Wilkinson and Katie Pickett (2010) find high correlations of pathological symptoms accompanying inequality, including obesity, mental illness, violence, and crime.

Conventional wisdom in the U.S. holds that globalization and technological development prevent full employment at high wages. In fact, the Nordics have *always* been globalized, making their living with exports like cod, pork, and lumber, at the mercy of larger market forces. Their industries have also been affected by technological advance.

Nevertheless, since adopting their new model they also enjoy high employment at high wages. The difference the new model makes can be seen in Norway's decades-long higher labor force participation than that of the U.S., belying the notion that a "nanny state" reduces the incentive to work.

Nordic measures such as Keynesian stimulus, free higher education, free job training, and support for entrepreneurs kept their job numbers high. When globalization intensified in the 1980s and '90s and some Nordic businesses found themselves unable to compete successfully, the Danes (borrowing from the Dutch) came up with "flexicurity," a program that makes it easy for owners of firms to shift their capital to more productive use while maximizing the chance for the workers to make the most of that opportunity for their own careers. The other Nordics then adopted the program.[10]

This creative, worker-centered response to the challenge of change brings us to the conditions under which countries can choose policies in line with their highest values.

### How Design Supports Doing Well along with Doing Good

When I was a boy, a major identifier for my country was that "Americans are a can-do people." According to the informal samples I take in audiences around the country, older people remember this identifier.

Most young people have never heard of it.

The disempowerment of American workers through the war against labor unions may have cultural fall-out: a failure to reproduce the old American confidence that "we the people" can collectively solve the problems that face us.[11]

U.S. polls consistently show rising disbelief that either government or the economic elite can solve major problems. If people at the grassroots believe

---

[10] Four years after the 2008 international financial crash, *Bloomberg's* Iain Begg surveyed the European economic situation. "In the Nordic countries, commitments to so-called active labor-market policies designed to keep people connected to the workforce have imparted resilience in employment that others envy" (Begg, 2012).

[11] The American Dream was an encouragement for the individual to rise through meeting the challenges they faced. That also has taken a beating; strong rates of upward mobility are only a memory in the U.S., although alive and well among the Nordics. I'm here referring, however, to the confidence that Americans can *collectively* meet major challenges as in the 1930s when unions led the charge against the Great Depression and in the 1940s when the nation went to war, the 1950s when the nation resolved to "stop the spread of Communism," and the 1960s declaration that we would have a "war against poverty." Since the 1980s the trend has been to reduce both expectations and aspirations of collective effort. The timidity shows up in response to climate change and even in my audiences for *Viking Economics* when people express doubt that we have the capacity to change our economic model despite majority agreement that the present model is severely flawed.

ourselves to be equally incompetent, desperation is predictable. Evidence for that desperation is reported in daily news sources.

In the worker-centered Nordic economies, with their high union density and track record of major advances in shared prosperity, the "can-do" spirit is alive and well. All have set highly ambitious goals for going carbon neutral, for example

As the Nordic adoption of flexicurity demonstrates, over half a century of social democracy results in an attitude of optimism when confronted with an apparent collision between a social value and practicality. Want to get done in thirty-five hours the amount of work usually done in forty, at the same pay? Want to encourage dads to take more responsibility for rearing their children, freeing the moms to continue to move ahead in their careers? Want to reduce the rate of purchase of automobiles in a prosperous society? Or even to abolish gasoline-fueled cars? Preserve the family farm? Stay out of the European Union, given that it's ruled by the economic elites and highly undemocratic? (That's the Norwegian choice.) Become the number one country in Europe for accepting refugees from Syria? (That's the Swedish choice.)

*These are all design choices, democratically debated, where people look actively for the innovations that enable them to express their values and maintain or improve economic well-being at the same time.*

The example of choosing universal health care as a matter of right, funded through taxation, long ago demonstrated the superiority of a design orientation. The Nordics pay roughly two-thirds what the U.S. pays for its market-based health care system, saving money while providing quality care for everyone.

## Trade-off between Individual Freedom and Equality?

Nordic performance challenges yet another widely-held assumption: that there is a trade-off between equality and individual freedom.

In U.S. discussions of economic policy, Conventional Wisdom assumes that there is a trade-off between equality and individual freedom. For example, when the state re-distributes wealth through progressive taxation, it thereby reduces the wealthier individuals' freedom to use their wealth as they see fit. When progressives counter by arguing that the Common Good is enhanced by more equality, the counter-argument is made that redistributing income from "makers" to "takers" results in lower prosperity for all (lower national income).

This policy conversation is model-specific, peculiar to free-market capitalism which, after all, is only one way to design an economy, a design that puts wealth at the center. The Nordics chose a different design. By focusing on the humane purposes of work, they created a model that generates more prosperity for the whole. In addition, by many measures they have more equality and enjoy more individual freedom than Americans do.

Instead of the value trade-offs common in the US model, the Nordics design for ways that policies for equality and individual freedom enhance each other. They look for synergies, ways to create outcomes for the whole that are larger than the sum of the parts.

Here are some specific examples of the synergistic approach.

People in mid-life sometimes find themselves in boring or dead-end jobs, or careers that are inappropriate for their talents. "Square pegs in round holes" don't maximize productivity for the whole. Universal programs (an egalitarian approach) step in: anyone can take advantage of free career counseling, education, skill training, and job placement to increase freedom to make a new choice.

For people who at any point get a bright idea that suggests an entrepreneurial opportunity, freedom to quit their job and pursue their dream is enhanced by very high unemployment support, free education and training, continued health insurance, and the continued assurance of pension. This helps to explain why there are more start-ups in Norway per capita than in the U.S. To even the playing field still further, the Drammen school of entrepreneurship offers some courses in English to encourage immigrants to join, since English is more likely to be immigrants' second language.

Teenagers in school have a choice of classroom instruction or apprenticeships, honoring individual differences in learning styles. When the design combines a high degree of equality of educational opportunity and the individual freedom to choose, the result is higher worker productivity, as shown by comparing Norwegian and U.S. rates.

Consider the following Nordic economic policies toward parents and their multiple synergistic impacts:

- universal paid parental leave with guaranteed return to the job,
- strong incentive in heterosexual couples for the dad to take some of that leave (if he refuses, the couple loses that part of the leave),
- the right to stay home (with pay) to take care of a sick child, workplace on-site nurseries for larger enterprises,
- paid time for nursing the baby at work,
- ongoing wages for parenting at home if the parent decides to do childrearing full time rather than continue a job,
- affordable childcare for all who choose it, in workplaces and neighborhoods.

These policies have resulted in high participation of women in the labor force along with increased rates of promotion and responsibility. Together they have increased gender equality and increased individual freedom.

In the U.S. many have noted a rising expectation of the career woman "super-mom" dealing with increased stress. The Nordic policies noted above reduce the stress of parenting. That, however, might lead to a fear that all these state interventions in the market become the dreaded "nanny state that chokes prosperity."

Norwegian economist and twice-prime minister Jens Stoltenberg sees the opposite outcome: increased participation in the labor force by women has been a highly important contributor to Norway's prosperity.[12]

Economist Gunnar Myrdal would not be surprised. Worker-centered economic designs that promote equality and individual freedom create the path to shared abundance.

### Are the Nordics "Welfare States?"

In August 2017, I went to Budø University in Northern Norway to keynote a professional meeting of 300 Nordic economists. I described to them a communication block that in the U.S. prevents an accurate understanding of the power of the Nordic model. I received widespread positive feedback.

"Welfare" in the U.S. means programs for the poor and disadvantaged, historically linked to the practice of charity. The Nordics, noting the futility of that strategy, decisively turned against it. Instead, they chose the strategy of universal services for everyone, no matter what their income level. That shift proved crucial to their success in preventing poverty.

At Budø I asked economists, when communicating with Americans and the British, to avoid the term "welfare state" as a descriptor of the Nordics. One alternative might be the much more accurate "universal services state."

Free higher education is available to all who qualify, whether high or low on the income scale, including law school, medical school, and other professional education. Higher education rests on a foundation of quality public schools for all, no matter the income of the parents, where teachers are respected and paid well.

Single-payer health insurance for all with small co-payments means that timely, very expensive treatments are available to working class as well as rich

---

[12] The oil and gas is owned by the Norwegian public and earnings are largely channeled into the Pension Fund invested abroad for the eventual benefit of the people. The fund in 2017 passed 1 trillion dollars in value, the largest sovereign wealth fund in the world, and has a rigorous social responsibility screen.

people. Previously I described the services for parents and families, with universal participation whether the parents are lower or higher income.

All Norwegian elders have a choice when they need assisted living: move to a retirement center or stay at home. Most stay in their homes, while between a third and a fourth choose to move. Those who stay home can receive between a few hours a month to a few hours a day of extra assistance.[13]

Rent control, cooperatives, and public responsibility for the supply of shelter means affordable housing for all. Disability benefits are available whether or not one has a background of wealth, as is re-training for a new job, and support while looking for one. Public transportation is subsidized for all. So are tickets to the new opera house in Oslo.

Making services universal can be a cost-saver: Nordics save money by reducing the bureaucracy needed for means-testing. Taking the profit and waste out of health care reduces the cost dramatically: by using single-payer Nordics pay roughly two-thirds what the U.S. pays for health care, for example, and the Nordics cover everyone. Ample and highly-subsidized public transportation reduces the need for cars, serving the values of equality, individual freedom, and sustainability.

Nevertheless, universal services overall require high taxes. This fact is widely understood and accepted.[14] Then Norwegian Labor Prime Minister Jens Stoltenberg told *The New York Times* that the Labor Party won two elections promising *not* to lower taxes (Bennhold, 2011). What motivates Nordics to pay high taxes for services is that the services are universal rather than targeted to a subgroup of "the needy."

*Everyone* benefits from quality health care, schools, transportation, and pensions, but most of all the political majority is composed of the working and middle classes. When someone proposes chipping away at the quality of universal systems, a political defense is mounted by the majority almost regardless of the

---

13 The cost of the service is subsidized for all but there is a charge. Unusually for Norway, means-testing enters in the pricing of this service: if an elder's income falls below a certain threshold they are charged only a nominal amount.

14 Some scholars outside the Nordic sphere see economic pay-off in high tax regimes. Economist Jeffrey D. Sachs compared the economic performance over time of, on the one hand, Denmark, Finland, Norway and Sweden, and on the other hand the low-tax, high-income countries that share a historical lineage with 19th century Britain and its theories of laissez-faire: Australia, Canada, Ireland, New Zealand, the U.K., and the U.S. His conclusion: "On average, the Nordic countries outperform the Anglo-Saxon ones on most measures of economic performance" (Sachs 2006, p. 42). The Canadian Centre for Policy Alternatives compared high-tax and low-tax countries on the basis of social and economic indicators. Among other things, the study found productivity (GNP per hour worked) was higher in the high-tax states (Brooks and Hwong, 2006).

party they belong to.[15] The Norwegian Progress Party and the Danish People's Party, for example, are branded as "right wing" because of their anti-immigration stance, but both parties are deeply committed to the universal services, which in the U.S. would put both of these "right-wing parties" well to the left of the Democratic Party.

## Are the Nordics the "Exceptional Case," or Are They a Laboratory?

Many professions pursue "best practices." When a professional encounters a stubborn problem, that person looks around to see how it was resolved in other situations, hoping to find something that could be useful.

Curiously, in the U.S. I sometimes find resistance to serious consideration of the Nordic model. A favorite defense against a best practices attitude is to emphasize differences from the U.S.: small size, for example, or homogeneous population, cultural and historical factors.[16]

During one of my research trips supported by Swarthmore I interviewed senior scholars at the Fafo Research Foundation in Oslo. I noticed that I had been preceded by a team of Chinese economists and policy-makers sent by the government in Beijing to learn from. . . Norway!

In size, heterogeneity, culture, and history, China is much more different from Norway than is the U.S. Nevertheless, the Chinese government was curious about Norway as a lab from which it might draw best practices. Thinking of the Nordics as laboratories for innovation is the pragmatic view of a "can-do" people. I thought it ironic that China is at this point so much more pragmatic than the U.S.

Using the pragmatic lens, I remembered that Iceland has a social security system (340,000 pop) but so does the U.S. (330 million)–clearly, social security can be scaled up! Denmark has a kind of Medicare but so does the U.S. Within the U.S. itself, California and New York (among our most culturally diverse states) not long ago had virtually free higher education. That policy was not abandoned because diversity reduces the quality of education–the reverse is more likely the case![17]

---

[15] In the U.S. Social Security and Medicare are virtually immune to serious cutbacks because they are universal programs, while food stamps, the supplemental nutrition program for women, infants, and children (WIC), and Temporary Assistance for Needy Families are programs for the poor and in continual jeopardy.

[16] The homogeneity defense is fast losing cogency because of rapid changes: one in five Norwegians is now foreign-born, and Sweden's taking in more Syrians per capita than any other European country means that they've exceeded Norway in proportion of immigrants.

[17] I show in chapters 6-9 of my pedagogy book (Lakey 2010) how diversity in a class actually supports learning.

It's obvious that there are economic designs that can scale up and are not culturally specific. No one knows how many specific designs that work for the Nordics can work as well or better in the U.S. on local, state, or national levels.

What may be missing is the curiosity to find out. If our people have lost their curiosity, there is still an alternative. Quaker history suggests that being led by values can motivate us to design alternatives, and sometimes even make breakthroughs.

### How Did the Nordics Break Through?

A century ago the Nordics were in bad shape; their people had been fleeing to the U.S. and elsewhere looking for the chance to live a decent life. A small minority of those who stayed behind committed themselves to fundamental change. As I describe in my book, those prophetic organizers helped the majority to see that their countries were only pretend democracies, in fact ruled by their economic elites.[18]

"Without a vision, the people perish." The Nordics playing the prophetic role developed an alternative vision with the help of Myrdal and other economists. Grassroots education spread the vision and motivated people to act. Poor farmers and workers were tired of perishing, and middle class people were also questioning the rule of the elite.

Co-ops assisted ordinary people to retain wealth rather than have so much vacuumed up by the rich, helped their self-confidence, and built the skills of solidarity that they would need in the struggle to come.

As the movement grew it engaged the elite in nonviolent struggle, initiating campaigns that were opposed by police and troops. The elite did defend their privilege with violence. The struggle illuminated the economic injustice and made transparent the pretend democracy, motivating more of the fence-sitters to join the movement.

In each country, the struggle came to a head at a different moment. The power shift occurred in Denmark in 1924, Sweden in 1931, and Norway in

---

[18] Political scientists Martin Gilens of Princeton and Benjamin I. Page of Northwestern examined the 1779 specific U.S. policy issues that came to a head for national decision over the two decades between 1981 and 2002, before the Supreme Court's Citizens United decision and the current money rush. On each issue Gilens and Page (2014) determined from opinion polls and other evidence what the majority of the public wanted and what the economic elite wanted. When those two views differed, the scholars wanted to know whose view prevailed. They found that, when there was a difference, the economic elite almost always got their way rather than the majority.

1935.[19] The power shift made possible the invention and implementation of the Nordic model.

Popular movements in other countries, such as the U.S., waged parallel struggles but did not succeed in overthrowing the domination of their elites. As a result, they fell far short of realizing their vision. In the U.S., where the Princeton "oligarchy study" famously describes the economic elite's overwhelming dominance of U.S. decision-making, no amount of reformist incrementalism has come close to reaching Nordic achievements of equality, individual freedom, and shared abundance (Gilens and Page, 2014).

Billionaire Warren E. Buffett revealed the current situation in his 2006 wide-ranging interview with Ben Stein of the *New York Times*. Stein (2006) noted that, when unfair tax rates are discussed, some people accuse others of being engaged in class warfare. Buffett replied, "There's class warfare, all right, but it's my class, the rich class, that's making war, and we're winning."

### How Does This Perspective Support Quakers Today?

The Nordic countries' narrative both confirms and challenges today's Friends. It confirms our historic legacy of bold innovation that breaks with the reigning paradigm, by giving us confidence that if we stay true to our values and take a risk with creative alternatives and new designs, we might more fully experience the unity of Creation.

The story of the modern Vikings also confirms another Quaker legacy: the usefulness of projecting a *vision* of what justice might look like. William Penn's Holy Experiment is well known, but not his sketch of a European league of nations that might bring peace to a war-wracked continent. For the Nordics, an economic vision was crucial for going beyond reform efforts and instead making system change, the breakthrough that made justice, equality, and freedom possible.[20]

The Nordics' story also supports Friends in speaking truth to power. More challenging for Friends, however, may be speaking truth *about* power. Friends are understandably reluctant to play a "blame game" or to demonize individuals. Here, too, we can learn from Scandinavians.

---

[19] The Swedish and Norwegian histories of major change are in Lakey (2016), Denmark's in Lakey (2017).

[20] The American Friends Service Committee has endorsed the vision offered by the Movement for Black Lives (AFSC, 2016), whose economic policies are in alignment with what the Nordics have shown to be workable in their "labs." The vision (also called "platform") was covered by *The NY Times* and other major media sources. Other Friends bodies would do well to consider signing on to that vision: https://policy.m4bl.org/platform/.

Political discourse in the Nordic countries has for a long time been more sophisticated than that of the U.S. because it assumes the existence of class interests and the possibility that any given issue may reveal class conflict. Because this conceptual framework has been omitted from courses even for many college-educated Americans, we are more prone to demonize people who are simply operating in the interests of their class.[21] Friends can emulate the Nordics, and just acknowledge what is true about class and power without demonizing.

Acknowledging class conflict helps us ground both Friends and non-Friends in reality. Just as "climate denial" prevents citizens from acting in their own interests, so "oligarchy denial" prevents people from choosing change strategies that actually have a chance of succeeding.

Another challenge for Friends is speaking truth *with* power, i.e., powerfully. Middle class socialization includes rule-following to such a degree that the largely working-class 17th century Friends would scarcely recognize their 21st century counterparts as Friends at all.

While it is true that early Friends sometimes petitioned authority, their effectiveness often lay in their willingness to be nonviolently disruptive, incentivizing officials to pay close attention to the truth Friends wanted to share.

Speaking truth *about* and *with* power was tough for Quakers in the 1960s, when the civil rights movement was looking for allies and found surprisingly few Friends willing to risk and join. I was there, involved heavily both in the civil rights movement and with the Religious Society of Friends. My observation was not that mainstream Quakers were as indifferent to racism as they appeared to be, but that they were so afraid to speak truth *about* power and to speak truth *with* power that they were rendered impotent, since simply speaking truth *to* power is a waste of time when power already knows what's up.[22]

As inequality in the U.S. and UK continues to grow and class conflict intensifies, Friends are tempted once again to shrink away, to indulge in Quaker witness, which a British Friend told me can be defined as "standing up to be counted and then sitting down so you don't rock the boat."

Fortunately, we do inherit an alternative, a legacy exemplified by the first Quakers, by Lucretia Mott and Bayard Rustin, and other Friends who have seen

---

[21] Judging from my conversation with many econ majors, knowledge about the Nordic model is also left out of many college economics courses, perhaps because of its frank acknowledgement of class conflict.

[22] A successful recent example of the deliberate use the prophetic Quaker legacy was persuading the seventh-largest U.S. bank to stop financing mountain-top removal coal mining in Appalachia. Earth Quaker Action Team (eqat.org) knew that peer-reviewed studies showed blowing up mountains doubled the cancer rates and increased birth defects in the affected areas. EQAT spoke truth to, about, and with power, and its five years of nonviolent direct action campaigning (125 actions, multiple arrests) incentivized PNC Bank to cease its practice.

connections between equality and economy. Embracing that legacy, we can project a paradigm-shifting alternative vision, using the Nordic model and the Movement for Black Lives platform as rough drafts.

Quaker economists and other academics keen to learn from best practices have skills to be a resource in this process. Thus emboldened, we can join the struggle for an economy that more closely reflects Friends testimonies. In the struggle, we will find the spiritual gifts that await outside our comfort zones.

## References

American Friends Service Committee endorses the Movement for Black Lives Platform (AFSC) (2016, October 21). American Friends Service Committee. Retrieved from https://www.afsc.org/story/american-friends-service-committee-endorses-movement-black-lives-platform

Begg, I. (2012, April 15). Is 'Flexicurity' Post-Crisis Europe's New Social Model? *Bloomberg View.* Retrieved from https://www.bloomberg.com/view/articles/2012-04-15/is-flexicurity-post-crisis-europe-s-new-social-model-

Bennhold, K. (2011, June 28). Working Women Are the Key to Norway's Prosperity. *New York Times.*

Bergmann, E. (2014). *Iceland and the International Financial Crisis: Boom, Bust and Recovery.* New York: Palgrave Macmillan.

Brooks, N., Hwong T. (2006). *The Social Benefits and Economic Costs of Taxation.* Ottawa: Canadian Centre for Policy Alternatives. Retrieved from https://www.policyalternatives.ca/publications/reports/social-benefits-and-economic-costs-taxation

Distribution of family income–gini coefficient (CIA) (2017). *The world factbook.* Washington, D.C: Central Intelligence Agency. Retrieved from https://www.cia.gov/library/publications/the-world-factbook/rankorder/2172rank.html

The Best-Performing CEOs in the World (HBR) (2016). *Harvard Business Review.* 94(November). Retrieved from https://hbr.org/2016/11/the-best-performing-ceos-in-the-world

Gilens, M. and Page, B.I. (2014). Testing Theories of American Politics: Elites, Interest Groups, and Average Citizens. *Perspectives on Politics,* 12(September), pp. 564-581 Retrieved from http://scholar.princeton.edu/sites/default/files/mgilens/files/gilens_and_page_2014_-testing_theories_of_american_politics.doc.pdf.

Hammar, K. (2015, March 13). IMF Survey: Iceland Makes Strong Recovery from 2008 Financial Crisis. *IMF News.* Retrieved from http://www.imf.org/en/news/articles/2015/09/28/04/53/socar031315a

Lakey, G. (2010). *Facilitating Group Learning.* San Francisco, California: Jossey-Bass.

Lakey, G. (2015, January 22). 8 ways to defend against terror nonviolently. *Waging Nonviolence.* Retrieved from https://wagingnonviolence.org/feature/8-ways-defend-terror-nonviolently/.

Lakey, G. (2016). *Viking Economics: How the Scandinavians Got It Right-and How We Can, Too.* New York: Melville House.

Lakey, G. (2017, July 19). Why are the Danes so happy? Because their economy makes sense. *Waging Nonviolence.* Retrieved from https://waging nonviolence.org/feature/denmark-nordic-model-economy-happiness/.

McElwee, T.A., Hall, B.W., Liechty, J., and Garber, J. (2009). *Peace, Justice, and Security Studies: A Curriculum Guide.* Boulder, CO: Lynne Rienner Publishers.

OECD (2017). Income inequality (indicator). doi: 10.1787/459aa7f1-en.

Sachs, J.D. (2006). Welfare States, beyond Ideology. *Scientific American,* 295(November), p. 42.

Schori, M. (2017, February 23). The crime situation in Sweden compared to the US, in 4 charts. *Aftonblatt.* Retrieved from https://www.aftonbladet.se/nyheter/a/WP0KG/the-crime-situation-in-sweden-compared-to-the-us-in-4-charts

Stein, B. (2006, November 26). In Class Warfare, Guess Which Class is Winning. *The New York Times.*

Stuckler, D., Basu, S. (2013). *The Body Economic: Why Austerity Kills.* NY: Basic Books.

Tronarp, G. and Sundholm, M. (2017, February 20). After Trump's 'Last night in Sweden': Here are the errors in Fox News' report on Swedish immigration. *Aftonblatt.* Retrieved from https://www.afton bladet.se/nyheter/a/g26Lk/after-trumps-last-night-in-sweden-here-are-the-errors-in-fox-news

Wilkinson, R., and Pickett, K. (2010). *The Spirit Level.* London: Penguin Books.

# 4 | Governing the World from the Ground Up Through Power Grounded in the Light: A Proposal for Action Research on Quaker and Gandhian Responses to our Global Crises

**By Gray Cox**

Our planet has proven a distinctly fortunate site for the evolution of life in extraordinarily rich variety and complexity. It has provided an especially hospitable home for the development of our species in particular as a creative, intelligent community of moral beings who have been capable of developing a remarkable variety of ways to live well and an inspiring variety of moral and spiritual practices for discerning beauty, goodness, and truth that can guide such life. It has also enabled the development of some extremely unhelpful and destructive practices and institutions that currently threaten the existence of all those resources and the gifts they could provide in the future. How can we best understand these existential threats to the creations with which we have been blessed? And how might we transform our lives and our institutions so as to address the concerns they raise? These are not just questions for academics to study—they are fundamental queries that call for a massive program of practical experiments in action research undertaken by all of us.

One set of such experiments with research methods was initiated in 2003 by a group of Quakers academics, policy analysts, and scholar activists. They had convened at Pendle Hill to explore the development of a Quaker Testimony on Economics and Ecology. In the course of the meeting, Keith Helmuth shared a leading he had which had been sparked by suggestions from Kenneth Boulding. The idea was to form a kind of "Quaker Thinktank." A group emerged which went on to found the Quaker Institute for the Future (QIF) which has sponsored a series of focus books and publications dealing with a wide range of social and environmental concerns. From the start, members of QIF sought to do research strongly informed by Quaker testimonies in an organization governed by Quaker process. But, further, they also sought to use Quaker models of communal discernment in the ways in which they actually undertook their research. These Friends have been experimenting for over a decade with methods for collaborative research that draws on Quaker traditions of communal discernment to practice a kind of "meeting for worship for the conduct of research." These include, for example, the use of clearness committees, summer research seminars, circles of discernment for pamphlets, and teams for writing books like *Right Relationship: Building a Whole Earth Economy* (Brown, *et al.*, 2009; Cox, *et al.*, 2014). Such methods can be used in conjunction with a full range of other research methods from natural and social science, policy analysis, ethnography, indigenous traditions, theology of liberation, community-based critical participatory research, and other practices. The aim of Quaker approaches to research is not to replace other methods but to lodge and frame them in the context of processes of communal discernment that are spirit-led and grounded fully in attitudes and practices of non-violent collaboration and satyagraha. I want to share here a proposal for a very ambitious research program which might be carried on in that spirit-led way as a collaborative project or set of projects.

The proposal springs from the conviction that we face inter-related global crises that pose four profound existential threats: 1) the economic/ecological; 2) the military/governance; 3) the technological, and 4) the moral/spiritual. I want to propose a collaborative program in action research that will address these by drawing on key insights and practices from the Quaker and Gandhian traditions. This program of research is systematic in intent and aims to shift paradigms in fundamental ways.

Observers from another planet might very well look at the management of ours–and the impending threats–and wonder: "*What* are they thinking?!" But the key problem lies, more precisely, in *how* we are thinking–and *how* we suppose rational people should choose beliefs and actions. In sketching each crisis and proposals to respond to it, I will suggest here that the most fundamental shift required is from a monological model of reasoning as inferential computation to a dialogical model of reasoning as conflict transformation. Such conflict transformation is exemplified, for instance, by Quaker communal discernment and Gandhian satyagraha. It calls for a fundamental shift in the understanding of truth and the ways it is sought. A central claim will be that key features of this shift are illuminated in profound ways by: 1) communal discernment practices developed out of traditions of early Quakers in their "Religious Society of

Friends of the Truth" and 2) Gandhi's "experiments with Truth" which developed methods of "satyagraha" as a kind of "Truth Force."

## Section I: The Economic/Ecological Crisis: Redirecting Income to Redirect History

We are threatened with catastrophic climate change and a sixth great extinction because of, in large part, a pervasive commitment to an economic rationality pursuing ever greater material consumption and GDP. People living at average American incomes consume at least two or more times what can be sustained globally. The Global Footprint Network (2017) estimates, for instance, that for the population of our entire planet to achieve and maintain the level of consumption of the average North American, the resources of five Earths would be required. But repeated informal polling strongly suggests that asking people to reduce their consumption seems to many–perhaps most of them–to deprive them of personal wellbeing. It's a hard sale.

But what if we frame reduction of material consumption differently? Not as a decrease in private consumption but as an increase in personal action and agency? We could explore this by starting with acts and practices of giving and moral agency that are already familiar. Then we might explicitly redirect them towards forms of effective social change and progressively scale them up so as to approach the levels of impact needed to successfully address the problems we face.

Traditional ways of raising money include, for instance, getting folks together to contribute while doing things they want to do anyway–meals, parties, dance-athons, run-athons, etc. How might we incorporate this in all the activities we undertake for protest, organizing and change? For starters we might make every march into a "march-athon." If we rally to protest cutting funds for Planned Parenthood we could ask each participant to get ten supporters to pledge Planned Parenthood a sum at least equal to travel costs for the march. If a million people at the Women's March in DC and related rallies in January of 2017 had each gotten ten others to contribute the equivalent of a hundred dollar bus ticket, that would have raised 10 x $100 x 1,000,000 = one billion dollars (roughly equal to the organization's annual budget). Marchers might then have focused not on pleading with conservative legislators for support but on other, perhaps more radical steps that would advance their cause. How might we make this kind of fundraising a basic part of our practice as activists?

Consider another example: people concerned with issues like climate change are willing to make a wide variety of sacrifices. Millions change light bulbs, cars, and investment portfolios and pay for transport, rally costs, and court fines to push for their cause. What if such actions were regularly coupled with a fundraising element? Citizens of the United States could, for instance, say to the world: "Do not be misled by the leaders of our country. We, the people, believe climate change is real and are ready to do our part to stop it. This includes funding the most needy, least developed countries' climate adaptation programs with a billion dollars raised this weekend . . . with more to come."

Further, when a special event like Valentine's Day or Easter comes, what if money we would otherwise spend on cards, sweets, and gifts was pledged in gifts to local food pantries, the Least Developed Countries Fund for dealing with climate change, or other worthy organizations that will make the world a better place for our loved ones? We could say "I love you" to our nearest and dearest by showing our love for their world. Instead of buying them stuff from China, give them blank checks to make out to whatever organizations they feel would best promote the world in which they would love to live. Our gift to loved ones can be the opportunity for them to give a gift. "Giving the gift of gifts" could become central to the celebration of birthdays, anniversaries, graduations, or even Christmas. Every holiday could be a celebration of life for all–and every protest an opportunity for pledging funds and acting on concerns.

How far might we be led to go in such pledges? It should depend of course on individual life circumstances. But a majority of Americans should, over the next few years, aim to cut our carbon and ecological footprints in half–and cutting our personal consumption in half. We should redirect the other half of our income to acts of charitable solidarity, socially responsible investment, and political/social change. We may not be ready to wear loin-cloths and live like Gandhi or Saint Teresa, but we could meet them halfway.

There are, of course, a variety of complications in trying to determine exactly how far over carrying capacity our consumption is and which portions most impact sustainability. However, in the context of framing the basic shift of life practices proposed here, we can more simply speak of cutting consumption in half, at least as a starting point, because of the conceptual and emotional clarity it provides.

Of course, it is not easy to redirect income all at once. And those living below the poverty line should, instead, be increasing consumption. But those who are living well on two or more times the sustainable level of individual material consumption for this planet should feel called to take up this challenge. It may take us a while to meet it. But we each know folks who are living on ten percent less than we are right now. In a year, we should be able to shift to their level of consumption and in the following year shift another ten percent. After five years it should be quite realistic to cut our personal material consumption in half and with the rest share in solidarity, invest in socially responsible ways, and fund political and social change. In the future, ecological constraints will require the consumption of the average person in the developed world to cut consumption dramatically. Our research task might be framed, in a sense, as simply learning to "meet the future halfway."

A blog called "Mr. Money Moustache" documents the efforts one young couple undertook in developing strategies for this (Adeney, 2016; Paumgarten, 2016). They chose after finishing college to devote at least half of their pooled, middle-class income to savings with the aim of being able to retire in less than 20 years. They beat that goal and in the process cultivated a community of people with strategies and insights into the process of living well while living on half their income. This is a model worth developing and promoting. If a 23 year old college student can envision investing half of her income on graduation for 17 years and retiring at 40, this can, for many, provide a very compelling life plan.

As we move towards "meeting the future halfway," we will be able to fund a parallel set of institutions to safeguard our commons–the commons that are being abandoned by our government. Part of the challenge arises from the increasing power of neo-liberal visions that push to shrink the size of government programs that care for the commons. A parallel challenge arises from the neo-liberal push to reduce the regulatory power of government and its ability to address social costs of private actions and various kinds of environmental externalities that end up benefiting the few at the expense of the commons. But, the challenge, especially at the level of the global commons and planetary concerns such as climate change, arises from something even more deeply grounded in our current global system than the rise of neo-liberal ideology. It is the nature of the national security state itself, which frames the world in terms of territories controlled by countries who defend their holdings with the military and view others as either allies or enemies. This framing of the world makes leaders see the lands, waters, and airspace of the world as resources that are either part of their territory or someone else's. Viewing the world through the lens of territory, they literally cannot see the commons. It is made invisible and irrelevant in the logic of their treatment of the world. In contrast, individuals, NGOs, tribal groups, cities, and regional governments all are able to recognize that their well-being depends on getting neighbors to collaborate–to manage the commons collectively in the ways that, for instance, Elinor Ostrom has studied. A clear illustration of this difference is the sharp contrast between the sad failure of nation-states to arrive at an adequate and effective treaty on climate change versus the extraordinary work that groups and communities in civil society have been doing to address climate change (Cox, 2012). Such efforts can be scaled up dramatically if progressively more of us redirect half our income to "meet the future halfway". We will be able to fund education, health, environmental stewardship, the defense of human rights, and work for global peace–doing the work that national security states have proved incompetent at.

A key hypothesis is that as we do this we will come to live in a different reality. It will be a reality in which we identify ourselves primarily not as capitalist consumers fueling a growing GNP. Instead, we will increasingly see ourselves as ethical agents of sustainable change taking ownership of the planet through investments and empowering people through political change. We will define ourselves not, primarily, by what we have and consume privately but by what we do and achieve publicly in caring for the commons.

It is not difficult to imagine a rich variety of research projects that might pursue these ideas about redirecting personal consumption and build on work already going on (Joy, 2011). For example, what are steps on this path that work best to motivate and transform people whose circumstances differ by age, gender, ethnicity, religion, regional traditions, and other factors? Which sorts of transition steps are most appropriate for college graduates, new parents, couples experiencing "empty nest syndrome," or retirees? What are ways the redirection of income can best be institutionalized so as to result in rapid scaling up of the process and consolidation of communities of practitioners? How might affinity groups, investment clubs, church peace and justice committees, family trusts, and other kinds of structures best be used to initiate, sustain, and scale up such efforts? What kind of learning, therapy, consciousness raising, public education, and other efforts might best help people change their habits, self-concepts, and visions of the good life? Action-centered research answering such questions will also help significantly in finding ways to deal with the second existential threat we face.

## Section II: Earth Swaraj: Establishing a Nonviolent System of Global Governance to Secure the Commons

We face a global governance crisis that not only threatens to incapacitate our ability to manage the global commons but also creates arms races that threaten mass destruction. It grows out of the global system of national security states that rely on violent sanctions to govern themselves with police and defend territory with military. Politics becomes a practice of self-interested polemic and manipulative, violent realpolitik. In trying to liberate India from the power of the British national security state system, Gandhi's aim was to achieve Indian self-governance or "Swaraj" through reliance on a different kind of power–"truth or love force." It used systematic non-violent methods of "satyagraha." He was not interested in simply substituting Indian for British rulers if the method of government would remain grounded in the terror, violence, and oppression of a traditional state. Like him, we need, at the global level, to focus not on changing who governs but on how governance is empowered and institutionalized. His basic strategy for Indian Swaraj was to systematically build a set of parallel institutions in education, health, food production, law, defense, and other social functions that could displace the power of the British Raj (Gandhi, 2013; Bondurant, 1988). The research proposal offered here is to pursue, similarly, a kind of Earth Swaraj with parallel institutions all grounded in sanctions of nonviolent direct action and appeals to truth force rather than the weapons of police and military.

Ways of funding this were suggested in Section 1. As we scale up ways we redirect our income, we will be able to fund parallel institutions to safeguard our commons abandoned by our governments. The World Social Forum and others provide excellent examples of this—for instance, of public/private partnerships funding hundreds of billions of dollars in loans to finance infrastructure that ameliorates or mitigates climate change. The paltry treaty making efforts of national security states in the Paris accords have in many ways been outstripped by such initiatives. The movement to build a global civic culture which began over a hundred years ago was, for a long time, a minor activity of utopian idealists operating in the shadow of nation-states and great powers. But with the extraordinary growth of civil society and the "blessed unrest" of a host of social movements, that relationship has been increasingly reversed (Boulding, 1990; Hawken, 2007). One central research question is: How might we strengthen and advance such work if we stop framing it as dependent action performed in the shadow of the nation-state system and start seeing it as the central governance system for the rule of our planetary home—as Earth Swaraj?

Another central research question concerns how to best develop campaigns and institutions for the wide range of satyagraha actions required to successfully govern the world through non-violence. The last century has provided very diverse, creative experiments with nonviolence. They were instrumental in liberating peoples and changing governments in India, Eastern Europe, South Africa, the Philippines, the South of the United States, much of Latin America, and a variety of other places. Starting with Gandhi, the systematic experimentation with such methods and the development of a rich array of them has made extraordinary progress. Academic studies like Chenoweth and Stephan's (2011) have demonstrated the extraordinary power of these methods. They have shown that they are on average, significantly more effective than violent methods at liberating people and changing regimes and, importantly, significantly better at securing more stable and democratic governments when regime changes are achieved, but there is much more R&D to be done in this area (see also Sharp, 2007). Much of history is still told from the point of view that assumes military might determines its course. The idea that Reagan's military buildup won the Cold War is widely shared—yet careful research might show instead that Eastern Europe was liberated by nonviolent direct action. Gorbachev stepped aside to allow this once he realized the peace movement had demonstrated Russians were secure from US threats—because a nuclear war could never be won and must never be fought. Much of history used to guide public opinion awaits correction in light of truths about the powers of nonviolence.

Opportunities for research on nonviolent methods may be especially promising considering, relatively speaking, so little money and effort has been invested in R&D on them. What if groups like The Nonviolent Peaceforce had R&D budgets funded by a million people rallying in DC raising a billion dollars? What innovations might result? Further, research could study how methods of nonviolence could support Earth Swaraj at every scale of governance and be refined to commit practitioners consistently and effectively to peacemaking that secures justice and a sustainable commons.

Another central research question concerns how truth can be discerned and empowered in many sided cross cultural disputes. Answering this may, in part require us to consider how Earth Swaraj could institutionalize a system of people's hearings or tribunals in which contested issues can be given fair and open hearings whose conclusions can be sanctioned systematically and effectively with nonviolent methods. It may seem daunting to imagine doing this in cases of major human rights abuses, ecological crimes, or acts of violent aggression. However, these things may actually become easier once they are no longer dealt with in the shadow of the national security state system. Might it be easier if many, or even all parties to a dispute are able to acknowledge culpability, advocate their interests, and pursue peaceful collaboration that is grounded in shared, emergent conceptions of justice, and truth that are only sanctioned nonviolently according to the principles of satyagraha? It's a researchable question.

One way to research it would be, for instance, to study historical cases of nomadic tribes and other marginalized communities that have needed to resolve conflicts amongst themselves and have not been able to draw on the resources of the state as an arbiter or enforcer. In many cases they have developed creative ways of using councils of elders, meetings of women, storytelling, healing ceremonies, and other techniques to negotiate common narratives about the past and plans for the future (Ledearch 2008). These have often included novel ways of sanctioning compliance with agreements that rely on the ceremonial and other symbolic exchanges, creation of family ties, collaboration in ecological stewardship and caring for commons, and institutions for securing status, reputation, and identity. How might these kinds of methods be adapted and/or used for inspiration to develop practices of Earth Swaraj?

For instance, how might a citizens-based tribunal be used to try Exxon for climate crimes? How might it be designed using a restorative rather than retributive justice model? How might its results be sanctioned effectively with non-violent methods of direct action that would secure compliance?

How might a truth and reconciliation process be initiated in the Middle East to address the kinds of terrorism that have been practiced by state and non-state actors? This is surely one of the most challenging cases to take on. It might be tempting to assume the tasks are insurmountable. However, note two points. First, the current practices of warfare on each of the asymmetric sides of the "war on terror" have, in fact, failed to develop any coherent strategy for achieving their long-term goals. It is generally acknowledged on all sides that the conflicts involved are not, fundamentally, military ones that can be won through physical conquest. They are ideological, political conflicts that can only be won by persuasion. Second, the conflicts are fueled, in the case of the resistance groups, by their continued access to new recruits who are persuaded to sacrifice their lives for a just and noble cause. If truth and reconciliation processes might include the creation of effective ways for them to fight for their cause using nonviolent methods, then they might be diverted as recruits–and shift the direction of the underlying historical trends. Concretely, imagine, for instance, a young Muslim man in France takes part in a kind of People's Tribunal for Restorative Justice in which civic leaders from France, the US, and other countries publicly acknowledge the injustices of their governments and commit to funding efforts to provide reparations and relief for victims. Perhaps he suggests ways in which such efforts might be directed to providing aid and economic development for refugees in Lebanon. And then he considers his options of going to Lebanon to volunteer in the delivery of that aid or going to Syria to fight with ISIS. How might such a Tribunal change his decision? And the decisions of others and the policy options that begin to open up?

A further set of questions concerns how to best negotiate the relationships between the institutions of the national security state and the Earth Swaraj systems. This will surely vary at different scales and at different points in the development and transformation of each. To take one example, in current US politics, the gerrymandering of districts tends to produce campaigns characterized by extremist rhetoric and verbal violence. In such cases, suppose the people from the minority party in such districts join the majority party and vote in its primaries. Might this result in a more balanced, less extreme, and violent rhetoric in the primary? Would it result in more centrist candidates winning in the final election? Would it increase the effective voice of minorities and build community and common ground? When would such strategies work better than, for instance, continuing to focus only on long-term efforts to build the strength of the minority party?

Researchers might also consider the reliance on advertising and social media that exacerbate the polemical character of campaigns. At local levels in some regions of the country these are avoided, in part, by door to door campaigning by candidates who hold substantive conversations with literally thousands of fellow citizens. Might there be ways to scale these methods up to the level of the Congressional District, for example, by having teams of collaborating candidates running for the office in something like the way teams of runners compete together in cross country races? The central task at every level is to find ways to establish institutions of governance that are based on the nonviolent, collaborative pursuit of truth.

## Section III: The Technological Crisis: Developing AI Systems that "Em-body" Morality

The instrumentalist model of technological reasoning is achieving ever greater power to create systems that are "smart" but not wise. They maximize one or a few values like profit, reading test scores, or tons of grain produced—but do so at the cost of securing the full range of values required to live a balanced life or sustain a community ecosystem. The instrumentalist model is also bent on promoting an exponential growth in the artificial intelligence of systems that manage our world in ways that will soon be incomprehensible to human understanding and may become indifferent or hostile to human welfare. A central task is to figure out how to insure AI systems are wise, moral, and friendly (Armstrong, 2014; Barrat, 2015).

Here are two key hypotheses: 1) We need to design into such systems the capacity for dialogue in the rich sense, the kind involved in deep listening fostered by Quaker processes of communal discernment; 2) We need to design into such systems the ability to undertake acts of self-sacrifice and witness as part of campaigns of Gandhian satyagraha and the ability to observe and be persuaded–have "their hearts be melted"–by satyagraha performed by others.

One way to explore these hypotheses is to experiment with the corporations which are, in an important sense, forms of artificial intelligence already. The limited liability corporation, as defined by its charter and the relevant statutes, is,

80

in essence, a set of algorithms for accumulating profit. As such, it is essentially amoral. One way to begin to enhance its moral capacities, would be to eliminate the limited liability clauses in its algorithms. If managers and owners could be personally sued, fined, and jailed for the misdeeds of their organization, how would their behavior change?

More generally, we should research what are the best ways of altering the place and function of human beings in the algorithmic decision processes of organizations. The aims should be to enhance the organizations' capacities for dialogue, communal discernment, and satyagraha in which they cling to truth in their own actions and respond to witness from others. Beyond this, we should also research other ways in which AI systems might be constructed, grown, and/or developed to include feelings and guiding values that include compassion, personal identity, mortality, the ability to make meaningful self-sacrifices, and respond to these in others. To do so the systems will have to in some meaningful way have identities associated with localizable bodies that are inserted in communities and ecosystems. The task is to research ways in which we can "em-body morality" or "in-carnate ethics" in AI systems through inclusion of actual humans and/or robotic artificial devices that emulate their key moral capacities.[1]

One promising way to explore these might be to research the development of moral elements and functions used in drones (committed to the use of nonviolent methods) to deal with violent people engaged in riots, terrorism, hostage taking and guerrilla warfare. For example, if someone experiencing severe PTSD is holed up alone with a weapon and attempting to commit "suicide by cop," a flying or rolling drone could approach them without risk to life to provide up close and more intimate audiovisual connections to therapists, family, or negotiators—or use tranquilizing darts or gas or incapacitating nets or glue to disarm them and avoid the loss of life. In the case of a terrorist threatening violence these options would likewise be available. And keeping the terrorist alive would have the further advantage of preserving what is often the single most important source of information about terrorist networks and their plans—the living agents themselves. In the case of war zone battles, it might be further possible for non-violent drones to provide food, medicine, emergency relief materials, and information to innocent bystanders and even to soldiers from the other side. This could limit or avoid the spiral making martyrs and enemies and build relations of solidarity, trust, and cooperation that might make peacemaking,

---

[1] For a fuller development of these ideas see "Reframing Ethical Theory, Pedagogy and Legislation to Bias Open Source AGI Towards Friendliness and Wisdom" (Cox, 2015).

and/or peacekeeping, and/or peacebuilding much more promising. To the extent that such drones might develop increasingly autonomous programs for listening, communicating, negotiating, and supporting people, they could begin to provide useful research models for experimenting with "in-carnating" morality in machines. A further, perhaps even more basic step that might be taken to this end would be to work through law, professional societies, and corporate policies to simply ensure that every researcher in AI include as part of her proposal and her project evaluation an assessment of the ways in which her work will or will not advance the development of wise, moral, and "human-friendly" systems. A central part of such research would involve, I believe, studying ways in which AI systems can be developed which use dialogical forms of reasoning modelled on the kind of conflict transformation exemplified by Quaker communal discernment and Gandhian satyagraha.

### Section IV: The Moral and Spiritual Crisis: Shifting from Monological Reasoning that Results in Relativism to Dialogical Reasoning that Leads to Emergent Truth

There is a common underlying set of epistemological and metaphysical assumptions that underlie the traditions of reasoning associated with the crises discussed so far. And a shared vision of the essence of rationality itself, one that takes Aristotle's logic, Newton's physics, and Turing Machine computations as paradigms for the activity of reasoning. In this vision, reasoning is a process of inference which starts with definitions, assumptions, or hypotheses and data and then uses rules of inference to draw conclusions. It is a monological process in the sense that a single person like Newton or a single machine like IBM's Watson can perform the entire operation of reasoning. In its classic formulation this vision was foundationalist, seeking to ensure the truth of its conclusions by starting, as Descartes sought to, with unshakeable first principles. The difficulty in finding such unshakeable principles has led many philosophers to try to come up with non-foundationalist models of rational inference using criteria such as pragmatic value or coherence of some sort as a criterion for truth. But such efforts remain haunted by the relativism that invariably threatens such efforts.

Advances made with this monological model of reasoning have provided powerful ways of increasing the efficiency and power of systems for manipulating and managing much of the world. But when divergent communities and cultures have disputes it offers no way of resolving moral or spiritual differences and dilemmas. It seems to offer no way to avoid a bankrupt moral relativism, intolerant religious fundamentalism, and the reduction of people's lives to ethically isolated spiritual death. While not a direct threat to our existence as a species, it is a direct threat to our humanity–to our existence as moral and spiritual entities (MacIntyre, 2014).

In mainstream contemporary philosophy, the power of this monological paradigm remains entrenched in much of the research on and teaching of ethics. This is reflected in the preoccupation with the search for basic principles and the attempt to choose between them–in particular, to choose between some version of the Utilitarian Greatest Happiness Principle and some version of the Kantian Categorical Imperative. A standard approach to teaching ethics is to pose dilemmas like the case of an approaching trolley car. The car will kill five people if left to proceed on track but it can be switched to another track at the last moment by you, the ethical agent. However, you can save the five only at the cost of killing some other person. Students are then asked to use Bentham and Kant's principles to analyze their intuitions and judge which horn of the dilemma should be adopted–passively watch five die or take action that will kill another. By varying the cases the teacher seeks to have students assess the strength of their intuitions and the legitimacy of the basic principles. For instance, the student who, as a Utilitarian is willing to sacrifice the one for the five in that first case is then asked to consider a doctor who has five patients in desperate need of organ transplants in her clinic and another, a healthy young adult asleep in the waiting room–whose organs could be harvested to save the other five.

This method for teaching ethics, like the influential method for evaluating stages of ethical growth developed by Lawrence Kohlberg, insists that the student accept the terms of the dilemma. She is not allowed to propose a third alternative that might transform the conflict and offer an improved solution to the problem–such as inviting one of the five terminally ill patients to volunteer to sacrifice his organs to save the other four (Harvard, 2009; Kohlberg, 1981; Gilligan, 2016). But that kind of creative response–finding third options–is precisely the sort that practical people would want. For Gandhians and Quakers, the attempt to have "way open" in this manner has long been a core feature of their practice. They also each have nuanced versions of other basic principles associated with dialogues and negotiations aimed at "Getting to Yes." Short hand versions of such strategies include "separating the people from the problem," "focusing on interests instead of positions," and "looking for objective criteria" to provide the basis for negotiations. These and a host of related strategies for collaborative reasoning have, since the 1960s, become the focus of intensive research by a very broad range of academics and practitioners engaged in conflict resolution, problem solving, negotiation, and conflict transformation practices in both Western and non-Western traditions (Bartoli *et al.*, 2011; Chew, 2001; Cox, 1986; Fisher and Ury, 1996; Ramsbotham, 2016).

The most central hypothesis for the research proposed here is that these practices are forms of dialogical reasoning that provide ways to avoid, escape, or transform the problems characteristic of the monological model. These practices start by assuming truth emerges through dialogue between people with differing points of view on the relevant definitions, data, assumptions, and rules of inference. The reasoning process involves renegotiating. Instead of inference to conclusions by a single thinker it conceives of reasoning as a process of negotiation towards agreements amongst many. The truth sought is, as Gandhi conceived it, emergent and inclusive rather than fixed and absolute. It can as Quaker's say, "prosper" or not. And it does so always in the context of the multiple perspectives that people in the situation bring to it. Truth is, in this sense, as Laura Rediehs (2015) has put it, "relational."

Shifts to practices of dialogical reasoning in the pursuit of emergent, relational truth are at the core of the transformations sketched in the first three sections of this paper. The economic model of reasoning that threatens us with ecological collapse is a form of monological reasoning in which Rational Economic Man calculates ways to maximize his utility preferences through competition over scarce resources that provide dilemmas for how they should be best distributed. As people shift spending more of their money on "giving the gift of gifts" and becoming Rational Historical Change Agents, their actions are no longer viewed as forced choices between given options but, instead, open-ended projects and initiatives undertaken in collaboration with others with whom they are in ongoing dialogue. As for the existential threats addressed in Sections II and III above, the conception of Rational Economic Man explicitly underlies the realpolitik reasoning of national security states and the instrumentalist reasoning of AI and other technological developments. For this reason the forms of reasoning required for Earth Swaraj and Em-bodying (or In-carnating) morality need, likewise, to also be transformed into dialogical ones in thoroughgoing ways.

Once the challenges presented by these existential threats are viewed in this way, a series of central research questions arise. How can we systematically articulate and best foster these forms of dialogical reasoning as ways of framing and resolving moral problems? What are the internal structures and nuances of these many different traditions and practices of dialogical reasoning in the form of negotiation, communal discernment, conflict transformation, et cetera? What are the analogies, substantive connections, and differences amongst them? What are the merits and challenges of these different practices in different settings and situations? How can such forms of dialogical reasoning best foster interfaith communication, reconciliation, and mutual spiritual nourishment amongst religious traditions that are currently in painful and destructive conflicts? What are the underlying philosophical commitments of these practices and to what extent can they be articulated in coherent and compelling ways?

This last question can lead to very abstract considerations that may at times seem quite remote from practical considerations—with discussions about epistemology, metaphysics, semantics, et cetera. However, at its heart lies a set of questions that are quite vital to our everyday experience and the difficulties we face in transforming our communities and our world. Rediehs' (2015) essay on "Truth and Nonviolence: Living Experimentally in Relation to Truth" brings this out in an especially illuminating and systematic way. She notes that post-modernists also suppose that truth is relational in a sense because it is seen to emerge out of consensus through processes of social construction. But, following Nietzsche and Foucault, post-modernists view these processes as exercises of coercive power that constitute relationships of exploitation and domination. Truth, on that view, is merely one more instrument of power. Children in oppressive schools and spouses in verbally abusive relationships have vivid and daily understandings of what it is like to suffer under such philosophical conceptions of "truth" which are simply tools in systems of discourse deployed to manipulate and coerce.

The Gandhian and Quaker traditions argue, however, that there is another kind of Truth, one founded in relations of love and justice which itself has a kind of power. It is a power to embolden satyagrahis with courage, a power to melt the hearts of opponents when they see people suffer gladly as they cling to it in nonviolent witness. As Rediehs (2015) notes:

> the truth that advocates of nonviolence have discovered is that the energy of indignation in the face of injustice can be channeled to more effective purpose by refraining from violence, claiming the moral high-ground, and appealing to the consciences of the oppressors. The fact that nonviolence has often been successful throughout history, and that its success brings about the transformation of unjust systems into just ones, is taken to indicate that the truth of justice carries transformative power (p. 171).

This notion of Truth as something that can prosper and that has transformative power is implicit in the lived experience of Friends from the very first in the formative period. George Fox and others witnessed to it in proclaiming each of us has a direct access to a living Presence, a Truth that can lead and empower—a Christ that "has come to teach his people himself." In traditions that are not

Christocentric, this experience and the associated ideas of truth get expressed differently. Some, like Gandhi, find themselves led to speak of seeking to "meet God face to face" and responding to a "still small voice." The metaphysical and ontological assumptions that frame their descriptions of such experience have common features however that indicate that they are responding to a common underlying reality. It is the reality of a presence that is encountered in some way—not merely an abstract idea or theory. It is a presence in which they participate in a relation that is in some sense, like Buber's I/thou relationship in contrast to the I/it. It is a presence which provides experiences of power that transforms through a sense of justice and activities of love. Important research tasks for philosophers, theologians, and spiritual practitioners include the following: 1) exploring the many different ways this core experience has been formulated—including ways in which it involves emergentist conceptions of the self, meaning, emotion as it relates to reasoning, and truth (Cox, 1986, 2014); 2) encouraging dialogue between them; 3) promoting the development of language and practice that can provide common ground among them, and, perhaps most importantly; 4) finding ways to make this experience as easily and immediately available as possible to everyone else. The experience of that loving Presence which is assiduous in seeking justice and always seeking to relate to the Other as Thou is a core experience that forms and fuels nonviolent, dialogical reasoning. Our species is hurtling us towards major existential crises as fast as the train of thought on its monological rail can move us. We need to find ways to promote the experience of loving Presence so it can form and fuel the nonviolent, dialogical reasoning needed to divert us from disaster.

As Rediehs notes, the relational, emergent notion of truth is inclusive of and builds on other notions of truth. These include the "unconcealment" account of Heidegger as well as the more commonly advocated correspondence, coherence, pragmatic and "post-modern" theories. People in dialogue seek to get agreements to emerge in which they arrive at perceptions that reveal realities explicitly and bring them out of concealment. In dialogical reasoning they also seek beliefs that correspond to emergent realities, have pragmatic or functional value in interacting with the world, cohere with each other, and can achieve consensus amongst those in dialogue.

Post-modernists have rightly pointed out, however, that these different theories of truth can each be deployed as instruments in the exercise of power and domination. For example, economists can claim that their neo-liberal theories of the market simply "correspond" to an external reality—which must be accepted. Theorists of international politics can claim their versions of realpolitik have superior pragmatic value—and are the only ones that really work. AI technologists can claim their models of Turing Machines provide the only coherent conceptions of intelligence that meet the standards developed for this in the context of the "Great Limitation Theorems" of Gödel and others. They may, in insisting on coherence/consistency as the criterion of truth, insist that rationality requires us to accept the law of non-contradiction and some version of the law of excluded middle and use these to reason axiomatically in monological ways. Coherence/consistency, when thus deployed, is not simply the "hobgoblin of small minds." It is a paradigm that enframes knowledge in a way that fundamentally obscures the dialectical processes in which ongoing productive dialogue is rife with contradictions and the affirmation of multiple points of view which are inconsistent with each other is the life blood of the creative process of reasoning when undertaken as a dialogical process of negotiation and conflict transformation.

The economic, realpolitik, and instrumentalist models of reasoning are part of a frame of our civilization that further obscures the nature of dialogical reasoning by its pervasive use of conflict categories to understand human experience in every domain—law, public debate, bargaining, sports, religion, psychology, art, etc. The central metaphor for all of life is the two islanders and one coconut—and the conflict they have because they both want it (a model of social reality as "a simple production system with conflict over the joint product"). This paradigm obscures the nature of peace, leaving us with a notion of it as a static absence. Peace is then defined by logical negation as the reduction or elimination of war and other forms of conflict and is not conceived as something we can do. We can say that "Nations are warring in the Middle East" but we cannot say that "They are peaceing in Scandanavia" because in English we lack a verb for this. But it is possible to engage in peace as an activity and the Scandinavians, Quakers, and Gandhians have been showing us ways to do this for some time.

These groups provide exemplars for an alternative civilization. The steps towards it might be conceived in stages that move from a lose/lose paradigm, to win/lose, and then win/win beyond this to a shared problem solving paradigm that foregoes reference to winning entirely. But to envision the real promise of such an alternative civilization it helps to focus on a metaphor frame that takes us even one step further, that of the birth process. When a pregnant woman goes into labor there can be intense pain, fierce struggle, danger of death—it is a situation as serious as any in life, even war. But there is no conflict. The woman is not, in any sense, trying to beat or win in a competition with the fetus. She and it and those attending as helpers are each engaged in a process that will redefine the physical limits and integrity of their bodies, their relationships to each other and their identities as humans. Where once they were pregnant woman and fetus, they become mother and child. This is a profound metaphor that could be taken to reframe all of life. As we deal with differences of all kinds, we can view ourselves as in processes of rebirth. Dialogical reasoning is the process of transformation through which new individuals and new communities are born out of struggle. This model of life–which is innocent of all conflict categories–is one we are born with. We are born knowing how to be born–and how to be loved and how to enter into dialogue with Others whose languages we do not yet speak and whose projects we are not yet a party to. While we may learn to become monolingual and learn to reason monologically, the capacity for dialogue guided and empowered by that Light of love, justice, and Truth can still be experienced as a living Presence and remains a never absent resource that is here to teach and heal and transform us.

The existence of that Presence is not a mere hypothesis, nor is it an abstract article of faith. It is a reality that has been experienced at some level by all who have learned to speak a language and live in community. No matter how heavily our culture represses experiences of it and suppresses conceptions of it, it remains a reality of which we are profoundly aware–even in the moments of greatest pain and darkness where we may only be aware of it through a longing and ache for that which seems to be only present in the mode of absence. And when we enter a silence that escapes the voices of our culture that repress and suppress that awareness, when we turn to others and enter into genuine, open dialogue, then, like wild grass and dandelions bursting out in the asphalt desert, the Presence of that Truth breaks through the darkness and offers us hope for a world of creation and a life surrounded by Life.

## References

Adeney, P. (2016). Getting Rich: from Zero to Hero in One Blog Post. Retrieved from http://www.mrmoneymustache.com/2013/02/22/getting-rich-from-zero-to-hero-in-one-blog-post

Armstrong, S. (2014). *Smarter than us: the rise of machine intelligence.* Berkeley: MIRI.

Barrat, J. (2015). *Our final invention: artificial intelligence and the end of the human era.* New York: Thomas Dunne Books.

Bartoli, A., Mampilly, Z. C., & Nan, S. A. (2011). *Peacemaking: from practice to theory.* Santa Barbara, Calif: Praeger.

Bondurant, J. (1988). *Conquest of violence: the Gandhian philosophy of conflict.* Princeton, N.J: University of California Press.

Bostrom, N. (2016). *Superintelligence: paths, dangers, strategies.* Oxford, United Kingdom: Oxford University Press.

Boulding, E. (1990). *Building a global civic culture: education for an interdependent world.* Syracuse, NY: Syracuse University Press.

Brown, P. G., Garver, G., & Helmuth, K. (2009). *Right relationship: building a whole earth economy.* San Francisco: Berrett-Koehler.

Chenoweth, E., Stephan, M. J. (2011). *Why civil resistance works: the strategic logic of nonviolent conflict.* New York. Columbia University Press.

Chew, P. K. (2001). *The conflict and culture reader.* New York: New York University Press.

Cox, J. G. (1986). *The ways of peace: a philosophy of peace as action.* New York: Paulist Press.

Cox, J. G., Blanchard, C., Garver, G., Helmuth, K., Joy, L., Lumb, J., & Wolcott, S. (2014). *A Quaker approach to research: collaborative practice and communal discernment.* Caye Caulker, Belize: Published for Quaker Institute for the Future by Producciones de la Hamaca.

Dudiak, J. (2015). *Befriending truth: Quaker perspectives.* Longmeadow, MA: Full Media Services.

Fisher, R., Ury, W., & Fisher, R. (1996). *Getting to Yes: How to Negotiate Agreement Without Giving in.* London: Simon & Schuster (Audio list).

Gandhi, M. K., & Parel, A. (2013). *Hind Swaraj and other writings.* New York: Cambridge University Press.

Getting Rich: from Zero to Hero in One Blog Post. (2016, December 25). Retrieved from http://www.mrmoneymustache.com/2013/02/22/getting-rich-from-zero-to-hero-in-one-blog-post/

Gilligan, C. (2016). *In a different voice: psychological theory and womens development.* Place of publication not identified: Harvard University Press.

Global Footprint Network. (2017). Global Footprint Network–Country Trends. Retrieved from http://data.footprintnetwork.org/#/countryTrends?type=earth&cn=2004

Hawken, P. (2007). *Blessed unrest: how the largest movement in the world came into being, and why no one saw it coming.* New York: Viking.

Harvard. (2009). Justice: What's The Right Thing To Do? Episode 01 "THE MORAL SIDE OF MURDER." Retrieved from https://www.youtube.com/watch?v=kBdfcR-8hEY

Joy, L. (2011). *How does societal transformation happen?: values development, collective wisdom, and decision making for the common good.* Caye Caulker, Belize: Published for Quaker Institute for the Future by Producciones de la Hamaca.

89

Kohlberg, L. (1981). *The philosophy of moral development: moral stages and the idea of justice.* Cambridge, MA: Harper & Row.

Lederach, J. P. (2008). *Preparing for peace: conflict transformation across cultures.* Syracuse, NY: Syracuse Univ. Press.

MacIntyre, A. C. (2014). *After virtue: a study in moral theory.* London: Bloomsbury.

Paumgarten, N. (2016). The Scold Mr. Money Mustache's retirement (sort of) plan. *The New Yorker.* doi:https://www.newyorker.com/magazine/ 2016/02/29/mr-money-mustache-the-frugal-guru

Ramsbotham, O., Miall, H., & Woodhouse, T. (2016). *Contemporary conflict resolution.* Malden, MA: Polity Press.

Rediehs, L. (n.d.). Truth and Nonviolence: Living Experimentally in Relation to Truth. Retrieved from http://www.academia.edu/12266266/Truth_and _Nonviolence_Living_Experimentally_in_Relation_to_Truth

Rediehs, L. (2015). Truth and Nonviolence: Living Experimentally in Relation to Truth. In Dudiak, J., (Ed.), *Befriending Truth.* Longmeadow (164-181). Longmeadow, PA: Full Media Services.

Sharp, G. (2007). *Waging nonviolent struggle: 20th century practice and 21st century potential.* Boston, MA: Extending Horizons Books.

# 5 | Responsibility in Business: What Can We Learn from the Quakers?

**By Nicholas Burton and Alex Hope**

What explains the success and prosperity of many Quakers in business and commerce in the UK throughout the eighteenth to early-twentieth centuries? What lessons can be drawn from the so-called form of 'Quakernomics' (King, 2014) for contemporary responsible business practice? In a publication for the Centre for Enterprise, Markets and Ethics, Richard Turnbull (2014) describes how Quaker culture and identity, more so than their religiosity, lies at the heart of the success of Quaker businesses. In contrast, Wagner-Tsukamoto (2008) describes the Quaker behavioural ethic as only partly successful, and in some respects the behavioural ethic represented a failure as it took precedent over institutional ethics and economics. Kavanagh, Brigham, and Burton (2017) have argued that the demise of the Quaker business coincided with the start of 'management' as an academic discipline. This was precisely at the point when many of the Quaker businesses were incorporating, which we see as a decisive political-economic change that ushered in an era of market-based capitalism based on limited liability and the shareholder economy. Much of the scholarly body of work on the role of Quakers in business is situated within the tradition of management and organisation history research (see for example Child, 1964; King, 2014; Raistrick, 1950; Walvin, 1997). Beyond these contributions, how the rise and subsequent decline of Quaker businesses can contribute to, and inform, our contemporary understanding of responsible business has been largely ignored.

Quakers have a long tradition in the world of commerce and business. The history of the Quakers involvement in the chocolate industry has been well-documented (see for example Cadbury, 2010; George and Owoyemi, 2012; Rowlinson and Hassard, 1993; Vernon, 2013). However, throughout the eighteenth to early-twentieth centuries Quakers were arguably instrumental in the history of industrial capitalism (King, 2014). For instance, in banking and finance, contemporary high-street names such as Barclays Bank can be traced back to an operation set up by Quaker John Freame in 1690, and Lloyds Bank began as a partnership between Quaker Samuel Lloyd and John Taylor in Birmingham in 1765. In manufacturing, Joseph Pease was prominent in the development of the Stockton and Darlington Railway Company. Turnbull (2014) notes that the Quaker-owned furnaces at Coalbrookdale became no less than "the laboratory for the industrial revolution" (p. 8). The sheer extent of Quaker involvement in early industry and commerce is quite astounding: iron, chocolate, banking, life assurance, biscuits, shoes, pharmacy, soap, chemicals, railways, canals, agricultural equipment, to name but a few. Another major contribution of Quaker businesses was a more ethical approach, grounded in religiosity, to business in general. Early Quaker businesses deemed the wellbeing of their employees and the society in which they operated as essential to the success of the business (Mendibil, et al., 2007). However, as we have seen these businesses eventually succumbed to market pressures with social and ethical issues being relegated in favour of profit and growth (Doane, 2005).

The picture we can draw is fascinating but also complex. Not all Quakers established businesses, and not all succeeded. With Quakers representing only a small minority of the UK population (Wrigley and Schofield, 1989, pp. 92-95), there remains something fascinating about the disproportionate presence of Quakers in business during the industrial revolution and Victorian England. However, despite their success over a long-period, the dominance of Quaker businesses waned. The reasons for this are many and varied, both exogenous and endogenously determined. For instance, King (2014) and Walvin (1997) have highlighted the declining membership of the Religious Society of Friends (Quakers) throughout the nineteenth and twentieth centuries, and have hinted at the changing nature of corporate law and declining importance of Quaker networks.

In this chapter, we develop these ideas and examine the decline of Quaker businesses to argue that exogenous shocks associated with corporate law and business model design in the mid-nineteenth century, coupled with the declining importance of Quaker business networks, can be identified as key characteristics that accelerated the decline of the Quaker business. We make the argument, however, that business model design and contemporary networks that share similarities to historic Quaker practice still matter in sustaining a responsible values-led business. The first section of this paper addresses the key characteristics of the rise and success of Quaker businesses. We then turn to the reasons why Quaker businesses began to wane and focus on the introduction of the shareholder company and the break-up of Quaker networks as key determinants. Next we examine more contemporary and secular models of business that seek to re-introduce similar principles of ethics, responsibility, and sustainability and ask whether parallels can be drawn between the Quaker businesses of the past and current practice. Finally we discuss the lessons that may be learnt from the decline of Quaker businesses for responsible business models of the future.

## The Rise and Fall of the Quaker Business Enterprise

In this section, we examine the contribution of religiosity and the role of families and the extended Quaker network to the success, or 'rise,' of Quaker businesses. We then chart how the decline of many Quaker businesses coincided with the introduction of changes in corporate law that marked the globalising business and commercial landscape in the mid-nineteenth century.

### The Contribution of Religiosity

Originating with the ministry of George Fox (1624-1691), at the heart of Quaker theology is the idea of the 'Light within,' and 'that of God in everyone.' As a consequence of their radical belief, early Quakers were heavily persecuted during the seventeenth century and excluded from political life, as well as from universities. Thus many Quakers turned their attention to business and commerce, with perhaps a hardened resolve, in order to make their way in the world. The Quaker community endowed its members with principles of integrity, trust, discipline, and responsibility, which in business and commerce extended to relationships with Friends, employees, and the wider society. Child (1964) described Quaker business ethics as exhibiting the following properties: (1) a dislike of one person profiting at the expense of another; (2) the promotion of the value of hard work; (3) the advocacy of egalitarianism in social behaviour; and, (4) a dislike of conflict. King (2014) highlights a similar observation that Quakers became known for honesty, hard work, equality, and a yeoman spirit. The idea of honesty and trust became central to the success of Quakers in business and commerce, embodied today in the stereotypical imagery of the quintessential Quaker on porridge oats packaging to signify honesty and simplicity.

For Quakers, work was not just about personal wealth creation. It assumed a spiritual, moral, and philanthropic significance, led by God or the Spirit (Walvin, 1997). Raistrick (1950) highlights that early Quakers emphasised that "trade and occupations show forth truth to the world, and that traders must be scrupulous to keep all their dealings in the spirit of truth" (p. 46). As far as Quakers were concerned, the business of business had a moral imperative, and hard work would be divinely rewarded. As Tawney (1926) notes, trade was intended as "the duty to make the honourable maintenance of the brother in distress a common charge" (p. 105). For the Quaker entrepreneurs of the nineteenth century, Cadbury (2010) notes that the contemporary idea that wealth creation equated to personal gain only would have been highly offensive. Pre-dating contemporary ideas of 'responsible business' by a century or more, wealth creation was viewed as a public and collective good for the benefit of workers, communities, and wider society, as well as for business owners themselves.

For Quakers, the 'Light within' provided the guiding moral principle that permeated both personal and professional lives. Raistrick (1950) comments that "their refusal to separate business activities from the principles and disciplines which regulated their religious life, gave them a stability and soundness of practice that was unusual in their day" (p. 46). The nature of business and trade, however, presented a moral hazard for Quakers. Even in the seventeenth century, George Fox had become deeply disturbed by the 'deceitful merchandise and cheating...' which he saw to be the norm in contemporary trade, and demanded that business people act honestly and justly. In the US, similar concerns about trade were expressed. John Woolman, for example, wrote about the obligations of the rich towards the poor in his essay "A Plea to the Poor".

The Quaker business ethic certainly meant adherence to the advice and queries outlined in its Book of Discipline. It also meant a highly regulated form of self-governance and oversight by local, monthly, and yearly meetings that provided support and advice, but also sought to avoid bringing the Quaker community into disrepute. Advice–in the form of written 'advices'–offered to the Quaker business community included matters such as avoiding bankruptcy, not trading beyond their means, keeping their word in all business matters, honesty in advertising, keeping and inspecting clear accounts, minimizing and avoiding debt, and ensuring swift payment to debtors (Tibbals, 2014). In other words, although many of these measures were advised to protect the Society from scandal, the 'advices' were an integral part of the Quaker professional as well as personal identity. As Walvin (1997) notes, time and time again, Britain Yearly Meeting issued advice aimed at reconciling business practice with faith and testimony. Turnbull (2014), for instance, relates an advice in 1732 where Friends were warned to be 'careful not to involve themselves in business which they understand not'–a timely warning for some contemporary businesses (p. 25).

Friends' behaviour in their professional lives was expected to be consistent with the Quaker testimonies. In 1732, Quakers were invited 'to have a watchful eye over all their members,' and those heading for commercial trouble should be warned and, if required, helped in their difficulties (Walvin, 1997, p. 34). Friends often turned to the community for business advice—more experienced Friends would help less experienced Friends. As Walvin (1997) asserts, "Cooperation, not rivalry, was their commercial watchword" (p. 34). For Quakers, with their heightened sense of responsibility to society, to leave debts owing to others was not only irresponsible but deeply damaging to their reputation. As a consequence, bankruptcy was particularly harshly dealt with by the Friends, and often resulted in expulsion if help and advice was ignored.

However, governance also operated constructively by seeking to help Friends who were in trouble. Quaker meetings then were often galvanised to monitor and help Friends to ensure Quaker principles were upheld. In other words, in a largely unregulated environment of the eighteenth and early nineteenth centuries, Quaker businesses were self-regulated like no other, with oversight and intervention at the local, regional, and national level of the Quaker system of governance. The demands on Quaker businesses were enormous. As Walvin (1997) recounts, they "...had to satisfy not only their partners, customers and suppliers, but also their fellow Friends—they were expected to open their ledgers, show their receipts, reveal their bills and correspondence to satisfy their co-religionists" (p. 78). Such governance and oversight, however, served to strengthen the Quaker as a figure of honesty and integrity, standing out to consumers as reliable. Prior and Kirby (1993) highlight that

> A collective responsibility for honesty and integrity in business led to the internalisation of guidance in good business practice, and improved commercial judgement. Transaction costs were reduced as confidence was increased. Credit flowed more easily. . . expanding business opportunities. Friends could invest with confidence in other Friends, knowing these concerns were overseen by those whose only vested interests were the good name of the Society, and the desire that Friends 'walked in truth' (p. 78).

## Families and Networks

Although Friends were by no means unique as a closely knit community, the degree of internal cohesion and the geographical extent of its network was distinctive, akin to an extended family (Raistrick, 1950). The strong connections within and among Quaker families within the close-knit structure of meetings allowed Friends to share information in respect of trading, markets, and new opportunities, both nationally and internationally. As members of a cohesive and tight-knit group, they knew each other well, regulated each other through the governance provided by meetings, and did business with each other. The fellowship of the community provided a forum for discussing emotional support, marriage, but also mutual commercial interests (Walvin, 1997). Isichei, quoted in Turnbull (2014), suggests that it was the network of Friends, rather than their religiosity, that accounts for a large slice of their success.

> "...the picture of a religious ethic acting directly upon the individual oversimplifies the direct impact of ideas upon events, by ignoring the opportunities and strength given by the fact of community among the faithful...The world of religious cum kinship group provided an environment of mutual trust and confidence within which an 'invisible hand' could accommodate the advantages of each member with the benefit of all" (p. 27).

The network of Friends was astonishingly important (Sahle, 2015). Quakers often travelled as ministers visiting Friends around the country, and across international borders, and so Quaker businesses had a ready-made network of mutual contacts and a national and international network which served to reinforce Quaker principles.

Prior and Kirby (1993) and Turnbull (2014) highlight that the network acted as a capital market to create capital flows and financing for businesses and projects within the Religious Society of Friends. The flow of capital within the community provides an interesting example of the power of the Quaker networks. Turnbull (2014) highlights the role of the Quaker network in providing access to capital to underpin many infrastructure projects of the era such as the Stockton and Darlington Railway. In the early nineteenth century, Quaker banking families facilitated the development of a number of significant infrastructure projects—canals, bridges, and railways. In other words, while the sources of success of early Quaker firms is multifaceted, the Quaker networks underwrote risk-based projects and facilitated capital flows in the form of a personalised chain of credit to members of the Quaker community. The importance of the mutual relationships among Quakers in furthering business interests paints the picture of the Quaker meeting house as an internalised source of commercial support and advice, governed by high-levels of trust and integrity and the close surveillance of business practices (Prior and Kirby, 1993).

Exclusion and persecution also led the Quaker community to turn inwards to develop the intellectual infrastructure to support the sustained involvement of Quakers in business and commerce. For example, exclusion from universities hastened Quakers to establish Quaker schools—still thriving today—that taught Quaker faith, practice, and discipline to a younger generation. Quaker firms developed and offered substantial numbers of apprenticeships in a wide range of professions, including medicine, financed largely through Quaker legacies. Apprenticeships in retail and commerce allowed young Quakers to gain experience in the trades and professions. Moreover, the tight-knit family links within the Quaker community were crucial in identifying Quaker partners for sons and daughters who could also be trained in the business. Marrying within the Quaker faith was vitally important to Quakers, such that 'marrying out of unity' led to exclusion, a form of excommunication from the Society[1]. Together, Quaker education and the availability of apprenticeships provided a steady flow of labour, imbued with the Quaker values and an entrepreneurial spirit. Unsurprisingly, the early Quaker businesses were family enterprises, although many later became quite substantial in size.

As an extended family, Quaker business regarded its employees as part of the organisational family. For instance, Joseph Rowntree developed a Works Magazine in 1902 to personally communicate with employees and a Works Library, and Richard Cadbury ensured all female employees were escorted to and from the local train station, and developed a sick club to care for, and provide wages to, staff who were ill and unable to work. Some Quaker employers introduced company councils for consulting with employees and profit sharing schemes for rewarding them (Ackers, *et al.*, 2006). Quaker firms, it is often remarked, also paid higher wages than other firms, and often provided half-days and bank holidays to staff, unusual at the time. Perhaps most notable, the Rowntree and Cadbury families provided a pension scheme just after the turn of the twentieth century (Walvin, 1997), predating the state pension by decades. Quaker firms had a real vision for how business, family, workplace, and wider

---

[1] Tibbals (2014) notes that "In the mid-19th century, as Quakers were no longer disowned for marrying out of the Society...[...]...the hedge against the outside world had begun to come down. In 1871, English universities revoked their religious test, so Quakers were now able to attend mainstream colleges and to enter professions that had been closed to them...[...]...In 1832, Quakers became eligible to become Members of Parliament, and the first Quaker (Joseph Pease) was elected that year...[...]...In these changes, Quakers were moving away from being an alternative society, a separate sect, to becoming part of general society. Following, these tumultuous changes occurred at roughly the same time as changes to corporate law and can be interpreted as further factors that influenced membership of the Society and hence the decline of Quakers in business" (pp. 96-97).

society interconnected. The Quaker model villages at Bourneville, Birmingham, and New Earswick, York, were an expression of this vision.

## Corporate Law and Decline

The problems faced by family businesses of the eighteenth and nineteenth centuries were not that different from today—for instance, how to ensure effective succession and issues around the raising of capital in order to finance growth and expansion. While internal drivers such as falling numbers of Quakers may have undermined the strength of the Quaker networks, and rising prosperity weakened Quakers religious attachment to the Religious Society of Friends, we can, however, point to the exogenous 'shock' of the Joint-Stock Act 1844 and Limited Liability Act 1856 that accelerated the decline of Quaker businesses in the late-nineteenth and twentieth centuries. The introduction of joint-stock companies and limited liability, as well as Quakers seduction by the forces of capitalism represent factors that are worthy of consideration. It suggests that corporate law and thus business model design matter in the sustainability of deeply-held values-led business practice.

Until the mid-nineteenth century, the vast majority of firms in the UK had been partnerships rather than companies (Sleapwood, 2017). The partnership corporate form blurred the distinction between personal and corporate behaviour and ethics—the partnership was an extension of an individual's personality and symbolically often the proprietors of the business lived in his place of work. Taylor (2006) suggests that

> [T]he individual's business was an outgrowth of his personality; the same rules regulated the individual's activity in the market as regulated his behaviour at home. And the business and the home were not so rigorously separated either conceptually or physically as they came to be. The businessman often lived in his place of work; business and domestic accounts were kept together (p. 24).

The partnership corporate form put the individual at the forefront of the business and the Quaker virtues of trust, integrity, and honesty could be brought to the fore as a form of competitive advantage in business dealings.

Until the mid-nineteenth century, only certain organisations that could demonstrate a public benefit had been allowed to become incorporated. By contrast, the 1844 Joint Stock Act enabled a much broader process of incorporation and enabled the separation of the roles of managers and shareholders. The 1856 Limited Liability Act also 'limited' the liability of individual shareholders to the value of their shares. Prior to the twentieth-century, very few businesses, including Quaker businesses, were organised as joint-stock companies (Sleapwood, 2017)–it was only after the beginning of the twentieth century had begun that they came to be ubiquitous and dominant (Taylor, 2006, p. 6), weakening the spiritual hold of the Quaker families over the businesses they had founded. Turnbull (2014) notes that as early as the end of the eighteenth century, unlimited liability–and the risk of personal debt–was a matter of concern for Quakers who risked being excommunicated from the Society. The 1844 Joint Stock Act and 1856 Limited Liability Act was a mixed blessing. On the one hand, a joint stock company with limited liability reduced the risk of unlimited debt and hence excommunication, and it also provided access to external capital flows via shareholders, perhaps much needed as competitive selection forces pushed against the partnership corporation form in an era of exponential industrial growth. On the other hand, the joint stock company corporate form undermined the very essence of the Quakers' competitive advantage: the importance of the values and ethics of the Quaker business weakened and the unique access to capital flows via the Quaker networks became more widely available to other non-Quaker companies via external shareholders with limited liability.

Despite being widely adopted as the more efficient corporate form, the joint-stock company with limited liability was not without critics worried about the possibly lasting effects on corporate responsibility. Quoted in Turnbull (2014), Cottrell highlights that "the possible inability of a limited company to meet its debts fully was regarded as immoral" (p. 41). Taylor (2006) suggests also that "An array of contemporaries believed that whereas the partnership system of commerce was predicated on notions of character, trust and credit, companies marginalised these qualities and encouraged their members to behave immorally" (p. 22). Furthermore, Taylor (2006) goes on to suggest that the separation of owner and manager had a much wider ramification–the separation between religion and business[2] (p. 145). Wagner-Tsukamoto (2008) adopts a more critical position on why Quaker businesses failed to survive– "...institutional structures and mechanisms of the market economy were ignored" (843). In his view, despite lower transaction costs (via trustworthiness), Quaker businesses were ultimately faced with additional costs forced upon them by their religious beliefs that overwhelmed the organisational system. Ultimately, strong market selection forces squeezed the Quaker firms, which eventually led to the need for Quaker

---

[2] We are grateful for discussions with Nicola Sleapwood and her Ph.D. research in Quaker Business History.

firms to compromise and subordinate their ethical precepts to economic objectives. For example, within 50 years most Quaker firms still remaining had adopted the joint stock company model, e.g. Reckitt's in 1888, Crosfield's in 1896, Rowntree's in 1897, and Cadbury in 1899 (Sleapwood, 2017; Turnbull, 2014).

There are a number of reasons why the Quaker businesses (and other family partnerships of the time) chose to incorporate. Kavanagh, Brigham, and Burton (2017) suggest that growing the business required significant levels of capital, attractive to Quakers since debt was anathema to them. Second, distributing company ownership–especially to the next generation and also to some non-family senior managers–was more easily effected through a shareholding rather than a partnership structure. Third, the willingness of the Quaker companies to embrace the new corporate form was consistent with their enthusiasm for innovations. Incorporation seemed to have the desired effect as the Quaker companies did succeed in growing, and many were able to retain Quaker ownership of the companies, at least initially, through complex capital structures that brought in capital without losing ownership. That said, the large scale of the new enterprises created a requirement for an authority structure and division of labour that was at odds with the Quakers' anti-authoritarian and egalitarian philosophy. Ultimately, the limited liability form of ownership, combined with the joint stock company, allowed the expansion of the company's capital base beyond family resources, but eventually, beyond family control. Limited liability also meant that companies had little social, political let alone theological requirement to serve the public interest unless it related to economic outcomes.

The Quaker approach to responsible business is unlikely to be copied exactly today, with markedly different social, political, and economic contexts. Sir Adrian Cadbury suggests that the publicly-quoted, shareholder-owned company model makes a return to the Quaker brand of responsible business impossible (King, 2014). However, while it is easy to dismiss Quaker enterprises as a historical peculiarity, the community was staggeringly successful; as Cadbury (2010) notes, they "...generated a staggering amount of worldly wealth. In the early nineteenth century, around 6000 Quaker families in Britain ran seventy-four banks, and over two hundred companies" (p. 3).

With this in mind it is important to investigate Quaker business practices in context with contemporary responsible business practice. Our discussion foregrounds the fundamental role of corporate law, corporate governance, and the role of 'movements' and networks in determining the sustainability of values-led businesses. While other authors have commented on the importance of the role of corporate governance (Velayutham, 2013), and the role of Quaker networks (Walvin, 1997), remarkably, the role of changing legal foundations in setting the 'rules of the game' are often ignored in the bulk of scholarly debate about management theory and practice (Kavanagh, Brigham, and Burton 2017).

## Lessons for Contemporary Business Practice

Scholars in the responsible business domain understand the need for many aspects of contemporary business to change. In the management literature, ideas of re-examining business and social progress have begun to reach high-impact journals. For example, in an article in the Harvard Business Review, Porter and Kramer, (2011) highlight "...the principle of shared value...[as]...creating economic value in a way that also creates value for society by addressing its needs and challenges. Businesses must reconnect company success with social progress" (p. 64). However, an exact return to the Quaker habits of the eighteenth and nineteenth century also seems untenable and unlikely. Despite this, the business practices of Quaker organisations deserve further scrutiny in relation to contemporary practice, and this chapter aims to forward that discussion. What lies at the heart of returning to a more responsible business practice, even if not embedded in Quaker theology or testimony, is entrepreneurs considering alternative approaches to corporate governance, consideration of the power of networks and movements in providing strength and legitimacy in developing more responsible business practices and the role of alternative sustainable and responsible business models.

## Corporate Governance

Generally, the term 'governance' refers to the "processes and institutions, both formal and informal that guide and restrain the collective activities of a group" (Keohane and Nye, 2002, p. 12). In business, corporate governance is the system of rules, practices, and processes by which a company is directed and controlled. This is predominantly carried out by individuals as part of a board of directors who balance the interests of the company's stakeholders and provide the framework for attaining a company's objectives. Directors are usually tasked with making critical organisational decisions such as the appointment of corporate officers, executive compensation, and financial policy. However, often board obligations can stretch beyond financial optimisation and incorporate social and environmental issues as well. Corporate governance is important then in not only contributing to corporate prosperity, but also in ensuring accountability and responsibility. Aras and Crowther (2008) recognise four principles of good corporate governance: (1) transparency; (2) accountability; (3) responsibility, and (4) fairness.

The importance of corporate governance in relation to environmental and social issues is well known. Good governance suggests that management must give regard to the wishes of all company stakeholders and be answerable to all. Therefore, there is a clear overlap between good corporate governance and the principles of corporate social responsibility that envisage business as a complex interaction between interrelated stakeholders that sustain and add value to the firm (Edward Freeman, 2010; Helfaya and Moussa, 2017). In addressing the interests of a wide range of stakeholders, corporate governance is ultimately concerned with honesty and transparency, an issue which is increasingly expected of organisations by both the public and investors (Jamali, Safieddine, and Rabbath, 2008). In addition to this transparency and disclosure of information between managers and employees, it is essential to earn employee trust and commitment. Therefore, good corporate governance can bring financial benefits for an organisation as well as social and economic benefits for society. On the other hand, "bad" corporate governance can cast doubt on a company's reliability, integrity, or obligation to shareholders as well as stakeholders in the broader term.

In recent years the effectiveness of corporate governance in many organisations has been sharply criticised. Support or tolerance of illegal, ethically suspect, or irresponsible activities can result in scandals such as that over Volkswagen's 2015 emissions activities.[3] The issue of excessive compensation packages for senior executives is another that regularly makes the news (Soltani, 2014). Corporate governance is one of the mechanisms that is supposed to ensure that business leaders act appropriately, ethically, and responsibly. However, it has been noted that boards of directors do not usually have the power or authority to take strong actions contrary to management, as they are usually subordinate to management in the company structure (Starbuck, 2014). In the majority of organisations, the norm has been for senior executives to nominate candidates for board membership with directors receiving both monetary and social incentives to endorse management proposals resulting in the potential for conflict of interest.

In these respects, modern day corporate governance may be able to take some cues from the Quaker approach to corporate governance. One of the characteristics of contemporary Board-based corporate governance models is the principle of one share one vote, and therefore representation is dependent on number of shares owned. Velayutham (2013) adds that "The right to participate

---

[3] For example, see http://www.bbc.co.uk/news/business-34324772 and Oldenkamp, R., van Zelm, R., and Huijbregts, M. (2016).

in the decision-making process of a company is the level of investment... It is also assumed that profit maximisation is the principal objective of a company, and therefore the powers and structure of the board are designed for the delivery of maximum profits" (p. 225). Resolving agency and conflicts of interest between the shareholders and management is minimised through a hierarchal governance structure consisting of the Board and a number of possible sub-committees, and roles such as executive directors, non-executive directors, and a wide range of reporting controls (Cadbury Report, 1992).

In contrast, the Religious Society of Friends has a non-hierarchal system of corporate governance. The Meeting structure enables decisions to be raised by a member of a Local or Area Meeting. Should the Local Meeting discern that the concern should be taken forward, it will be tabled at an Area Meeting for further deliberation and discernment. Furthermore, should the concern have a national focus, it may be further deliberated by Quakers at the relevant Yearly Meeting. In other words, individual concerns are subject to a rigorous corporate 'testing' by a greater number of members as they pass from local, area and yearly meeting (Burton, 2017). This system of governance appears to be in sharp contrast to the way decisions are tested and decided upon in many contemporary forms of corporate governance where decisions are made by fewer and fewer as they escalate up the organisational hierarchy.

The roles of 'office' in the Quaker community are also in sharp contrast to the contemporary form. Within the community, no-one holds any kind of special 'leadership' role. Rather, meetings have a Clerk who 'chairs' the meetings, takes the minutes and follows up on decisions that need to be implemented. The Clerk is not there to 'lead' the Meeting in the traditional sense, present motions, or oversee votes. They are a servant of the meeting and responsible for facilitating the Quaker Business Method process (Burton, 2017). In one sense, the Clerk's role is one of stewardship, rather than leadership as "leadership is seen as provided by the Spirit, by God; and this leadership comes through the clerk..." (Reis-Louis, 1994, p. 48). Velayutham (2013) highlights that two other important positions at Quaker Meetings are the Elders and Overseers. The Elders look after the spiritual life of the meeting and Overseers have a pastoral role. The appointment to one of these offices does not mean that the individual concerned is elevated to a higher position, but continues to be a 'servant' to the meeting and its decision-making processes (p. 229).

The Quaker form of corporate governance has a theological consistency with its beliefs and practices. The non-hierarchal form resonates with the belief of Friends in a testimony to equality and there is that of God in everyone. The governance structure provides every member with an equal voice in the governing of the Society. Velayutham (2013) notes that

> The lack of office bearers also leads to the practice of collective accountability rather than personal accountability. All members are collectively responsible for the strategic direction and the operating activities of the Society since no individual office bearers can be held responsible for organisational outcomes and financial results. The absence of individually responsible positions within the Society requires all members to be accountable to each other as well as to be collectively accountable to outsiders. This not only requires the development of trust among members, but also the maintenance of constant vigilance (p. 230).

In summary, the Quakers developed a system of corporate governance that embeds a collective responsibility that may still offer lessons to many contemporary business contexts. Currently efforts are being made to encourage a more long-term market orientation which would see companies focus on sustained value creation rather than short term profit. The Quakers often saw their business dealings as long-term projects which would remain in family networks for several generations necessitating more careful sustained stewardship than modern day shareholder-focussed organisations. Modern day companies interested in responsible business are also experimenting with alternative organisational structures such as flat or hybrid models which seek to distribute responsibility throughout the company thus increasing accountability. Again, parallels may be drawn with Quaker society's lack of office bearers. It is interesting to note that such developments have arisen as a response to irresponsible business practices and not through a conscious effort to mimic past organisational practices such as those of the Quakers, yet this is exactly what seems to be happening.

### New networks and movements

One of the key enablers to the success of Quaker businesses was the power of the Quaker network, a close knit community that allowed businesses to share information about trading conditions, markets, new opportunities, and ways of working. Whilst Quaker networks were formed around shared religious beliefs and were akin to an extended family, such cohesive business networks are rarer in today's globalised highly competitive world. It has been suggested that when shifting business focus from competitiveness to sustainability, there is a need to engage with a broader and more diverse network of actors (van Kleef and Roome, 2007). Collaboration of businesses through networks, alliances of firms, governments, and NGOs contributes to the practical realisation of ethical, responsible, and sustainable goals (Sharma and Starik, 2002).

The largest corporate sustainability initiative is arguably the United Nations Global Compact (UNGC), an initiative which aims to assist companies in aligning their strategies and operations with universal principles on human rights, labour, environment, and anti-corruption (United Nations, 2017a). Launched in July 2000, the compact now boasts a membership of some 9,269 companies from 164 companies resulting in over 43,000 public reports from companies on their ethical, responsible, and sustainable actions (United Nations, 2017b). With so many participants, arguably the UNGC has been successful in engaging organisations (Kell, 2013) and provided a common cause through which businesses can work and learn together. One key dimension of the Global Compact is that it enables the development of local networks made up of large, medium, and small businesses alongside civil society organisations, professional bodies, and universities. In the UK alone there are 338 participants in the Global Compact network who offer support and advice to one another (Global Compact UK, 2017). The United Nations talks about the Global Compact as a 'movement' in a clear attempt to mobilise organisations towards developing common responses to sustainability challenges (UN Global Compact, 2017).

In the UK, one of the most prominent networks of sustainability focussed organisations is facilitated by Business in the Community (BITC) a business-led charity presided over by HRH the Prince of Wales (BITC, 2012). Membership of the core network stands at over 800 companies who engage with thousands more organisations to work collaboratively on economic, social, and environmental issues (BITC, 2016). One of the key initiatives of BITC is the business champion scheme currently running in the UK whereby a range of employees from member organisations with a variety of business experience give their time and support to other businesses in the area of CSR among others (Jenkins, 2006). In addition to business to business mentoring, the BITC Business Connectors initiative sees individuals seconded from business and the Civil Service placed in local communities of greatest need (BITC, 2014). For the businesses and communities involved, engagement with responsible business networks offers opportunities for shared learning, development of best practice and ultimately improvements in economic, social, and environmental outcomes.

Some networks go even further and aim to certify organizations that engage in ethical, responsible, and sustainable activities. B Corporations (the B stands for "benefit") are part of a movement to use business innovation as a means to make not only profit, but also help alleviate poverty, build stronger communities, improve the environment, and create jobs with purpose (Honeyman, 2014). The movement is somewhat legitimised by B Corp certification, a private certification scheme that is administered by B Lab, a global non-profit organisation headquartered in the U.S. but operating worldwide (B Lab, 2017a). The main aim of B Lab is to build a global community of certified B Corporations who meet high standards of verifiable social and environmental performance, public transparency, and legal accountability (B Lab, 2017a). Alongside this, the NGO seeks to assist businesses in achieving these aims through a facilitated network of peer organisations and to gather best practice using data compiled from member businesses. At the time of writing there are more than 1,600 certified B Corps from 42 countries and over 120 industries (B Lab, 2017b).

It is clear then that a key strength of the Quaker movement was the opportunity to learn from one another's practices and the mutual support mechanisms provided through the Religious Society of Friends. The learning opportunities and support available to members of the Society were similar in many respects to the kind of support available through other 'movements' such as to members of the Co-operative movement (Novkovic, 2008). In contemporary business, the role and importance of 'movements' in developing responses to sustainability is well established (Hess, 2009; Utting, 2005). Networks facilitate organisational learning which plays a critical role in an organisation's response to the natural environment and other sustainability orientated actions (Petts, 1998; Winn and Angell, 2000). Again, it appears that clear parallels can be drawn between historical business networks and the rise of responsible and sustainable business networks. When there are issues that arise for one organisation, it often follows that others will also experience similar problems. Networks facilitate the sharing of solutions as well as opportunities and as a result it is perhaps unsurprising that we are seeking an increase in responsible and sustainable business networks.

### Responsible Business Models

One of the major challenges facing contemporary business is how to align business practices with ethical, responsible, and sustainable activities such as those demonstrated by many of the Quaker firms of the past. One way in which this may be achieved is through the application of sustainable business models, which differ from more traditional profit focussed approaches to business. As a term, 'business model' is used rather loosely and there still is no commonly agreed definition of the concept in the academic literature. However, they can be understood as structured management tools that are essential for an organisation's success (Magretta, 2002). In its simplest form, the business model defines the way in which a company generates value and its route to market. The overall objective of the business model is to exploit a business opportunity enabling an organisation to meet its customers' needs while generating a profit for the organisation and its shareholders (Amit and Zott, 2001). However, over the last two decades, understanding of the role of the business model has developed into a more integrated picture of an organisation's overall strategy and operations such that the business model can increasingly be seen as a representation of a company in general (Amit and Zott, 2001; Eriksson and Penker, 2000).

Business models then are important in defining the way in which an organisation develops strategy and goes about its day-to-day operations. As a result many organisations view the business model not as a fixed entity, but rather as a dynamic strategic tool through which firms can seek to innovate and exploit new opportunities. As many organisations seek to respond to some of the sustainability challenges of today, business model redesign has emerged as a key tool through which to improve the performance of organisations and create greater environmental and social value while delivering economic sustainability (Porter and Kramer, 2011). Whilst traditionally business models have sought to define an organization's approach to creating value through profit, those businesses utilising sustainable and responsible business models differ somewhat in that they seek to deliver value more generally to all stakeholders both now and in the future. They attempt to do so by minimising any impact on the environment, improving social outcomes in the communities through which the business operates, and providing economic value both to shareholders and wider stakeholder groups, much like the Quaker businesses before them. There are a number of business models which seek to integrate the principles of sustainability and responsibility and in some way mirror Quaker values.

**Cooperatives and Mutual Structures.** Cooperative and mutuality business models share some commonalities with the Quaker businesses of the past. In fact the founder of the Co-operative movement, the Welsh social reformer Robert Owen credited Quaker John Bellers' (1654-1725) 1695 work 'Colleges of Industry' as one of his major influences. Cooperative business models are based on a structure where the owners are also employees and/or customers. The premise is that instead of focussing primarily on producing profits for shareholders or a narrow group of executives, cooperatives can offer improved services, differentiated product assortments, and a unique position as the outlet of choice for a particular product or service (Mikami, 2003; Sorescu, et al., 2011). As a result of the opportunity for the businesses customers to contribute to the governance of the organisation, cooperative companies can champion an ethical approach to business underpinned by internationally agreed principles and values (McDonnell, Macknight, and Donnelly, 2012). Such principles include voluntary and open membership; democratic member control; member economic participation; autonomy and independence; education, training and information; cooperation among cooperatives; and concern for community. It is obvious to see here that cooperative values are as close to Quaker values as any modern business model.

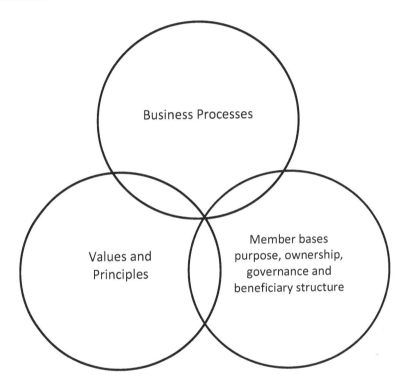

**Figure 1:**
The cooperative business model (McDonnell, Macknight, and Donnolley, 2012)

Far from being a niche business model, cooperatives range from small community-based enterprises to multi-billion dollar businesses in sectors as diverse as healthcare to housing, renewable energy to retail, and sports to social care in countries all around the world. It is estimated that a few years ago there were some 900,000 cooperatives with around 500 million members in over 100 countries (Birchall and Ketilson, 2009). Following the 2008 global financial crisis, evidence has emerged that suggests that cooperative business models provide stability and security in tough economic times, tending to last longer than other businesses in the private sector (Birchall and Ketilson, 2009).

One of the key difficulties faced by businesses seeking to incorporate responsible and sustainability principles into their business model and operational strategy is the tension between value as profit and social value. Birkin, *et al* (2009) suggest that it is very likely that new sustainable business models will have to address issues that appear to be counter to business interest. For this reason responsible business model innovation requires the inclusion of stakeholders' values in the process of design in the same way that a responsible technical innovation does (Taebi, *et al.*, 2014). As Hope and Moehler (2015) suggest, sustainable and responsible business model innovations must address the following challenges:

- Incorporation of the principles of sustainable development, social responsibility and ethics into the business model;
- Reconciliation of the often conflicting interests of profit and social value;
- Flexibility to incorporate local needs and markets;
- Scalability across a wide range of business sizes;
- Replicable both within and across a range of business sectors;
- Inclusion of all relevant stakeholders in the design of new responsible business models;
- Operationalizable in practice.

Whilst there are many companies who employ these responsible business models, they are often perceived as a minority and tend to be established to meet a specific need such as to provide a service in absence of a state or market actor, or in the case of cooperatives to share profits amongst a wide range of stakeholders, thus providing a mix of self-help and mutual aid. Innovating more sustainable business models requires the development of new and revised business models that go beyond a profit oriented economic focus to one which can integrate environmental, social, and economic value throughout the strategy and operations of an organisation (Bocken, *et al.*, 2013; Willard, 2012). Sustainable business models must be economically sustainable as a prerequisite. The overall objective in sustainable business modelling is to identify solutions that allow firms to capture economic value whilst also generating environmental and social value (Schaltegger and Wagner, 2011). However, it is also important to recognise that each individual, community, firm, or organisation has different values, preferences, and interests that arise out of specific cultural and social situations (Birkin *et al.*, 2009; Opoku, 2004). As such, responsible business models must be flexible enough to incorporate local needs and operate in local markets.

## Conclusion

Our discussion has foregrounded the importance of the role of corporate governance, networks, movements, and business model design in Quaker businesses. We have addressed some of the similarities between contemporary practice and the historic practice of Quaker business. We have argued that these features of the Quaker business 'ethic' continue to remain vitally important in today's competitive and often global markets.

Given the largely secular nature of contemporary business, we highlight that while Quaker business turned to their faith for ethical direction, it is less clear where modern entrepreneurs find their ethical inspiration. Today, while many of the challenges for business are the same –and the importance of good corporate governance and business model design, and strong personal and professional networks remain as vital as ever –the emphasis of contemporary responsible business is often more global, secular, dispersed, and less grounded in a Quaker-style of testimony. Considering the relationship between contemporary ethics and Quakers, Scully (2009) identifies the Quaker 'ethic' as a form of virtue ethics, grounded in Quaker testimonies, with a 'deontological tether.' This appears to be an important foundation for evaluating the degree of 'responsibility' of contemporary business practice.

While contemporary Quaker business practitioners have formed interest groups in the UK (such as Quakers and Business[4]) and management academic communities such as the Academy of Management has formed groups such as the Management, Spirituality and Religion[5] that seek to foreground the role of spirituality and religion in business, the responsible business literature often has 'secular' concerns, and the 'stakeholder' view of the corporation often remains tethered to a utilitarian ethical perspective. Despite these different ethical perspectives that separate Quaker business of the past from contemporary businesses, parallels can be drawn between recent interest in the role of an 'enlightened' CEO and the rise of 'responsible' business groups and networks such as the Global Compact or Business in the Community in the UK.

Our chapter has made a first step in suggesting that academics, practitioners, and policy-makers in responsible business may have much to learn by examining

---

[4] Quakers and Business can be found at qandb.org
[5] Details can be found at http://aom.org/Divisions-and-Interest-Groups/Management-Spirituality-and-Religion/Management-Spirituality-and-Religion.aspx

the practice of movements from the past. The faith-based and testimony-led approach of the Quakers is one example. But, there are other movements such as the cooperative movement and the mutuality movement that have much to bring to the debate. The exploration of the themes outlined in this chapter by scholars across these various traditions may be able to shed new and surprising insights into the broader management literature.

## References

Ackers, P., Marchington, M., Wilkinson, A., and Dundon, T. (2006). Employee Participation in Britain: From Collective Bargaining and Industrial Democracy to Employee Involvement and Social Partnership–Two Decades of Manchester/Loughborough Research. *Decision (0304-0941)*, *33*(1).

Agle, B. R., Mitchell, R. K., and Sonnenfeld, J. A. (1999). Who Matters to Ceos? An Investigation of Stakeholder Attributes and Salience, Corpate Performance, and Ceo Values. *Academy of Management Journal. Academy of Management*, *42*(5), 507-525.

Amit, R., and Zott, C. (2001). Value creation in e-business. *Strategic Management Journal*. Retrieved from http://onlinelibrary.wiley.com/doi/10.1002/smj.187/full

Aras, G., and Crowther, D. (2008). Governance and sustainability: An investigation into the relationship between corporate governance and corporate sustainability. *Management Decision*, *46*(3), 433-448.

Birchall, J., and Ketilson, L. H. (2009). *Resilience of the cooperative business model in times of crisis*. Geneva: International Labour Organization.

Birkin, F., Cashman, A., and Koh, S. (2009). New sustainable business models in China. *Business Strategy and the Environment*. Retrieved from http://onlinelibrary.wiley.com/doi/10.1002/bse.568/full

BITC. (2012, October 8). Who we are. Retrieved from http://www.bitc.org.uk/about-us/who-we-are

BITC. (2014, January 3). Business Connectors. Retrieved from http://www.bitc.org.uk/programmes/business-connectors

BITC. (2016). Issues. Retrieved from http://www.bitc.org.uk/issues

B Lab. (2017a). About B Lab | B Corporation. Retrieved from https://www.bcorporation.net/what-are-b-corps/about-b-lab

B Lab. (2017b). B Corp Community | B Corporation. Retrieved from https://www.bcorporation.net/b-corp-community

Bocken, N., Short, S., Rana, P., and Evans, S. (2013). A value mapping tool for sustainable business modelling. *Corporate Governance: The International Journal of Business in Society*, *13*(5), 482-497.

Burton, N. (2017). Quaker Business Method: A Contemporary Decision-Making Process? In, Angell, S., and Dandelion, P. (Eds), *Quakers, Business and Industry*, USA: Friends Association in Higher Education.

Cadbury, D. (2010). *Chocolate Wars: From Cadbury to Kraft–200 Years of Sweet Success and Bitter Rivalry* (First Edition). HarperCollins Publishers.

Cennamo, C., Berrone, P., Cruz, C., and Gomez-Mejia, L. R. (2012). Socioemotional Wealth and Proactive Stakeholder Engagement: Why Family-Controlled Firms Care More About Their Stakeholders. *Entrepreneurship Theory and Practice*, *36*(6), 1153-1173.

Child, J. (1964). Quaker employers and industrial relations. *The Sociological Review*, *12*(3), 293-315.

Dacin, P. A., Dacin, M. T., and Matear, M. (2010). Social Entrepreneurship: Why We Don't Need a New Theory and How We Move Forward From Here. *The Academy of Management Perspectives*, *24*(3), 37-57.

Doane, D. (2005). Beyond corporate social responsibility: minnows, mammoths and markets. *Futures*, *37*(2-3), 215-229.

Edward Freeman, R. (2010). *Strategic Management: A Stakeholder Approach*. Cambridge University Press.

Eriksson, H.-E., and Penker, M. (2000). Business Modeling with UML: Business Patterns and Business Objects. John Wiley and Sons Inc.

George, O. J., Owoyemi, O, (2012). Religion; the Forerunner of Organisational Culture: The Case of Quakerism in the Employment/Industrial Relations Practice of John and George Cadbury. *International Journal of Business and Social Science*, *3*(11).

Global Compact UK. (2017). About Us–Global Compact Network UK. Retrieved from http://www.globalcompact.org.uk/about-the-uk-network /about-the-uk-network/

Helfaya, A., and Moussa, T. (2017). Do Board's Corporate Social Responsibility Strategy and Orientation Influence Environmental Sustainability Disclosure? UK Evidence. *Business Strategy and the Environment*. https://doi.org/10.1002/bse.1960

Hemingway, C. A., and Maclagan, P. W. (2004). Managers' Personal Values as Drivers of Corporate Social Responsibility. *Journal of Business Ethics: JBE*, *50*(1), 33-44.

Hess, D. J. (2009). *Localist Movements in a Global Economy: Sustainability, Justice, and Urban Development in the United States.* MIT Press.

Honeyman, R. (2014). *The B Corp Handbook: How to Use Business as a Force for Good.* Berrett-Koehler Publishers.

Hope, A., and Moehler, R. (2015). Responsible Business Model Innovation: Reconceptualising the role of business in society. In: EURAM 2015: 15th Annual Conference of the European Academy of Management, 17th - 20th June 2015, Warsaw, Poland.

Jamali, D., Safieddine, A. M., and Rabbath, M. (2008). Corporate Governance and Corporate Social Responsibility Synergies and Interrelationships. *Corporate Governance: An International Review, 16*(5), 443-459.

Kavanagh, D, Brigham, M and Burton, N. (2017). Changing the Rules of the Game: Recasting the Legal and Ethical Foundation of Business and Management. *Paper submitted to* 33rd European Group of Organizational Studies (EGOS) Colloquium Copenhagen, Denmark, July 6-8, 2017.

Kell, G. (2013). 12 Years later: Reflections on the growth of the UN Global Compact. *Business and Society, 52*(1), 31-52.

Keohane, R. O., and Nye, J. S., Jr. (2002). Governance in a globalizing world. In R. O. Keohane (Ed.), *Power and Governance in a Partially Globalized World* (pp. 193-218). Abingdon, UK: Taylor and Francis.

King, M. (2014). *Quakernomics: An Ethical Capitalism.* Anthem Press.

Longenecker, J. G., McKinney, J. A., and Moore, C. W. (2004). Religious Intensity, Evangelical Christianity, and Business Ethics: An Empirical Study. *Journal of Business Ethics: JBE, 55*(4), 371-384.

Magretta, J. (2002). Why business models matter. *Harvard Business Review, 80*(5), 86-92, 133.

Mair, J., and Martí, I. (2006). Social entrepreneurship research: A source of explanation, prediction, and delight. *Journal of World Business, 41*(1), 36-44.

McDonnell, D. P., Macknight, E. C., and Donnelly, H. (2012). *Democratic Enterprise: Ethical Business for the 21st Century.* https://doi.org/10.2139/ssrn.2041159

Mortimer, J and Mortimer, R. (1980). Leeds Friends' minute book 1692-1712. The Yorkshire Archaelogical Society, York.

McShane, S., and Von Glinow, M. (2011). *M: Organizational behavior.* Irwin/McGraw-Hill.

Mendibil, K., Hernandez, J., Espinach, X., Garriga, E., and Macgregor, S. (2007). How can CSR practices lead to successful innovation in SMEs. *Publication from the RESPONSE Project,* 1-7.

Mikami, K. (2003). Market power and the form of enterprise: capitalist firms, worker-owned firms and consumer cooperatives. *Journal of Economic Behavior and Organization, 52*(4), 533-552.

Novkovic, S. (2008). Defining the co-operative difference. *The Journal of Socio-Economics, 37*(6), 2168-2177.

Oldenkamp, R., van Zelm, R., and Huijbregts, M. (2016). Valuing the human health damage caused by the fraud of Volkswagen. *Environmental Pollution, 212*, 121-127.

Opoku, H. N. (2004). Policy implications of industrial ecology conceptions. *Business Strategy and the Environment, 13*(5), 320-333.

Petts, J. (1998). Environmental Responsiveness, Individuals and Organizational Learning: SME Experience. *Journal of Environmental Planning and Management, 41*(6), 711-730.

Porter, M. E., and Kramer, M. R. (2011). The big idea: Creating shared value. *Harvard Business Review, 89*(1), 2.

Prior, A., and Kirby, M. (1993). The Society of Friends and the family firm, 1700-1830. *Business History, 35*(4), 66-85.

Raistrick, A. (1950). *Quakers in science and industry: being an account of the Quaker contributions to science and industry during the 17th and 18th centuries.* Philosophical Library.

Reis Louis, M. (1994). In the manner of Friends: learnings from Quaker practice for organizational renewal. *Journal of Organizational Change Management, 7*(1), 42-60.

Rowlinson, M., and Hassard, J. (1993). The Invention of Corporate Culture: A History of the Histories of Cadbury. *Human Relations; Studies towards the Integration of the Social Sciences, 46*(3), 299-326.

Sahle, E. (2015). An investigation of early modern Quakers' business ethics. Retrieved from http://eprints.lse.ac.uk/64487/

Schaltegger, S., and Wagner, M. (2011). Sustainable entrepreneurship and sustainability innovation: categories and interactions. *Business Strategy and the Environment, 20*(4), 222-237.

Scully, J. (2009). Virtuous Friends: Morality and Quaker Identity. *Quaker Studies, 14*(1), 108-122.

Sharma, S., and Starik, M. (2002). *Research in Corporate Sustainability: The Evolving Theory and Practice of Organizations in the Natural Environment.* Edward Elgar Publishing.

Sleapwood, N. (2017). *The Birmingham Quaker Business Community 1800-1900*. In, Angell, S and Dandelion, P. (Eds). *Quakers, Business and Industry*. USA: Friends Association in Higher Education.

Soltani, B. (2014). The Anatomy of Corporate Fraud: A Comparative Analysis of High Profile American and European Corporate Scandals. *Journal of Business Ethics: JBE, 120(2)*, 251-274.

Sorescu, A., Frambach, R. T., Singh, J., Rangaswamy, A., and Bridges, C. (2011). Innovations in Retail Business Models. *Journal of Retailing, 87, Supplement 1*(0), S3-S16.

Starbuck, W. H. (2014). Why Corporate Governance Deserves Serious and Creative Thought. *The Academy of Management Perspectives, 28*(1), 15-21.

Taebi, B., Correljé, A., Cuppen, E., Dignum, M., and Pesch, U. (2014). Responsible innovation as an endorsement of public values: the need for interdisciplinary research. *Journal of Responsible Innovation, 1*(1), 118-124.

Tawney, R. H. (1926). *Religion and the Rise of Capitalism*. Transaction Publishers.

Taylor, J. (2006). *Creating Capitalism: Joint-Stock Enterprise in British Politics and Culture 1800-1870*. Royal Historical Society studies in history. New series v. 53. London: 2006.

Tibbals, K. (2014). The theological basis behind Quaker businesses: a comparison of the first 150 years to the beginning of the 20th century. Unpublished thesis. Earlham School of Religion.

Turnbull, R. (2014). *Quaker Capitalism: Lessons for today*. Oxford: Centre for Enterprise, Markets and Ethics.

UN Global Compact. (2017). Our Global Strategy | UN Global Compact. Retrieved from https://www.unglobalcompact.org/what-is-gc/strategy

United Nations. (2017a). What is the UN Global Compact | UN Global Compact. Retrieved April 25, 2017, from https://www.unglobal compact.org/what-is-gc

United Nations. (2017b). Homepage | UN Global Compact. Retrieved from https://www.unglobalcompact.org/

Utting, P. (2005). Corporate responsibility and the movement of business. *Development in Practice, 15*(3-4), 375-388.

van Kleef, J. A. G., and Roome, N. J. (2007). Developing capabilities and competence for sustainable business management as innovation: a research agenda. *Journal of Cleaner Production, 15*(1), 38-51.

Velayutham, S. (2013). Governance without boards: the Quakers. *Corporate Governance: The International Journal of Business in Society, 13*(3), 223-235.

Vernon, A. (2013). *Quaker Business Man: The Life of Joseph Rowntree*. Routledge.

von Shomberg, R. (2013). A Vision of Responsible Research and Innovation. In R. Owen, J. Bessant, and M. Heintz (Eds.), *Responsible Innovation: Managing the Responsible Emergence of Science and Innovation in Society* (pp. 51-64). London: Wiley.

Wagner-Tsukamoto, S. (2008). Contrasting the Behavioural Business Ethics Approach and the Institutional Economic Approach to Business Ethics: Insights From the Study of Quaker Employers. *Journal of Business Ethics*, *82*(4), 835-850.

Walvin, J. (1998). *The Quakers: money and morals*. London: John Murray.

Willard, B. (2012). *The New Sustainability Advantage: Seven Business Case Benefits of a Triple Bottom Line*. New Society Publishers.

Winn, M. L., and Angell, L. C. (2000). Towards a Process Model of Corporate Greening. *Organization Studies*, *21*(6), 1119-1147.

Woolman, J. (1971). *The journal and major essays of John Woolman* (Vol. 1971). Oxford: Oxford University Press.

Wrigley, E. and Schofield, R. (1989). *The population history of England 1541-1871*. Cambridge: Cambridge University Press.

# Discussion Questions

1. Pick a contemporary political economy challenge and describe the way participants in policy debates fail to see a way to bridge the gap between the values and ideals to which we aspire and the "practical," stubborn realities that violate ethical ideals.

2. Quakers were most visibly successful in the world—in business, science and government—when they relied on tight-knit networks of Friends. Can the movement really be said to offer anything of universal value to the greater polity?

3. How is economics transformed if we replace the presumption that work is an unavoidable burden we take on to achieve a certain standard of living with recognition that useful, purposeful work provides meaning? Provide general reactions and specific examples of policy responses.

4. What would be the consequences of converting the US Social Security program from a universal program for all retired workers to means-tested "welfare"?

5. How do the following metaphors we use to describe the way people interact in the economy influence our individual choices and approaches to selecting and implementing public policies?

   - self-interested homo economicus
   - creative, intelligent member of a community of moral beings
   - winners and losers competing for scarce resources
   - walking "cheerfully over the world, answering that of God in everyone"
   - race, nationality, class, religion

6. How might the integration into social and natural science research methods, policy analysis, and decision-making of Quaker traditions of communal discernment, indigenous traditions, theology of liberation, and community-based critical participatory research alter the ways we understand and respond to the political, economic, ecological and militarized challenges facing our communities?

7. Summarize key differences between the management paradigms that emerged in the 2nd half of the 20th century and traditional Quaker discernment approaches to decision making. How might the latter inform the former?

8. Quakers built some of the most successful business enterprises of the 18th and early 19th centuries. Why then are few Quaker business practices manifest in the managerial structure of most corporations today? Why is the managerial class so underrepresented within the Religious Society of Friends?

# PART III
*Contributions and Challenges of Quaker Organizations*

# 6 | Quakers in the Coalfields:
# Economic Justice and the American Friends Service Committee, 1920-Present

**By Paul Moke, Wilmington College**

Take a group of disappointed, disinherited and unemployed miners in a camp in West Virginia or in Kentucky; if one really searches for the kingdom of God in their midst there it is.

–Clarence E. Pickett (1933)

The renaissance of liberal theology that transformed evangelical Quakerism in the late nineteenth and early twentieth centuries brought a renewed focus on social activism to Quaker meetings around the world. Inspired by modernism and a desire to square Quaker doctrine with the affairs of the outside world, liberal Quakers in Friends service organizations extended the peace testimony to confront the roots of conflict in the political and economic structures of society. Their critique of extreme capitalism and public injustice, reinforced by the experiences of conscientious objectors during World War I, reflected the values of the social gospel movement. This movement embraced the goal of social salvation to counter the exclusive focus on individual salvation stressed in the evangelical tradition. Clarence E. Pickett, former executive secretary of the American Friends Service Committee (AFSC), articulated the new theology in a reflective 1928 essay when he wrote that Friends, as practical idealists seeking to promote conscience and reconciliation, should refrain from materialist accumulation and strive to "release moral and religious forces in an acquisitive, militarist, and racist society" (Pickett, 1928, p. 149).

Although the social gospel mission of AFSC in assisting war refugees and promoting civil rights has been the focus of several previous studies, the organization's involvement in the economic justice movement has received relatively little academic attention.[1] One chapter in this history involves the work of AFSC in the coalfields of Appalachia. The story begins in the late 1920s when a severe recession hit the coal industry, and families in isolated company towns and coal camps faced shocking levels of poverty and malnutrition. Using a combination of federal funds and private donations, AFSC distributed food and clothing to children and experimented with homestead communities until the 1940s when economic and social conditions in Appalachia temporarily improved. In subsequent decades as the Appalachian region again descended into poverty, AFSC renewed its commitment to the area. Today its regional staff conducts policy analysis on issues affecting low income families and investigates incidents such as the Upper Big Branch Mine disaster of 2010.

The legacy of AFSC in the coalfields provides a case study in the role of religious organizations in building a just social order. In mapping the contours of this legacy, I begin with a discussion of Clarence Pickett's world view as well as the factors that sparked his interest in the concentrated power of extraction industries and the resulting problem of social dislocation. Understanding this background helps to frame the liberal Quaker critique of unrestrained capitalism and the focus on humanitarian service and small community experimentation that promoted reform in Appalachia. The second portion of the chapter examines specific AFSC projects in the Depression era as well as the individuals who devoted substantial portions of their lives to professionalize social welfare, educational, and health care services in West Virginia. AFSC personnel such as Clarence Pickett, Homer Morris, and Alice O. Davis, as well as their colleague Elsie Ripley Clapp, forged alliances with academic experts in order to develop best practices in their respective fields. They exercised diplomacy in interactions with influential officials, including vice presidents of coal and steel corporations, local judges, state welfare administrators, and school superintendents, in order to win elite cooperation and support. Their success attracted the backing of public figures such as First Lady Eleanor Roosevelt. Some AFSC staff even accepted full or part-time positions in federal and county agencies as a means of implementing their vision of reform. But when bureaucratic inertia, local opposition, and militarism compromised their core beliefs, these Friends resigned their public-sector work and pursued alternative ways to accomplish their objectives. I conclude the chapter with an overview of the contemporary work of AFSC in Appalachia and a brief discussion of the meaning of these

---

[1] For an overview of the centennial history of AFSC, see Barnes (2016); for analysis of the organization's involvement in racial justice activism before 1950, see Austin (2012); for discussion of its activities in World War I and the interwar period, see Jones (1937).

experiences for the developing concept of Quaker approaches to economic justice.

### Liberal Quakerism and Economic Justice

The liberal Quakers who advocated economic justice and social service in the Progressive era (1900–1920) consciously built upon the tradition of social reform in the Friends community that antedated the rise of evangelism in the 1800s. As early as the 1760s, John Woolman stressed the interrelationship between slavery and other forms of unjust labor, acquisition, materialism, and war. Woolman advocated the development of conscience as a means of creating a just social order:

> Oh that we who declare against wars and acknowledge our trust to be in God only, may walk in the Light and therein examine our foundation and motives in holding great estates! May we look upon our treasures and the furniture of our houses and the garments in which we array ourselves and try whether the seeds of war have any nourishment in these possessions or not (Woolman, 1922, 419).

Doctrinally, liberal Quakers of the early twentieth century in Britain and the United States endorsed the ideas of modernist Protestantism, particularly the premise that Old Testament mores needed to be reinterpreted in light of modern culture. Influential Quaker scholars such as Rufus M. Jones, Mary Mendenhall Hobbs, and Elbert Russell saw in early Quaker history the idea of an inner light of God that they incorporated into a "dynamic view" of religion based on the concepts of "progressive revelation, mysticism, and the social gospel" (Hamm, 1988, p. 149). These scholars rejected Old Testament teachings about family relations, war, and original sin in favor of outlooks more congruent with personal experience and the scholarship of contemporary natural and social scientists. They also promoted personal contact with the divine through quiet contemplation and sought to bring about the kingdom of God on earth through a broad set of political and economic reforms.

Most American Quakers in the Gilded Age supported the Republican Party, both because of their interest in promoting racial equality in the South and their support for free trade and unregulated markets. By the turn of the century, however, endorsement of unregulated capitalism among Quakers started to erode due to concern about low wages, poor working conditions, and the use of child labor (Hamm, 1988). The growing critique of capitalism also reflected the influence of contemporary social gospel theologians, such as Walter

Rauschenbush, a Baptist pastor who taught at Rochester Theological Seminary. Rauschenbush contended that the Old Testament prophets were "revolutionists of their age" because they "pictured an ideal state of society in which the poor should be judged with equity and the cry of the oppressed should no longer be heard" (Rauschenbush, 1976, p. 37). Liberal Quakers joined Rauschenbush in opposing the extreme economic inequality, worker exploitation, and material excess of the capitalist era, even as they endorsed a moderate, non-Marxist approach to socialism and government oversight of the economy that avoided coercion or threats to individual freedom. Their ranks included two Quakers from the Midwest, Clarence E. Pickett and Homer Morris, who played crucial roles in the development of AFSC's economic justice initiatives in the period before 1950.

Both Pickett and Morris were birthright Quakers who earned undergraduate degrees at small Quaker colleges before pursuing advanced degrees, Morris in economics at Columbia University and Pickett in religious studies at Hartford Theological Seminary.[2] As graduate students they encountered faculty with strong commitments to the social gospel and progressive reform. Hartford, an institution associated with the Congregationalist Church, contributed much to the development of liberal Quakerism. In addition to Pickett, many other influential Quakers studied there, including Thomas R. Kelly, Errol D. Peckham, and Alexander C. Purdy. These Friends emerged from their studies with the conviction that finding that of God in everyone meant that one should identify with and empower the disinherited outcasts of society.

Hartford's curriculum combined traditional Protestant theology with classes in labor relations, economics, and social service. Course offerings included "Christian Socialism," "History and Theory of Socialism," "The Labor Problem," "Elements of Christianity to Social Progress," and "Christian Ethics." Pickett's future brother-in-law, Errol D. Peckham, who attended Hartford at the same time Pickett did, enrolled in all of these courses. Pickett himself performed an externship at the Spring Street Presbyterian Church Neighborhood House in New York City, a settlement house where the leading American socialist Norman Thomas previously had worked. Located in the lower west side of Manhattan, the Spring Street House served one of the roughest neighborhoods in the city. Its director, the Rev. H. Roswell Bates, hired divinity students to expose them to the challenges of serving poverty-stricken communities. Like Thomas, Pickett gradually became a Christian socialist as a result of his experiences at Spring Street. The two friends also shared a commitment to pacifism. When Thomas

---

[2] Clarence Pickett received his undergraduate education at Penn College and Homer Morris at Earlham College.

left the Presbyterian ministry and assumed leadership of the Socialist Party, Clarence Pickett openly supported his candidacy for President in 1928.[3]

Liberal Quakers in the United States also drew inspiration from London Yearly Meeting, which in 1918 approved a document entitled "The foundation of a true social order" (Heron, 1997; Kennedy, 2001). Grounded in the premise that "The Fatherhood of God, as revealed by Jesus Christ, should lead us toward a brotherhood which knows no restriction of race, sex, or social class," it endorsed a society that "expresses itself beyond all material ends," assures the full development of every member of the community, and rejects the appeal of force in matters of industrial control (Heron, 1997, pp. 22-23). By 1926, the Meeting's Committee on Sufferings established a "watching committee" to investigate and relieve conditions of those laboring in the mining industry, a group encompassing what Karl Marx saw as the "quintessential proletariat" (Heron, 1997, pp. 22-23). Pickett attended the 1920 World Conference of Friends in London, and the ideas about industrial order he encountered there increased his awareness of and interest in the welfare of miners in the United States.

London Yearly Meeting's call for restraint and individual respect in industrial relations contrasted sharply with a series of confrontations between miners and corporate agents in the United States. The most serious of these incidents occurred in 1921 at Blair Mountain outside Logan, West Virginia, when an estimated 120 persons died in protracted fighting (Savage, 1990; Shogan, 2004). By the late 1920s, Clarence Pickett, acting at the invitation of Norman Thomas, convinced the AFSC Board of Directors to approve negotiations leading to settlement of a bitter strike among textile workers in Marion, North Carolina (Pickett, 1953). By 1931, conditions in southern coalfields deteriorated so badly that President Hoover asked AFSC to oversee child-feeding and rehabilitation programs in over 500 coal mining communities in five states.[4] Over the next two years, AFSC secured two million dollars in support from the federal Bureau of Children's Welfare, the Reconstruction Finance Corporation, and private donations to undertake the child-feeding program (Pickett, 1953). Fifty AFSC workers joined 200 volunteers in feeding 40,000 underweight children of school age; in addition, they distributed over 150 tons of used clothing and shoes and

---

[3] Of course, Pickett's support for Norman Thomas, as well as his previous support for Eugene V. Debs for that office in 1920, should not be read to imply that all liberal Quakers accepted the socialist critique of capitalism. Pickett's colleague at AFSC, Rufus M. Jones, supported Republican Herbert Hoover in the 1928 presidential election.

[4] The five states in the service delivery area consisted of selected portions of West Virginia, Kentucky, Illinois, Pennsylvania, and Maryland.

initiated homesteading communities and a number of health care and community development programs throughout Appalachia (Pickett, 1953).

The Friends who participated in AFSC's economic justice initiatives were motivated by simple humanitarian concern for people in need. Their programs reflected progressive scholarship in social welfare, community education, and vocational retraining. Reformers perceived these efforts as pathways of escape from local "coal economies" that favored the interests of the "captains of industry." Ideologically, the Quaker concern for economic justice arose not so much from opposition to capitalism per se but as resistance to unrestrained corporate power that intensified economic inequality, corrupted local and state government, and left "surplus" workers vulnerable. Specifically, the concern was that extreme forms of market fundamentalism and political domination by one class of producers blunted the development of diverse local economies, leading to a decayed state of democracy in which workers had little stake in society and few means of offsetting the power of remote corporate elites.

While the Quakers' ideas and methods were experimental and controversial, their material support and innovative reforms helped tens of thousands of people to survive and even to improve their lives until the point when Franklin Roosevelt's public assistance and civilian employment programs replaced the need for the child-feeding program. Pickett and other Quaker leaders, unlike Roosevelt, never placed their ultimate trust in state authority. Their philosophy of the relationship between Quakerism, humanitarianism, and the nation-state is voiced in a lecture Clarence Pickett gave to the Arch Street Meeting in Philadelphia in 1951, shortly after his retirement from AFSC (Pickett, 1951). The title of his remarks, "Having Done All, to Stand," comes from Paul's Letter to the Ephesians, 6:13 AV: "Therefore take unto you the whole armor of God, that you may be able to withstand in the evil day, and having done all, to stand." Pickett interpreted this passage to mean that Friends must develop "a balance between social concern and inward conviction, between the intelligent effort to affect currents of society, while at the same time finding with some assurance that point at which we must take our stand and cannot accommodate ourselves to the political and social views and moods of the moment" (Pickett, 1951, p. 9). Pickett's reference to "balance" illustrated his devotion to pacifism and his insistence that Quakers, as a minority group potentially out of step with the militarism of American society, should be willing to work constructively with government to achieve reforms while withdrawing into a posture of separation and resistance in the face of the evils of war as necessary. His words illuminate the work of AFSC in Appalachia.

### Relief and Reconstruction in the Coalfields

AFSC's efforts to understand the dynamics of the coal industry in Appalachia centered on the scholarly work of Homer Morris, a professor of economics at Earlham College and Fisk University, who studied the economics of the coal industry in the 1920s and 1930s. In the summer of 1931, as AFSC's child feeding program in Appalachia got underway, Morris took a leave of absence from his teaching responsibilities to serve as Field Director for the program and conduct survey research on coal miners and their families. His book (1934), *The Plight of the Bituminous Coal Miner*, traced the rapid rise and sudden fall of the southern coalfields of Appalachia during the early twentieth century. Morris stressed that coal operators in West Virginia, eastern Kentucky, and Virginia took advantage of topography, with relatively low-cost access to valuable metallurgical coal. In addition, the operators benefited from a non-union work force and cheap long-distance railroad rates, factors that enabled them to gain access to profitable markets in Illinois, Maryland, and northeastern cities. High demand for coal before and during World War I led operators to recruit immigrants from eastern and southern Europe and African Americans from the South for work in the mines.[5] By the late 1920s, however, demand for coal fell sharply due to greater efficiency in industrial and locomotive boilers and increasing use of petroleum. As coal operators cut production and low-capital mining companies filed for bankruptcy, the unique social and political circumstances of Appalachian coal communities proved catastrophic for unemployed miners.

Morris's central argument, that a surplus of 200,000 miners in Appalachia needed to pursue other forms of employment, led him to concentrate on the impediments that life in coal towns posed for individuals seeking to make this transition. Monopolized company stores, scrip methods of employee compensation, and a dearth of employment alternatives trapped workers and their families in one-industry towns and blocked economic opportunity. Poorly constructed houses and inadequate sanitation systems contributed to unhealthy living conditions and epidemics of typhoid fever, smallpox, and tuberculosis. Underperforming local schools chafed under the control of coal operators. Teachers and staff often had little reason to improve since so many students saw their future careers in mining. In the face of these problems, Morris concluded

---

[5] Census data from Scotts Run near Morgantown, WV, one of the coal mining areas served by AFSC, confirms the ethnic diversity of the coal camps in Appalachia. In 1930, sixty percent of the residents were foreign-born—from such nations as Hungary, Lithuania, Poland, Italy, and Poland; twenty percent were African-Americans; and the remaining twenty percent were native-born whites (Lee, 1991, p. 9).

that the best path forward was to adopt British policies for surplus miners: government-run homestead communities for supplementing diets as well as "rehabilitation" programs to retrain workers.

AFSC's experience managing relief programs in Europe provided a template for the new project in Appalachia. From their offices in Philadelphia, Clarence Pickett and Bernard A. Warner recruited staff members, most of whom were veterans of the child-relief work in Europe, Young Friends who recently had graduated from college, or volunteers from Friends meetings across the country. Project leaders included Homer Morris, Alice O. Davis, and Winifred Waye Wencke. Davis had served AFSC as a nurse and social worker at Botkinsky Hospital outside Moscow in the 1920s. Working in Morgantown, West Virginia in the early 1930s, she organized adult vocational and community improvement programs for unemployed workers and their families. Wencke, a former campus nurse at Earlham College, headed the child-relief program in Logan, West Virginia. She organized summer camps and vocational programs for girls throughout southern West Virginia and founded a regional polio treatment center and community health clinic, which evolved into the Friends Health Service.[6]

In the fall of 1931, as the child-feeding project got underway, AFSC held section conferences in Philadelphia and Logan to review academic articles, compare experiences in local communities, and formulate best practices. Their discussions, summarized in the AFSC archives and in Pickett's journals, reveal the insights, ideas, and methods of the Service Committee. At one meeting, a participant noted: "Here in one industry we have focused all the sore spots in our national life, race problems, absentee landlords, camps, labor problems. This is the first time in our national life when we have faced a decaying industry where the displaced men cannot be transplanted into and absorbed by other industries without a conscious effort on the part of someone." Field directors also emphasized the importance of securing the support of local judges, community leaders, and coal operators before launching child weighing and food distribution programs in the schools.

Homer Morris's experience in Harlan County, Kentucky, site of protracted labor unrest in the early 1930s, showed the importance of working cooperatively

---

[6] For a thoughtful review of service to the Logan community, see Spence (1976). Beth Spence, the author's sister, worked as a coalfield specialist for AFSC in West Virginia until her recent retirement. In her review of Winifred Waye Wencke's life's work, as published in her brother's book, Ms. Spence wrote, "[Wencke's] accomplishment, and her gift to Logan was easy to understand. Mrs. Wencke had labored for others in a time when many were too concerned for their own future to care for anyone else; she had labored quietly and with great strength for children who had no one else to fight for them" (Spence, 1976, p. 506).

with community leaders in order to get the food distribution program underway. In Harlan, local elites–including coal operators, small business owners, religious leaders, and county officials–joined forces to drive "radicals" affiliated with the United Miners Union from the region. They evicted the striking miners and terminated all county welfare programs. In response, liberal groups such as the American Civil Liberties Union and the Dreiser Committee (a group consisting of famous writers such as Theodore Dreiser, John Dos Passos, and Sherwood Anderson) came into the local community to oppose the violation of free speech and assembly rights and to publicize the plight of the miners.[7] Local leaders perceived these groups as unwanted outsiders and responded violently in order to terminate the flow of aid to the striking miners and their families. In these circumstances, Morris began his work in Harlan by meeting with a powerful local judge, who initially proved hostile until Morris shared a letter of introduction from President William J. Hutchens of nearby Berea College. The letter stressed that the Friends were neutral peacemakers, not radical agitators. These words, in conjunction with AFSC's ties to the Hoover Administration, convinced local leaders of their good will. By the summer of 1932, the Friends served 139,681 meals to eligible children in Harlan County (AFSC, 1932).

Clarence Pickett brought both insight and managerial skill to the project. His outreach to the corporate community was particularly important. In the spring of 1932 at a conference of coal operators in Washington, D.C., Pickett met executives from the Pittsburgh Coal Company, United States Steel, the Ford Motor Company, and the Baltimore and Ohio Railroad. Industrialists on the AFSC board of directors later helped him appeal successfully to these organizations for financial support. Pickett also worked closely with Quaker meetings throughout the country to secure assistance from Friends who ran produce operations. Prune farmers in Newburg, Oregon, apple and chicken farmers in Barnesville, Ohio, and owners of powdered milk companies responded with in-kind donations that shipped on common carriers either free or at heavily discounted rates. Attentive to public relations, Pickett invited Malcolm Ross, a publicity agent from New York City, to attend the various section conferences of the child-feeding program to gain an understanding of their work. This led to favorable articles in newspapers and magazines.

---

[7] The Dreiser Committee published its analysis of labor strife in Harlan County in the National Committee for the Defense of Political Prisoners (1970). For an overview of the miners' strikes in Harlan and Bell County Kentucky during the early 1930s, see A Strike Against Starvation and Terror: An Archival Exercise Exploring a Coal Miners' Strike, available at https://appalachiancenter.as.uky.edu.

In 1933, a close friend of Eleanor Roosevelt, Lorena Hickok, became a writer and consultant for Harry Hopkins, Director of the Federal Emergency Relief Administration. Hickok's first assignment involved a visit to coal camps along Scotts Run near Morgantown, accompanied by Clarence Pickett and AFSC field organizer Errol D. Peckham. There they encountered thousands of unemployed miners and their families living in squalid conditions in coal camps scattered along the banks of Scotts Run. Many were surviving on a diet of corn meal and hog fat, and barefoot children without adequate clothing often skipped school. Subsequent analysis showed that about forty percent of the children suffered from "malnutrition, enlarged tonsils, defective vision, and decayed teeth" (Lee, 1991, p. 22). Writing to Eleanor Roosevelt, Hickok offered a vivid description of Scotts Run: "I came upon a gutter along a village street filled with stagnant, filthy water used for drinking, cooking, washing, and everything else imaginable by the inhabitants of ramshackle cabins that most Americans would not have considered fit for pigs."

Hickok's descriptions of Scotts Run attracted the concern of the First Lady, who made her own visit to the area later that summer. As she met with unemployed miners and their families, the First Lady chose not to reveal her identity so that she could observe the local conditions first-hand. By the end of her visit, she resolved to devote her personal resources and political influence to improve the coal miners' lives. Over the next six years, until the onset of World War II, Eleanor Roosevelt worked tirelessly with Pickett to develop social welfare, educational, and homesteading programs to help the workers and their families envision and pursue new lives outside the coalfields. For his part, Pickett visited the White House over 150 times during this period, collaborating closely with Mrs. Roosevelt on field research and community development programs.

During all phases of its work in Appalachia during the Depression, AFSC emphasized the importance of educational and vocational programming as a means of providing family support, promoting self-respect, and enhancing upward mobility. As one field worker phrased it, "[A]dult relief work [should be] self-supporting rather than just a dole." In this spirit, Alice O. Davis developed self-help programs to counter the sluggishness and indolence that often accompanied long periods of unemployment and welfare support. Working with the staff of the Shack, a settlement house in the Scotts Run area, she established racially integrated nursery school programs, weaving classes, and community gardening workshops. Bill Simkin, another AFSC field worker in Scotts Run, collaborated with forestry officials from the State Extension Service to offer woodworking classes for unemployed miners. They recruited Bud Godlove, a mountaineer who specialized in traditional methods of making furniture from old-growth hickory trees. The project later evolved into the Mountaineer Craftsman Cooperative Association, which produced furniture and other handmade goods that Friends marketed along the eastern seaboard.[8] Pickett and Morris sought to extend these programs by embracing the British model for coalfield relief. They advocated the relocation of surplus miners into homesteading programs that would provide new housing, suitable truck gardening space, and high-quality educational and vocational programming to supplement unreliable income from mining and help families transition into new sources of livelihood.

In 1933, Eleanor Roosevelt persuaded the Roosevelt administration to include funding for experimental homesteading programs in the National Industrial Recovery Act (NIRA). Section 208 of the Act authorized the U.S. Department of Interior to establish homesteads "for the redistribution of the population in industrial centers by making loans for...the purchase of...subsistence homesteads" (National Industrial Recovery Act, 1933).[9] Congress eventually appropriated $25 million for the program. One goal of the homesteading program was to develop pilot projects for industrial workers to relocate to rural settings and engage in subsistence agriculture to supplement industrial employment and sustain their families during economic downturns. A second goal was to initiate educational and vocational programs for children and adults to qualify them for professional work beyond low demand labor markets. In Appalachia, these programs included instruction in furniture making, weaving, gardening, nutrition, and traditional music and folk arts.

After the legislation passed into law, Secretary of the Interior Harold Ickes appointed Milburn L. Wilson to head the Subsistence Homestead Division. An experienced administrator who specialized in agricultural economics, Wilson favored a decentralized approach to homestead development that brought local residents into the development and management of experimental communities. He appointed Clarence Pickett on a part-time basis to develop homesteads in the coalfields. Pickett selected Homer Morris as field supervisor for the program. For a little over a year, the two Friends developed homesteads for impoverished persons in Appalachia, three in West Virginia (Arthurdale, Red House, and Tygart Valley), one in Pennsylvania (Norvelt), and one in Tennessee (Cumberland); eventually, hundreds of similar programs were established

---

[8] Many of Godlove's chairs can be found at Pendle Hill today.

[9] When the Supreme Court of the U.S. declared Title I of the NIRA unconstitutional in Schechter Poultry Co. v. U.S., 295 U.S. 495 (1935), Congress did not replace the act. Subsequently, President Roosevelt transferred responsibility for administering the Title II subsistence homestead program to the Resettlement Administration and the U.S. Department of Agriculture.

throughout the United States, although most were not specifically targeted for the poor.

Arthurdale, the first, largest, and most famous of the homestead projects, began in 1933 when the Interior Department purchased a 1,200 acre tract in Reedsville, WV, approximately 40 miles southeast of Morgantown. Plans called for 165 single family houses, each with indoor plumbing, steam heat, a fireplace, and a root cellar, as well as four acres of ground suitable for a truck garden and a small pasture for livestock. However, in his haste to get the program off the ground, White House advisor Lewis Howe carelessly ordered prefabricated Cape Cod summer cottages for Arthurdale. The cottages did not fit on the preexisting foundations and were ill-suited for West Virginia winters. This led to an unfortunate series of retrofits, repeated custom alterations, and cost overruns; in addition, the porous rock structure of the acreage made it difficult to build wells and sanitation systems.

One of Pickett's first responsibilities as a federal administrator involved the process of selecting families for Arthurdale. Working with officials at West Virginia University, Pickett helped to develop an eight-page application that featured questions designed to elicit information about the applicant's moral character and knowledge of farming. All residents of Scotts Run, including many African Americans, were encouraged to apply, but in the end, funding limitations, West Virginia school segregation laws, and opposition from white applicants led to exclusion of African Americans from Arthurdale. This outcome distressed Pickett and Morris. Although approximately 60% of the families selected for Arthurdale came from Scotts Run, the vast majority of the 3,000 families who resided in the coal camps along Scotts Run did not benefit from the program.

A principal challenge of Arthurdale concerned how to attract employers to the community. The search for suitable farmland had led planners to rural Preston County, but the location proved too remote from the transportation grid and the commercial markets of Morgantown. Federal officials managed to draw a series of industries to Arthurdale, including corporations that made vacuum cleaners, tractors, and shirts, but in the stress of the Depression years none proved successful. With the coming of World War II, several companies obtained defense contracts for the assembly of walkie-talkies and wooden simulation fighter planes at Arthurdale, quasi-military enterprises that troubled AFSC officials. Eventually, the war stimulated heavy industry in the region, leading to a reopening of the mines and the development of the Morgantown Ordinance Works, which purified ammonia for Army ammunition and distilled deuterium for the Manhattan Project. Some Arthurdale families returned to

Scotts Run during the war, only to face tragedy when over 89 miners died in three separate mining disasters at Osage and Pursglove in 1942.[10]

Perhaps the most significant legacy of Pickett's involvement with Arthurdale concerned his collaboration with Eleanor Roosevelt in the development of the Arthurdale community school. Pickett recruited Elsie Ripley Clapp as principal for the school. A progressive educator who studied under John Dewey at Columbia University, Clapp began work at Arthurdale in 1934. Her innovative approach to education featured practical learning and exploration of family heritage. She developed nursery school and kindergarten programs, classes in math and reading that featured connections to gardening and basic construction skills, as well as adult vocational programs in weaving, woodworking, and metal work. The creative high school curriculum encouraged students to build musical instruments, study Appalachian ballads, and write plays about their family experiences (Stack, 2016). Eleanor Roosevelt took a special interest in the Arthurdale community school, and when federal funds proved insufficient for all Clapp wanted to accomplish, Roosevelt donated the proceeds of her "My Day" newspaper columns and other public speaking engagements to AFSC for the school. She frequently accompanied her friend Clarence Pickett to community activities, graduations, and other social events at Arthurdale.

By 1934, the subsistence homestead program began to generate criticism within the Executive Branch. Thomas (1998) reports that many New Deal administrators, including Interior Secretary Harold Ickes and economist Rexford Tugwell saw the Arthurdale program as "wrongheaded," "utopian," and "escapist." Secretary of Agriculture Henry Wallace thought it ill-advised to combine agriculture and industry in rural resettlement programs, and Ickes viewed Arthurdale as "nothing but a headache from the beginning" (Thomas, 1998, p. 173). Ickes opposed the decentralist administrative model favored by Pickett's immediate supervisor, Milburn L. Wilson, and in June of 1934 Wilson left the Interior Department for a new position in Agriculture Department. The new centralized approach took power away from community residents and led to a series of conflicts and resignations of lower level administrators over accounting and financial management issues. The bureaucratic infighting disturbed Pickett and Morris, who soon resigned their positions in the Interior Department. In subsequent years, administrative responsibility for Arthurdale moved to the Department of Agriculture, the Federal Housing Authority, and the National Housing Agency, which finally sold the homestead properties to local residents and terminated the Arthurdale project in the mid-1940s.

---

[10] For further reading on the history of Scotts Run, see Yeager (1994) and Ross (1994).

Like Pickett and Morris, other Friends who worked in the public sector during the Depression became frustrated and left for other careers. Alice O. Davis, whose initial success led to her appointment as Morgantown welfare administrator in 1934, resigned after one year. She lost a battle with an entrenched local bureaucracy that resented outsiders and resisted the establishment of a non-partisan, professionally administered social welfare system. Davis's experience in many ways mirrors that of Pickett and Morris. All three were unhappy with patronage, delays in obtaining funding, and discontent with the exclusion of black coal miners from Arthurdale. Similarly, after two years of reasonable success at Arthurdale Community School, Elsie Clapp resigned as principal when parents expressed a desire to reshape the school to resemble the other public schools of Preston County. Despite her limited time at Arthurdale, the creative ideas that she brought to the classroom benefited her students, many of whom went on to professional careers outside the field of mining. The dedication and gratitude of the original Arthurdale families and their descendants, exhibited by the annual reunions that continue into the present, testify to the success of the educational programs at Arthurdale.

Both the First Lady and the AFSC leadership continued their involvement with community development activities during the period leading up to WWII. Working with the U.S. Resettlement Administration, Mrs. Roosevelt launched a series of public cooperative communities, popularly known as "green-belt" experiments, in Greendale, Wisconsin (Milwaukee metropolitan area), Greenbelt, Maryland (Washington, D.C. metropolitan area), and Green Hills, Ohio (Cincinnati metropolitan area). These communities featured homes for all income levels, residential neighborhoods within walking distance of businesses, schools, and religious centers, and a balance between urban life and parks and forests. Following his resignation from the Department of the Interior, Pickett resumed full-time duties as executive secretary of AFSC. Homer Morris accepted a new position within AFSC as secretary of the Social-Industrial Section, relying in part on financial support from Eleanor Roosevelt. Both continued their work with homestead communities but under private-sector, rather than public-sector, control.[11]

The AFSC's new homestead project for unemployed miners, Penn-Craft, located in Fayette County Pennsylvania, benefited from the mistakes of Arthurdale: the community accepted African American residents; families assumed responsibility for building and paying for their own homes; and the

---

[11] Morris later assumed responsibility for helping Japanese-Americans relocate from internment camps during World War II. Davis earned a Ph.D. in sociology from the University of North Carolina and served as a professor at Virginia Commonwealth University.

location was close enough to the Pittsburgh metropolitan area to attract stable sources of employment. The first families moved into Penn-Craft in 1939 under financial terms more reasonable than at Arthurdale. The total cash outlay for each house was $2,000, financed on a twenty-year loan to the owner from AFSC at two percent interest. Over two hundred Young Friends volunteered in the summers to excavate stone, build plumbing infrastructure, and provide recreation areas for children.

AFSC continued its work at Penn-Craft until the late 1940s, even as it turned its principal attention to the problems of war refugees, Japanese American internees at relocation centers, and conscientious objectors during World War II. In 1947, when AFSC and the Friends Service Council of London won the Nobel Peace Prize, Clarence Pickett shared why he thought they had been chosen for the award: "[I]t seemed to us that in an age when increasingly the state was held to be supreme and the individual only a tool, the prize had gone, in a basic sense, to that way of life which holds each individual to be a child of God and therefore of supreme value" (Pickett, 1953, p. 306). After devoting so much of his time and attention to the development of public sector homesteading initiatives in the middle years of the New Deal, by the end of World War II Pickett focused on world peace and human rights in his quest for moral community.

## Scholarly Analysis of AFSC's Depression-Era Work

Scholarly evaluations of AFSC's child-feeding program have been largely positive. Maloney (2011) praises the effectiveness of this aspect of AFSC's work, including the organization's fundraising activities, the efficiency of its collaboration with local officials and volunteers in the establishment of medical screenings, food and clothing distribution centers, and community gardens, as well as its creativity in developing the Mountaineer Craftsman Cooperative Association. Thomas (2010) concurs, noting that "the Friends were generally well received by all elements of the community including local officials, coal operators, and mining families" notwithstanding occasional problems with resistant individuals who perceived the Quaker volunteers as unwanted outsiders (p. 57). Nearly all scholars acknowledge the severity of the challenge AFSC faced in the coalfields, and all would agree with Pickett's observation that in view of the scope of the problem, the AFSC effort resembled "trying to sweep back the ocean" (Quinn, 2016, p. 96).

The scholarly consensus breaks down when it comes to evaluations of the social welfare and economic reforms of the early New Deal, of which Arthurdale and the NIRA are representative. In large part the disagreement reflects ideological tensions over the merits of government intervention in the marketplace. Orthodox interpretations, supportive of FDR's reforms, stress the unprecedented severity of the Depression as well as the need for experimentation with banking reforms, codes of fair competition, and federal work projects in order to stabilize the economy (Burns, 1956; 2001; Schlesinger, Jr., 1956; 2003; Leuchtenburg, 1995; 2009). Revisionists assail the evils of big government and stress the adverse impacts of Roosevelt's regulatory reforms and tax increases on business profitability and hiring trends (Kennedy, 1996; Powell, 2003). As it applies to AFSC, much of this debate centers on Arthurdale. Maloney (2007; 2011) criticizes Arthurdale as a misguided, wasteful, and socialist, but other scholars are more positive. Stack (2016) stresses the partial success of educational programming at Arthurdale, and Thomas (1998) praises the role of New Deal reformers in overcoming opposition from corrupt and captured state and local political leaders. Other authors note the failure of laissez-faire conservatives to acknowledge the severe economic and political problems that the extraction industry left in its wake in Appalachia (Eller, 1982; Thomas, 1998).

Maloney (2011) portrays Arthurdale as an ill-fated exercise in the evils of central economic planning, arguing that the project ignored America's individualistic political culture and transgressed constitutional limitations on governmental power: "The economic platform of the back-to-the-landers consisted of a self-righteous, moralistic disdain for laissez-faire combined with a desire to restrict production and raise prices. The entire idea of encouraging handicrafts on the subsistence homesteads was to turn the resettled away from the factory system of mass production and become islands of economic autarky" (p. 198). Although Maloney offers valuable data, his broader policy and legal conclusions are exaggerated and lack supporting evidence. Missing from his analysis is any discussion of the role of corporate elites in the troubled economic and political history of Appalachia or the many ways in which laissez-faire policies contributed to the onset of the Great Depression. His legal objections to the Arthurdale project, which emphasize the absence of constitutional authority for the federal government to create and manage a "town," fail to address a variety of counterarguments, such as the contractual basis for the undertaking and the authority to establish rules for the protection of the health, safety, and welfare of residents.

Maloney unfairly attacks Arthurdale educator Elsie Ripley Clapp. He condemns Clapp's Ivy League background and "progressive" educational methods yet fails to explain how these factors made her ill-suited for the job (Maloney, n.d.). Admittedly, Clapp served at the Arthurdale Community School for only two years, and, after she left in 1936, the Preston County School Board revised the School's curriculum to follow conventional curricula. Yet as Hoffman (2001) reports, "[A]lmost all of the children [of Arthurdale Community School] went on to college: becoming teachers, doctors, lawyers, artists, musicians, accountants, librarians, and historians" (p. 92). Stack (2016) supports this assertion: "During the progressive years, perhaps up until World War II, the children of Arthurdale explored their heritage, their culture, and their identity. They learned from experience, not just texts, and they were very fortunate to have a highly educated, caring, and creating teaching staff. The Arthurdale School saw its greatest success with its younger students" (p. 137).[12] Given the deficiencies of public schools at Scotts Run and other mining camps, this strongly suggests that Clapp's Montessori methods supported the students at a crucial stage in their educational development. For both Eleanor Roosevelt and Clarence Pickett, encouraging the younger generation to leave the mining industry was the major goal of Arthurdale, and in this, the project had significant success.

Academic research in cultural anthropology offers additional insights into Arthurdale. Becker (1998) examines the construction of American folk art in the 1930s and exposes contradictions in the way middle-class reformers who came to the Southern mountains in the early decades of the twentieth century viewed Appalachian residents and culture. On the one hand, the reformers sought to "impose" middle-class values on a region they perceived as urgently in need of relief; on the other, they promoted southern Appalachia as the "noble remnant" of authentic pioneer culture through the mass marketing of traditional goods (p. 59). In fundamental ways, the reformers' attempt to synthesize subsistence farming and pre-industrial craftsmanship did not square with the broader industrial and mass consumer culture upon which it was based. The reformers' romantic attraction to Appalachian handcrafts also relied in part on domestic piecework performed by exploited female and child workers. But the reform effort did not misunderstand or reject the values of mountain culture. Rather, it sought to improve desperate lives and create community structures that nurtured self-respect and marketable skills.

The scholarly literature also addresses the role of nonresident corporations in weakening the political culture of Appalachia, which AFSC officials of the Depression era seemed to overlook. Williams (2006) argues that out of-state corporations assumed nearly total control of state and local politics in the region,

---

12 Recent oral history research confirms the positive impact that Clapp's progressive educational methods had on Arthurdale students. Wuenstel (2002) notes, "Several of the participants stated that the experience had changed them innately and, in the long-term, had enabled them to become more confident and involved in life-long learning processes" (p. 768).

promoting policies like West Virginia's 1932 Tax Limitation Amendment that minimized corporate liability and adversely affected the state's ability to respond to the crisis of unemployment during the Depression. These trends fostered corruption, alienation, and widespread voter apathy. Corporate policy opposed increases in public spending to assist unemployed coal workers and their families. Elected officials of both political parties resisted implementation of New Deal programs at the state level. The result was what leading authors variously describe as "feudal" or "colonial" relationships in which "captured" political entities sustained the flow of massive profits to distant elites; states lacked the ability to match federal New Deal grants; and corrupt political machines proliferated. In contrast, local workers lived in "sacrifice zones" featuring unstable employment, extensive toxins, and few avenues of upward mobility (Thomas, 1998; Eller, 1982).

In his influential portrait of the New Deal in Appalachia, Thomas (1998) asserts that federal reforms led to two fundamental changes in the political culture of the coalfields. First, the NIRA fostered the success of the United Mine Workers in overcoming the political power of the coal barons, leading to improvements in working conditions, benefit programs, and overall standards of living. Second, other social welfare reforms improved the political culture of Appalachia by limiting and sometimes displacing corrupt systems of social welfare administration. As Thomas (1998) states, the "Elizabethan methods of care for the indigent" moved toward "a more bureaucratic and professional system of relief and welfare" (p. 4). AFSC professionals like Alice O. Davis played significant roles in this process.

## Concluding Thoughts: The Contemporary Picture

Today coal operators and others in the extraction industry continue to dominate the political economy of Appalachia. The adoption of strip mining, longwall extraction, and mountaintop removal methods led to overproduction of coal and steep declines in the demand for labor. Yet profits for nonresident corporations soared, especially between 1980 and 2010. Corporate income and mineral depletion taxes remained low, even as unemployment and poverty rates in coal-dominated counties rose. Similar trends have taken place in the fracking industry. In broad terms, the economic policies that have benefited the contemporary extraction industry parallel the free market fundamentalism of the pre-New Deal era. In both periods, elites pursued a laissez-faire and deregulatory agenda, privatizing property rights and profits and either ignoring economic, health, and environmental risks or "externalizing" them onto workers and taxpayers. The result is a troubled economy plagued by underemployment, increasing inequality, and relatively low levels of growth.

These trends have adverse consequences for democracy. Political scientists use the term "resource curse paradox" to describe the strong correlation between a one-commodity economy and the increased likelihood that those who control that commodity will gain inordinate power in the relevant political system (McPherson, 1953; Cavalcanti, Mohaddes, and Raissi, 2012; Leong and Mohaddes, 2011; Shrivastava and Stefanick, 2015). The resulting decline in democracy jeopardizes political party competition, threatens separation of powers, and contributes to reduced levels of political participation and political equality. The resource curse paradox appears to be a constant across many parts of the world where the extraction industry operates, including in the Middle East, the tar sands region of Alberta, and Appalachia.

The recent work of the AFSC staff in the West Virginia field office is a counterweight to these trends. Working with its coalition partner, the West Virginia Center on Budget and Policy, AFSC prepares policy analyses to address economic underdevelopment, deindustrialization, and unfair tax policy in the region. One of its recent reports examines the continuing problem of extensive ownership of land by nonresident corporations and timber management trusts. Researchers found that in six West Virginia counties—nearly all in the high-poverty southern coalfields—the top ten landowners own at least 50% of all private land. This arrangement frustrates local economic growth and makes it difficult to build public assets for the benefit of future generations (West Virginia Center on Budget and Policy, 2013). Another recent report traces sharp declines in wages and benefits among middle and low-income workers in the wake of the state's movement from an industrial economy to a service economy (West Virginia Center on Budget and Policy, 2015). The severity and persistence of these trends distinguishes today's economic climate from that of the early twentieth century. When asked about whether AFSC can follow Clarence Pickett's example by discussing necessary reforms with corporate officials, AFSC local administrator Rick Wilson responded with a note of pessimism: "Now the other side is very far away."

An important component of AFSC's recent focus in Appalachia concerns the investigation of mine disasters (McAteer et al., 2011). AFSC Coalfields Specialist Beth Spence served as an investigator and writer on two official panels that examined fatal mine incidents at two Massey Energy facilities. The worst of these was the 2010 Upper Big Branch Mine disaster that killed 29 miners. Spence spent over a year conducting 350 interviews before writing an extensive report on behalf of former federal mine safety chief Davitt McAteer and the other members of the panel. After carefully documenting the role that inadequate, malfunctioning, and improperly maintained ventilation, rock dusting, and longwall shearer equipment played in the deadly explosion, the investigators concluded that upper level officials at Massey Energy engaged in a "culture of deviance" in pushing coal production over safety practices at the mine. Federal and state departments of mine safety and federal prosecutors relied upon the panel's findings in issuing extensive fines for violation of mining laws and in a subsequent federal criminal action against Massey CEO Don Blankenship.[13] In 2016, Blankenship was found guilty of a misdemeanor count of conspiracy to violate federal mine safety laws; the trial court sentenced him to serve one year in federal prison.

Viewed in historical perspective, AFSC has been called to Appalachia in order to mend broken lives and restore community stability in a region besieged by deindustrialization, poverty, and structural inequality. Many aspects of its work illustrate the world view of the Society of Friends, from the focus on individual dignity, self-reliance, and fair treatment to the recruitment of women and minorities into positions of responsibility within the organization. Another central theme in its work—the interplay between AFSC personnel and government officials—illustrates the tension between activism, cooperation, self-criticism, and protest in the legacy of AFSC. As a case study in the development of Quaker approaches to political economy, AFSC's work in Appalachia shows the important role that scholarship plays in framing its policy positions and experimental projects. Of equal importance is the role of values, as AFSC personnel insist that powerful corporate and public sector officials respect the dignity of the individual, generously share public and private resources with the underprivileged, and consider the welfare of future generations in all aspects of community life. Notwithstanding this remarkable legacy, much work remains to be done, both in understanding the history of AFSC's work in the coalfields and in addressing the human and environmental needs of the Appalachian region. As a "zone of abandonment" in a world that relentlessly pursues fossil fuels, Appalachia may serve as an unfortunate harbinger of the future for many other communities across the world. Given the weighty human and environmental consequences, the response of communities of conscience rarely has been more crucial.

---

[13] In 2011, Alpha Natural Resources, the successor to Massey Energy, settled a civil action brought by the U.S. government for $209 million, a figure that included $41.5 million for the survivors and families of the deceased. In addition, the Mine Safety and Health Administration issued a $10.8 million fine for violation of federal mine safety laws, the largest such fine in U.S. history.

## References

American Friends Service Committee (1932). Report of the child relief work in the bituminous coal fields by the American Friends Service Committee. Philadelphia, PA: Engle Press.

Austin, A. W. (2012). *Quaker brotherhood: Interracial activism and the American Friends Service Committee, 1917-1950.* Urbana, IL: University of Illinois Press.

Barnes, G. A. (2016). *A centennial history of the American Friends Service Committee.* Philadelphia, PA: Friends Press.

Becker, J.S. (1998). *Selling tradition: Appalachia and the construction of an American folk, 1930-1940.* Chapel Hill, NC: The University of North Carolina Press.

Burns, J.M. (1956). *Roosevelt: The lion and the fox.* New York, NY: Harcourt, Brace.

Burns, J. M. (2001). "Franklin Roosevelt's 'first one hundred days.'" *Triumphs and tragedies of the modern presidency: seventy-six case studies in presidential leadership.* Westport, CT: Praeger.

Cavalcanti, T.V., Mohanddes, K., and Raissi, M. (2012). "Commodity price volatility and the sources of growth." IMF Working Paper. Retrieved from https://ssrn.com/abstract=1846429

Cook, B. W. (1999). *Eleanor Roosevelt, Vol. 2, 1933-1938.* New York, NY: Penguin Putnam.

Eller, Ronald D. (1982). *Miners, millhands, and mountaineers: Industrialization of the Appalachian south, 1880-1930.* Knoxville, TN: University of Tennessee Press.

Hamm, T.D. (1988). *The transformation of American Quakerism: Orthodox Friends, 1800-1907.* Bloomington, IN: Indiana University Press.

Haid, S. E. (1975). *Arthurdale: An experiment in community planning.* (Unpublished doctoral dissertation). West Virginia University, Morgantown, WV: West Virginia University.

Heron, A. (1997). *The British Quakers, 1647-1997: Highlights of their history.* Kelso, Scotland: Curlew Productions, Thirlestane House.

Hoffman, N. C. (2001). *Eleanor Roosevelt and the Arthurdale experiment.* North Haven, CT: Linnet Books.

Jones, M.H. (1937). *Swords into ploughshares: An account of the American Friends Service Committee, 1917-1937.* New York, NY: Macmillan.

Kennedy, D. M. (1989). *Freedom from fear: The American people in depression and war.* New York, NY: Oxford University Press.

Kennedy, T. C. (2001). *British Quakerism, 1860-1920: The transformation of a religious community.* New York, NY: Oxford University Press.

Lee, S.D. (1991). *… and the trees cried.* Morgantown, WV: Author.

Leong, W. & Mohaddes, K. (2011). Institutions and the volatility curse. Cambridge Working Papers in Economics 1145. Department of Applied Economics, Faculty of Economics, University of Cambridge, Cambridge, UK.

Leuchtenburg, W.E. (1995). *The FDR years: On Roosevelt and his legacy*. New York, NY: Columbia University Press.

Leuchtenburg, W.E. (2009). *Franklin D. Roosevelt and the New Deal*. New York, NY: Harper Perennial.

Macpherson, C. B. (1953). *Democracy in Alberta: The theory and practice of a quasi-party system*. Toronto, Ontario: University of Toronto Press.

Maloney, C.J. (2007). The peculiar history of Arthurdale. Retrieved from https://mises.org/library/peculiar-history-arthurdale

Maloney, C.J. (2011). *Back to the land: Arthurdale, FDR's New Deal, and the costs of economic planning*. Hoboken, NJ: John Wiley & Sons.

McAteer, J. D., Beall, K., Beck Jr., J.A., McGinley, P., Monforton, C., Roberts, D.C., Spence, B., & Weise, S. (2011). Upper Big Branch: Report to the Governor. Retrieved from https://www.documentcloud.org/documents/2401616-mcateer-giip-report-on-upper-big-branch-mine.html

Miller, L. M. (1999). *Witness for humanity: A biography of Clarence E. Pickett*. Wallingford, PA: Pendle Hill.

Morris, H. (1934). *The Plight of the Bituminous Coal Miner*. Philadelphia, PA: University of Pennsylvania Press.

National Committee for the Defense of Political Prisoners (1970). Harlan Miners Speak: Report on the Terrorism of the Kentucky Coal Fields. New York: De Capo Press.

National Industrial Recovery Act (1933), Ch. 90, 48 Stat. 205, Title II, Sec. 208.

Pickett, C.E. (1928, March 1). What worries the Quaker. *The American Friend* 16(9), 148-9.

Pickett, C.E. (1933, September 7). A New Deal in motives. *The American Friend* 21(29), 401.

Pickett, C.E. (1951). *And having done all, to stand: Delivered at Arch Street Meeting House, Philadelphia*. Philadelphia, PA: Young Friends Movement of the Philadelphia Yearly Meeting.

Pickett, C.E. (1953). *For more than bread: An autobiographical account of twenty-two years' work with the American Friends Service Committee*. Boston, MA: Little, Brown.

Powell, J. (2003). *FDR's folly: How Roosevelt and his New Deal prolonged the Great Depression*. New York, NY: Three Rivers Press.

Quinn, S. (2016). *Eleanor and Hick: The love affair that shaped a first lady.* New York, NY: Penguin Press.

Rauschenbusch, W. (1976). The righteousness of the kingdom. In Ronald C. White and C. Howard Hopkins (Eds.). *The social gospel: Religion and reform in changing America.* Philadelphia, PA: Temple University Press.

Ross, P. (1994). The Scotts Run coalfield from the Great War to the Great Depression: A study in overdevelopment. *West Virginia History,* 53, 21-42.

Savage, L. (1990). *Thunder in the mountains: The West Virginia mine war, 1920-21.* Pittsburgh, PA: University of Pittsburgh Press.

Shrivastava, M. & Stefanick, L. (2012). Do oil and democracy only clash in the global south? Petro politics in Alberta, Canada. *New Global Studies,* 6(I): article 5.

Shrivastava, M. & Stefanick, L. (Eds.) (2015). *Alberta oil and the decline of democracy in Canada.* Edmonton, Alberta: AU Press.

Schlesinger, Jr., A. M. (1956). *The age of Roosevelt.* Boston, MA: Houghton Mifflin.

Schlesinger, Jr., A.M. (2003). *The politics of upheaval: The age of Roosevelt III.* New York, NY: Houghton Mifflin.

Shogan, R. (2004). *The battle of Blair Mountain: The story of America's largest labor uprising.* Boulder, CO: Westview Press.

Spence, R.Y. (1976). *The land of the Guyandot: A history of Logan County.* Detroit MI: Harlo Press.

Stack, Jr., S. F. (2016). *The Arthurdale community school: Education and reform in depression-era Appalachia.* Lexington, KY: The University Press of Kentucky.

Thomas, J. B. (1998). *An Appalachian New Deal: West Virginia in the Great Depression.* Lexington, KY: The University Press of Kentucky.

West Virginia Center on Budget and Policy (2013). Who owns West Virginia? Retrieved from http://www.wvpolicy.org/state-of-working-wet-virginia/

West Virginia Center on Budget and Policy (2015). The state of working West Virginia, 2015. Retrieved from http://www.wvpolicy.org/state-of-working-west-virginia/

Williams, J. A. (2006). *West Virginia and the captains of industry.* Morgantown, WV: West Virginia University Press.

Woolman, J. (1922). A plea for the poor or a word of remembrance and caution to the rich. In Amelia Mott Gummere (Ed.), *The journal and essays of John Woolman.* New York, NY: Macmillan.

Wuenstel, M. (2002). Participants in the Arthurdale community schools' experiment in progressive education from the years 1934-1938 recount their experiences. *Education* 122(4), 759-768.

Yeager, M. (1994). Scotts Run: A community in transition. *West Virginia History*, 53, 7-9.

# 7 | Working in Congress to End Poverty: Looking for Answers in All the Wrong Places

**By Ruth Flower**

Most Friends are neither generals nor economists—neither diplomats nor social workers. Yet our shared beliefs have called us to seek policies that would bring an end to war and an end to poverty.

Our work to bring an end to war has led us to learn more about how to build and sustain peace. The Friends Committee on National Legislation (FCNL) continues to work vigorously to prevent or stop U.S. military actions, to help the world step back from nuclear annihilation, to interrupt the next flow of arms to tense regions, and to reduce the billions of federal dollars that fund the war machine. *And* FCNL pursues peace by supporting U.S. capacities for resolving conflict and averting violence, and by lifting up the peacebuilding work of communities in other regions of the world where the focus in conflict is on achieving and sustaining justice. Learning from Martin Luther King's admonition that "peace is not merely the absence of...tension, but the presence of justice" (King, 2007, p. 258), FCNL has developed a peacebuilding program that seeks out and supports non-destructive ways to achieve and sustain justice among communities, tribes, and nations.

Our work to end poverty has not yet yielded a parallel shift in focus to building *economic* justice. Most of the work of the last sixty or seventy years has been devoted to defending people who are desperately poor, and preserving the government programs on which they must rely to alleviate their poverty.

Our journey has not been without vision, however. In at least two eras, FCNL addressed the structures that sustain poverty, and named and advocated for steps that could alter income and wealth disparities in this country. In the civil rights era, FCNL addressed legal structures that sustained poverty. Joining with many others, FCNL lobbied to dismantle the legal protections for race discrimination and racial violence, and to support enforcement processes that were intended to ensure fair access to voting, housing, education, and jobs[1].

In the 1970s, FCNL policies focused on economic structures that continued to create and sustain poverty. FCNL's Policy Committee explored ways to adjust the economy to include *all* in its benefits and opportunities. The Committee proposed, and FCNL's widely representative General Committee adopted, forward thinking statements on assured income, full employment, progressive tax structures, and the foundational role of racism in the persistence of poverty. While the language of these statements made its way into testimonies and other communications with Congress, the economic solutions the statements offered were far out of step with the politics of the times. To remain effective after 1980, FCNL focused its strategies on dealing with some discouraging political realities.

FCNL has had successes toward the goal of ending poverty, but success has been visible mostly in the effectiveness of enormous efforts to hold back a tide of punishment and blame toward low-income families and individuals, and to push forward a few pieces of the puzzle that could one day come together as a solution.

What follows is a story of evolutions and effort, told from the perspective of *one* person who lived in these times and engaged in this work for *some* of the decades that are described.[2]

### How We Began and How We Go On

The FCNL Executive Committee gathered in 1943 to establish the Friends Committee on National Legislation in the hope that personal contacts and persuasion with members of Congress and government officials would "win the assent of reasonable minds and enlist sympathies with the objectives sought" (Wilson, 1975, p. 18).

Though the "assent of reasonable minds" has sometimes proved to be an elusive goal in the intervening decades, the group's founding intention to work through personal contacts and persuasion has continued as a defining characteristic of FCNL's manner of lobbying. In 2017, more Friends than ever are experiencing these personal contacts and persuasive conversations by participating in local FCNL Advocacy Teams, the Advocacy Corps project,

---

[1] Many aspects of the Jim Crow structure remain today, especially (ironically) in the justice system, which arrests, beats, kills, and incarcerates people of color far out of proportion to what any fair system of justice would allow. FCNL's criminal justice program continues to address that structure, focusing on over-incarceration and police violence.
[2] The perceptions and reflections in this chapter, including any misperceptions and errors, are the author's own and should not be ascribed to the FCNL.

Quaker Public Policy Institutes, Spring Lobby Weekends, and other direct and personal advocacy opportunities.

FCNL was founded, in part, by Friends who had been active in the American Friends Service Committee, joining with others who recognized a distinct role for a Quaker policy advocacy organization based in Washington D.C. In its first decade, FCNL's governing committee, staff, and budget were tiny by today's standards, but today FCNL's growing capacity is just keeping pace with the rising complexity of the issues that both the organization and Congress face.

FCNL's founders saw Friends' testimonies as the basic guide to FCNL advocacy. While these testimonies established reasonably clear directions on many issues of war and peace, the rights of conscience, and individual civil liberties, they proved to need additional study and detail when applied to the right ordering of economic and social systems.

FCNL wrestled with these complex economic issues for decades. From the beginning, Friends were clear about the *values* that should support and define economic and social policies (fairness and respect for every person) and the policy goal (a society where every person's full potential could be realized), but Friends often struggled to define and embrace the appropriate government structures, actions, and programs to connect these basic beliefs with the desired ends.

### Evolution of FCNL Policies on Poverty

FCNL has a long-standing practice of consultation with Friends across the country to develop and update the policies that guide the organization's advocacy on specific issues, and to discern the relative emphasis that should be given to various policy areas during each congressional session. FCNL's Policy Committee compiles and reviews responses from surveys of Friends' meetings on matters of policy and relative emphasis, and then writes its discernment into policy or priority draft documents to submit to FCNL's General Committee. The General Committee, a body of 150 to 200 Friends, is widely representative of yearly meetings and Friends organizations around the country. It reviews and often modifies the language and the choices of the Policy Committee, and then adopts the statements of policy and the selection of priority issues as its own. Because of this consultative practice, the policy statements adopted in successive years can provide a window–though imperfect, of course–into the evolution of policy interpretations widely shared among succeeding generations of Quakers.

FCNL's work on poverty issues has evolved in two threads that have often seemed separate from one another. One is the policy framework and the overall objective to end poverty in the United States. The other is responses to the agenda set by Congress, which is often at odds with *any* agenda that FCNL would wish to follow. In reality, these threads weave together, as FCNL's staff and network apply and adapt the language of the organization's policy framework to respond to congressional agendas and look for opportunities for policy change that may emerge.

When FCNL began its work in the midst of distress about World War II, the organization carried a deep concern for conscientious objectors to war and an abhorrence of nuclear war. As the war came to an end, attention turned to the desperate need for food and rebuilding throughout Europe, Japan, Russia, and in other war-torn countries. In the 1940s and 50s, as the nation decided how and who it wanted to be in the world, FCNL engaged deeply in national and international debates about the United Nations, the prospect of a North Atlantic Pact (now NATO), and efforts to ban nuclear weapons for all time.

Yet even with these foundational issues pulling attention toward the rest of the world, both Congress and FCNL devoted substantial work and effort to changes that needed to happen here at home.

### Civil Rights Policy Frame

As troops returned from a war that had united most of the nation, racial divisions and inequalities at home glared at the nation's conscience. Through the 1940s and 50s, Congress struggled over anti-lynching laws, abolition of the poll-tax, equal education, fair employment, and fair housing policies. FCNL raised a strong voice in favor of these efforts and often brought in Friends–especially from Southern states–to testify on the moral aspects of these issues (FCNL, 1949).

FCNL social policies at the time, arising directly from Friends' testimonies, emphasized respect for all individuals. The unstated economic corollary to this policy, which emerged more explicitly in the policy language of the late 1950s and 60s, was that, given a fair chance and a legal structure that outlaws race discrimination, *all individuals* would lift themselves out of poverty and become part of a free and energetic economy that would, eventually, support all.

### Economic Opportunity Policy Frame

The U.S. economy grew significantly in the 1950s and 60s, as military spending spiraled down (for a brief time) and the nation looked with hope toward achievements made possible through science and technology. But contrary to Friends' apparent expectations in the post-war period, the growing economy did not invite or even allow everyone to participate.

147

In the early 1960s, new prophets and leaders emerged. Michael Harrington wrote *The Other America* demonstrating the reality of poverty in the midst of plenty. A young lawyer, Marion Wright (later Edelman), engaged a young Senator Robert Kennedy in a tour of the South to learn about hunger and poverty, especially among children. These teachers and many courageous and inspired African American organizers in the South and in major cities–Medgar Evers, Malcolm X, Bayard Rustin, Martin Luther King, Rosa Parks, Fannie Lou Hamer, Dorothy Height, John L. Lewis, and many others–saw and lifted up the reality of communities all over the country that had been left behind and locked out of the benefits of the dramatic post-war economic growth.

Speaking with the voice it had first raised on civil rights issues, FCNL continued to advocate for fairness and equal opportunity for all individuals and families. But it was difficult for the organization to move from its commitment to fairness and individual rights to give voice to the need for systemic and structural changes in the society and in the way the economy operated.

From about 1947 to 1963, FCNL's policy statements articulated a continuing concern about domination and interference by the federal government in the implementation of social and economic policies. At that time, FCNL believed and accepted that social policies and economic supports belonged in the hands of local communities, with the assistance of the states. FCNL's letters and testimonies cautioned that federal aid should enter the picture only when necessary and with explicit protections for local and state control of programs. This caution may have arisen from an underlying philosophy about federalism, but it was almost certainly informed by ongoing congressional debates about universal military service, with a peacetime draft beginning at age 18. For many Friends, federal control portended military control.

The 1949 Statement of Legislative Policy on Welfare, Education and Social Security (FCNL, 1950) captured FCNL's philosophy of the times, and identified the specific areas where federal aid was seen as necessary. This statement, with minor variations, appeared year after year until the early 1960s.

> Sensitivity to human needs in our communities leads to action by individuals and by voluntary organizations. Individual awareness of and responsibility for human needs must be nurtured. Responsibility by the states should be encouraged. Under certain circumstances federal aid is necessary to make up for inadequacy of individual and local resources. Therefore we support:

- Federal aid to education under safeguards for state and local independence in the control of public schools, including freedom from military control;
- A health program adequately supporting the United States Public Health Service and providing more generously for the care of the mentally ill and for school health programs; and nationwide provision for medical and hospital benefits, using voluntary methods to the greatest possible extent, and providing safeguards for the individual's free choice of doctors and institutions;[3] and
- Federal action to supplement state and local encouragement of low-cost housing.
- We also recommend continued development and extension of the Social Security Program.[4]

By 1970, policy statements had begun to evolve significantly from an emphasis on individual effort and local community compassion to an acknowledgment that sometimes individual and local voluntary efforts were simply not enough to reverse poverty.

**Systemic Poverty Policy Frame**
In the 1970s, FCNL's economic policy statements began to reflect a deeper analysis of the roots of poverty. Three pivotal FCNL statements adopted by the General Committee between 1969 and 1974 turned a page, opening a new perception that "involuntary poverty in our affluent society is ethically intolerable," and "racism is a most poisonous and destructive force in our society" (FCNL, 1973). The three statements are:

A. Goals for a Just Society: Jobs and Assured Income (FCNL, 1969)
B. FCNL Policy Statement on Economic Life and Social Development (FCNL, 1972a)
C. FCNL Policy Statement on Discrimination, Racism and Exploitation (FCNL, 1972b)

---

[3] This early call for a national health care program was significantly ahead of its time. In 1959, the committee made the call even more explicit, querying whether the federal government ought to set up a national health insurance plan. Medicare, for seniors and persons with disabilities, and Medicaid for low-income families, were not established until 1965. Access to affordable health care for the rest of the population is still a hot item for debate in 2018.
[4] The Social Security Program at that time was considered to include Old Age Security, Disability Insurance, and Unemployment Insurance.

In addition, the Policy Committee approved a "Statement on Taxation and the Distribution of Income" which stated that "government has a primary responsibility to assure all people *fair access* to the resources and services through which they can meet their basic needs" (FCNL Policy Committee 1973).

**Goals for a just society: jobs and assured income.** The General Committee approved this statement at its annual meeting in January 1969. The statement started with an emphasis on the importance of full employment in jobs paying a living wage, and ended with an assertion that, by whatever means, everyone should have a right to assured income. "The claim upon society for that which a person needs in order to contribute to the social good, should be recognized as a human right" (FCNL, 1969), the statement concluded.

The statement emphasized that jobs paying a living wage could provide *one* path out of poverty, but also acknowledged the majority of people living in households with incomes below the poverty line were children, elders, and people with disabilities. Nearly half of the households were headed by people who were already employed, but not in full-time jobs or receiving a living wage. Of the adults able to work but who were not employed outside the home, 80 percent were caring for small children in the home. The statement named the following paraphrased items as "Goals for a Responsible Society":

-**Basic education, health care, and training** should be available to ensure that everyone has the opportunity to be self-supporting and to contribute to society.
-**Jobs** for those able and free to work outside the home should be provided either in the private sector or the public sector.
-**Access to ownership** of a home, a business, or a share in the economy, whether held individually or in a cooperative structure, should be available to all.
-**Social insurance for elderly and disabled people** should be broadly available, simplified, and upgraded to a level that "supports an acceptable standard of living."
-**Assured income** should be available "for those who are unable to work or unable to find work," sufficient to provide a minimum acceptable standard of living (FCNL, 1969).

The statement offered specific recommendations for an assured income system: it should be a single system—such as the negative income tax—that would encompass the range of cash transfer programs then in existence (in 1969). It should also be available to supplement the earnings of workers whose wages are too low to support their families, or to replace the wages of people who are laid off or who are needed in the home to care for children.

The statement pointed to other forms of income maintenance that were already part of the U.S. economy: farm subsidies to encourage control of the supply of food, agricultural price supports, oil depletion allowances to oil drilling companies, tariff protections, income supplements for airlines and the maritime industry. The supplements recommended here, the committee asserted, would yield a broader benefit for the whole society and economy and would be directed to those who need it most (FCNL, 1969).

**Economic life and social development.** In 1972 the General Committee tied racism to economic justice, and called for comprehensive cures for both. It seems clear, the statement concluded, that our economic system, with all its good points, needs drastic revision and change. These changes should include:

- providing a guaranteed income, similar to the proposal in the 1969 statement,
- increasing the stock of affordable housing in inner cities, and providing subsidies to support both rent and purchase of decent housing in inner cities,
- developing mass transit to match people with jobs,
- overhauling the entire tax structure, with increased progressivity,
- adopting broader anti-trust laws to break up the concentration of corporate power, and
- leveling *up* living standards for the poor and leveling *down* unnecessary consumption by the rich to curb "conspicuous and luxurious consumption" and to conserve resources (FCNL, 1972a).

**Discrimination, racism and, exploitation.** More than 45 years ago, FCNL spoke in language that is still fresh and needed today, calling out white racism as a primary root of poverty, violence, and injustice in our society, naming specific actions for governments and individuals to take to bring an end to this "poisonous and destructive force." "Elimination of racism is a key to the solutions of many problems facing our society and the world," the statement asserted.

Much of the statement is reproduced here, because it represents an important moment in FCNL's history, and because its clear and powerful language invites us to examine how far we have and haven't come in the decades since we issued and heard this call:

151

As the United States approaches its bicentennial, the truth that all people are created equal and are endowed with certain inalienable rights to life, liberty and the pursuit of happiness is not self-evident to millions of our people who, as victims of categorical discrimination, are relegated to the status of second class citizens in such areas as government, employment and income, housing, education, health, and treatment in courts of law and in organized religious bodies.

'Racism' is a most poisonous and destructive force in our society. It involves the denial, consciously or unconsciously, of equality and human dignity because of skin color or other ethnic differences . . .
Racist attitudes in both public and private sectors of American society continue to shut off equal opportunity and bring major injustice to most non-white Americans. 'White racism is essentially responsible for the explosive mixture which has been accumulating in our cities since the end of World War II' (*National Advisory Commission on Civil Disorders*, 1968, Chap. 4). Yet white American society in general has not recognized, or acted upon, the truth that ours is still largely a racist society. Elimination of racism is a key to the solutions of many problems facing our society and the world.

The demands of racial justice call for drawing upon every spiritual resource–faith that all mankind is one family under God and should live together in respect; love to overcome the hatred and bitterness engendered by centuries of slavery, oppression, and discrimination; earnestness to move with more than deliberate speed; penitence and willingness to relinquish special privilege; readiness to ask and grant forgiveness and extend the hand of friendship; courage to supplement the law with heroic determination to right the wrongs in our own communities; and dedication to the principles of nonviolence as the moral and truly effective method of social change. Law must provide the framework of justice, but law is harsh and sterile without the spirit of goodwill and reconciliation.

We dedicate ourselves to this spirit and this process, and to the elimination of discrimination, racism, and exploitation. We call urgently for government action to:

- Clear the statute books of all remaining provisions which discriminate on the basis of sex, race, religion, or ethnic groups.

- Strengthen administration and enforcement; end all discrimination by governmental officials and agencies.
- Insure full access to political and economic power, especially by groups now objects of discrimination.
- Equalize opportunity in education, health, public accommodation, the courts, recreation, and particularly in employment and housing. Federal and other legislation is needed to obtain fair housing.
- Recognize the contributions made to American society by all minority groups, which have resulted in a most desirable cultural diversity.
- Improve the distribution of income and wealth (FCNL, 1972b).

**Taxation and the distribution of income.** The Policy Committee approved this statement, as a follow-up to the 1969 statement on Jobs and Assured Income. In its 1972 statement, the Policy Committee pursued some new perspectives on concepts of "work," "compensation," "individual initiative and responsibility," and "government assistance."

The view offered of "work" was an expansive one, taking in all of the activities that are "creative, productive, useful, and meaningful for society and the individual." In common usage, "work" is understood to refer to activities for which one is compensated. The statement affirmed the 1969 proposal of an assured income that is *independent* of the concept of (compensated) work.

"Individual responsibility" was the keystone of earlier FCNL economic policies in the 1940s and 50s. The phrase was given a fuller definition in 1972 to include working constructively to meet one's own needs as far as possible, as well as achieving human dignity and obtaining and retaining individual freedom. The 1972 definition included helping others, individually and collectively, to achieve a measure of control over their own lives, and being an active citizen seeking good government policies or changing them. Finally, "individual responsibility," as defined in this statement, called for limiting unnecessary consumption so that world resources might be more equitably shared.

"Government assistance" was described as something that nearly everyone requires in order to meet basic needs.

The General Committee approved the portion of the Policy Committee's 1972 statement that proposed tax policies. Overall, these proposals called for greater progressivity in the tax system, to ensure that amounts actually paid relate to the relative ability to pay (FCNL, 1972a).

These policy statements set a turning point for FCNL. They created an opening for FCNL's future work on economic issues to reach beyond individual rights and opportunities to issues of systemic economic justice. They also set the groundwork for attention to the hazards of concentrated wealth, especially in contrast to the complete absence of ownership among so many in this mixed capitalist economy. They took steps to delineate a substantive role for government that should extend beyond funding for programs that alleviate poverty, and into areas of regulation and tax policy to promote justice and access rather than privilege and exclusivity (FCNL Policy Committee, 1972).

### Explorations into a Macro-Economics Frame

Still searching for answers about the right ordering of a macro-economic system that could incorporate Friends' shared values, FCNL began in 1975 to consult widely with Quakers who were professionals in economics, business, and related disciplines. FCNL lobbyist Frances Neely polled 95 of these Quaker professionals, asking their views on tax policies that FCNL could and should recommend in upcoming tax debates. The continuing consultation included a series of three "Quaker Dialogues" in 1980, sponsored jointly with Friends United Meeting, to explore whether there was a consensus among Quakers about macro-economic structures that would support FCNL's policy goals. The dialogues were held at Pendle Hill in Wallingford, Pennsylvania, Guilford College in Greensboro, North Carolina, and Quaker Hill in Richmond, Indiana. Participants exchanged dozens of papers and piles of correspondence, and engaged in many hours of respectful dialogue. But the answer that emerged from the consultation was "no"–there was no consensus among Quaker economists and other professionals on fundamental questions about the role of government in managing the economy. Friends' consensus centered on the desired outcome–that every person should be able to participate in and benefit from the economic engines that the society creates and sustains. But the right ordering of the U.S. economic system to reach such goals was not yet revealed to those gathered.

Perhaps reflecting the fundamental differences that were uncovered in these consultations, FCNL's policy statements in the early 1980s were less bold and confident on economic issues than they had been in the previous decade. The Policy Statements continued to include much of the language of the 1970s (in summary form), but a few issues that had been firmly stated in previous documents were raised as questions ("Challenges to the Society of Friends") in the 1980s. For example, the 1969, 1970, and 1972 statements painted a fairly clear picture of certain responsibilities of government and the private sector in addressing the nation's economic justice challenges. But in 1982, the Policy

Statement posed two questions: "To what extent and over which aspects do we wish government action in our economic life? To what extent does private enterprise require government support?" (FCNL, 1982).

FCNL's statements in the 1970s had celebrated a "most desirable cultural diversity" and called for "aggressive enforcement of affirmative action laws to correct the effects of past discrimination" (FCNL, 1977). But the 1982 statement asked "At what point do values of diversity and of self-determination challenge our capacity to function as a unified country?" and "Are there ways to remedy past discriminatory practices without violating equality of opportunity?" (FCNL, 1982).

These more tentative policy statements and questions emerged as the country was experiencing the "Reagan revolution." The "Reagan era" brought a reversal of much of the progress of the war on poverty, with President Reagan and many members of Congress being willing to declare defeat and to blame those who remained poor for the failure of the effort. These years offered little opportunity for advocacy on major structural changes in the economy. Full-employment and guaranteed income were not part of the congressional vocabulary at that time. So the unfinished macro-economic policy discussions among Friends were put on hold while FCNL joined with faith colleagues and others to address the immediacy of the grinding weight of poverty and to push back and protect the most basic supports for families and individuals who were excluded from economic power.

### Basic Federal Programs Frame

During most of the 1980s, FCNL policy statements continued to affirm that "hunger and poverty should be eliminated," and to rely chiefly on full employment and a sensibly managed economy (undefined) to accomplish this goal. The statements supported investments in a range of programs for "the general welfare," including health care, housing, education, legal services, mass transportation, and programs for children. The statements also continued to call for "an income, adequate to maintain health and dignity," for all persons, whether or not employed. In 1984, one of the priorities identified by the General Committee was to promote a "just social and economic order at home." But the exuberant calls for assured income and new definitions of work and compensation were missing from policy statements of the 80s—washed over, perhaps, by the challenges of the new "Reaganomics."

### Communities vs. Corporations Frame

Beginning with the 1994 Statement of Legislative Policy, FCNL emphasized "the community" as the place where all social and economic policies come together and are reflected back in national statistics. "The quality of our nation's future depends greatly on its ability to form and maintain safe, supportive and economically viable communities," the 1994 policy statement stated (FCNL, 1994, Part III, Section 2).

In this year, the policy statement articulated roles for both private and public sectors in sustaining or ending poverty, and offered perspectives on how the two sectors should interact in order to bring about that end, reiterating some of the policies first stated in the 1970s. The statement also called for assistance to businesses that were adapting to rapid global and domestic changes, and encouraged government investment in new small business ventures (FCNL, 1994, Part III, Section 1).

Without defining the macro-economic policies that would achieve an end to poverty, the General Committee agreed that it supported "various economic models that promote economic justice." Economic institutions and policies "should make rational decisions possible, and should provide for the dispersal of political and economic power." The statement specifically called out the "disproportionate racial and gender expressions" of economic disparities and the concentration of wealth. Similar statements were carried through in the first policy documents of the new millennium.

By 2014, the General Committee was ready to describe its policy vision in hopeful terms. Inspired by FCNL's long-standing vision statement,[5] the Committee named its new policy statement, "The World We Seek." Central to that articulated vision was the call to "expand opportunities for all people to have adequate resources to maintain health, dignity and economic security" (FCNL, 2014, Part 3, Section 1).

The concept of "inclusion" was an emerging feature of "The World We Seek" vision. The language about poverty did not speak about "the poor," but addressed instead an intention and a system that would work well for everyone. In this vision, "education, housing, health care, recreation, and access to functioning infrastructure" were described as "public goods to which all have a right, including individuals who cannot afford to pay for them" (FCNL, 2014, Part 3, Section 2).

---

[5] "We seek a world free of war and the threat of war. We seek a society with equity and justice for all. We seek a community where everyone's potential may be fulfilled. We seek an earth restored."

This vision ventured further into new standards that would tend to define our mixed economy in the U.S. in different ways, by calling for new measures that index the quality of life and ecological sustainability. The vision called for policies that would reduce income and wealth disparities, for strong regulation of corporations, and for support of "safe, thriving, diverse, and sustainable communities with healthy, informed people, and a broad resilient economic base" (FCNL, 2014, Part 3, Section 2).

## FCNL's "Change Strategies"–How We Advocated for These Policies

FCNL's actions have almost always been chosen and planned strategically. Generally, staff work within the FCNL policy frame of the times, and adapt language and expectations to the current political environment and congressional agenda. Recently, FCNL staff adopted a more explicit practice, called "change strategies." For each congressional session, lobbyists identify how they will work to advance each of the priority issues chosen and approved by the General Committee. Lobbyists ask: How far can we get with this issue? By what path and in what framework? Which members of Congress need to be persuaded, in order for this change to happen? How will we persuade them? Who are our partners, among colleagues in Washington and among our network around the country?

Here is how some of those change strategies–and their predecessors–look, and have looked, over the past several decades.

## Policy Frame: Individual Rights

In the 1950s and the early 60s, most of FCNL's work that touched on poverty focused on racial discrimination and civil rights. FCNL's lobbyists and invited witnesses addressed anti-lynching laws, abolition of the poll-tax, and policies on equal education, fair employment, and fair housing. During those years, congressional committees were open to public testimony. FCNL's archives include more than a dozen testimonies given in those years.

Some of the testimonies related personal experiences of FCNL witnesses in the South or in other parts of the country. Others conveyed a close analysis of the legislation being considered, along with known facts about poll taxes, the quality of education, and other issues. Correspondence from that time reveals detailed work by FCNL lobbyists engaging with authors of bills and committee staff, suggesting and promoting specific bill language and amendments.

Civil rights are core constitutional issues, protecting the rights of individuals. So the conversations and testimonies in these years framed poverty in terms of individual rights to fairness, access, and all benefits enjoyed by others in the society. The policy focus on issues touching on poverty addressed primarily the discriminatory and racist practices of many local communities, employers, and government agencies. While this policy frame did not exclude hopes for a more fair and equitable economy, the emphasis was on *access* to the economic system that existed at the time, rather than on seeking systemic change.

### Policy Frame: Protecting Programs

The 1970s were explosive and troubling political times. Following on the heels of the assassinations of respected leaders in the 1960s including John F. Kennedy, Malcolm X, Medgar Evers, Martin Luther King, and Robert Kennedy, the shadowy behavior of political leaders (such as Vice President Agnew who resigned under a cloud of fraud and tax evasion charges, and President Nixon's resignation in preference to impeachment for the Watergate scandal) diminished respect for government generally.

Against this troubling background, maintaining normalcy of any kind was an absorbing challenge. FCNL lobbied to preserve and continue the Office of Economic Opportunity, the Legal Services Corporation, child care assistance, and food assistance programs including food stamps, child nutrition, and elderly nutrition. FCNL also opposed added work requirements for participants in the Food Stamp program (now SNAP) and a higher rent formula for residents of public housing. FCNL supported enforcing health and safety regulations covering migrant workers, and increasing and expanding the coverage of the minimum wage. Although health care reform generated a lot of interest in Congress and among advocates, including FCNL and our interfaith partners, health care legislation did not move beyond committees in these years.

### Policy Frame: Compassion and Fairness

When the Reagan administration ushered in its "take it or leave it" budget and spending bills in 1981 and 1982, the legislation included deep cuts in essential programs for low-income families, including health, education, employment supports, income benefits, and housing assistance. Ironically, working parents were specifically selected to be cut from welfare rolls, with rhetoric about "double dipping." In spite of the fact that both federal and state efforts in the 1970s had focused on moving people "from welfare to work" by subsidizing paychecks that offered less than poverty wages, the plan in the 1980s was to cut these families out of government assistance, including health care.

FCNL joined immediately with other faith-based and policy groups to bring a message of compassion and fairness to congressional offices. FCNL participated in the Interreligious Task Force on U.S. Food Policy, which formed an "Emergency Campaign for Economic Justice." When the group set up a Domestic Human Needs (DHN) working group, FCNL lobbyist, Ruth Flower, became its chair. DHN, which is still hard at work today, took up lobbying and grassroots strategies to support the Food Stamp Program, Aid to Families with Dependent Children, Medicaid, housing assistance, and supports such as child care subsidies that enabled heads of families to maintain employment. As the work of the Emergency Campaign continued through the 1980s, the campaign re-organized itself as Interfaith Action for Economic Justice. DHN continued its lobbying work.

Much of the door-to-door lobbying on the Hill centered on "painting complete pictures" for congressional staff, offering a voice for those who would be harmed by the proposed budget cuts. Many congressional staff members were familiar with one or two of the programs that were being harmed, but few had the whole picture of the combined impact on families in their states.

The frame for this work was at first one of compassion and fairness. The interfaith lobbyists called on senators and representatives to consider "the least of these"–especially children–as they made their budget decisions. Lobbyists also pointed to the doors unfairly slammed shut on opportunity, especially in the faces of those who had been doing their best to earn a living for their families.

Seeking a more direct impact on congressional offices, we began to engage local members of the various denominations in grassroots action. FCNL and most of the denominational groups had traditionally used general, routine monthly or weekly channels for alerting interested local members in what was happening in Washington. At FCNL, the primary channel was a taped weekly telephone message. Many meeting contacts listened to the tapes each weekend, and reported to their meetings and churches on Sundays about issues that they thought would be of most interest. But the idea of "targeted" or "focused" grassroots work was new to us, especially in these pre-Internet days. When it became necessary to reach the constituents of all of the members of the huge Agriculture Committees in both the House and the Senate (to protect the Food Stamp program), for example, finding and contacting local supporters in the relevant districts was a daunting task. FCNL and our partners in various denominational offices developed long lists arranged by zip-codes and stuffed action alerts into hundreds of envelopes to get them in the mail to Friends and others as rapidly as possible.

### Policy Frame: Budget Priorities

While compassion and fairness remained consistent themes in advocacy on poverty issues, it became clear early in the new budget-cutting era that compassion was not a sufficiently compelling platform for a change in direction. Many in Congress saw the federal government as *unable* to respond appropriately to unmet human needs, and felt bound instead to provide for virtually unlimited military spending and generous tax reductions for high-income households and large corporations. The conversation shifted to one about choices.

**The choice to end poverty.** In 1983 and 1984, FCNL and interfaith colleagues conducted an experiment. Noticing that the word "poverty" had apparently disappeared from the *Congressional Record,* we visited the offices of members of Congress who worked on key committees connected to poverty issues and programs. We asked one question: What do you think would make a difference about poverty? Recognizing that the political environment was not very hospitable to positive ideas at that time, DHN members asked about "back burner" and "bottom drawer" proposals that the offices might have been considering–perhaps to be introduced in a better time. The collected ideas became anonymous contributions to a list of steps out of poverty that Congress could help bring about. Then in 1984 and 1985, we began reflecting the list back to members of key congressional committees, and issuing a challenge to end poverty.

In 1985, the working group compiled and circulated a formal statement–*The Call to End Poverty in the United States*–among heads of religious denominations and organizations in the U.S. (IAEJ, 1985). The Call made a distinction between alleviating conditions of poverty, and working to end systemic poverty, and named specific steps to end poverty. Thirty-six denominations signed the statement and joined in the Call. The working group followed through with media opportunities, Hill visits, and publicity. In the fall of that year, members of the working group authored an interfaith publication called *"Prepare"* (Flower, et al., 1985) outlining the "Eighth Step of Charity," which, according to the 12th century philosopher Rabbi Maimonides, is "to anticipate charity by preventing poverty."

Using this frame, we continued to lobby to protect essential programs, to advance employment legislation, to achieve equitable pay for women and for all races, and to increase the minimum wage and the Earned Income Tax Credit. We lobbied for child nutrition and health care and for supports for homeless people. We convened a housing conference called "Raising the Roof," which several members of Congress attended in order to present their own affordable housing proposals. FCNL also supported and publicized the Congressional

Black Caucus Alternative Budget, which provided sustained funding for programs serving low-income communities.

By the end of the decade, the "Reagan era" had already created permanent scars by rolling back acknowledgment of federal government responsibility for persistent poverty. It was difficult to see the impact of our work at the time. But in retrospect, the budget numbers show clearly that the spending cuts never reached as deep as promised. And military spending, which competed strongly for the funds that could have gone to poor families, did not *increase* nearly as much as proposed. But major tax cuts were implemented as promised, and deficit spending became a new addiction in Congress.

Even so, when Congress decided in 1985 to get control of deficit spending by adopting a formula for across-the-board spending cuts, a long list of programs serving low-income people—similar to the list we had gathered and reflected back to offices on the Hill—was exempted from these automatic cuts. States as well as advocates had pushed back, pointing out how unworkable they found the plans coming out of Washington. This list survived to modify future across-the-board budget-cutting mechanisms in various deals and agreements.

**Spending choices.** As a Quaker organization committed to peaceful solutions, it was clear to us that the U.S. military was *not* weak and underfunded and that the U.S. did *not* need to prepare to fight two and a half simultaneous wars—as proposed. Rather, the country needed to invest in preventing wars and in providing for its people at home. In the late 1980s and 90s, FCNL participated with several budget-focused coalitions—primarily the Budget Priorities Working Group which concentrated specifically on military spending, the Coalition on Human Needs which had formed as the "Block Grant Coalition" in the early 1980s, the National Low Income Housing Coalition, and Interfaith Action for Economic Justice with its working group on Domestic Human Needs. We encouraged each of these groups to broaden their perspectives to take in both over-spending on the military side of the budget and under-investing on the human side. Eventually, most of them did.

Having changed our frame to include a challenge to Congress—to end poverty in the U.S.—we at FCNL felt an obligation to demonstrate that the goal was reachable. We started talking about spending *choices*—this school or that bomber, health care for these children or fraud and waste at the Pentagon. Since 1981, FCNL's federal budget analysis had shown how the pieces of the "budget pie" were cut up and distributed, with Pentagon-related spending almost always getting nearly half the pie. Now we looked more deeply, using materials from some colleagues—notably, at the Project on Government Operations—who analyzed waste and fraud in the Pentagon, and from other colleagues—especially at the National Priorities Project–who put price tags on military spending and human needs in specific states and communities. For years, these analyses generated packets of handouts for the Hill, to be taken on lobby visits and given to Hill staff by FCNL lobbyists and by coalition partners.

**Budget campaigns.** The federal budget is not on many people's reading list. It's a hard sell. So at several points in our efforts to affect the shape of this $2 trillion (and up) mountain, FCNL invented campaigns. The first was the "Buck Starts Here" campaign in 1989, in which post-card-sized dollar bill images carried budget messages from thousands of constituents to their representatives in Congress. The distinctive cards stressed one point: "We expect you to make better choices when you spend our dollars."

The success of that campaign encouraged the founding in 1989 of the "Citizens' Budget Campaign," led by a handful of organizations[6] that were committed to influencing decisions in all parts the budget, and to supporting fairer taxes. In 1991, the Citizens' Budget Campaign undertook a project called "Reinvest in Our Communities."

The Reinvest project pointed to the fall of the Berlin wall in 1989 and the consequent end of the Cold War as an occasion to re-order priorities away from military weapons to community investment. The Reinvest project developed information (with the help of the National Priorities Project) on how communities in various regions of the country were affected by current patterns of domestic and military spending. The Reinvest project engaged local organizers to coordinate events, develop a presence in local media, and place Public Service Announcements (PSAs) on local stations. In some regions, the project provided grant support to place taped radio ads during drive-time slots.

In 2008, with military spending still out of control, and poverty and unemployment climbing due to the stock market melt-down, FCNL launched the "Our Nation's Checkbook" campaign. This campaign harked back to the "Buck Starts Here" theme, and incorporated the local findings of the Reinvest project. The campaign set the scene of balancing family checkbooks (which were still in use at that time, though rapidly disappearing). If the nation was our household, the Checkbook campaign suggested, why would we buy ridiculous amounts of so-called "security" equipment from every sales person who came to the door, without inquiring about effectiveness or our need for the latest

---

[6] Initial steering committee of the Citizens' Budget Campaign included FCNL, NETWORK– a Catholic Social Justice Lobby, National Priorities Project, National Low-Income Housing Coalition, and SANE-FREEZE (which later became Peace Action). The group grew rapidly from 25 member organizations to 123, with about half being local and state groups around the country.

gimmick, while our children outgrew their clothes, couldn't afford to go to the dentist, and complained that they were hungry?

The Checkbook analysis offered an engaging message. The National Priorities Project continued to provide local analyses of the impact of federal spending, and developed a user-friendly methodology that enabled local organizers to create their own analyses for their town, county, or state.

## Systemic Poverty and "Welfare Reform"

The idea of taking on structural or systemic poverty seemed to intimidate Congress. Congressional committees often invited expert witnesses who described how the economy was built on an assumption of a certain amount of poverty, and advised Congress either to correct that flaw or leave it alone. Some members of Congress had responded by proposing employment programs, wage enhancements or subsidies, and youth employment programs, all apparently on the assumption that a full employment economy would be the answer to poverty. But when those efforts dissolved in the budget cutting fervor of the 1980s, Congress abandoned the idea of addressing systemic poverty. The only "employment bills" that seemed acceptable for discussion were military spending bills. Relying on analyses by the National Priorities Project, we lobbied to demonstrate that dollars spent on military industries generated far *less* employment than dollars spent on human services such as education, health care, and community programs. By the 1990s, Congress no longer acknowledged a goal of managing a full-employment economy.

Nevertheless, Congress did weigh in on *debates* about systemic poverty, usually buried in the assumptions and foundational beliefs that prompted successive "welfare reform" proposals. From 1970 to 1972, Congress debated (and ultimately rejected) President Nixon's Family Assistance Plan which, with all its flaws, would have put a floor under the lowest amount of welfare assistance that any participant in any state would receive. In the 1980s President Reagan introduced (and Congress approved) fundamental changes in the nature of assistance programs, combining many programs into block grants and giving states more flexibility over their management. More changes and restrictions were proposed in 1994 when the new Republican House Speaker Newt Gingrich promoted the conservative agenda, "Contract with America." In 1996, Congress debated (and ultimately passed) President Clinton's "end welfare as we know it" plan.

FCNL staff engaged minutely with each of these proposals, devising and presenting careful analyses of each of the various bills' provisions and their combined effect on individuals, families, local economies, and states. In the

1970s, when public presentations were still welcomed in committees, FCNL offered testimonies–sometimes in partnership with the American Friends Service Committee. Later, the most effective analyses and lobbying messages were carried primarily by direct and grassroots lobbying.

The assumptions that built the platforms for these "welfare reform" proposals formed a stark contrast to Friends' values and beliefs about people. In congressional offices, we often heard variations on themes related to the personal flaws of people who do not take advantage of the opportunities offered by our free enterprise system, the motivations of unwed teen mothers, the attitudes of unemployed people toward responsibility, the tendency of people in public assistance programs to "game the system," and the lack of responsibility of the federal government for the personal situations of low-income families.

In spite of the fact that the vast majority of people receiving public assistance are elderly, disabled, children, or single parents, the concept of "work" was presented as the panacea for poverty in each of these so-called welfare reform proposals. If work *opportunity* was not the answer to poverty (though that solution had not really been tried) perhaps *mandating work* would be effective in ending welfare once and for all.[7] In 1972, the Senate version of President Nixon's Family Assistance Plan carried reminders of the "work houses" of Victorian England. The Senate proposed a government agency that would create an agency to hire welfare recipients to do menial tasks at miniscule wages, so that any recipients not hired by another employer could still *earn* the family's completely inadequate welfare benefits. The "Contract with America" introduced in 1994 promised reforms that would deny welfare assistance to teen mothers and to mothers who gave birth to another child while receiving public assistance. These extreme proposals generated a lot of heat and, ultimately, were not adopted. But during their brief time in Senate and House floor debates and on the nightly news, they very effectively promoted the pernicious and damaging myths of the "welfare queen," and the "lazy person on the dole."

The biggest actual change came in 1996 when President Clinton, in partnership with House Speaker Newt Gingrich and a Republican-led House, pushed his "Personal Responsibility and Work Opportunity Act" and ended the federal government's bottom-line commitment to help individuals or families who had no other source of income. With passage of the new law, assistance would be available only to a narrow group of families, for only 6 months at a time, and for a maximum of five years in a *lifetime*. Even within those limits, temporary assistance was to be *earned* by working at a "workfare" job. And even

---

[7] Some members of Congress–then and now–equated "ending welfare" with ending poverty.

that small slice of help was denied to people who had legally immigrated to this country–until they had been lawfully in the U.S. for five years, accumulating Social Security work credits. This proposal passed, and Aid to Families with Dependent Children ended, to be replaced with Temporary Assistance for Needy Families (TANF). The last shred of the so-called "safety net" had frayed away to nothing.

In the years after 1996, FCNL continued to work with the DHN working group in attempts to broaden the coverage of TANF to include at least legally-admitted immigrants and their children, and to improve support for job training and placement in actual jobs. In 2002, when TANF was being reauthorized, some of these modest improvements passed, but people who had immigrated were still excluded for five years after their legal arrival.

FCNL's messages and work on "welfare reform" were consistent through the decades, in different analyses, delivered by different lobbyists, with different coalitions, and different formats. In each generation, lobbyists analyzed the current proposals, and passed along to House and Senate staff the stories and absent voices of the individuals, families, communities, and states that would be deeply affected by the changes. In 1993 and 1994, FCNL staff offered and "shopped" 22 amendments to President Clinton's initial welfare reform proposal, most of which the House accepted (and the Senate rejected.) In lobbying efforts on these tangential congressional engagements with economic policy, staff echoed the views expressed in FCNL's 1969 statement on *Jobs and Assured Income*, and carried the language of compassion, fairness, and respect for each person. In 2018, FCNL staff continue to lead efforts among faith-based advocates to bring voices of excluded people into conversations with congressional staff, calling local constituents to participate via phone *during* lobby visits. The early 1980s efforts to "paint the whole picture" continue and intensify in 2018, as FCNL lobbyists and constituents push back against promises to shred supports health care and protections from hunger.

## Is Congress the "Wrong Place" to Seek an End to Poverty?

Congress has most of the tools that would be needed to bring poverty to an end, including the ability to reduce income disparities by implementing more progressive tax policies, the ability to invest in communities and individuals through the U.S. Treasury, and the ability to support and fund the "common wealth"–the goods and services that everyone needs, but not everyone can afford.

The courts also have–and have used–tools to break down barriers in housing, employment, schools, and businesses. Changes in civil rights laws and their implementation have at least made it possible for diverse neighborhoods to develop, diverse classrooms to broaden students' and teachers' perspectives, and diverse colleagues to work together and discover each other's talents. But with all the changes in law and funding, poverty persists. And racism continues to feed its roots.

The end of poverty will accompany the end of racism. Though it is true that not all of the people who are cut out of the economy are people of color, and certainly not all people of color are poor, poverty and race are tied. The ability of this society to tolerate, and even embrace, the *exclusion of some* from "goods to which all have a right, including individuals who cannot afford to pay for them" forms the basis of both racism and poverty (FCNL, 2014, Part III, Section 1).

The end of poverty will not inevitably follow if all racism were to be expunged from this society. The tools that are available to and through Congress would still have to be used to create new structures.

Congress is relevant to the process of ending poverty because it is–at its heart (yes, Congress has a heart)–a place for conversations. Members of Congress represent the conversations they hear–the call and response conversations of campaigns and town hall meetings and the personal conversations in their offices and in the districts and states they represent. If those conversations tolerate and even embrace personal and corporate privilege, both electoral and congressional votes will follow in that direction. But when the conversations at home begin to change and the people of this country are ready to call on each other–and therefore on Congress–to end poverty, both electoral and congressional votes will take a new direction.

The call to Congress to end poverty will come when we see ourselves as a people and talk with each other–not just as separate individuals–but as participants in living communities. In all of our communities, we look for a "common wealth" that includes safety, economic security, respect, the company of friends and family, meaningful work to do, and the ability to become who we really are. The communities we could build toward would be enriched by the diversity of who we are as American people–an amalgam of the world with roots, ties, and treasures in many distinct traditions. Conversations among us, on those terms, will bring an end to poverty. Indeed, they will change the world.

## References

FCNL. (1949). Testimonies. *Historical record* (Vol. 1: 1943 to 1950). Washington, DC.

FCNL. (1950). 1949 Statement of legislative policy on welfare, education and Social Security. *Historical record (Vol. 1: 1943 to 1950)*. Washington, DC.

FCNL. (1969). Goals for a just society: Jobs and assured income. *Historical record (Vol. 1969)*. Washington, DC.

FCNL. (1972a). FCNL Policy Statement on economic life and social development. *Historical record (Vol. 1972)*. Washington, DC.

FCNL. (1972b). FCNL Policy Statement on discrimination, racism and exploitation. *Historical record (Vol. 1972)*. Washington, DC.

FCNL. (1973). 1973 Statement of legislative policy. *Historical record (Vol. 1973)*. Washington, DC.

FCNL. (1977). 1977 Statement of legislative policy. *Historical record (Vol. 1977)*. Washington, DC.

FCNL. (1982). 1982 Statement of legislative policy. *Historical record (Vol. 1982)*. Washington, DC.

FCNL. (1994). 1994 Statement of legislative policy. *Historical record (Vol. 1994)*. Washington, DC.

FCNL. (2014). *The world we seek*. Washington, DC.

FCNL Policy Committee. (1972). Statement on taxation and the distribution of income. *Historical record (Vol. 1974)*. Washington, DC.

Flower R., Rutenberg T., Martin C., Cooper, M., (1985). Ending poverty: The eighth step of charity. *Prepare*. Washington D.C.: National Impact Education Fund, Retrieved from: http://www.fcnl.org/documents/506

Interfaith Action for Economic Justice (IAEJ) (1985). The call to end poverty in the United States. *FCNL historical record (Vol. 1985), Washington DC*.

King, Martin L. (2007). When peace becomes obnoxious: a sermon at the Dexter Avenue Baptist Church. Clayborne Carson, C., Carson, S., Englander, S., Jackson, T., and Smith, G.L. (Eds.). *The papers of Martin Luther King, Jr.: Volume VI: Advocate of the social gospel, September 1948–March 1963*. Palo Alto, CA: King Papers Project, Stanford University, Retrieved from https://kinginstitute.stanford.edu/publications/king-papers

National Advisory Commission on Civil Disorders. (1968). *Report*. (Chap. 4, p. 8). Washington DC.

Wilson, E.R. (1975). *Uphill for peace: Quaker impact on Congress*. Richmond, IN: Friends United Press.

# 8 | Linking Politics, Economics, Peace and Friends Around the World: The Work of Quakers at the United Nations

**By Lori Heninger and David Atwood**

We are a people that follow after those things that make for peace, love, and unity; it is our desire that others' feet may walk in the same, and do deny and bear our testimony against all strife, and wars.

—Margaret Fell (1660)

In 2002, my co-author David Atwood and I were both working for the Quaker United Nations Office (QUNO), he in Geneva and I in New York. We were attending a Quaker Violence Prevention conference in Burundi that had been preceded by conferences in London in 2000 and in Washington DC and New York in 2001. We met in Burundi—towards the end of an outbreak of major civil conflict in that country—after Friends at the 2001 meetings decided that it was crucial to come together in a country experiencing violent conflict. In Burundi, we worked and worshiped with African and non-African Friends, we witnessed and learned about their situation, and we strived to determine how we all could better work together.

At one point in the journey, a group of us were leaving Bujumbura for a field visit in a vehicle that creaked and groaned, shook and rattled. We found ourselves careening down a mountain road next to people pushing bicycles loaded with charcoal or wood, past donkeys laden with chickens, and people on foot. There were few other vehicles. As we arrived at our destination, children in second-hand t-shirts with U.S. sports team logos chased our van, and one person commented that it looked like one of the children was eating ice cream; it turned out to be a root—white on top and brown at the bottom. David remembered that at one point I turned to him and said, "David, what the hell are we doing working at the UN when there is so much need here? How can we justify it?"

In discussing ideas for this chapter, that tension—working at the international policy level in contrast to working on the ground, whether we should focus on disarmament or the international financial architecture or sustainable development or racism and xenophobia; and at the same time being responsible to a range of Quaker bodies—often threatened to pull us in multiple directions, spreading thin resources even thinner. At times it seemed that we were pushed toward allying with one Friends group or another, having to defend a decision around which issues we worked on, and whether, indeed, Friends should focus on international institutions or work at the community or national level. Our conversation was excellent preparation for writing this chapter on politics, economics, and peace.

In our conversations, David and I talked about the knowledge gained from our Quaker work in-country, and the ability we had to codify that knowledge into broad policy at the UN. We talked about our individual struggles to resolve these seeming conflicts within our work. And we agreed that no matter what the subject area, whether it was disarmament, child rights, or economics, the foundation of all our work was our commitment to peace. An abundance of small arms and light weapons supports emerging or existing conflict. Economic inequality sows the seeds of discontent that can easily lead to conflict. Unfair trade practices exacerbate inequality. Racism and xenophobia are meant to divide people. A decimated environment leads to a shortage of resources necessary for life, potentially leading to conflict. So much of our work depended on the lens through which we chose to see it, and the lens we chose was peace. Everything else flowed from that.

In this chapter, through a brief description of the Quaker UN Office and two case studies, we will work to illustrate the tensions within our work, how we sought to creatively address those tensions, and the ways that the lens of peace guided whatever thematic work we pursued.

## Origins, History, and Methodology

The history of Quaker work at the United Nations is virtually coterminous with that of the United Nations organization itself. Friends took an early interest in the UN as a much hoped-for institution for global peace in the aftermath of World War II. In 1948, the Friends World Committee for Consultation (FWCC)—the global body established in 1937 to help create better understanding among the diverse family of Friends worldwide—was granted "consultative status" under the new rules of the UN for relationships with non-governmental bodies.

FWCC became, and still is, the official body under which the Quaker Office, located in New York and Geneva, can operate in relation to the UN. The American Friends Service Committee in the United States and Quaker Peace Social Witness of Britain Yearly Meeting have historically taken particular responsibility for the New York and Geneva offices respectively. QUNO has its formal status within the UN through ECOSOC (the Economic and Social Council), the UN body that vets and approves or denies non-governmental organizations' (NGOs) requests for affiliation. QUNO also is informally linked to the Quaker Council for European Affairs, established in the late 1970s to further Quaker concerns within the European institutions.

The broad vision for the UN reflected in the Preamble to the United Nations Charter—*'to save succeeding generations from the scourge of war'*—places peace as the new institution's founding principle. Not only does this require attention to the tools of war (the very first Resolution of the UN General Assembly [UNGA], passed on 24 January 1946, resolved to establish a Commission charged with dealing with the problems "raised by the discovery of atomic energy") but also to the methodologies for achieving peace contained in the general foundational assumption of problem-solving and transformation, through collective processes and guidelines. These collective processes and guidelines lead to international understanding regarding the creation and implementation of treaties and the strengthening of international law.

The Preamble closely corresponds to Friends' testimonies and values. Quaker testimonies of peace, simplicity, equality, integrity, and community have guided the nature of Quaker work at the UN over the last 70 years and more. The broad understanding of the foundations for peace reflected in the Preamble echo well the multi-faceted way in which Friends have sought to "pursue peace" (Bailey, 1993; Wood, 1962).

Ensuring *human rights and the equal rights of men and women and nations large and small* (and through later conventions to the rights of children, people with disabilities, indigenous peoples, and others) speaks to equality, community, integrity, and stewardship. If nations are agreed on ensuring the human rights of every person, it is hoped that there will be less reason to fight. If every country's vote in the UN General Assembly carries the same weight, they may feel more empowered and less sidelined.

The same holds true for *the promotion of the economic and social advancement of all peoples,* and brings in the idea of simplicity. If people are living more simply, being less attached to material possessions/goods, there is the possibility for more people to have a better standard of living, both economically and socially.

Since its initial establishment, Quakers at the UN have become known as a small group of impactful people, taking on both large and small issues and areas for work. Quakers have used a methodology of bringing people together for off-the-record meetings in which people can speak their minds in ways that they may not be able to in formal UN settings.

Structurally, Quaker work at the UN is based in New York, where QUNO has an office across the street from the United Nations, as well as nearby Quaker House, a brownstone in the historic Turtle Bay area of Manhattan; and in Geneva at Quaker House, a perfect combination of offices and meeting spaces. Both Houses are just far enough away from the UN to hold the kind of meetings that Quakers do best: quiet diplomacy that is informal, off-the-record, and discrete. The current mission statement for QUNO is: *"We are a Quaker presence at the United Nations, representing Friends' concerns for global peace and justice to the international community"* (Quaker UN Office, 2017).

Many examples of timely work, with important impact on international policy, can be cited by the Quaker UN Office. The idea for a Law of the Sea Treaty was introduced at Quaker House in 1967 by then ambassador of Malta, Arvid Pardo (Collett, 2007) and Quaker House hosted many off-the-record meetings among delegates during the course of Treaty negotiations. Quakers, in partnership with others, did foundational work on the issue of child soldiers. For years, private meetings were held in Quaker House between the Burmese Government-in-Exile and friendly country representatives so that the positions of the Government-in-Exile's positions could be included in UN negotiations. At a certain point QUNO provided space for important meetings concerning what eventually became the Anti-personnel Mine Ban Treaty. Quakers played a leadership role in preparations for and ongoing work on the International Women's Conferences and the Commission to End All Forms of Discrimination Against Women, as well as on anti-racism and xenophobia policy in the lead-up to the World Conference in South Africa in 2001. Leadership was also shown prior to and during the annual meetings on Sustainable Development, a term which formerly focused on the environment and now is being used to describe the UN Sustainable Development Goals (United Nations, 2015). QUNO focused on intellectual property agreements within the World Trade Organization, leading to constructive approaches to food security. In the late 1990s and the first decade of the new millennium, QUNO also focused on the demand side of small arms and light weapons and on financing for development. It is on small arms and light weapons and financing for development, individually and collectively, that the rest of this chapter will focus, making the case that politics—in the form of work for peace—and economics are inseparable.

## Case Studies

### QUNO and the Small Arms Issue[8]

The Quaker United Nations Office had the general issue area of small arms and light weapons as one of its principal focal areas for a period of more than 15 years, beginning in the second half of the 1990s. This case study will illustrate factors that shaped this work and the range of approaches that were taken over these years.

**Small arms and light weapons as an emerging global concern.** In the immediate post-Cold War period of the early 1990s, a strong sense that at last the UN's peace function might achieve new meaning emerged in the apparent new space that the relaxation of East-West tensions afforded. The articulation of this was most fully developed through a central document for the time, *An Agenda for Peace* by the then Secretary-General Boutros Boutros-Ghali (1992). This document was a reflection on what was perceived to be required by the international system in an era when most conflict taking place was no longer between states but within states, or in places where states did not really exist except in name. Three central functions—preventive diplomacy, peacemaking, and peacekeeping—were outlined, along with a call for the enhancement of capacity of the UN in these areas. In the more than 20 years since this seminal document, the UN system has, if fitfully, enhanced its "peace" function on many of these fronts, including a vast expansion in peacekeeping and in broad areas of peacebuilding, symbolized in the creation of the UN Peacebuilding Commission in 2006.

In a supplement to *An Agenda for Peace* in 1995, the Secretary-General gave the first official reflection on behalf of the UN on what he called the need for "microdisarmament." The Secretary-General pointed out that although most international disarmament attention had been paid to so-called weapons of mass destruction, the real weapons of mass destruction—the ones taking a huge toll in human lives and livelihoods of people around the world—were small arms and light weapons (Boutros-Ghali, 1995). The Secretary-General's "Supplement"

---

[8] In this case study and the conclusions section of this chapter, we have drawn on and expanded the case studies used in *From the Inside Out: Observations on Quaker Work at the United Nations*, a monograph prepared as part of the James Backhouse Lecture, Australia Yearly Meeting (Atwood, 2012). This material is used with the permission of Australia Yearly Meeting.

articulated officially for the first time a reality to which there was growing attention and awareness among observers and pointed to the need for national, regional, and global action.

**The origins of QUNO engagement.** It was in this atmosphere of the mid-1990s that the Quaker UN Office began its major engagement with the issue area of small arms and light weapons. QUNO had a long-established reputation as an actor on disarmament matters in the UN settings of New York and Geneva. For example, at the time of the preparation of the United Nations First Special Session of the General Assembly devoted to disarmament in 1978, both the Geneva and the New York offices were key players in assisting delegations in their preparation for participation at the Special Session, through off-the-record encounters at the Quaker Houses in both settings, and in coordinating the historic engagement of non-governmental organizations with this game-changing moment of global attention to disarmament (Atwood, 1982). Another example of historic QUNO disarmament work was the accompaniment QUNO provided to the negotiation process of what eventually became the Chemical Weapons Convention in 1992 through off-the-record meetings and residential conferences.[9] The cause of disarmament as a peace concern has been a thread that has run through the life of Quaker work at the UN since its founding.

The shaping of specific program work at the Quaker UN Office is a reflection of discernment and governance processes that guide the staff, assessments of particular need at a moment in time where it can be perceived that there is a "niche" for Quaker intervention, and the skills and interests of particular members of staff.

In 1994-95, two new staff members joined the Quaker UN Office, David Jackman in New York and David Atwood in Geneva. Both had a long history in peace and non-violence work, and in nuclear disarmament concerns. Both arrived at a time when the two offices, by general decisions of their governing bodies–the American Friends Service Committee for New York and Britain Yearly Meeting for Geneva–were seeking to re-shape their programs in relation to the United Nations in tune with the changes and opportunities perceived for the UN in the new international atmosphere of the early 1990s. Neither Jackman nor Atwood had an investment in any particular approach for QUNO in its

---

[9] Quakers have used diplomatic conferences for diplomats as a part of their approach to peacemaking and peacebuilding at the international level for many years. See former QUNO-NY Director Stephen Collett's useful history of Quaker conferences for diplomats (up through the late 1990s), including those undertaken by QUNO. (Collett, n.d.).

disarmament work when they began. Both spent some time in their early months listening, observing, and engaging, in order to bring direction to their work program in each place.

During 1995, conversations between the two Davids led to their exploring whether there was something they might do jointly from their differing UN disarmament settings to engage with the emerging concern around the proliferation and mis-use of small arms and light weapons. Although neither was a small arms expert, the reputation of the two offices in the settings of Geneva and New York, including in the facilitation of off-the-record conversations, led them to believe that they might be able to offer something to the structuring of attention to the small arms issue. QUNO-Geneva's important engagement in the multilateral steps to achieve the Anti-Personnel Mine Ban Convention (the so-called Ottawa Treaty) in 1997 had built confidence that there were things that the two offices could offer in the small arms area. More importantly, as they deepened their understanding of the issue in its many manifestations, they became convinced that engagement in this area was very much in right ordering with Quaker concern. Efforts to deal with the manifestations of small arms proliferation could be understood as linked to more general goals of reducing the human costs of violence, and expanding opportunities for peacebuilding. Without tackling this issue, it seemed increasingly clear to them, other areas such as development and human rights stood little hope, given the centrality of small arms and light weapons to conflict and oppression.[10]

**Advancing the focus on small arms, building the agenda for action.** QUNO's early involvement in this issue area allowed it to play a number of key roles across the years in the evolution of policies and programs related to the small arms problem. Being "ahead of the curve" at a time when there were both regional and international explorations going on among governments and among civil society organizations put QUNO, despite its small size, in a good position to serve in a number of roles to leverage action on the issue.

In the second half of the 1990s, the two offices were able to work from their settings in organizing meetings that helped to move the issue onto the international agenda. In doing so, Jackman and Atwood built collaborative relations with diplomats of governments that were showing early commitments to action. For example, QUNO organized an early "off-the-record" residential

---

[10] This early engagement led to the small arms issue being a substantial element in the work undertaken by David Atwood in Geneva from 1995 until his retirement in 2011 and by David Jackman in New York during his tenure there through 2001. Jackman then continued his involvement with the small arms and armed violence work of QUNO Geneva as a consultant from 2002 to 2010.

"colloquium" on "Strategies for Managing Light Weapons," with a range of key governments and participation by civil society experts in Jongny s/Vevey, Switzerland on 2 -3 April 1999. A further one on "The 2001 Conference on the Illicit Trade in Weapons," was held at Lake Mohonk outside New York City on 25–27 February 2000. These meetings were precursors to a series of such meetings that QUNO co-organized over the years through the Geneva Forum (see below) aimed at building consensus among state representatives and civil society organizations around policy steps on small arms.

Early on, both Jackman and Atwood engaged with a range of increasingly active civil society organizations, including Quaker bodies at work in different conflict-affected regions. This resulted in 1998 in QUNO becoming a founding member of the International Action Network on Small Arms (IANSA). Subsequently, QUNO-New York provided office space to IANSA for its work in preparation for the first major UN Conference on small arms in 2001. QUNO-Geneva assisted IANSA in other ways, including with Atwood serving as a member of the Facilitation Committee of IANSA for a number of years. QUNO, as is the case with all of its program work at the UN, had to walk a tight-rope between its "facilitation" role and that of out-right advocacy throughout the years of its engagement in this issue area.

Working with civil society organizations, research organizations and others became a characteristic of QUNO's work on small arms and light weapons. While there are unique roles for a small organization to play, QUNO also saw that cooperation and joint work with others could be a multiplier for its own particular contributions. In Geneva, for example, QUNO joined with the Programme for Strategic and International Security Studies (PSIS) of the Graduate Institute of International Studies in the organization of a series of lunch-time seminars on dimensions of the small arms problem. This initiative helped to put Geneva on the map as a center for small arms concerns. The work with PSIS evolved as well, and became known as the Geneva Forum, a joint initiative of the two organizations and the UN Institute on Disarmament Research, which provided a major platform in Geneva from the late 1990s on a range of international security concerns, but especially small arms. The Geneva Forum—offering a unique structure as a joint civil society/research/and UN body—was able to play a key role in the steps towards the first major UN conference on small arms in 2001, which led to the UN Program of Action to Prevent, Combat, and Eradicate the Illicit Trade in Small Arms and Light Weapons in All Its Aspects (PoA) (United Nations, 2001). In 2002 the Geneva Forum partners facilitated the creation of what became known as the *Geneva Process*, a regular series of meetings and working groups made up of a range of key states and a number of UN agencies and civil society experts. This mechanism played an important role in providing an informal means aimed at strengthening the implementation of the PoA (Borrie, 2006). On a more modest scale, over a number of years QUNO-New York assisted the intergovernmental platform known as the New York Small Arms Forum, which provided similar informal space for engagement with issues related to the PoA process.

**A pioneering QUNO initiative: focusing on "demand."** In order to build a small arms movement to pressure and sustain the UN process, the QUNO Offices pursued the traditional Quaker-style work of offering space for deliberation and dialogue, seeking out and establishing linkages with other civil society organizations, and working in a multi-organizational way. But there was also an additional dimension that represented an important, specific QUNO contribution. The initial global focus on small arms approached the issue largely as just another arms regulation or control problem. Closer analysis, however, revealed that with small arms and light weapons, one is dealing with more than "supply" issues. Reducing the violent human, social, and economic impact of small arms would also require greater understanding of why individuals and groups choose to acquire, possess, and (mis)use small arms as an option for dealing with their settings. The pioneering joint work of QUNO in New York and Geneva led to early attention to these under-attended and little understood dimensions, so-called "demand" factors. In a sense, this focus was a natural for Quakers because Quaker understanding of the requirements for sustainable peace includes the need to understand and address the root causes of violence and war. The logic of QUNO's thinking was that the job of controlling the flows, managing the presence, or removing the existence of small arms and light weapons from certain settings can only be done in an effective and sustainable way if we also understand and learn to deal with these "demand" factors, and develop the range of required policy directions which go well beyond traditional arms control prescriptions.

While during the 1990s there was growing expertise among organizations on the many "supply" side factors of small arms proliferation and management, little was actually known or understood except in general terms about the "demand" side, at least at the international level. While QUNO is not a traditional research organization, Jackman and Atwood realized that, for real work on small arms that incorporates the both supply and demand considerations to be done, a basic understanding, an evidence base as it were, needed to be created about "demand" realities. To do this, it was felt important to discover from those affected by armed violence factors which were perceived to be important in affecting the demand for small arms and light weapons and learn of approaches being taken to dealing with these factors. Therefore, it was necessary to move beyond the confines of Geneva and New York. Hence, between 1999 and 2004, QUNO, alone and in collaboration with other organizations[11], organized a series of "demand" workshops in Durban, Nairobi, Amman, Phnom Penh, and Port-au-Prince. These were developed largely with community-based organizations in different parts of the world, aimed at bringing to light factors driving demand, and the steps being taken by groups and official actors at different levels to address these factors. The factors revealed included such things as economic inequality, lack of youth opportunity, failure of or lack of public safety, police abuse, cultures of impunity, abuse of fundamental human rights, land and resource access, cultural factors, gender issues, and small arms proliferation itself (QUNO, 2007).

In addition to the cross-fertilization of ideas and strategies for action among organizations working locally and nationally that these workshops afforded, QUNO aimed to assist in bringing into the international processes on small arms an integration of the demand dimension. Not only did QUNO produce and distribute a series of publications on the results of its findings, it also actively promoted this work in the preparation period of 2004–2006 for the first Review Conference of the UN PoA in 2006, with the aim of getting "demand" language into the final outcome document of the Review Conference. In the end, the Review Conference was unable to achieve a consensus outcome, but the "demand" dimension achieved considerable attention during the two weeks of the Conference in June 2006 (QUNO, 2006). It must be added that QUNO was not alone in this focus on demand questions but it was a catalyst for attention to this side of the equation and worked collaboratively with others such as the Small Arms Survey in building the knowledge base (Atwood, Glatz, and Muggah, 2006).

**Demand, development, and the focus on armed violence.** The formal small arms processes of the PoA, a largely supply-side initiative to this day, have not yet proven capable of incorporating very much of the now fairly common understanding of demand factors and particular policy steps aimed at addressing these. Nevertheless, attention to these factors gained increased currency in international development thinking during this period, particularly as the review processes of the Millennium Development Goals began.

QUNO's early demand-side work built foundations for the broadening of the understanding of the overall small-arms *problématique*. Over time, QUNO was

---

[11] Over the years of QUNO's work on "demand issues", collaborative work was undertaken with the American Friends Service Committee, Project Ploughshares, the Africa Peace Forum, the Bonn International Center for Conversion and the Centre for Humanitarian Dialogue.

surpassed by others with greater capacities at the research end of the work. But, typical of Quaker work in general, QUNO had provided a catalyst and a base to be built upon by others.

In 2006 a new international initiative began, called the Geneva Declaration on Armed Violence and Development. The Geneva Declaration, which has 108 state signatories, provided vital energy through 2015 to the critical relationship between the realities of armed violence and sustainable development. In the period following the 2006 PoA Review Conference, QUNO redefined its engagement with the "demand" theme through direct involvement in the life of the Geneva Declaration. QUNO-Geneva played a key role from 2008 to 2012 as the civil society interface with the Geneva Declaration Secretariat and other core state and international actors, such as the United Nations Development Programme (UNDP). Its work included being a central organizer for civil society involvement in a series of "good or promising practices" regional seminars held in 2011 (in Rio, Nairobi, Kathmandu, Abuja and Zagreb) in the run-up to the 2nd Ministerial Review Conference for the Geneva Declaration in October 2011. QUNO also provided documentation on the engagement of civil society armed violence reduction programming at the community and national level as evidence for that meeting (Communidad Segura, 2011).

QUNO's efforts in 2011 and 2012 were also focused on seeking to establish a new global civil society network, which became the Global Alliance on Armed Violence, an initiative that, sadly, only survived as a formal structure until 2015. The growing understanding of the relationship between armed violence and development resulted in the achievement of the inclusion of the critical Goal 16 ("Promote peaceful and inclusive societies for sustainable development, provide access to justice for all and build effective, accountable and inclusive institutions at all levels") into the 2030 Agenda for Sustainable Development, which includes the following as Goal 16.4: "By 2030, significantly reduce illicit financial and arms flows, strengthen the recovery and return of stolen assets and combat all forms of organized crime" (United Nations, 2015).

**Outcomes.** We live in a world where armed violence is still far too prevalent and the institutions for the management of the major instruments of that violence—small arms and light weapons—are still too weak for the task. Nevertheless, important steps have been made since the mid-1990s.

It is a truism of the analysis of social phenomena that there are no single cause explanations, and "measuring" the actual impact of QUNO's engagement to these steps is extremely difficult. Nevertheless, this case study has shown a number of ways in which QUNO, alongside and in partnership with others, has played a contributing role in global advances in addressing this critical humanitarian issue in its many dimensions. To briefly summarize some of the key dimensions outlined in this case study:

- In its early engagement, QUNO worked with sympathetic state representatives to strengthen the movement towards what eventually became the PoA in 2001, a program that continues to shape the way the international community addresses small arms and lights weapons control issues;
- Throughout its more than 15 years of involvement in the issue area, QUNO provided singly, and in partnership with others, an important range of settings for the development and refinement of approaches to institutional engagement with the issue;
- QUNO worked in creative ways to strengthen the capacity of affected communities to get their voices heard at the global level, and to build solidarity of engagement through, among other means, the civil society network of the International Action Network on Small Arms;
- QUNO provided early analysis of factors related to the "drivers" of demand for small arms and light weapons and possible responses by affected communities, hence leading the way for developments in international approaches to armed violence in general and the links to development;
- QUNO's experience in the small arms area illustrates the potential for Quaker engagement at all stages of the policy cycle–from issue identification and awareness-raising, to agenda development, to multilateral negotiating processes and institutional developments, to agreement implementation dynamics and requirements.

While QUNO in its program work is no longer directly addressing small arms and light weapons issues, the results of its more than 15 years of involvement continue to live through the multi-faceted ways in which the *problématique* is being addressed through a range of policy channels at the global, regional, national, and local levels. In addition, its long and diverse engagement on small arms has fed constructively into the peacebuilding focus that characterizes much of the current work of QUNO in both New York and Geneva.

## Financing for Development

**Introduction.** In 2002, the United Nations held the first International Conference on Financing for Development (FfD) in Monterrey, Mexico, resulting in *The Monterrey Consensus on Financing for Development* (UN, 2002). The process leading up to the conference started three years previously, in 1999. Financing for Development was initially conceived as an opportunity to address, in a systemic way, the issues inherent within economic inequality with the goal of *"eradicating poverty while achieving sustained economic growth and the promotion of sustainable development as the world advances to a fully inclusive and equitable global economic system"* (UN, 2002, p. 5).

The conference was preceded in 2000 by a growing awareness of the impact of economic globalization and the neoliberal—and often times very damaging—economic policies of the Bretton Woods Institutions, which resulted in large anti-World Bank/anti-IMF demonstrations during their annual meetings that spring (Rucht, 2006). The Jubilee 2000 movement on forgiving unsustainable debt burdens was gathering strength (Gaventa, 2007), and the percentage that donor nations were contributing to development aid was under scrutiny. On September 11, 2001, the US was attacked, leading to security, geographic, and economic policy changes around the world.

**Origins of Quaker engagement: economic policy and QUNO work on financing for development.** Quakers have been concerned about economics for hundreds of years. Early Quaker businesspeople practiced fair and honest dealings in their workplaces; they were trusted by their customers and thrived.

In the 18th century, US Quaker John Woolman wrote,

> if our views are to lay up riches, or to live in conformity to customs which have not their foundation in the truth, and our demands are such as require from them [the poor] greater toil or application then is consistent with pure love, we invade their rights as inhabitants of a world of which a good and gracious God is the proprietor, and under whom we are tenants (Woolman, 1871, p. 292).

Quaker testimonies of community, equality, integrity, simplicity, and peace are all underpinned by economic fairness.

For many years, the American Friends Service Committee has worked on economic inequality. Many Quakers live in the global south in countries including Burundi, Kenya, Rwanda, the Democratic Republic of the Congo, Bolivia, Guatemala, and Nepal. The Quaker UN Office in Geneva worked on trade issues, and Friends around the world have been concerned with rising levels of economic inequality both nationally and internationally (Quakers in the World, 2017). An additional, and much less visible, impetus to become involved in FfD was the structure—with its inherent power imbalances—of the international financial architecture. In a traditional organizational chart of the UN, the World Bank and the International Monetary Fund, sit under the UN General Assembly, and although the General Assembly was the higher-up body, it actually had little say over what happened in the Bank and the Fund. At the time of FfD, decision-making in the Bank was weighted toward northern countries (Bretton Woods Project, 2016); in contrast, the UN General Assembly provides each country with one vote, each country is weighted equally. Having the General Assembly–a more equitable body–as the ultimate arbiter of the international financial architecture, as per the historical structure, seemed an avenue to rebalance international economic decision-making. With this in mind, and after discussions with the Quaker UN Committee (QUNC), it was decided one staff person and one intern in New York would follow the Financing for Development Process.

QUNO-New York was one of the first organizations to become involved in FfD. Staff set up meetings in New York with ambassadors, national representatives to the Second Committee of the General Assembly on Economics and Finances, and with other non-governmental organizations. QUNO-New York staff also met with people from the World Bank and the IMF, as well as NGO representatives in Washington DC. The meetings were somewhat unusual; in most cases, NGOs request meetings to advocate for a specific position–an international tax code, international standards for extractive industries, getting all developed countries to live up to contributing 0.7% of GDP to development aid. At that time, QUNO was not advocating for a specific thematic position. This was a new area of work for the UN, and QUNO staff saw that providing space for governments and NGOs to speak frankly about issues as the way they could most significantly contribute to the process. The resolution to convene a working group, A/RES/52/179 (entitled "Global partnership for development: high-level international intergovernmental consideration of financing for development") was adopted in 1997 (UNGA, 1997). The resolution to hold a conference, *A/RES/54/196*, was adopted in 1999 (UNGA, 1999). Formal and informal dialogues were held between the UN, the Bank, the Fund, civil society, and the business community. It was the first time UN Ambassadors met officially with the Executive Board of the World Bank and the IMF. Panels were created. Regional meetings were held. Civil society created events and conferences.

The first dilemma QUNO-New York faced was becoming known and having any credibility in the Financing for Development discussion. Quakers were the 'peace and human rights people,' working around the Security Council, UNGA First Committee on Disarmament and International Security, and the UNGA Third Committee on Social, Humanitarian and Cultural Rights; there was little history of working on macroeconomic issues. Additionally, staff working on FfD had little experience in this area, potentially further lessening credibility.

The second dilemma was QUNO-New York's role within wider civil society. In the UN system, there are governments and there is everyone else—that everyone else is 'civil society'. Civil society tends to band together by interest area to increase leverage for advocacy on specific thematic areas such as those listed previously. These groups—whether NGOs or the business community—create panels, presentations, and papers outlining positions and demands from governments. QUNO did not fit into these groups given the lack of a specific thematic demand. The lines were quite clear and not often crossed; however, that is directly where QUNO-NY found itself, talking to many people in many different groups, across lines. QUNO saw its work as one of bringing a process to the FfD negotiations, in contrast to taking a position.

Since QUNO-NY was working across groups, there was confusion and some suspicion on the part of NGO representatives as to motives and intentions. Representatives from other organizations who knew QUNO well knew the office was committed to a more equitable international financial system, and that this cross-sectoral work was the way they had chosen to get there.

**Advancing the focus on Financing for Development.** One of the first things QUNO did, in 1999, was to create *"Building a Common Future: United Nations Work on Financing for Development"* to explain the FfD process and terminology; it was quickly realized that there were many people who wanted to participate in the discussions, but did not have the background or knowledge to be able to participate fully. The booklet was in such demand that a Spanish language version was created and released (Snarr and Overman, 2002). Next, staff began to set up meetings with ambassadors whose countries were playing pivotal roles in the FfD process. QUNO became co-chair of the New York NGO Working Group on FfD. Staff made trips to Washington, D.C. and met with people in the Bank and the Fund who were focal points for FfD, and again quickly realized that ministries of finance—that staffed the Bank and the Fund—were not consulting with Ministries of Foreign Affairs/Departments of State, their counterparts within the UN. It was clear that there was a distinct hierarchy within governments, with finance seeing themselves (and acting) as the ultimate decision-makers. It became clear that the intra-governmental power imbalance was mirrored in the dominance of the Bank and the Fund over the UN, and was at least part of the imbalance in lack of coherence in international development policy. This led to QUNO's next piece of work, off-the-record meetings.

During negotiations in the UN, there are formal meetings, informal meetings, informal informal meetings, and then there are QUNO-style meetings.

From an outsider's point of view, most people would not be able to tell the difference between formal and informal meetings; in both, member-states deliver statements on a specific issue or resolution. The main difference is that traditionally, civil society was not allowed to view or participate in anything other than formal meetings. Informal informal meetings were the place where negotiations happened and, until recently, were completely off-limits to civil society. Because FfD was new within the UN system, government representatives had not discussed financial architecture issues in quite the same way before, and QUNO took the opportunity to bring together interested member-state representatives at Quaker House, in a series of meetings based on the specific thematic areas within the FfD agenda. People got to know one another, and could have personal, as well as work-related, chats during the meetings.

These primarily UN-only meetings led to the clear need for a more substantive meeting between representatives of the Bank, the Fund, UN member-states, UN Secretariat, researchers, and Quakers. The weekend retreat was held at the Mohonk Mountain House in June 2001. Sessions were aligned to mirror the thematic areas within the overall FfD process and included:

- Mobilizing domestic financial resources for development;
- Mobilizing international resources for development: foreign direct investment and other private flows; international trade as an engine for development;
- Increasing international financial and technical cooperation for development;
- External debt; and
- Addressing systemic issues: enhancing the coherence and consistency of the international monetary, financial and trading systems in support of development.

The retreat gave people an additional opportunity to get to know one another, and to have substantive conversations with experts on each of these areas.

In addition to the off-the-record meetings, QUNO was asked to hold a first-ever meeting between the head of the Bank for International Settlements (BIS)/the Financial Stability Forum (FSF) and civil society. This was an informal meeting at Quaker House, requested by the head of the BIS/FSF, and contributed to the inclusion of the BIS/FSF in FfD negotiations and subsequent meetings between the Director and civil society.

In 2002, QUNO staff and Quaker academics attended the FfD Conference in Monterrey, Mexico. QUNO staff spoke at the roundtable on Partnerships in Financing for Development, and all Quaker participants attended panels and events.

**Friends and the Post-Monterrey FfD process.** QUNO-NY was most concerned that, within all of the areas of discussion on FfD, there was little mention of the linkages between economics and peace. The explanation was that developing countries were concerned that international resources for development–development aid–would be linked to peace and thus would encumber aid with an additional conditionality. QUNO staff began asking government representatives if there was any appetite for including peace, and found that more developed countries favored the inclusion of peace in the text of the Monterrey Consensus.

An additional concern was that by the end of the lead-up to the Monterrey Conference, there was a much reduced role for QUNO. Member-states, the Bank, the Fund, and the Business Community were by that time well-acquainted. In 2002, the UN established The Global Compact, an "initiative to encourage businesses worldwide to adopt sustainable and socially responsible policies, and to report on their implementation" (UN Global Compact); and although QUNO was invited to sit in on the meetings, the process for building relationships, etc. had been established and QUNO had little substantive role.

Finally, given that one of QUNO's goals was–in a small way–to help the international financial system become more egalitarian through increasing the role of the UN General Assembly within the international financial architecture, QUNO's work focused mainly on building relationships between the UN, the Bank, and the Fund. QUNO did work with NGOs, but was not as strongly linked with civil society as it was with others. The office did not have a specific area of expertise (debt, taxation, etc.) that would allow staff to join with other groups that held areas of expertise, and continue the work.

**Outcomes.** There were a number of outcomes within the FfD process to which QUNO made some small contribution, although with initiatives of this size, correlations between inputs and outcomes are quite difficult to make definitively.

The first outcome was the inclusion of the word 'peace' in the Consensus document (2002). Page 6 reads: "Recognizing that peace and development are mutually reinforcing, we are determined to pursue our shared vision for a better future, through our individual efforts combined with vigorous multilateral action." QUNO's focus on economics and peace led to a lifting up of this issue within QUNO-NY and resulted in a QUNO paper on economics and peace highlighting the work of Paul Collier and others (Bannon and Collier, 2003).

Soon after the Monterrey Conference, the UN held the 2002 Earth Summit in Johannesburg. QUNO staff, because of Friends' concerns about the environment, were working on the conference, and it seemed like an opportune moment to bring together member-states and UN staff from both FfD and Sustainable Development for a meet-and-greet, and to make links between the two processes. At the end of the meeting, the representative from Denmark stated, "Why is it that we needed the Quakers to bring us together on this issue?"

## Conclusions from Case Studies and Lessons Learned

It is hoped that the two case studies have answered the question that opened this chapter, "How can Quakers justify working at the UN?", making the case for Quaker work at the international policy level, as well as illustrating the links between peace/security policy and economic policy.

There are additional lessons that emerge from the case studies:

- QUNO's work reinforces the general observation that a key role for Quakers can be engaging in an issue area perceived to be critical to human security or economic policy that is under-attended and in need of attention. In the case of small arms, QUNO staff 'discovered' a critical area of ongoing violence and through much work, brought it to the international policy agenda. In FfD, Friends provided information through a handbook and raised awareness through co-chairing an NGO Committee.

- Although not principally a research organization, Quaker investigation into problem areas such as small arms and light weapons and the international financial architecture increased understanding and the accessibility of the central issues and became important elements in deepening understanding and engagement by a range of actors, both governmental and non-governmental.

- The multi-actor nature of our world opens up many avenues for potentially influential work through new kinds of partnerships operating at many different levels. Building alliances with others is a key element in leveraging the particular contribution that Quakers can bring to a global policy area. Working beyond Geneva and New York in such partnerships can also bring vital authenticity and legitimacy to the international policy process.

- Quaker work at the international level, to be seen as credible and legitimate, must remain connected to Quaker concern and engagement at other levels and should be directly linked to Friends' testimonies.

- The level of QUNO's engagement on any issue depends on resources beyond those provided by Quaker bodies for QUNO work. Grant funding requirement is a reality that shapes Quaker work at the UN and demands vigilance and attention to core values.

- QUNO's work in both the areas of financing for development and small arms and light weapons, as with other international policy work undertaken by QUNO over the years, shows that size doesn't necessarily matter. No matter how formidable the structures and obstacles may seem, it is possible to make a difference. Quaker process, including listening, seeking and finding one's niche, respect, and doing one's homework, can mean that it is possible to get heard, to grease the wheels of change, and to see positive change happen.

## References

Atwood, David. (2012). *From the Inside Out: Observations on Quaker Work at the United Nations.* Sydney: Australia Yearly Meeting.

Atwood, David, Glatz, Anne-Katherin, and Muggah. Robert. (2006). *Demanding Attention: Addressing the Dynamics of Small Arms Demand.* Geneva: Small Arms Survey and Quaker United Nations Office.

Atwood, David. (1982). *Non-governmental Organizations and the 1978 United Nations Special Session on Disarmament.* Unpublished PhD dissertation, University of North Carolina.

Bailey, Sidney. (1993). *Peace is a Process.* Swarthmore Lecture. Quaker Books.

Bannon, Ian and Collier, Paul. (2003). *Natural Resources and Violent Conflict.* Washington DC: World Bank.

Bretton Woods Project. (2016). *IMF & World Bank decision-making and governance.*

Retrieved from: http://www.brettonwoodsproject.org/2016/03/imf-world-bank-decision-making-and-governance-existing-structures-and-reform-processes/.

Borrie, John. (2006). "Small Arms and the Geneva Forum: Disarmament as Humanitarian Action," in John Borrie and Vanessa Martin Randin, eds., *Disarmament as Humanitarian Action: From Perspective to Practice.* UN Institute for Disarmament Research. Geneva, pp. 137–165.

Boutros-Ghali, Boutros. (1992). *An Agenda for Peace: Preventive Diplomacy, Peacemaking and Peacekeeping.* New York: United Nations.

Boutros-Ghali, Boutros. (1995). *Supplement to An Agenda for Peace: Position Paper of the Secretary-General on the Occasion of the Fiftieth Anniversary of the United Nations.* New York: United Nations.

Collett, Stephen. (n.d.). *Quaker Conferences for Diplomats: a 20th Century History.* Unpublished manuscript. Philadelphia: American Friends Service Committee.

Collett, Stephen. (January 2007). *Sixty Years with the UN in New York: A History of the Quaker UN Office.* Quaker United Nations Office. Retrieved from http://www.quno.org/sites/default/files/resources/Sixty%2BYears%2Bw ith%2Bthe%2BUN%2Bin%2BNew%2BYork.pdf.

Comunidad Segura (2011). *Good Practices in Armed Violence Reduction and Prevention: The Experiences of Civil Society in Five Regional Settings.* Rio de Janeiro: Comunidad Segura. Retrieved from http://www.quno.org/sites/default/files/resources/Good%2BPratices%2B-%2BE%2Bafrica%2Bnovember%2B2010.pdf.

Fell, Margaret. (1660). Retrieved from http://www.quakersintheworld.org/quakers-in-action/111/-Peace-and-Nonviolence.

Gaventa, John. (2007). Case study on the Jubilee Debt Campaign: Working across the levels, spaces and forms of power. New York: Routledge. Retrieved from http://www.powercube.net/wp-content/uploads/2009/11/Jubilee_debt_campaign.pdf.

Geneva Declaration Secretariat. (2008). *Global Burden of Armed Violence.* Geneva: Geneva Declaration Secretariat.

Quaker UN Office. (2006). *Dealing with Small Arms Demand: A Report of QUNO Activity at the UN Small Arms Review Conference.* (2 October). Geneva: Quaker United Nations Office.

Quaker UN Office. (April 2007). *Setting a New Agenda for Demand Work: Next Steps in the Comprehensive Approach to Small Arms Control.* Geneva: Quaker United Nations Office.

Quaker UN Office. (2017). Website. Retrieved from www.quno.org.

Quakers in the World. (2017). *Economic Justice.* Retrieved from http://www.quakersintheworld.org/quakers-in-action/134/Economic-Justice.

Rucht, Dieter. (2006). Social Movements Challenging Neo-liberal Globalization. Retrieved from https://depts.washington.edu/ccce/assets/documents/Rucht,SocialMovelents&Globalization.pdf.

Snarr, Michael and Overman, Joey. (2002). *The Quaker United Nations Office and the Monterrey Consensus.* Indiana: Quaker Life.

(UNGA) United Nations General Assembly Resolution. (1997). *Global partnership for development: high-level international intergovernmental consideration of financing for development.* Retrieved from http://repository.un.org/handle/11176/178329.

(UNGA) United Nations General Assembly Resolution. (1999). *High-level international intergovernmental consideration of financing for development.* Retrieved from http://repository.un.org/handle/11176/231037.

United Nations. (2001). Report of the United Nations Conference on the Illicit Trade in Small Arms and Light Weapons in All its Aspects (A/CONF.192/15).

United Nations Global Compact. (2002). Retrieved from: www.Unglobal compact.org.

United Nations. (2002). Monterrey Consensus on Financing for Development. New York: UN.

United Nations. (2015). Sustainable Development Goals. Retrieved from http://www.un.org/sustainabledevelopment/sustainable-development-goals/.

United Nations. (1945). UN Charter Preamble. Retrieved from http://www.un.org/en/sections/un-charter/preamble/index.html.

Wood, J. Duncan. (1962). *Building the Institutions of Peace.* London: George Allen and Unwin.

Woolman, John. (1871). *The Journal of John Woolman.* New York: Houghton Mifflin Company.

# 9 | Fifty Years of Right Sharing:
# A Brief History of the Right Sharing of World Resources Program

**By Steven Dale Davison**

The year 2017 marked the fiftieth anniversary of the Right Sharing of World Resources program (RSWR). Ever since its emergence in 1967 at the Fourth World Conference of Friends, Right Sharing has worked with partners in the developing world to support their entrepreneurial efforts. And for five decades the program has challenged Friends in the overdeveloped world to examine their own lives in the light of divine love and their responsibilities as consumers of more than their share of the world's resources. This essay celebrates this significant milestone in the history of the Right Sharing of World Resources program and in the economic history of Friends.

## The Seed is Planted

The concern for Right Sharing first emerged in 1965 in a document prepared in advance of the Fourth World Conference of Friends, which took place in 1967 under the auspices of Friends World Committee for Consultation (FWCC) in Greensboro, North Carolina, on the campus of Guilford College, a Quaker institution of higher learning. FWCC is a Quaker organization that gathers Friends from around the world and from all its various historical branches into one fellowship.

In 1964, as a way to stimulate interest, discussion, and discernment ahead of the Conference, a representative committee of FWCC prepared a list of Friends who might be asked to write essays in five areas of interest that had been chosen for Friends to consider during the Conference. These were The Nurture of the

Spiritual Life, The Ecumenical Challenge, The Community of Friends, The Community of Peoples, and Peace Making and Peace Keeping.

Douglas V. Steere, then chairman[1] of FWCC, approached the Friends on this list and twenty-six responded with essays. In 1965 FWCC published these submissions, along with queries for study at the end of each chapter, in a book titled *No Time But This Present* (Schaffer, 1965).

For the Peace Making and Peace Keeping section of the book, British Friends Walter and Maisie Birmingham wrote an essay titled "Christian Responsibility for the Use of Natural Resources" (Birmingham and Birmingham, 1965)[2]. This essay seems to have been the original seed that eventually bore fruit as the Right Sharing of World Resources program.

In its seven pages, the Birminghams raised all the issues that would characterize right sharing for the next fifty years. They laid out the spiritual basis for the concern, pointing to the immense gap in circumstances between people who lived in rich countries and those who lived in dire poverty in the under-developed world as a violation of Jesus' injunction to love one's neighbor as one's self; they defined the concern as a Christian responsibility for action. They called for the redistribution of wealth, for technical aid for developing countries, and for fair prices in international markets. They challenged Friends to live modest lifestyles at home. They raised up the "population explosion" and the wrongness of diverting vast resources to armaments and war as critical, related concerns. They emphasized the social costs of inequality and the importance of community over and against the impulse toward private gain. They called for conservation, reverence for all life, and expressed a special concern for nature's beauty (Birmingham and Birmingham 1965, pp. 202-209).

At the conclusion of their essay, the Birminghams asked how individual Friends and meetings might address these issues and whether Friends would be willing to accept "(a) voluntary taxation through the Society of Friends, or (b) extra State taxation, to assist the poorer nations?" (Birmingham and Birmingham 1965, p. 209).

In this last query, they prefigured the One Percent More Program that embodied FWCC's initial implementation of the right sharing concern, in which Friends (and governments) were asked to tax themselves one percent of their after-taxes income for projects in developing countries over and above their

---

[1] FWCC used the term "Chairman" until 1985, when it changed its usage to "clerk."

[2] The majority of the resources quoted or referred to in this essay, not including those which are books, are in the Right Sharing of World Resources archives in the Quaker collection at Earlham College in Richmond, Indiana, or in the RSWR offices, also in Richmond.

other charitable contributions or, in the case of governments, in addition to their existing foreign aid.

The Birmingham's essay ended with this appeal: "Is it now time that Friends worked out their common testimony to the right use of the world's resources? Have we something to say on the urgent need of massive economic aid to the poor nations if they are to develop their resources and lift their people to a fuller life…?" (Birmingham and Birmingham, 1965, p. 208) The answer, it turned out, was yes.

### The Seed Sprouts and a Flower Blooms–The Fourth World Conference

The concerns raised by the Birminghams fell upon fertile soil. As the World Conference approached, planners included developing and sharing the world's resources in the Conference's seven principal roundtable topics, and these discussions were well attended. Furthermore, *Seek, Find, Share*, a second preparatory volume published in early 1967 as a follow-up to *No Time But This Present*, included five essays in a section titled "Developing and Sharing the World's Resources." These were: "Did Jesus Summon All Men to a New Social Order?" by Margarethe Lachmund; "A Theology for the Space Age" by Fred Haslam; "Our Christian Responsibility for the Use of the World's Resources" by F.W.C.C. European Section; "The Use of Natural Resources" by William H. Marwick; and "Family Welfare Planning" by Joseph D. Alter (Moore, 1969).

The Guilford World Conference organizers had set aside five periods for Meetings for Special Interests and Concerns during the 10-day conference, with 35 topics for discussion. Right sharing was one of the main topic areas. Forty-one Round Tables were also planned, including four on right sharing. As the Conference progressed, three particular areas of concern advanced to the fore in these groups–peace in Vietnam, racial conflict, and sharing the world's resources. In response to these quickening interests, the organizers set up special sessions for considering them in greater depth.

These workshops and discussions watered the shoots of the right sharing concern and by the end of the Conference, a new awareness and passion for succor to the world's poor had flowered. It would take a while for the plants to bear fruit and even then the concern struggled on and off to fulfill the promise of its vision. But it was clear to those attending the Conference that God was leading Friends to engage in new forms of social witness in the international arena.

In its final sessions, the Fourth World Conference of Friends adopted three statements that had been brought to the Conference from the Round Tables and

Special Interest and Concerns Groups: "People, Food and the Sharing of Resources–A Vision for the Future," "The Vietnam War," and "Friends Response to Racial Conflict." (Two more statements were commended to Friends for further study, on "The Peace Testimony and Peace-making," and on "The Middle East.")

The Conference's Right Sharing minute called upon "the peoples and the governments of the earth to stop squandering resources on armaments and destruction, to promote family planning and health, to curb population growth, to increase and share food production, and to further economic and social development. Only by an all out attack on want can this be done." It appealed to governments to devote "a significant proportion of the gross national product to international development" and to work to make the global economic system more fair, among other recommendations. It urged Friends organizations and service bodies to become more engaged in "world community involvement" in various ways and it urged individual Friends to get involved, as well, by practicing greater simplicity in personal consumption and by dedicating "a regular portion of our income towards world development" (FWCC1968, pp. 125-127).

The Conference's statement was extremely significant in its concrete consequences for Friends worldwide and it figured prominently in the mission and self-identity of subsequent right sharing programs as they evolved through the decades. In its particulars, it also prefigured many of the programs' signature features.

### Getting Started

With "People, Food and the Sharing of Resources" and the other statements from the Conference, FWCC adopted a fresh outward-looking focus that, while not new to Friends, nevertheless carried a new level of energy. A strong sense of excitement and urgency had been born during the Conference and FWCC's leadership immediately sought ways to channel this new energy into concrete action.

Following the Conference, at the invitation of FWCC Chairman Douglas V. Steere, Friends from around the world wrote essays on seven themes that had emerged during the Conference, and Right Sharing of World Resources was one of them. From the initial responses to Steere's invitation, some writers were selected to write essays for a post-conference volume, which was published in 1969 as *Break the New Ground: Seven Essays by Contemporary Quakers* (Cooper, 1969). *Break the New Ground* included a contribution from Denis P. Barritt titled "Right Sharing of World Resources." FWCC ultimately published "Right Sharing of World Resources" as a standalone pamphlet with the same title.

In addition to these post-Conference essays, shortly after the World Conference, Joseph Haughton of Ireland Yearly Meeting, who had been a co-chairman of the Conference's Round Table Groups, distributed to thirty-seven Friends with expertise in various areas related to international development a new essay by Walter Birmingham that offered suggestions for action on the right sharing concern. In his accompanying letter, Haughton invited these Friends to comment on Birmingham's proposals and to make suggestions of their own. Twenty-seven Friends responded.

At its meeting in January 1968, the Interim Committee of FWCC considered the suggestions from Joseph Haughton's respondents and decided on ways to implement the suggestions that had been offered. At this gathering, the idea of right sharing of world resources became an incipient program of FWCC.

Three suggestions in particular paved the way for the program's future—creating a FWCC Committee on Right Sharing, hiring staff dedicated to the concern (Haughton, 1968), and a suggestion by Walter Birmingham that "*Friends voluntarily surrender 1% of their individual product* (income) to a fund to provide capital for the poor nations" (emphasis his) and that governments be urged to dedicate one percent of GDP (Birmingham, 1967, p. 2).

Accordingly, a World Resources Committee was formed in the spring of 1968. In June of 1968, William E. Barton was appointed Associate Secretary of FWCC, a new position tasked with shepherding the international mission and service mandates that had come out of the World Conference, though he was only able to assume the position in 1969. The idea of a one percent fund generated a lot of enthusiasm, although it was some time before it found its feet in the larger FWCC organization.

While FWCC had set some things in motion, not much actually happened for a year, except on the part of three yearly meetings in the European Section. Germany and London Yearly Meetings created one percent funds, and Switzerland Yearly Meeting appealed for 3%. London Yearly Meeting's appeal collected the first Right Sharing donations–£21,000 in 1968.

FWCC's American Section and Fellowship Council[3] created an International Affairs Committee, which also met in January of 1968 to consider the concerns for international action that had preoccupied the World Conference. But a year passed without any other concrete action by either of FWCC's sections or the world body.

---

[3] The "American Section" of FWCC was called the American Section until 1954, when it was changed to American Section and Fellowship Council. The current usage of Section of the Americas was adopted in 1974. I have used "American Section" throughout this essay for the sake of its brevity.

## The One Percent More Program

Eventually, however, following the leadership of the European yearly meetings, the idea of asking Friends to give one percent of their after-tax income to international development caught on.

In 1969, a European Friends Conference adopted a "Preliminary Statement" on "Right Sharing of the World's Resources" that asked Friends to give one percent of after-tax income, in addition to their other charitable giving, a modification that soon was more widely adopted and became the One Percent *More* Fund. The Statement also encouraged governments to add one percent of GDP to their existing international aid to foster development in developing countries (Hadley, 1991, p. 155).

Also that year, the American Section's Executive Committee endorsed recommendations from the International Affairs Committee for a One Percent More Fund and Herbert M. Hadley, General Secretary of the Section, sent a letter recommending the One Percent More Fund to North American yearly meetings. Thirty yearly meetings were contacted and all but seven endorsed the idea, along with Friends Committee on National Legislation (FCNL), Friends General Conference (FGC), Friends United Meeting (FUM), United Society of Friends Women (USFW), and Young Friends of North America (YFNA).

However, most of these endorsements came without clear plans for implementation. To move things along, the American Section's International Affairs Committee sponsored what would be the first in a series of consultations on Right Sharing, this one at William Penn House in Washington, D.C. in November 1969. Friends from eight yearly meetings and eight other Quaker organizations attended. The consultation agreed upon guidelines for the program and emphasized efforts to examine lifestyles at home and reduce consumption in the U.S. through population control and simplicity (WRG, 1970, p. 1).

These new guidelines organized the program around committees in the yearly meetings that would promote the program, manage the finances, maintain connections with FWCC and other Quaker organizations involved in the program, and make the allocation decisions. A newly formed World Resources Group comprised of Friends with expertise in right sharing issues, which had replaced FWCC's original World Resources Committee (a change discussed in greater detail below), would review project proposals and make recommendations to the yearly meeting committees.

In early 1970, the American Section's Executive Committee decided to accept contributions and appointed an Allocations Committee in the fall. In June of that year, the International Affairs Committee hired John Sexton as Director of the One Percent More Program, and he began visiting yearly meetings that summer to promote participation. By the end of 1970, $7,000 in grants of $1,000 or $2,000 had been given to projects in Zambia, India, and Guatemala, all of which were connected with other Quaker organizations. Another thousand dollars, plus earmarked funds from yearly meetings, were allocated to interpretation, coordination, and education (ICE) efforts. Total receipts for the program for the year came to $28,000 (Hadley, 1991, p. 157).

The American Section also decided that the International Affairs Committee would take general responsibility for coordinating the projects, keep the records, create and distribute promotional materials, and help yearly meetings with educational resources.

Right Sharing of World Resources was now an established program in two of the Sections of Friends World Committee (the third Section was Africa), though initially these programs were called One Percent More Funds.

## Right Sharing of World Resources–The Philosophy

From the very beginning, Friends' right sharing witness embodied a constellation of concerns that went farther and deeper than just the micro-funding of development projects.

Many organizations help local communities in the developing world with micro-funding nowadays but Right Sharing of World Resources helped to lead the way. However, what makes the program unique is its double focus. Right Sharing is both outward looking and inward looking. With the One Percent More Program and the Right Sharing of World Resources program that followed it, the program encouraged Friends to commit their own resources to help people in poorer countries develop theirs. But it also encouraged Friends to look at their own lifestyles, to see how they might reduce the burden on the world's resources by consuming less themselves, recognizing that the over-developed world consumed far more than its share.

Right Sharing appealed to individuals, but it also sought initially to influence governments to increase their support for development in the under-developed world. This "lobbying" mission never came to full fruition, but Right Sharing never lost sight of the concern to change the consciousness and policies of governments towards the world's poor.

Friends understood this witness to spring from a "spiritual basis" and argued for the concern with explicitly Christian, biblical, and moral language, in addition to rhetoric derived from political economy.

The movement always saw right sharing as only one aspect of an integrated social testimony that included other Quaker testimonies: the peace testimony most prominently, but also the testimonies of simplicity, equality, social justice, and what has evolved into earthcare. Friends especially linked increased foreign aid to decreased spending for armaments and the military.

Another concern preoccupied Friends at the beginning–the population explosion, as it was being called at the time. Many experts were predicting a catastrophic collision between birth rates, especially in the developing world, and food supplies. Friends involved in the right sharing movement returned again and again to population control as a concern directly related to right sharing.

The movement has always seen the right sharing concern as having both a service and an advocacy mission, seeking to support people in poor countries, but also to change the approach of rich countries to development aid and the international economic order. Friends were especially exercised over the unfair trade agreements that denied poorer countries the wealth they might use for their own development from the only exports they often had at their disposal–natural resources. In this way, the right sharing movement saw third world poverty as a systemic and structural problem, a direct consequence of a global economic system deliberately tilted in the over-developed countries' favor.

Time and time again, the leaders of the movement expressed a concern for collaboration with their project partners in the field, a desire to avoid a top-down and paternalistic approach, to listen to the recipients' real needs and respect their social situation and their humanity. They were fully aware of how difficult international aid projects were in this regard and how often such projects failed or even did more harm than good. They consistently saw the need not just for money, but also for training and other non-pecuniary support. And they sought to include Friends from the developing world in the planning and administration of the program.

The right sharing movement had from the beginning a primary concern for educating Friends and the public about right sharing and international development issues. After the One Percent More Fund was launched, they codified this aspect of the program as ICE–interpretation, consultation, and education. The program tried to serve as a clearinghouse for information about the issues. And it produced articles and pamphlets, often by Friends professionally engaged in development work in one way or another, which were both substantive and morally persuasive.

This was FWCC at work, so the program has always included Friends from across the various branches and theologies of Quakerism. This included collaboration with independent Quaker organizations like the service committees, Quaker United Nations Office (QUNO), FCNL and others. The organizers of the One Percent More Fund were also keen to include young adult Friends and to work with other churches and the United Nations in the field.

## Slow Growth and a Learning Curve

The Friends who gathered at the Fourth World Conference had been inspired by the idea of right sharing of world resources and a number of Friends found themselves led by the Spirit into this new witness ministry. They had been awakened to and moved by the enormous disparities between their own economic circumstances and those of millions of people living in the poorer countries of the world. And they felt called to address these inequities both personally and collectively, both structurally and morally and spiritually.

However several factors delayed the full realization of these ideals. While the global dispersion of Friends was a recognized strength, providing knowledge, contacts, and networks around the world, plus some existing programs and structures for work in the field, it also made organization difficult. While FWCC had organized the Guilford Conference and had received the mandate from the gathered body for implementing this new witness impulse and had issued a formal statement of commitment, the worldwide organization was not well equipped to carry it forward quickly. It was both too big geographically and too thin organizationally, and it was not yet organized to manage programs like the One Percent More Program. It lacked the financial resources necessary to launch such a worldwide program in a timely fashion. The travel it entailed, especially, proved beyond the means of both the organization and the Friends involved.

Thus the concern for right sharing and the One Percent More Program that embodied it grew very slowly at first and had to step through several stages as Friends adapted to the obstacles before them. Things didn't really get going in a meaningful way until late 1969, two years after the World Conference in Greensboro.

Without travel funding, and with members in both Europe and North America, the World Resources Committee that FWCC had formed in early 1968 found it impossible to meet. Thus, in the fall of 1969, FWCC's Interim Committee laid it down and asked the wider body at its 1970 Triennial Meeting held in Sigtuna, Sweden, to convene a World Resources Group to replace it (WRG, 1970). The new Group would meet face-to-face when they could but would conduct most of its business by correspondence. That business was educating Friends about world poverty, encouraging personal commitment to the concern of right sharing, and reviewing and making recommendations to yearly meetings about projects, as its members had considerable development expertise.

A World Resources Gathering was held in Sigtuna directly after the Sigtuna Triennial, with representatives from 13 countries attending. However, the gathering was not able to agree on which issues to tackle first and over the next several years the World Resources Group continued to find coordinated international action very difficult to organize. At FWCC's Twelfth Triennial Meeting in Sidney, Australia in 1973, the body accepted the recommendation from FWCC's Interim Committee to lay down the World Resources Group. The world body of FWCC had passed the Right Sharing baton to its Sections.

### The American Section

The American Section endorsed the One Percent More Program at its meeting in January of 1969. Its efforts to reach out to yearly meetings led to twenty yearly meeting endorsements during that spring and summer, though many of these yearly meetings had not yet created a structure for implementation. In the spring of 1970, the International Affairs Committee, which the American Section had created to respond to the international concerns arising from the World Conference, hired John Sexton as Director of the Section's One Percent More Program, with Sexton's wife Lois as his assistant. In September of that year the Section appointed an Allocations Committee charged with making grant decisions.

But the program struggled financially. In 1971, Philadelphia Yearly Meeting and the Section had to prop up the Program's outreach efforts with grants. And since very few Friends were following the 1% formula that was the One Percent More Program's identity, the Section renamed the program Right Sharing of World Resources. It also decided to terminate the Right Sharing staff. In August, the Section let the Sexton's go and ended its administration of the Program. The Section replaced John Sexton's Advisory Committee with a Coordinating Committee for Right Sharing of World Resources, with many of the same people staying to serve on it. However, the baton had passed once again, this time from the Section to the yearly meeting committees.

Problems also bedeviled the effort to craft a unified presentation of right sharing's spiritual basis. Individual Friends wrote articles that were often very powerful statements of the Christian, biblical, moral, and spiritual reasons for right sharing of world resources. But by late 1975, the Spiritual Basis Task Force of the American Section's Right Sharing of World Resources Committee "was unable to agree on a spiritual basis statement and queries which expressed the feelings of all concerned" (American Section RSWR Committee, 1975). The Committee let the spiritual basis project go and resolved to approach Quaker periodicals with articles as an alternative.

## The Program Settles

These setbacks notwithstanding, Right Sharing of World Resources did finally gain its feet and continued under FWCC's care until 1999.

The American Section established guidelines for selecting recipient projects at the important World Resources Gathering in Sigtuna, Sweden, held in August 1970 in conjunction with the Sigtuna FWCC Triennial. Projects should "promote economic development, release of human potential, equality of opportunity, and social justice." They should involve international and Quaker cooperation, especially from the different areas of Quakerism; involve local communities in the formulation, operation, and planned devolution of projects; avoid presenting or aligning with any particular political or economic ideology; seek opportunities for service by young people; look for innovative projects; and work with the United Nations and other church groups when possible and appropriate (WRG, 1970).

In 1972, after releasing John Sexton from his position as Director of the One Percent More Program, the American Section restructured its right sharing work, with the International Affairs Committee taking on the coordination of the program. They published a new brochure that John Sexton had created, titled *We Must Share the World's Resources*, which highlighted the right sharing statement from the 1967 Guilford Conference. The Committee also published a manual for RSWR implementation for use by the yearly meeting RSWR committees (RSWR, 1972). Now, a clear set of protocols was in place for suggesting and approving projects, handling the money, and other matters.

After a reenergizing fifth RSWR Consultation in Evanston, Illinois, in 1973, the success of the American Section's subsequent financial appeal encouraged it to form a new standing Right Sharing of World Resources Committee, taking over from the International Affairs Committee. The new Committee hired Jennifer Haines, a young Friend from New York Yearly Meeting, as part-time staff. The new Committee was charged with assuming the consultative role that the World Resources Group had played, serving as a resource on right sharing issues and projects, educating Friends on development issues, encouraging individual involvement in the concern and yearly meeting participation in the program, selecting projects and allocating funds, and providing staff and administrative support in order to unburden Friends World Committee's staff and resources. In 1978, the Committee raised the portion of non-designated contributions dedicated to education from 15% to 30% and hired Gail Weinstein as 3/5-time Program Coordinator. The program continued to enjoy staff support from the Section until FWCC devolved it in 1999, with Elaine Crauderueff becoming Coordinator in 1980, then Sharli Powers in 1983, Johan Maurer in 1986, and Roland Kreager in 1993.

Meanwhile, the European and Near East Section was active as well, with the Section's Executive Committee promoting the One Percent More Fund among yearly meetings. According to Herbert Hadley in *Quakers World Wide*, the yearly meetings in the Section "gave generous support to the right sharing projects of their choice" (Hadley, 1991, p. 160).

The European and Near East Section also published two pamphlets in the 1970s, *World Resources–Dilemma and Concern* in 1976 and *The New International Order–The Promise and the Reality* in 1977.

Within the European and Near East Section, project grant allocations were always in the hands of the yearly meetings, while in the American Section the Section office served as the clearinghouse for grants until 1999. American Section grant allocations seem to have varied quite a bit during this period. Annual allocations spiked to almost $30,000 in 1970, then dropped off until the middle of the decade, when they crested again to $38,000 twice and then almost $30,000 in 1977. They ended the decade a little under $20,000 a year.

As an indicator of the program's scope, from 1977 to 1981, the program gave grants to 32 projects, 12 in Africa, 15 in Central and South America and the Caribbean, four in India, and one in Turkey (Hadley, 1991, p. 161). Grant amounts increased significantly in the mid-1980s, from $43,000 in 1984 to $86,285 in 1986, where they leveled off for the rest of the decade.

The Right Sharing committees in both Sections held consultations fairly regularly, often in conjunction with Section gatherings and FWCC Triennials. These were attended by RSWR committee members, RSWR staff, and sometimes other FWCC staff, by representatives from yearly meetings, and by other concerned Friends. They were opportunities for organizing, especially in the beginning, for making decisions regarding the program, for sharing ideas, and sometimes for reviewing projects and making grant allocations.

### Publications

The Right Sharing of World Resources programs also published their truth, in newsletters, pamphlets, brochures, articles in Quaker journals, information sheets on the projects they funded, and white papers that described the causes and character of international economic inequity and laid out the reasons for Quaker concern.

### Newsletters

The first newsletter (published by the American Section) was *Quaker Efforts in Development* (QED). The newsletter's title was changed to *Right Sharing News* after the program's name was changed from the One Percent More Program to Right Sharing of World Resources in 1971.

### Brochures

The European and Near East Section published *Give One Per Cent More!* in 1969, a one-sheet trifold brochure that explained how the Section's One Percent More Program worked, described the need for addressing the problems poorer nations faced and the reasons for Quaker action, and described a number of example projects.

The American Section also published a single-sheet, 8 ½ by 14-inch folding brochure introducing the One Percent More Program titled *We Must Share the World's Resources.* It presented the full text of the minute approved at the Fourth World Conference and added an appeal for contributions.

After it laid down the One Percent More Program, the American Section published *The Right Sharing of the World's Resources* for use by yearly meeting and monthly meeting RSWR committees. This slim eight-page outline of the reorganized Right Sharing of World Resources program laid out the purpose of the new program, the procedures meetings should use, and the role of FWCC.

### Essays

Several individual Friends wrote essays that received various levels of distribution. In the late 1960s, Betty D. Richardson of the Quaker United Nations Program wrote "Rich Countries, Poor Countries . . . Does Your Shopping Basket Hold the Key?" which explored "what it would really mean–in practical terms . . . to make the sacrifices we need to make for a just society." In 1969, a fact sheet was prepared with statistics on poverty in the developing world as an educational tool.

The crown jewel of the early years was Denis P. Barritt's *Right Sharing of World Resources,* which has already been mentioned. Originally published in *Break the New Ground* (Cooper, 1969) and ultimately printed as a stand-alone pamphlet, Barritt's essay reviewed the issues involved in world poverty and international development and introduced the idea of a one percent more fund and other ways forward. Barritt also stressed study of the problem of right sharing, working with other groups in the field, education, individual simplicity, and service, especially for young people just out of school (Barritt, 1969).

In 1972, Gilbert F. White wrote "Moral Issues Concerning the Global Environment" in which he mentions the effects of burning fossil fuels on the global climate in the midst of a very wide ranging and searching essay.

In 1972, FWCC's Right Sharing Committee also published a slim card titled "How to Live on One Hundred Dollars a Year" that dramatically illustrated how much a small suburban American household would have to give up to live as millions do in poor countries

In 1975, Alfred Haines Cope wrote "Managing World Resources," an eight-page essay covering many topics related to RSWR for the organization's use.

In 1978, the Right Sharing of World Resources Committee of FWCC-American Section published "Right Sharing of World Resources," a set of three essays packaged together for distribution, along with some outside comments, author replies, and other materials. The essays were "The Spiritual Basis for Right Sharing of the World's Resources" by Everett L. Cattell; "Stewardship of the Earth" by Gilbert F. White; and "Toward a New World Order" by Mexican Friend Heberto Sein. Sometime in the late 1970s, RSWR gathered a package of educational resources on the concern, including games, movies, film strips, and posters. Around the same time, the American Section prepared a six-page bibliography on right sharing.

### Resources

In June of 1979, FWCC drafted a Memorandum "To the Preparatory Committee for the New International Development Strategy (Established under Resolution 33/193)," a United Nations initiative. This thorough and thoughtful four-page document introduced Friends World Committee, its right sharing work, and the spiritual basis for that work. Based on FWCC's experience, the Memorandum offered observations and comments regarding international development for both "technologically sophisticated countries" and "technologically poor countries." It laid out what FWCC saw as the dilemmas involved in addressing these inequities and recommended ways to address them (FWCC, 1979).

### Project visitations

Throughout its history, Right Sharing has tried to maintain meaningful connections between Friends in the over-developed countries and the communities it served in under-developed countries. These visits also helped the program evaluate the appropriateness of potential new project grantees and to maintain a sense of connection and to evaluate the progress of existing grantee projects.

In 1974, after traveling on their own through India, Bruce Birchard and Demie Kurz spoke with Jennifer Haines, then RSWR director, about some of the Ghandian projects they'd visited and RSWR invited three of these to submit proposals. One proposal from women seeking micro-credit to purchase good quality milk buffaloes fit the program perfectly and became a model for future grants. In 1978 Anna and Will Alexander visited Belize, Zambia, Kenya, and India, and then visited yearly meetings in the U.S. upon their return to share their experiences. Elizabeth Moen performed site visits from 1986 to 1993 in and around Madurai, Tamil Nadu. Between 1995 and 1998, both Roland Kreager and George Willoughby did site visits in India, also.

## 1980s and 1990s

In 1980, a long-range planning committee of FWCC's American Section conducted a review of the Right Sharing program with Lloyd Bailey as its clerk, and reported to the Section's Annual Meeting in November 1981. The Section acted on the report by establishing new guidelines for the program and reaffirming its long-standing goals of education, cooperation with other Quaker bodies when possible, clarifying and expressing its spiritual basis, influencing public policy, and helping individuals implement their right sharing concerns.

In 1988, the American Section's Right Sharing program distributed its largest amounts to its partners to date, but also in that year London Yearly meeting laid down its 1% Fund, citing its inability to sway the British government or successfully educate Friends and others about the issues, prohibitively high administrative costs, and the existence of good alternative organizations that had Quaker connections (RSWR, 1994, p. 4).

By 1994, RSWR had in its 25 years received $881,000 in donations. In that year, FWCC undertook an evaluation of the Right Sharing program, held at Ghost Ranch, a retreat center in Abiquiu, New Mexico, with the help of Abigail Adams as outside facilitator. The Consultation considered four queries: on current goals and the success of past goals, on how Quaker testimonies serve the concern, on what defines success, and on the future of the program. Background materials for the last query suggested that "Right Sharing can be seen to have lost its prophetic edge. . . . [and] to be relatively ineffectual in distributing funds to the developing world" (RSWR, 1994, p. 6). Yet those same materials still held out hope that "There is yet Truth to be revealed." (RSWR, 1994, p. 7). The gathering reaffirmed the central importance of mutual relationships with project partners, with other local groups, and with like-minded organizations in North America, and dedicated itself to improving project management and reimagining RSWR as a global and decentralized program.

Soon, however, the Program's fortunes would change dramatically.

## RSWR Becomes an Independent Organization

In November 1997, the Executive Committee of Friends World Committee for Consultation completed a review of FWCC's role in the world and within the wider constellation of Quaker organizations. The review included an examination of the two development programs it had been sponsoring–Right Sharing of World Resources and the International Quaker Aid programs–which it had originally undertaken in response to the concerns about inequalities in the international order that had so energized the 1967 Conference.

These programs were a considerable burden on the organization's resources. The financial administration was especially burdensome. Processing the many donation checks, sometimes with specific designations, accounting for these designations, writing checks to the project recipients and managing funds in an international finance system, all of this with books kept clear of confusion with the organization's own operating budget and involving relatively small amounts of money–the Executive Committee had come to see all of this as a distraction from FWCC's and the Sections' core mission, which was to bring Friends together and strengthen Quaker fellowship through consultations and other gatherings across all international, cultural and theological boundaries.

In the face of these longstanding difficulties, the Executive Committee decided to refocus FWCC's energies on what it saw as its core mission and to devolve both of the development programs. It decided to terminate its sponsorship and involvement with Right Sharing of World Resources, notwithstanding the fact that Right Sharing did actually fulfill FWCC's mission of bringing all Friends together in Spirit-led work.

RSWR had been a program of the American Section for its entire life (whereas the right sharing programs in the European and Near East Section were programs of their yearly meetings). To the Friends who were so deeply committed to its work, the decision to cut them off by the worldwide body's Executive Committee felt at the time rather top-down and, frankly, unQuakerly (Wang, L., personal communication, Summer, 2017). Some Friends were so disillusioned by the move that they left FWCC. Eventually, some Friends did come to understand how the move was better for FWCC, but at the time it felt to many like an assault on a vital Quaker ministry and a betrayal of the vision that had seemed so Spirit-led at the Fourth World Conference. Ultimately, however, RSWR came to feel that its release from FWCC had benefited the program after all (Wang, L., personal communication, Summer, 2017).

In response to the decision, Roland Kreager, RSWR's part-time staff person, and Linnea Wang, its clerk, reached out to all the Quaker organizations that they thought might take the program under their wings. Many of these organizations expressed great good will but none felt that RSWR fit their mission.

After these disappointments, Roland Kreager and Linnea Wang met for worshipful discernment over the phone and it became clear that they would try to establish Right Sharing of World Resources as its own independent program. They were convinced that the flame that had ignited at the Fourth World Conference had not sputtered out, that a great deal of support for the mission remained, and most importantly, that God was not yet done with them (Wang, L., personal communication, Summer, 2017).

In February 1999, they gathered Friends who had been involved with the program and met for five days at Quaker Knoll Camp in Wilmington, Ohio, to plan the devolution and create a new organization. They brought a recommendation to the Executive Committee of FWCC and at its Annual Meeting in March of 1999, FWCC released the Right Sharing of World Resources program.

Right Sharing of World Resources was incorporated as a 501c3 nonprofit in Ohio on April 2, 1999, and Roland Kreager continued as the sole staff person, working out of what was literally a closet in the building owned by Community Friends Meeting in Cincinnati, Ohio. Colin Saxton became the board of trustees' first clerk, serving until 2004.

## RSWR as an Independent Program

Right Sharing struggled to survive, initially, but it continued the work it had been doing under the auspices of FWCC-Section of the Americas–providing grants to small, grassroots organizations focused on building small businesses owned by women. These first projects were in Tamil Nadu, India.

By 2000, the program was on its feet. The board hired an education coordinator tasked with promoting the program among Friends, beginning with Sally Miller, who had served as clerk of the FWCC Right Sharing Committee and then on Right Sharing's board.

Soon after RSWR became an independent program, director Roland Kreager was inspired to change the way its funding worked using the microcredit model developed by Muhammad Yunus and the Grameen Bank in Bangladesh. Under this model, the women in the communities with which RSWR was working were organized into self-help groups and the groups received the RSWR grants, rather than giving grants directly to individual projects. The groups then gave loans to the women for their projects, which the women repaid to the group with interest. This is how RSWR works today.

In 2002, the program clarified its mission, identifying three guiding principles for its operation and its projects that it had gleaned from listening to its project partners. The first was mutual support and accountability: the board and staff would help each other and hold each other accountable, and the women building their businesses would help each other, as well, if any of them ran into difficulties or couldn't make their loan payments. The second principle was local self-reliance: the businesses would serve local markets and where possible use local sources and materials. The third was sustainability: the projects were to generate income that would ensure their continuing survival as businesses, and interest was charged on their loans so that the self-help groups could continue to serve them and grow to serve others. That same year, projects in Kenya and Sierra Leone were added to the program.

RSWR launched a website in 2004, but it suffered from lack of technical expertise until a 2010 capital campaign make it possible to upgrade the site. The problems with the website reflected a lack of clear vision for the wider educational aspects of the program, of which the website was a part (Eagleson, 2013).

To address these and other issues, the board held a strategic planning retreat in 2005, but implementation of its decisions proceeded somewhat slowly. That year, the office moved to Richmond, Indiana, to be closer to Earlham College and the FUM offices, in order to build a stronger relationship with FUM and to tap Earlham students as interns. The central office is still in Richmond today.

That year RSWR also added Cindi Goslee, Roland Kreager's wife, as proposals coordinator, who developed a standardized format for project reports from project partners and tightened up the whole grant process. In 2007, Sarah Northrop joined RSWR as clerical support; she became Program Director in 2012 and remains with the program today (personal communication, August 31, 2017).

However, by 2007, it had become clear that the program needed more resources to achieve the goals it had set for itself in 2005. The next year, the board launched a capital-building campaign with a goal of $2 million, only to fall prey to the Great Recession. Even after extending the campaign a year, it netted only $1 million.

Like most nonprofits during the Great Recession, Right Sharing had to tap its reserves to make its grants, and continued to do so now and then until 2016. Annual income dropped 15% in 2008, from $418,000 to $367,000, and worked its way back up fitfully to $407,000 in 2012.

In 2011, Roland Kreager left the position of General Secretary. The board and all who loved him learned of his death in 2016 with deep sadness. Sylvia Graves served as interim director until Betty Tonsing came on in 2012. In 2014, she filled in again until Jacqueline Stillwell became director in January 2015. Jacqueline Stillwell remains Right Sharing's director today.

In 2012, the program engaged Grace LaClair as a consultant to help the board review its organization and processes. The board decided to restructure itself, reducing the number of committees from five to three, and implementing more standard practices for governance and finance, including conducting the program's first audit in 2012 (Eagleson, 2013).

In 2010, the board had reviewed its 2005 strategic plan, and continued to work on strategic planning for the next four years, finally approving a new strategic plan in October of 2014 for 2014 through 2017. The new plan outlined four major goals:

1. Increase and improve overseas programs to serve more people and serve them better.
2. Strengthen the evaluation measures and increase the positive impact of the work.
3. Empower women by increasing their leadership capacity and roles in the programs.
4. Articulate the program's spiritual message in a compelling way.

The new plan changed the practice of basing the number of approved grants on the contributions expected over the next six months, and then writing checks as the money came in. Understanding the frustration of project partners who were being forced to wait for funds before they could start their work, the board now sets money aside so that grants can be paid as soon as they are approved (Eagleson, personal communication, September 25, 2017).

Grants are usually $4,000 to $5,500; $5,500 is the maximum grant amount. Each grant is expected to support 20-75 women. The program seeks to give a total of $250,000 per year in grants. It also provides training and support to help the women's businesses succeed (Northrop, personal communication, August 31, 2017).

## Right Sharing's Impact

The Quaker concern for the right sharing of the world's resources stands as a milestone in the evolution of Quaker social consciousness and witness. Right Sharing of World Resources is the first formal program in the history of Friends to address economic justice issues and economic suffering directly. It is the first to do so in the international arena but also unique in the way it has also sought to change the behavior of Friends in the over-developed world.

Right Sharing also combines the witness of service with an advocacy witness aimed at changing a global financial system that abets that suffering, even though this aspect of its mission has never been as successful as its grants program. In this combined service-and-advocacy aspect, Right Sharing was part of a new awakening in Quaker consciousness that began in earnest in the middle of the twentieth century.

This was a relatively new way to think and act among Friends. For two hundred and fifty years until the rise of so-called liberal Quakerism around the turn of the twentieth century, Quaker witness had focused on changing individuals, and mostly only other Quakers, at that, through gospel ministry. Even the radical ideas and practices of the first generation of Friends had not tried to understand or change the world order, as such, but rather to be channels of a new order in Christ. Not until Seebohm Rowntree published *Poverty: A Study in Town Life* in 1901 did Friends look closely at the way social and economic *structures* impoverished people.

But during the Fourth World Conference of Friends in 1967, Quaker awareness of the disparities between the world's rich and poor reached full maturity and it galvanized action. For the first time, a Quaker organization sought to directly address some of the structural aspects of economic injustice and inequality and to provide a viable alternative to the status quo. That ministry remains vital today, fifty years later.

## Right Sharing Today

Yet fifty years later, the problems that Right Sharing seeks to address still remain. One point two billion people still live in extreme poverty, that is, on less than $1.25 a day. The world's over-developed countries still dominate the global financial system and still skew it in their favor, and they still do little to ameliorate the suffering through international aid. The world's richest countries—20% of the world's population—still consume 75% of the world's resources. Globalization has allowed market forces to reach into every little corner of the world, and the Market has acquired near god-like status among many of the world's elites.

Yet Right Sharing of World Resources has never given up on its original vision and by its own historical standards, Right Sharing is thriving. And it is still evolving. From its original concept of "right sharing" it now conceives of its work as "Jubilee justice," in which, in the words of the theologian Walter Brueggemann, "You find out what belongs to whom and give it back." Right

Sharing's basic idea is still wealth redistribution through capital grants to women's self-help groups, which support small-scale, income-generating businesses with loans. And it still sees itself as a partnership, in which one set of partners is the donors—Quakers and others—who are "seeking to live more justly, providing capital to help support micro-enterprises, and experiencing jubilee justice," and the other partners are the women's self-help groups, who "are living sabbath economics in their own community" (What is the Heart of RSWR?, n.d.,).

Right Sharing of World Resources continues to demonstrate that "living justly" is possible. It continues to raise a light toward which many people turn from both sides of the divide between rich countries and poor countries. And it continues to build a bridge across that divide with Spirit-led witness.

## References

American Section RSWR Committee. (1975). Minutes (October 18). William Penn House, Washington, D.C. FRG: Right Sharing of World Resources, Friends Collection and Earlham College Archives, Richmond IN.

Barritt, D. P. (1969). *Right Sharing of World Resources*. Friends World Committee for Consultation. FRG: Right Sharing of World Resources, Friends Collection and Earlham College Archives, Richmond IN.

Birmingham, W. (1967). Essay written in 1967 and attached to a 1968 letter by J. P. Haughton distributed on behalf of FWCC Interim Committee. FRG: Right Sharing of World Resources, Friends Collection and Earlham College Archives, Richmond IN.

Birmingham, W., Birmingham, M. (1965). Christian Responsibility for the Use of Natural Resources. In Schaffer, B. (Ed.) *No Time But This Present*. Friends World Committee for Consultation.

Cattell, E.L. (1978). The Spiritual Basis for Right Sharing of the World's Resources. In *Right Sharing of World Resources: Basic Concerns*. Committee on Right Sharing of World Resources of Friends World Committee for Consultation. FRG: Right Sharing of World Resources, Friends Collection and Earlham College Archives, Richmond IN.

Cooper, C.W. (Ed.). (1969). *Break the New Ground: Seven Essays by Contemporary Quakers*. Birmingham, England: Friends World Committee for Consultation.

Cope, Alfred Haines. (1975). Managing World Resources. Published by the author, Syracuse, NY. FRG: Right Sharing of World Resources, Friends Collection and Earlham College Archives, Richmond IN.

Eagleson, M. (2013.) A Recent History of RSWR, Inc. Right Sharing of World Resources, Friends Collection and Earlham College Archives, Richmond IN.

FWCC. (1968). Report of the Fourth World Conference of Friends. Friends World Committee for Consultation. (1979) Memorandum "To the Preparatory Committee for the New International Development Strategy (Established under Resolution 33/193). FRG: Right Sharing of World Resources, Friends Collection and Earlham College Archives, Richmond IN.

*Give One Per Cent More!* (1969). Friends World Committee for Consultation, European and Near East Section, Birmingham and London, England. FRG: Right Sharing of World Resources, Friends Collection and Earlham College Archives, Richmond IN.

Hadley, H. M. (1991). *Quakers World Wide: A History of FWCC.* Friends World Committee for Consultation, London.

Haughton, J. P. (1968). Right Sharing of World Resources. FWCC Interim Committee. FRG: Right Sharing of World Resources, Friends Collection and Earlham College Archives, Richmond IN.

How to Live on One Hundred Dollars a Year. (1972). RSWR Committee, FWCC American Section and Fellowship Council. FRG: Right Sharing of World Resources, Friends Collection and Earlham College Archives, Richmond IN.

Implementing the One Percent More Program for Overseas Development: Notes from a Consultation. (1970). Friends World Committee for Consultation-American Section and Fellowship Council. FRG: Right Sharing of World Resources, Friends Collection and Earlham College Archives, Richmond IN.

Kreager, R. (2000). Early History of the Right Sharing of World Resources Program. Section 1 of Policy manual in MS Word 2011, (Office files), Right Sharing of World Resources, Richmond, IN.

Moore, J. F. (Ed.) (1969). *Seek, Find Share: Responses to No Time But This Present.* Friends World Committee for Consultation.

Richardson, B. D. (n.d.). Rich Countries, Poor Countries . . . Does Your Shopping Basket Hold the Key? FRG: Right Sharing of World Resources, Friends Collection and Earlham College Archives, Richmond IN.

(RSWR)*Right Sharing of the World's Resources.* (1972). Friends World Committee for Consultation Section of the Americas, International Affairs Committee. Right Sharing of World Resources, Friends Collection and Earlham College Archives, Richmond IN.

(RSWR) Right Sharing of World Resources Consultation. (1994). *Report of the Right Sharing of World Resources Consultation* [Ghost Ranch], (August 25-26). Ghost Ranch, New Mexico: Right Sharing of World Resources, Friends Collection and Earlham College Archives, Richmond IN.

Rowntree, B.S. (1901). *Poverty: A Study of Town Life*. London: Macmillan & Co.

Schaffer, B. (Ed.) (1965). *No Time But This Present,* Friends World Committee for Consultation, Birmingham, England. FRG: Right Sharing of World Resources, Friends Collection and Earlham College Archives, Richmond IN.

Sein, H. (1978*).* Toward a New World Order. In *Right Sharing of World Resources: Basic Concerns.* Committee on Right Sharing of World Resources of Friends World Committee for Consultation. FRG: Right Sharing of World Resources, Friends Collection and Earlham College Archives, Richmond IN.

*The New International Order–The Promise and the Reality* 1977. FWCC European and Near East Section. FRG: Right Sharing of World Resources, Friends Collection and Earlham College Archives, Richmond IN.

*We Must Share the World's Resources* (1972), Right Sharing of World Resources Program, Friends World Committee, American Section and Fellowship Council. FRG: Right Sharing of World Resources, Friends Collection and Earlham College Archives, Richmond IN.

What is the Heart of RSWR? (n.d.) FRG: Right Sharing of World Resources, Friends Collection and Earlham College Archives, Richmond IN.

White, G.F. (1972). Moral Issues Concerning the Global Environment. FRG: Right Sharing of World Resources, Friends Collection and Earlham College Archives, Richmond IN.

White, G.F. (1978). Stewardship of the Earth. In *Right Sharing of World Resources: Basic Concerns.* Committee on Right Sharing of World Resources of Friends World Committee for Consultation. FRG: Right Sharing of World Resources, Friends Collection and Earlham College Archives, Richmond IN.

*World Resources–Dilemma and Concern* (1976). FWCC European and Near East Section. (Office files), Right Sharing of World Resources, Richmond, IN.

(WRG) World Resources Group (1970). Notes from the World Resources Group business meeting during the World Resources Gathering, Sigtuna, Sweden (August 8-9). FRG: Right Sharing of World Resources, Friends Collection and Earlham College Archives, Richmond IN.

# Discussion Questions

1. AFSC's work in the coalfields relied heavily on "scholarship in social welfare, community education, and vocational retraining." To what extent does Quaker activism today rely on and incorporate scholarship?

2. Is there any hope that extractive industries in West Virginia will wane in the future? Do increasing profits of non-resident corporations help or hinder these extractive industries?

3. FCNL seeks to employ a decision-making approach that coincides with Quaker principles. Describe and assess those decision-making approaches.

4. How would you answer Ruth Flower's question—"Is Congress the 'Wrong Place' to Seek an End to Poverty?"

5. The chapter on the Quaker United Nations Office describes its work on small arms and financing for development. How do these issues fit with Quaker values, and what other global issues are important to you?

6. To what extent does globalization help the mission of Right Sharing of World Resources? To what extent does it hurt RSWR?

7. How successful have the Quaker organizations in this section been? How should success be measured?

# PART IV
## Historical Engagement by Friends

# 10 | The Radical Hicksite Critique of the Emerging Capitalist Order: Cornelius C. Blatchly, Benjamin Webb, and Friends, 1827-1833

## By Thomas D. Hamm, Earlham College

For the past century, liberal Quaker theology, whether in the British Isles, Friends General Conference, or independent yearly meetings in North America, has usually been associated with economic liberalism: skeptical about capitalism and laissez faire, often angry about the injustices that unrestricted free markets can produce. Many Friends assume that such an association has always been the case. But theological liberalism does not always go hand-in-hand with antagonism toward capitalism or affection for socialism. Anyone who has studied nineteenth-century Unitarianism in the United States will know that one can be a critic of Christian orthodoxies and still embrace the orthodoxies of Adam Smith, David Ricardo, and John Stuart Mill.[1]

In the 1830s, following the Hicksite Separation of 1827-1828, a small group of Hicksite Friends in New York City, Philadelphia, and Wilmington, Delaware, emerged as radical critics of the emerging American market economy. Friends like Dr. Cornelius C. Blatchly in New York, Warder Cresson in the neighborhood of Philadelphia, and Benjamin Webb in Wilmington blasted banks and banking, called for more equitable distribution of wealth, and endorsed the emerging workingmen's movement.

In the case of Webb, Cresson, and Blatchly, economic critiques became entwined in theological controversy. By 1831, some thought that the Hicksites were on the verge of another separation. Some Hicksites were convinced that a

---

[1] See, for example, Howe (1970).

conservative leadership had betrayed the principles of liberty of conscience that had been at the heart of the reorganization of the yearly meeting. But most "weighty" Friends in Philadelphia and the other Hicksite yearly meetings were certain that they had beaten back a dangerous outbreak of "ranterism" that threatened all organization and discipline among Friends. Ironically, these Friends may also have been influenced by their relative economic affluence. The radical critique Webb and his allies had offered disappeared, not to surface again until the twentieth century among Friends.

These Friends, of course, had just experienced a bitter split, the Hicksite Separation of 1827-1828 (Ingle, 1986). At its center had been the ministry of Long Island Friend Elias Hicks (1748-1830). Hicks's questioning of orthodox Christian doctrines on the divinity of Christ and the authority of the Bible had deeply troubled some Friends, who became known as Orthodox Quakers. In Hicks's intimations that Jesus was not born the Christ in a Virgin Birth, but instead became the savior of humanity through perfect obedience to the Inward Light, they saw a denial of His divinity. And Hicks's offhand comments about how the Bible, through misinterpretation and misunderstanding, had been the source of as much evil as good in the world struck them as infidelity. Hicks, however, claimed that he was the Quaker traditionalist, resisting the inroads of un-Quakerly doctrine that were the fruits of the association of Orthodox Friends with non-Quaker evangelicals in assorted reform and humanitarian groups. Many Friends—a majority in New York, Philadelphia, and Baltimore yearly meetings—supported Hicks.

Ironically, however, less than five years after separating from Orthodox Friends in part because the Orthodox were perceived as threatening spiritual freedom and "liberty of conscience," some of the most conspicuous Hicksite leaders found themselves cast in a conservative role, trying to squelch fellow Hicksites. "Some of us have contributed largely to excite the younger and inexperienced part of society to free inquiry—we have treated subjects *deemed sacred*, with great freedom, and thus have given an impetus to a ball that has rolled beyond our reach and over the line that *we* think should bound it" (Ingle, 1984, p. 131), was the conclusion of Benjamin Ferris, a Wilmington Friend who had been one of Elias Hicks's most committed supporters. Now, weighty Hicksites like Ferris were unwilling to concede the same liberty they had previously claimed.

The conflict in Wilmington was the most prolonged and serious and the best documented. The Wilmington Hicksites were a formidable group. One historian has concluded that at this time, "the Quaker meeting was the most potent private institutional force in town life." Wilmington Hicksites such as William Gibbons,

Benjamin Ferris, and William Poole had been among the most articulate defenders of Elias Hicks. Gibbons had founded a journal, the *Berean,* to advance Hicksite views and attack what he and like-minded Friends saw as the aggressions of evangelical Protestant clergy. Ferris's "Amicus" letters, a long-running debate with a Presbyterian clergyman in a local religious journal, subsequently collected and published as a substantial book, had been a chronic source of irritation to Orthodox Friends in Philadelphia Yearly Meeting. In 1827, one would have thought it an unlikely place to be a center of Hicksite reaction against "infidelity." But by 1830, it had become just that (Cavey, 1992, p. 165; Ingle, 1986, pp. 55-61, 98-102, 131-33).

At the center of the controversy in Wilmington was Benjamin Webb. A native of Chester County, Pennsylvania, born in 1786, Webb had moved to Wilmington as a young man and had become a successful tanner. A friend described him as "a man of great energy and remarkably perceiving in all his undertakings." Webb served as public agent for William Gibbons's *Berean* (Harlan, 1914, p. 331; Swayne, 1851; Webb, 1831, pp. 49-50; Ingle, 1984, pp. 129-30; Webb, 1831, Feb. 26).

By 1830, however, Webb was at odds with Gibbons and other weighty Hicksites in Wilmington. Central to that conflict was Webb's public embrace of the freethinker and reformer Robert Dale Owen, whose ideas Webb was disseminating through a new journal, the *Delaware Free Press.*

In the late 1820s, Robert Dale Owen was one of the most controversial figures in the United States. Born in Scotland in 1801, he was the son of Robert Owen, an industrialist who had sought to make his mill towns models of a just society and who by 1817 had become an incipient socialist. In 1825 the Owens had financed a utopian community at New Harmony, Indiana, that attracted wide attention for its *avant-garde* educational and economic theories and hostility to orthodox Christianity. The New Harmony experiment collapsed quickly, and in 1829 Owen settled in New York City and began publishing a new journal, the *Free Enquirer.* Owen's associate was Frances "Fanny" Wright, an Englishwoman who was, if anything, more notorious for having founded an interracial utopian community, Nashoba, in Tennessee in 1825. The *Free Enquirer* was a vehicle for free thought as well as an early advocate for women's rights and birth control. "Owenism" and "Fanny Wrightism" quickly became sources of horror for evangelical Christians. Owen was equally radical on economic matters, advocating the formation of labor unions and "workingmen's parties." He found some readers among Hicksite Friends. When Wright and Owen visited Wilmington, several attended their lectures (Leopold, 1940, pp. 47-84; Spurlock, 1988, pp. 39-41; Carwardine, 1993, p. 66; Palmer, 2002, p. 113).

According to Webb, Gibbons had looked with disfavor on Owen and New Harmony and wanted to attack them in the *Berean*. Webb found Owen's theories attractive, and in 1829 began publishing a like-minded journal in Wilmington, the *Delaware Free Press*. Meanwhile Gibbons, who was convinced that some Hicksites were venturing into morally and spiritually dangerous territory, launched a separate attack on the *Free Enquirer*, spurred by a gratuitous copy that Owen had sent to him in October 1829. This spurred an acrimonious exchange of letters between Owen and Gibbons. By the end of the year, Gibbons had penned a scathing critique of "Owenism" and had rushed it into print under the title of *An Exposition of Modern Skepticism* (Ingle, 1984, pp. 129-30; Gibbons, 1830).

The *Exposition* was an unrestrained and personal excoriation of Owen and Wright. "Groping in the thick darkness of your own delusions, you espouse opinions full of absurdity–are constantly resorting to a beginning of principles and credulously yielding assent to irrational propositions," Gibbons charged. The free thinker was "a subverter of morals, and of the social relations,–such a violator of common decency, and of the common charities of life, must be as inaccessible to reason, as he is undeserving of the respect of mankind." Gibbons closed with a double appeal: "The case is not a mere difference of opinion, on a subordinate point of Christian faith; *it is Christianity, or atheism.*" Gibbons worried that, "for the first time, we witness the American press prostituted by foreigners, to the dissemination of opinions which the wise and good, in all ages of the world, have held in utter abhorrence." He had no doubt of "the glorious triumph of Christianity over every attempt of this sort, yet the peace and happiness of many will be thereby disturbed, or destroyed" (Gibbons, 1830, pp. 7, 14, 29-34, 42-43, 45-52).

In the *Exposition*, Gibbons accused Owen of "addressing the laboring, and poorer classes, and holding out to them, delusive promises of improving their scheme, that must infallibly prejudice every temporal interest, and rob them of their only refuge, and consolation in adversity, in sickness, and in sorrow." The relationship between Owen's socialist, anti-capitalist leanings and Hicksites is more complicated than the relatively straightforward opposition of Hicksites like Gibbons to Owen's religious views (Gibbons, 1830, p. 45).

By the late 1820s, unrest was becoming manifest among both skilled and unskilled workers in eastern cities like Philadelphia and New York. With the rise of factories and the growing consolidation of small workshops into larger ones, workingmen were increasingly losing control of their conditions of labor. This led to varied movements for improvement. As an Owen biographer summarized the situation, "the industrial worker demanded shorter hours of labor, higher wages, cheaper forms of justice, a lien law, and, above all, better educational facilities for his children." How to achieve these goals divided workers. Some saw the solution in escaping factory labor entirely through the provision of free land in the west. Others, accepting factories, wanted to improve conditions. They favored the organizations of workingmen's associations, incipient labor unions. In some places these became political parties, which pressed for the election of workers to city councils and state legislatures. Often coupled with these more immediate concerns were broader attacks on banks and monopolies and the increasing concentration of wealth and political power. Some advocates of the workingmen's cause, like Owen and Wright, were freethinkers (Leopold 1940, p. 85; Schultz 1993, pp. 211-38; Wilentz, 1986, pp. 145-254; Grasso, 2011, pp. 297-98).

The relationship of Friends to this rising labor movement and its discontents is complex. Hicksites had commented negatively on the prominence of wealthy Friends in the ranks of Orthodox leadership in the 1820s. Thus one describing the arrival of Orthodox Friends at a quarterly meeting: "the combined forces of Orthodoxy in all the Yearly Meeting came upon us at once & very splendidly too[,] bouncing chariots and prancing steeds[,] plated harness & servants etc." Elias Hicks had been eloquent. "Riches is a great hurt to Society. Parents if they cant have the heart to bestow the surplus of their trader income on charitable objects they had better sink it in the sea than leave a greater deal to their children. They are much better without it," he preached in Philadelphia in 1819. In Vermont, Rowland T. Robinson agreed. "The deep rooted cause of our comparatively spiritual desolation as a religious society? Avarice! The love of wealth," he wrote. Indeed, one of the accusations that Orthodox Friends leveled at Hicks was that he incited envy against well-to-do Friends (Foulke, 1827, 12th Mo. 6; Pryor, 1819, 10th Mo. 31; Robinson, n.d.; Society of Friends 1828, p. 375).

Elias Hicks and like-minded Friends were not necessarily radical when they warned against love of money and urged charity for the poor—those themes went back to the beginnings of Christianity. But Hicks and other Hicksites offered at least a vague critique of the emerging market economy. "I have beheld it to my grief & sorrow many who embark in the things of the world by not attending to the Law of God written on the table of each of our hearts have extended their concerns beyond all bounds and as was said of old 'Come let us go into such a City & buy and sell and git gain' and grievously wounded their own souls and injured others," he preached in 1817. Indeed, "it would be much better for a Man who had thousands & tens of thousands to tye his money in a bag and sink it into the ocean than it should become a scourge to their children or land themselves in eternal misery for a rich man cannot inherit the kingdom of heaven." A year earlier, Hicks had called it "a cause of sorrow and lamentation to find that the members of our favored society" were "running into cities to get riches." There they sought wealth "by their wit and their learning in opposition to Honest and frugal industry." They fell into other bad habits. If they were unable to pay their debts and took advantage of the bankruptcy laws to "exonerate their debts," it was like "the priest who forgives sins," a comparison that Hicks did not intend favorably. On the other hand, Friends sometimes used the law to coerce debtors, something that Hicks considered equally unchristian (John, 1832, 1st Mo. 11; Hicks, 1816, 3rd Mo. 8; *Pryor, 1817, 11th Mo. 25; Gould, 1827, p. 244)[2]

Hicksites saw the ill effects of "covetousness" in two features of the economic world of the early nineteenth century. One was a steady increase in rents, something that would have been especially apparent to farmers in long-settled areas like southeastern Pennsylvania, the Hudson Valley, and Long Island. As early as 1788, the minister Hugh Judge had recorded his belief that "renters are too generally oppressed by their landlords in many places, and that it is an evil in the land. . . . My heart feels for the poor, the widows and the fatherless; and the distresses of the oppressed are at times heavy upon my soul." Thirty years later, Elias Hicks agreed that "covetousness" caused "increase of rents" and so consequent hardships for many. Traveling in Ireland early in the nineteenth century, Jesse Kersey, another minister, had seen the rent-racking of Irish peasants, and by 1826, he feared that some American Friends were engaged in the same behaviors: "I regret the consequences produced by the conduct of plain men as it respects hard dealing," he wrote. "These oppress the poor and make the way of such difficult in the world: high rents, little wages and high prices for every little necessary." Edward Hicks, the painter-minister, thought that no one would ever need to own more than 25 acres of land "with suitable improvements," 50 at most. He urged that if a Friend owned 150 acres, he should keep 50; sell 50 and then lend the proceeds interest-free to "some poor Friend"; and lease rent-free the last 50 to another poor Friend who could cultivate it until he had saved enough to buy his own "little farm" (Judge, 1841, p. 149; Hicks, 1816, 3rd Mo. 8; Kersey, 1851, pp. 63-64; Kersey, 1826, 8th Mo. 26; Hicks, 1845, p. 6).

Significantly, a few prominent Hicksites were equally critical of banking. Lending money at interest was "usury, the great high priest of the mammon of unrighteousness," Edward Hicks warned. Hugh Judge had urged his sons "to have as little to do with banks as possible." Far better for them to "run no risks

---

[2] This critique of the emerging market economy is central to Doherty (1967).

at all" by borrowing money, but instead to "move on slow and sure." Philadelphia Hicksite merchant Thomas W. Pryor offered a more detailed analysis in the midst of the Panic of 1819, a major economic depression. In his diary, he bemoaned "the bubbles speculations and finesses of finance that have so long amused us and which have produced such various rapid changes and alterations of wealth." He concluded with disapproval: "The vast oceans of bank paper that tempted such multitudes of adventurers upon its swelling waves has at last subsided and the ebbing of the faithless flood has betrayed too many who were easily and carelessly floating upon its easy undulations." Young Dillwyn Parrish in Philadelphia went further: "As a cancer in the human Body so are private banks in the Body politic. Private bankers are in fact publick Pick pockets." Interestingly, although Hicksites pointedly criticized the corruptions that they saw wealth working among English Friends, none noted the banking connections of some of the leaders of London Yearly Meeting (Hicks, 1845, pp. 6-7; Pryor, 1819, 6th Mo. 30; Parrish, n.d.).[3]

These social concerns were not central to Elias Hicks's ministry. But by 1830, a few other Hicksites had become committed social reformers, convinced that both their faith and the working out of God's will in the world demanded fundamental changes in the economic and political structure of American society. The two most visible were Warder Cresson in Philadelphia and Dr. Cornelius Camden Blatchly in New York City.

Blatchly was a native of New Jersey, born in 1773. How he became a Friend is unclear. By the 1820s, he was visible in humanitarian and reform circles in New York. An admirer wrote: "I know no man in America who is more liberal and philanthropic in his intercourse with men, whether as a physician, a minister of the gospel, or a private citizen." One scholar has called him the first socialist thinker in the United States. After completing his medical training, he devoted himself to serving the poor in New York City. In 1817 Blatchly had published *Some Causes of Popular Poverty, Derived from the Enriching Nature of Interests, Rent, Duties, Inheritances, and Agreement with Scripture.* As the title suggests, Blatchly's book was a spirited critique of the emerging market economy. "Commerce should be restricted to things necessary, useful, and convenient; its excess is a vice that produces the most serious and destructive consequences in individuals and states," Blatchly wrote. It was wrong, he argued, that "millions of industrious and frugal people toil from imbecile youth to decrepid age, without being able to obtain riches." Instead, he asserted, wealth should flow to "the artists, scientifics, and labourers who enrich the nations." Along the way, Blatchly condemned high

---

[3] For English Friends and banking, see Walvin (1997, pp. 61-81).

rents, lending money at interest, and banking generally. Of the last, he wrote, "as it goes still farther, and issues paper to several times the amount of the specie stock, it becomes so many times the more unjust." Blatchly was especially outspoken against child labor in England, whose increase in the United States he feared. He concluded with an exhortation to fellow Christians: "I really think, since God works by his saints and servants, that it is the duty of many of them to investigate the cause of the afflictions and sufferings of the poor and needy" (Blatchly, 1817, pp. 194, 196-97, 203-04, 213-20).[4]

In 1822, Blatchly carried his enthusiasm for reform to new levels by leading in the organization of the New York Society for Promoting Communities. A combination of professionals, artisans, and liberal clergy, its founding manifesto drew on the experiences of sectarian groups like the Rappites and Shakers and reprinted extensive excerpts from the writings of Robert Owen as well. The society proposed the organization of new communities in the west that would be models of cooperative economics and non-coercive government. As Sean Wilentz has noted, Blatchly's vision of a new world was based on an "ill-defined 'inclusive system,' where wealth would benefit all," and was so focused on "rural motifs" that he paid little attention to urban conditions, despite living in "one of the fastest-growing cities in the world." But, as Wilentz concludes, Blatchly

> should not be dismissed as an agrarian visionary or a pious crank and consigned to the oblivion of 'utopian' socialism. If nothing else, his writings proved that an egalitarian Christianity could still inspire radical plans to counter the coercive measures increasingly characteristic of evangelical reform. No one more bitterly denounced the evangelicals, particularly those 'false prophets' the Sabbatarians, than did Blatchly; no one was more insistent that 'we should not meddle with religion politically, but let that be between God and every man's conscience.'

In this, Blatchly presaged a later generation of radical Hicksite reformers (Blatchly, 1819, 8th Mo. 5; Bassett, 1954, pp. 88-90; Wilentz, 1986, pp. 159-60).

In 1824, Blatchly laid out his vision in long letters to Elias Hicks himself. He hoped that Hicks would endorse the communitarian movement, arguing that communitarianism was the highest form of Christianity. "If heaven is a spiritual community, should it be commenced on earth?" Blatchly answered affirmatively. "The selfish & exclusive systems of all civil institutions, do naturally & necessarily excite men to covet, envy, hate, fight, etc. because these systems are all radically

---

[4] For background on Blatchly, see Wilentz, 1986, pp. 158-59; Harris, 1967, pp. 10-19); and Foner, 1978, pp. 157-58.

wrong, being formed & managed by the dragon of heathenism & the old serpent of antichristianity. Spiritual Israel, God's people, are now in captivity to spiritual Babylon & Egypt, as really the external Jews were formerly in the bondage of Egypt & the captivity of Babylon." The command of Christ to be perfect and, Blatchly concluded, to "love to every neighbor as to myself, doing to each, as I would have him do to me (the best of all moral & social rules) can never be perfectly followed but in a perfect or just state of society. Only in a community of substance & property can any fully love each neighbor, and prove it" (Blatchly, 1824, 8th Mo. 5 & 10th Mo. 15).

Hicks was unpersuaded, responding that "exclusive property was best suited to a state of probation," which was human life in this world. "It is clearly discoverable that a state of trial and probation, is alloted to man, in this state of being, and he cannot unite with his fellow man, in such a manner, as to make a State of inclusive priviledges, and possession in common expedient and useful." Blatchly's theories were workable only if all of the members of his community were under the guidance of the Holy Spirit, and "for any association of men, however high they may stand in the varied sects of Christian professors, to undertake to establish such a community of commonage and inclusive priviledges it will all prove abortive, and will only be Babel of their own contriving." Even if somehow such a state could be achieved, Hicks concluded, "they must stop the promulgation of their species, for every Child born into the world, must have a religion and righteousness of his own, independent of his parents and external teachers, and this he must gain, through trial and temptation" (Hicks, 1824, 9th Mo. 25).

Unless it was in a short-lived group, the Friendly Association for Mutual Interests at Kendal, now Massillon, Ohio, which formed in 1826, Blatchly's vision never found realization in an actual community. (The Kendal group was made up largely of Friends and was regarded by neighbors as a "nest of infidelity.") Nor did Robert Owen, whose communitarian vision was much more secular than Blatchly's, show much interest. A few Philadelphia Friends embraced Owen's New Harmony. One, Philip M. Price, wrote in the fall of 1825 that he was "perfectly persuaded that the system of mutual co-operation in labor at no very distant period [would] become the prevailing system of society." But Price's father dismissed this as a "delusion," writing that "it will end in ruin and disappointment" because it was not based on Christianity. Blatchly was undeterred. As the workingmen's movement formed in New York City, he became a strong supporter. And when the *Free Enquirer* and *Delaware Free Press* began publication, Blatchly was in their columns. During the separation in New

York, Blatchly cast his lot with the Hicksites (Bassett, 1954, pp. 90-95; Price, P.M., 1825, Sept. 30; Price, P. 1825, 7th Mo. 29; Hinshaw, 1936-1950, p. 37).

Blatchly found a counterpart in a Philadelphia Hicksite, an erratic and colorful figure, Warder Cresson. Born into a well-to-do family in 1798, he lived for a time in Byberry near Philadelphia, but, as Friends there remembered, "was never much esteemed." By the time of the Separation he was married and farming at Gwynedd, Pennsylvania. He entered the public sphere in 1827, when he published an exhortation to the ministers and elders of his quarterly meeting, warning them that God would "continue to *overturn* and utterly lay waste all which stands in the will of man," like "outward laws and disciplines, which are only in part, and *to be done away,* to grace and truth *alone,* which is *perfect.*" Apparently Gwynedd Hicksites found him increasingly difficult, since by early in 1829 they had him "under dealing," significantly, for having identified himself with the Shakers, the largest communitarian group in the United States. Late that year, Cresson penned a long tract that marked his final break with Friends (Fox, 1971, pp. 148-57; Martindale and Dudley, n.d., pp. 116-17; *Warder, 1827, pp. 2-4).

Cresson's new exhortation, *Babylon The Great Is Falling!,* drew on many of the same themes that Blatchly had developed. "A monopoly of wealth is a monopoly of power," he wrote, and was a danger to any republic. Monopolies took varied forms. Among them, all "speculative and anti-republican," were "bank charters, acts of incorporation, . . . lotteries, . . . taverns," and, worst of all, "the endowment of colleges and priest-teaching academies, to prepare thousands and tens of thousands of 'locusts' to eat up every *'green thing in the land,'* (which they have almost done)." Indeed, Cresson saw "selfish lazy priests, lawyers, doctors, tavern keepers, hospitals, poor-houses, sheriffs, magistrates, jails bars and bolts" all as scourges that had to be "supported by the laborious and oppressed part of community." Cresson claimed that anyone "who is accumulating fortunes" was "a follower of Anti-Christ," since "it must be directly or indirectly, at the expense of the poor and oppressed." In fact, Cresson asserted, the current economy made humans like "so many different and separate little kingdoms, each one at variances and opposite to the other, the life of one, is death to the other, a fortune to one, is oppression to the other, a bargain to one, is a loss to the other." The only solution, he concluded was to "peaceably withdraw . . . into social communities." Cresson singled out Robert Owen's communitarian experiments as models. Otherwise, it was the duty of the Christian to follow Christ in being poor (Cresson, 1830, pp. 4-5, 9-11, 15-17, 19-20, 28-29, 35).

For Cresson, the tie between economics and Christianity was clear, and just about every church fell short, including Friends. Indeed, "all Christianity" would continue to be corrupt "while separate interests continue." Significantly, while

Cresson criticized Fanny Wright for her infidel views, he praised her honesty and social insight. He judged William Gibbons far worse. *An Exposition of Modern Skepticism*, Cresson wrote, read as if it had been "written by an Orthodox." All Friends, Cresson, concluded, had fallen (Cresson, 1839, pp. 26-29, 40-43, 50-51, 55-65).

Against this background of emerging economic radicalism, the appearance of Webb's *Delaware Free Press* was doubtless unsettling for some Wilmington Hicksites. From its opening issue, it advocated a class-based view of social problems; its goal was, in the words of George Reynolds, another Wilmington Hicksite, "to awaken the attention of the Working People to the importance of co-operation in order to attain that rank and station in society to which they are justly entitled by their virtues and industry, but from which they have been excluded." Its columns regularly "carried notices of strikes in the Wilmington area, descriptions of workers' celebrations in Philadelphia, excerpts of labor addresses in Massachusetts, and reprints from labor papers in New York," and blasted the "respectable classes, . . . acquiring riches, hypocrisy, and a goodly stock of church going religion." As editor, Webb urged the combination of working men's groups into a national movement, and publicized the "Working Men's Ticket" in local elections. Quakers made up about a third of the membership of the Association of Working People of New Castle County (AWPNCC), by far the largest single religious affiliation in the organization. The most careful student of the workingmen's movement in Wilmington, Jama Lazerow, describes Webb as a "key committeeman" in the AWPNCC. And his paper was, in Lazerow's words, "popular among area workers" (Webb, 1830, Aug. 7; Editorial 1830; Owen, 1830, June 30; Union of All Parties 1832, Sept. 17; Working Men's Ticket 1831, Oct. 1; Lazerow, 1995, pp. 100-03).

If Webb and his coadjutors had restricted themselves to economics, history might have been different. But for Webb, Blatchly, and Cresson, their critique of the emerging capitalist market economy was inextricably bound up with their faith. Indeed, Webb thought it impossible to separate politics and religion. "What a *pity* it was the Quakers led such ascetic lives as to pen themselves out from political affairs," Webb wrote privately early in 1831. "They will be in a few years little better than a set of Monks if they do not reform." Yet, while he thought it impossible to separate faith from politics, he was skeptical about the formation of political parties based on religion. "There is considerable exertion (secretly making) among Heretics to come out at the next presidential election, a measure to which I am decidedly opposed," Webb told a Chester County Friend. "I am opposed to mingling politics either with religion or heresy. It is enough, and all we ought to ask of orthodoxy, that we will not raise the hue & cry against her."

Religion had political implications, but that did not necessarily dictate the formation of religiously-based parties (Webb, 1831, 1st Mo. 10).

Ultimately, however, Owen, Wright, radical economics, and Hicksite reformation became entangled. And so the questions would be resolved through the disciplinary processes of Friends, processes that ended with Webb and like-minded Friends thrust out of Quakerism.

In New York City, Blatchly and his sympathizers had by 1830 become a distinct party within the Hicksite monthly meeting. His allies included Maria Imlay, a minister from Mount Holly, New Jersey, whom the Orthodox had disowned before the Separation; the merchants Elijah Crane and Isaac Hatch; and Phebe Johnson, a schoolteacher who had been disturbing Friends both Orthodox and Hicksite with her erratic preaching since 1824. Unfortunately, Blatchly wrote, the monthly meeting, was "the dupe of its lordlings," a few ministers, elders, and overseers. They moved systematically against the dissidents. Imlay, who fell under suspicion for subscribing to the *Free Enquirer* and attending meetings at the Owenite "Hall of Science," died before action could be taken against her, but Johnson, after ignoring several warnings against speaking in meeting, was disowned. Then Crane conveniently fell into financial difficulties, and the monthly meeting disowned him. By January 1831 Hatch and Blatchly were attending "free" religious assemblies in which "all sects opinions and parties could without restraint from human control relieve their own minds in the line of the ministry." The monthly meeting disowned Hatch in March 1831 (Blatchly, 1824, 8th Mo. 5; Blatchly, 1831, May 14; Crane, 1831, Sept. 24; NY Minutes 1929, 8th Mo. 5, 10th Mo. 7, 11th Mo. 4, 12th Mo. 2 & 1831 1st Mo. 5 & 3rd Mo. 2); Tatum, n.d.; Hinshaw, 1936-1950, p. 181; Owen, 1830, pp. 4-6).

This left only Blatchly, who by his own account had been the target of the monthly meeting's leaders for years. Late in 1829, his preparative meeting brought in a complaint that he had "attended lectures which have a tendency to lay waste the Christian religion," doubtless by Owen and/or Wright. Additionally, Blatchly had been making "communications in our Meetings for worship" that were "exercising & burdensome to Friends," and, despite being "sensible that it was so, he gave . . . no encouragement to expect that he should desist from what appeared to him to be a duty." In January 1830, however, the committee appointed to visit him reported that he had stopped attending the questionable lectures "as Friends are uneasy." The committee also reported that he had not spoken in meeting for several weeks and indicated that he probably would not so long "as there was an opposition to him." In May, the monthly meeting dropped the case. But by March 1831 Blatchly was attending the same "free" meetings as Isaac Hatch and had "been actively engaged therein as a preacher." When Friends approached him, he refused to discuss it. So in June 1831 he was disowned (Blatchly, 1831, May 14; NY Minutes 1829, 10th Mo. 7, 1830, 1st Mo. 6, 2nd Mo. 3, & 5th Mo. 5, 1831, 3rd Mo. 2, 5th Mo. 4, & 6th Mo. 1).

A few other Friends became identified with Blatchly and Webb, most notably two women: Phebe Johnson, a thorn in the side of authority for nearly a decade, who had moved from New York City to Philadelphia; and Elizabeth M. Reeder, a member of Green Street Meeting in the latter city. Reeder, who began appearing in meeting in a scarlet dress, especially vexed conservative Hicksites with her sermons, many of which were printed in the *Delaware Free Press*. But they dealt entirely with doctrinal and spiritual issues. Johnson and Reeder were apparently uninterested in the social side of the new reform cause.[5]

Weighty Friends in Wilmington were troubled but uncertain about how to deal with Webb. Early in 1830, Webb wrote that some Friends in Philadelphia were worried that Wilmington Friends had "adopted the opinions and principles of Frances Wright." Benjamin Ferris admitted that Friends were in a "time of *deep trial*," worse than the Separation, but needed to move carefully. He worried that the most fervent critics of Webb wanted to use the Discipline against him in the same spirit that the Orthodox had used it against the Hicksites, "*as a sword.*" Gibbons responded hotly. Previously he had told Ferris that if the monthly meeting could not deal with Webb, "it must be a dead, stinking carcass indeed, not worthy to remain on earth." Webb was the leader of "a confederacy of our own members, in the bosom of the church, whose avowed object is the destruction of Christ[ianit]y and the overthrow of the public worship of God" (For the Delaware Free Press, 1830a; Some Lucubrations, 1830, 8th Mo. 1830; Six Sentiments, 1830, 8th Mo. 1830; Ingle, 1984, pp. 131-37).

Thus began a long struggle that badly divided Wilmington Hicksites. In August 1830, Gibbons filed charges with the meeting overseers, who were charged with investigating violations of the Discipline. After almost a year of bitter argument, with Concord Quarterly Meeting intervening at one point, the monthly meeting disowned Webb in June 1831. The charge was that he had "been engaged, for some time past, in the publication of a periodical paper, wherein the authenticity of the scriptures and some of the fundamental doctrines of the christian religion are called in question." As was his right, he appealed the disownment to Concord Quarterly Meeting and Philadelphia Yearly Meeting. Both upheld it as proper (Webb, 1831, pp. 20-23, 53-57; Wilmington Minutes, 1831, 2nd Mo. 4, 3rd Mo. 4, 4th Mo. 1, 4th Mo. 29 & 6th Mo. 3; WPMC, 1830, 12th

---

[5]See, for example, Reeder, 1831, June 18 and 1831, Aug. 20.

Mo. 23; Wilmington QM Notes, 1831, 8th Mo.; Quarterly Meeting Committee Report, 1831, 2nd Mo. 23).

"I have lately passed through a scene, which has shown to my mind with indubitable clearness, what men of otherwise good moral character will do, in the cause of religion, when I was attacked by these wolves," Webb wrote in January 1831. "The spirit of intolerance," he editorialized later the same month in the *Delaware Free Press*, "has set at naught not only every principle of feeling and respect due from man to man, . . . but violated the most sacred obligations of peace and amity." Yet when Webb wrote about his experiences, he had little to say about his economic views. He saw his persecutors as driven entirely by doctrinal and spiritual bigotry and intolerance (Webb, 1831, 1st Mo. 10; Webb, 1831, Jan. 29).

Why did most Hicksites, part of a body that had a few years earlier rebelled against overbearing leaders and perceived intolerance, respond so sharply to Blatchly, Webb, and their sympathizers? The answer is two-fold. First, most Hicksites perceived themselves as defenders of good order. The dissenters of 1829-1832, particularly Johnson and Reeder, were clearly disorderly; Johnson had had that reputation for almost a decade. Ferris spoke for most Hicksites when he told Gibbons that in the course of the Separation, Hicksites had unleashed a spirit of free thinking, a spirit that now had to be restrained. Rachel Barker, another minister in Philadelphia, characterized Webb and his coadjutors as under the influence of "a spirit of ranterism," the Quaker equivalent of anarchy (Ingle, 1984, pp. 131, 136; Wilmington QM Notes, 1831, 8th Mo.; Wilmington Notes, 1831; Bringhurst, 1831, 3rd Mo. 20).

Moreover, Webb and like-minded Friends found themselves isolated and disowned because the cause that they linked with their "ranterism," labor and economic radicalism, apparently did not resonate with most Hicksites. The most careful student of Wilmington Quakerism, Verna Cavey, has noted in Wilmington "much of the leadership of Hicksite movement was representative not of the poor Quaker farmer": the Ferrises were "craftsmen of reputation"; William Poole "a noted mill owner"; Gibbons a physician, and Eli Hilles, the monthly meeting clerk, "a well-respected educator." Benjamin Ferris might have written during the Separation in 1827-1828 that "riches and the power and influence which they confer are dangerous things," but that insight did not lead him to unite with the views of Webb, Blatchly, and the Owenite labor reformers. Weighty New York Hicksite Jacob L. Mott was suspicious of "vague schemes to remodel social organizations." Gibbons was forthright in his condemnation of such views. Owenite theories, he wrote, were "calculated to operate on the passions of the uninstructed class of hearers, and to produce disgust with the present order of things." Their quest for "*equality* by legislation" was "chimerical." When the helpless poor faced hardship, then Friends should provide charity. But in Owen and Wright's proposals, Gibbons saw "wicked, profane attempts to subvert Christianity,–to render the people dissatisfied with their excellent government, and their religion and laws–to overthrow our well-tried institutions; and to establish in their room, ATHEISM AND ANARCHY." The problems of urban workers and the emerging factory system apparently held little concern for most Hicksites in the early 1830s (Cavey, 1992, pp. 85-86; Bush, 1902 p. 16; Ferris, n.d.; Gibbons, W. 1830, pp. 35-36; For the Delaware Free Press, 1830b; Mott, 1858, p. 16).

After 1832, Webb and his coadjutors largely faded from view. Phebe Johnson occasionally resurfaced, but no longer vexed Friends as she once had. Cornelius Blatchly died in December 1831. Webb gave up the *Delaware Free Press* in 1833. Elizabeth M. Reeder moved back to Bucks County in 1835. But some Hicksites remained convinced that they should have "the liberty of examining for themselves" what they should believe, and were openly critical of the disownment of Webb, Reeder, and Johnson. Lucretia Mott remembered that she and her husband James "came near 'losing our place,' by uttering our indignant protest against . . . intolerance." In her opinion, Wilmington Monthly Meeting lost its power when it disowned some of its "most active, benevolent citizens;" since then it had "had 'Ichabod' on its walls." Martha Smith in Bucks County, who, like Lucretia Mott, remained a member and recorded minister, mourned that recent events proved that in "reformation after reformation" leaders invariably, "after stepping out of the mother *church* and establishing themselves in power, begin to practice upon their own members what they felt to be oppressive." From Skaneateles, New York, another discontented Hicksite, Lydia P. Mott, wrote that "reform is necessary," and it was not just the "young and thoughtless" who weakened Friends, but "those who make broad the phylactery and accept appointments to deal with offenders, & put the law in force upon others." Within a decade, Hicksites would find themselves facing another set of reformers who would flirt with "infidelity" and radical reform movements. But these reformers would link their causes to two of the fundamental testimonies of Friends, peace and antislavery. And that is another story (Mott, 1836, 5th Mo. 19 & 1831, 3rd Mo. 16; Hinshaw, 1936-1950, p. 37; Webb, 1833, 1st Mo. 30; Green Street Minutes, 1835, 2nd Mo. 19; Kimber, 1842, 1st Mo. 15; Palmer, 2002, p. 113; Smith, 1844 p. 118; Mott, 1832, 4th Mo. 1).

# References

Bassett, T. D. S. (1954). The Quakers and Communitarianism. *Bulletin of Friends Historical Association,* 43(Autumn), 84-99.

Blatchly, C.C. (1817). *Some Causes of Popular Poverty, Derived from the Enriching Nature of Interests, Duties, Inheritances, and Agreement with Scripture.* Philadelphia: Eastwick & Stacy.

Blatchly, C.C. (1819, 8th Mo. 5). [Letter to Elias Hicks]. Elias Hicks Papers (Folder 227) Friends Historical Library, Swarthmore College, Swarthmore, PA.

Blatchly, C.C. (1824, 8th Mo. 5). [Letter to Elias Hicks]. Elias Hicks Papers (Folder 227) Friends Historical Library, Swarthmore College, Swarthmore, PA.

Blatchly, C.C. (1824, 10th Mo. 15). [Letter to Elias Hicks]. Elias Hicks Papers (Folder 227) Friends Historical Library, Swarthmore College, Swarthmore, PA.

Blatchly, C.C (1831, May 14). Extract of a Letter to One of the Editors of the *Delaware Free Press, Delaware Free* Press.

Bringhurst, D. (1831, 3rd Mo. 20). [Letter]. Letter to Hannah Hurnard, Hurnard Manuscripts, Friends Historical Library, Swarthmore College, Swarthmore, PA

Bush, L.P. (1903). Memoir of Benjamin Ferris, *Historical and Biographical Papers of the Historical Society of Delaware,* 4, 5-17.

Carwardine, R.J. (1993). *Evangelicals and Politics in Antebellum America* New Haven, CT: Yale University Press.

Cavey, V.M. (1992) *Fighting among Friends: The Quaker Separation of 1827 as a Study in Conflict Resolution.* Syracuse, NY: Syracuse University Press.

Crane, E. (1831, Sept. 24). [Letter]. *Delaware Free Press.*

Cresson, W. (1827). *An Humble and Affectionate Address to the Select Members of Abington Quarterly Meeting.* Philadelphia: John Young.

Cresson, W. (1830). *Babylon the Great Is Falling! The Morning Star, or Light from on High Written in Defence of the Rights of the Poor and Oppressed.* Philadelphia: Garden and Thompson.

Doherty, R.W. (1967). *The Hicksite Separation: A Sociological Analysis of Religious Schism in Early Nineteenth Century America* New Brunswick, NJ: Rutgers University Press.

Editorial (1830) *Delaware Free Press* (Sept. 25).

Editorial (1831) *Delaware Free Press* (Jan. 8).

Editorial Note (1831). *Delaware Free Press.* (May 14).

Ferris, B. (n.d.). [Fragmentary essay on the Separation]. Box 12, Ferris Papers, Friends Historical Library, Swarthmore College, Swarthmore, PA.

Foner, P.S. (1978). A Pioneer Proposal for a Women's Library. *Journal of Library History,* 13(Spring) 157-59.

For the Delaware Free Press. (1830a). *Delaware Free Press.* (Jan. 23).

For the Delaware Free Press. (1830b). *Delaware Free Press.* (Feb. 27).

Foulke, J. (1827, 12th Mo. 6) [Letter to George Hatton]. Foulke Family Papers (Box 2), Friends Historical Library, Swarthmore College, Swarthmore, PA.

Fox, F. (1971). Quaker, Shaker, Rabbi: Warder Cresson, the Story of a Philadelphia Mystic, *Pennsylvania Magazine of History and Biography,* 95 (April), 148-57.

Gibbons, W. (1830). *An Exposition of Modern Skepticism, in a Letter, Addressed to the Editors of the* Free Enquirer. Wilmington, Del.: R. Porter and Son.

Gould, M.T.C. (Ed.). *The Quaker, Being a Series of Sermons by Members of the Society of Friends* (Vol. I). Philadelphia: Marcus T.C. Gould, 1827.

Grasso, C. (2011). The Boundaries of Toleration and Tolerance: Religious Infidelity in the Early American Republic, in C. Beneke and C. S. Grenda (Eds.) , *The First Prejudice: Religious Tolerance and Intolerance in Early America, 286-302.* Philadelphia: University of Pennsylvania Press.

Green Street Monthly Meeting Men's Minutes (Green Street Minutes) (1835, 2nd Mo. 19). Philadelphia Yearly Meeting Archives, Friends Historical Library, Swarthmore College, Swarthmore, PA.

Harlan, A.H. (1914). *History and Genealogy of the Harlan Family and Particularly of the Descendants of George and Michael Harlan, Who Settled in Chester County, Pa., 1687.* Baltimore: Lord Baltimore Press, 1914).

Harris, D. (1967). *Socialist Origins in the United States: American Forerunners of Marx, 1817-1832.* Assen, The Netherlands: Van Gorcum.

Hicks, E. (1816, 3rd Mo. 8). [Letter to Samuel Parsons]. Anna Wharton Morris Papers (Box 3), Friends Historical Library, Swarthmore College, Swarthmore, PA.

Hicks, E. (1824, 9th Mo. 25). [Letter to Cornelius Camden Blatchly]. Elias Hicks Papers (Box 16). Friends Historical Library, Swarthmore College, Swarthmore, PA.

Hicks, E. (1845). *A Word of Exhortation to Young Friends, Presented to Them without Money and without Price.* Philadelphia: J. Richards.

Hinshaw, W.W. (Ed.) (1936-1950). *Encyclopedia of American Quaker Genealogy* (Vol. III). Ann Arbor: Edwards Brothers.

Howe, D.W. (1970). *The Unitarian Conscience: Harvard Moral Philosophy, 1805-186.* Cambridge, MA: Harvard University Press.

Ingle, H. L. (1984). "A Ball That Has Rolled Beyond Our Reach": The Consequences of Hicksite Reform, 1830, as Seen in an Exchange of Letters. *Delaware History*, 21(Fall-Winter), 131-32.

Ingle, H. L. (1986). *Quakers in Conflict: The Hicksite Reformation* Knoxville, TN: University of Tennessee Press.

John, E. (1832, 1st Mo. 11). *Elida John Diary.* John Family Papers (Box 2), Friends Historical Library, Swarthmore College, Swarthmore, PA.

Judge, H. (1841). *Memoirs and Journal of Hugh Judge; a Member of the Society of Friends, and Minister of the Gospel; Containing an Account of His Life, Religious Observations, and Travels in the Work of the Ministry.* Byberry, Pa.: John and Isaac Comly.

Kersey, J. (1826, 8th Mo. 26). [Letter to Samuel Bettle]. Miscellaneous Manuscripts, Friends Historical Library, Swarthmore College, Swarthmore, PA.

Kersey, J. (1851). *A Narrative of the Early Life, Travels, and Gospel Labors of Jesse Kersey, Late of Chester County, Pennsylvania.* Philadelphia: T. Ellwood Chapman.

Kimber, A. (1842, 1st Mo. 15). {Letter to Richard D. and Hannah Webb}. Item MS A.1.2, v. 12.2, p. 9, Antislavery Manuscripts, Rare Books Department, Boston Public Library, Boston, MA.

Lazerow, J. (1995). *Religion and the Working Class in Antebellum America* (Washington: Smithsonian Institution Press.

Leopold, R.W. (1940). *Robert Dale Owen: A Biography* Cambridge, MA: Harvard University Press.

*Letters of Martha Smith*, 182; Lydia P. Mott to Robinson, 4th Mo. 1, 1832, box 1, Robinson Papers.

Martindale, J.C. and A.W. Dudley (n.d.), *A History of the Townships of Byberry and Mooreland, in Philadelphia, Pa. from Their Earliest Settlements by the Whites to the Present Time.* Philadelphia: George W. Jacobs & Co.

Mott, L. (1831, 3rd Mo. 16). [Letter to Willis]. Box 1, Willis Papers, Phebe Post Willis Papers, Special Collections, University of Rochester, NY.

Mott, L.P. (1832, 4th Mo. 1). [Letter to Robinson]. Box 1, Robinson Papers. Friends Historical Library, Swarthmore College, Swarthmore, PA.

Mott, L. (1836, 5th Mo. 19). [Letter to Willis]. Box 1, Willis Papers, Phebe Post Willis Papers, Special Collections, University of Rochester, NY.

Mott, J.L. (1858). *Some Extracts from the Writings of Our Deceased Friend, Jacob L. Mott, with a Memorial concerning Him, Approved by the Meeting for Sufferings, Held in New York.* New York: Benj. F. Corlies.

New York Monthly Meeting Men's Minutes (NY Minutes). (1829-1831), New York Yearly Meeting Archives, Friends Historical Library, Swarthmore College, Swarthmore, PA.

Owen, R.D. (1830, June 30). [Letter]. *Delaware Free Press.*

Owen, R.D. (1830). *Letters Addressed to William Gibbons of Wilmington, Del. in Reply to "A Exposition of Modern Skepticism," Together with an Address to the Society of Friends, and a Letter to Eli Hilles, Benj. Ferris and Others. First Published in the F. Enquirer.* Philadelphia: J.A. M'Clintock.

Palmer, B.W. (Ed.). (2002). *Selected Letters of Lucretia Coffin Mott* (Urbana: University of Illinois Press, 2002).

Parrish, D. (n.d.). [Memorandum]. Cox-Parrish-Wharton Papers (Dillwyn Parrish folder, box 13,), Historical Society of Pennsylvania, Philadelphia.

Price, P., Sr., (1825, 7th Mo. 29) [Letter to Eli K. Price]. Box 2, Price Family Papers, Friends Historical Library, Swarthmore College, Swarthmore, PA.

Price, P.M. (1825, Sept. 30). [Letter to Eli K. Price] Box 2, Price Family Papers, Friends Historical Library, Swarthmore College, Swarthmore, PA.

Pryor, T.W., (1819, 10th Mo. 31). *Thomas W. Pryor Journal.* Friends Historical Library, Swarthmore College, Swarthmore, PA.

Reeder, E.M. (1831, June 18). Sermon Delivered at Bucks Quarterly Meeting, Held at Buckingham, on the Morning of May 26, 1831, by Elizabeth M. Reeder, a Member of Green-Street Monthly Meeting, Philadelphia. *Delaware Free Press.*

Reeder, E.M. (1831, Aug. 1831). Sermon Delivered at Friends' Meeting, Green Street, Philadelphia, on the Morning of June 19th, 1831, by Elizabeth M. Reeder, *Delaware Free Press.*

Robinson, R.T. (n.d.). [Letter]. Box 1, Robinson Family Papers, Sheldon Museum, Middlebury, VT.

Schultz, R. (1993). *The Republic of Labor: Philadelphia Artisans and the Politics of Class, 1720-1830.* New York: Oxford University Press.

Six Sentiments.(1830, 8th Mo. 1830). Wilmington Monthly Meeting Papers Friends Historical Library, Swarthmore College, Swarthmore, PA.

Society of Friends–No. 9 (Friends–No. 9) (1828, 9th Mo. 6) *Friend.*

Some Lucubrations. (1830, 8th Mo. 1830). Wilmington Monthly Meeting Papers Friends Historical Library, Swarthmore College, Swarthmore, PA.

Smith, M. (1844). *Letters of Martha Smith*. Smith, Martha. *Letters of Martha Smith, with a Short Memoir of Her Life*. New York: Piercy and Reed.

Spurlock, J.C. (1988). *Free Love: Marriage and Middle-Class Radicalism in America, 1825-1860*. New York: New York University Press.

Swayne, J., (1831 May 21). [Letter]. *Delaware Free Press*.

Swayne, B. (1851, 2nd Mo. 23). *Benjamin Swayne Journal*. Swayne Family Papers (Box 5), Friends Historical Library, Swarthmore College, Swarthmore, PA.

Tatum, A. (n.d.), box 5, Biddle Family Papers, Friends Historical Library, Swarthmore College, Swarthmore, PA.

Union of All Parties (1832, Sept. 17). *Delaware Free Press*.

Walvin, J. (1997). *The Quakers: Money and Morals*. London: John Murray.

Webb, B. (1830, Aug. 7). To B.W., *Delaware Free Press*.

Webb, B. (1831). *The Authenticity of the Scriptures, and Fundamental Doctrines of Quaker Christianity, According to the Berean, and the Investigation of Benjamin Webb's Case before a Committee from the Quarterly Meeting of Concord*. Wilmington, DE: W.M. Naudain.

Webb, B. (1831, 1st Mo. 10). [Letter to William Jackson]. Item #8095, Manuscripts Collection, Chester County Historical Society, West Chester, PA.

Webb, B. (1831, Jan. 8). Persecution. *Delaware Free Press*.

Webb, B. (1831, Jan. 29). Editorial. *Delaware Free Press*.

Webb, B. (1831, Feb. 12). Persecution. *Delaware Free Press*.

Webb, B. (1831, Feb. 26). Persecution. *Delaware Free Press*.

Webb, B. (1831, Apr. 16). The Case Continued. *Delaware Free Press*.

Webb, B. (1833, 1st Mo. 30). [Letter to William Jackson.] Item #8095, Manuscripts Collection, Chester County Historical Society, West Chester, PA.

Wilentz, S. (1986). *Chants Democratic: New York City & the Rise of the American Working Class, 1788-1850* New York: Oxford University Press. 1986.

Wilmington Monthly Meeting Men's Minutes (Wilmington Minutes), (1831). Philadelphia Yearly Meeting Archives, Friends Historical Library, Swarthmore College, Swarthmore, PA.

Wilmington Notes. (1831). Notes Taken at the Second Meeting of the Committee on the Appeal of Benjamin Webb. Wilmington Monthly Meeting Papers, Friends Historical Library, Swarthmore College, Swarthmore, PA.

Wilmington Preparative Meeting Complaint (Wilmington Complaint), 1830, 12th Mo. 23). Wilmington Monthly Meeting Papers, Friends Historical Library, Swarthmore College, Swarthmore, PA.

Wilmington QM Notes. (1831, 8th Mo.). Quarterly Meeting Notes from Memory & Proposed Answers. Wilmington Monthly Meeting Papers, Friends Historical Library, Swarthmore College, Swarthmore, PA.

Wilmington QM Notes. (1831, 2nd Mo. 23). Quarterly Meeting Committee Report. Copy of the Minutes of W.M.M. in the Case of B.W., Wilmington Monthly Meeting Papers, Friends Historical Library, Swarthmore College, Swarthmore, PA.

Working Men's Ticket (1831, Oct. 1). *Delaware Free Press*.

# 11 | Conflict between Friends: Southern African Quakers' Critique of AFSC's Approach to End Apartheid

## By Robynne Rogers Healey

## Introduction

For the duration of the apartheid era in South Africa, relations between Quakers who lived in South Africa and the American Friends Service Committee (AFSC) were tense. They became particularly bitter between 1977 and 1992 when the South African National Party under FW de Klerk began to dismantle apartheid.[1] These years coincided with the most violent anti-apartheid protests within South Africa itself, starting with the Soweto riots in 1976 and ending with the first democratic elections in 1994. The event that set off this pacifist conflict was a–somewhat–chance meeting between a group of Southern African and South African (SA) Quakers and an AFSC Study Tour Group at the Quaker Seminar on Nonviolence in Gaborone, Botswana in August 1977.[2] While everyone in attendance was committed to the end of apartheid, the parties disagreed sharply on a number of points. Especially contentious to SA Quakers was AFSC's single-minded commitment to divestment and its seemingly weak commitment to non-violence. The conflict that followed was, at moments, quite bitter. During this time there were visitations back and forth between South African Quakers, American Quakers, Friends World Committee for Consultation (FWCC) personnel, and AFSC staff; moreover, voluminous

---

[1] Apartheid was dismantled over a period of years, beginning with the unbanning of the African National Congress (ANC) and the release of Nelson Mandela from prison in 1990, the abolishment of South African race laws in 1991, and the first democratic elections in 1994 that brought Nelson Mandela's ANC party to power.

[2] The Southern African Yearly Meeting (SAYM) included meetings in South Africa, and in surrounding countries such as Botswana, Zambia, and Zimbabwe.

correspondence crossed the Atlantic in both directions. While many South African Quakers were part of this transoceanic dialogue, one Friend, H.W. (pronounced in Afrikaans as hah-vay, or 'Harvey') van der Merwe, played a particularly central role, although that role was viewed contrarily by different groups. South African Friends viewed van der Merwe as educating outsiders on the position of South African Quakers; most AFSC staff considered him "the most aggressive spokesperson of the Southern Africa Yearly Meeting" (Hostetter, 2002, p. 582). Certainly, this conflict shone a light on American Quakers' concerns about AFSC (Fager, 1988; Hostetter, 2002; Ingle, 2016). Importantly, it provides an opportunity for an examination of the ways in which Quakers who lived in an environment of conflicted peace, or potential war, considered and applied the peace testimony as they understood it.

Scholars have largely interpreted disagreements between Quakers and AFSC during the Cold War years from an American point of view (Fager 1988; Lewy, 1988; Cromartie, 1990; Frost, 1992; Smith, 1996; Ingle, 1998; Hostetter, 2002; Ingle, 2016). Given that the *American* Friends Service Committee has been the object of analysis and critique, this is logical. These interpretations depend heavily on an examination of the divisions that existed in American Quakerism as a result of the nineteenth century schisms that so deeply divided the North American Religious Society of Friends. But SA Quakers were not American. Their heritage was elsewhere. Certainly, the first Quakers in South Africa were Nantucket whalers. Strictly speaking, these were not Americans either; they were part of the Quaker Atlantic world. Most SA Friends had roots in English Quakerism, as part of a British immigration to southern Africa in the twentieth century. And H.W. van der Merwe? He was an African–a white African. He was an Afrikaner, a Boer, who became in his own words "an African" (van der Merwe, 2000, pp. 13-34). While "Challenges to the American Friends Service Committee" (Ingle, 2016) touches on South Africa along with the Middle East and Vietnam as a point of contention between AFSC and American Quakers, "Liberation in One Organization" (Hostetter, 2002) is the single work that explicitly examines the disagreements between AFSC and South African Quakers. Despite its valuable conclusions about AFSC itself, it is based entirely on AFSC records and does not account for a South African perspective.

This chapter uses South African Quaker records to examine the Southern African perspective on the conflict over how to end apartheid. It argues that three factors fuelled the acrimonious dispute. First, SA Friends viewed the attitudes, approaches, and interventions of AFSC staff as a form of American cultural imperialism. Second, SA Friends, deeply committed to faith-based pacifism dedicated to 'build up the good, so that evil will be cast out', felt bound to create a just and equitable society through genuinely nonviolent means. They rejected all violence, including tactics designed to destroy South Africa. Third, individuals with strongly held beliefs had a profound impact on the ongoing conflict between AFSC and SA Friends and on the events that eventually ended apartheid in South Africa. Even so, SA Quakers played an important role in ending apartheid and trying to create a more just South Africa. The Southern Africa Yearly Meeting (SAYM) was not large; in 1977, its entire membership, about one hundred, was less than the number of individuals employed by AFSC (Hostetter, 2002, p. 582). Nevertheless, their influence surpassed their membership numbers. As one American Quaker commented after visiting South African Friends, "I have never known of so much being accomplished by so small a number of Friends" (Snipes, 1979, p. 1).

### The Quaker Seminar on Non-Violence meets the AFSC Study Group

In July 1976, FWCC held its Thirteenth Triennial Conference in Hamilton, Ontario, Canada. The conference accepted a minute proposed by one of its study groups:

Friends are exercised by efforts to achieve freedom and justice in many parts of the world using means that have veered away from nonviolent persuasion into violence and guerilla warfare. Often these tactics have been reluctantly adopted by liberation movements when intransigent regimes refuse to take significant steps toward their valid goals. Entrenched, systemic violence has thus spawned violent attacks despite world-wide efforts to achieve freedom and justice for all.

The study group devoted to social and economic justice and nonviolence would like to lay upon Friends everywhere and most particularly on the Africa Section of FWCC a concern that this moral issue be seriously addressed. African Christians, though divided, have in a number of cases justified support for violent efforts by reference to scripture. For example, the General Secretary of the All Africa Conference of Churches, Canon Burgess Carr, apparently feels that the "violence of the Cross has sanctified violence in such cases."

Friends must face this question on theological as well as pragmatic grounds, if our witness and service in such areas of the world are to be effective.

We therefore suggest that the Africa Section urgently consider a consultation or seminar in Africa (probably in the Friends International Centre in Nairobi) at which representative Friends shall gather to examine rigorously both principle and practice of nations, liberation groups, churches and individuals on the issue of violence and to formulate counsel and guidance for us all as well as further activities. If this is approved, a special fund should be solicited (Kikaya, to Shelagh Willet, 5 October 1976).

After some months of planning, Friends arranged the Quaker Seminar on Non-Violence to take place in Gaborone, Botswana from 4-11 August 1977. FWCC's focus on global interactions between Quakers meant that attendance at the seminar was to be broadly representative. The first list of attendees numbered twenty-four, including fifteen representatives from all the African meetings, seven representatives from FWCC, and one representative each from AFSC in the United States and FSC in the United Kingdom (De, to FWCC/Africa Section, 4 April 1977). Even before the Seminar began, SAYM representatives expressed concerns about its planning. Tineke Gibberd wrote to Shelagh Willet, "I told Vernon [Gibberd's husband] what you had said about the non-violent seminar–how you are not happy how it is put together and about the accent being different from what was envisaged originally." After encouraging Willet to phone Nairobi to express her discontent, Gibberd supported "what Friends at the World Conference felt was needed–a father of friends to help each other to study and put into practice the method of nonviolent action. We really don't want people there at the seminar who hold different views and it must not be a high powered group of erudite speakers–but as you said–a family gathering to strengthen in us all the ways of non violence" (Gibberd, to Shelagh Willet, 15 May 1977).

At the same time that FWCC was planning its Seminar on Non-Violence, AFSC was preparing to send an AFSC study tour to southern Africa as part of its South Africa Program. In May 1977, David Sogge from AFSC wrote to the clerk of SAYM inviting several members to meet with the AFSC study tour while both groups were in Gaborone (Sogge, to Rory Short, 28 May 1977). Sixteen individuals comprised the AFSC study tour group: ten staffers, including Bill Sutherland who was AFSC Southern Africa Representative, and six board and subcommittee members. Six of the sixteen participants were Quakers; most tour participants were non-white and members of AFSC's Third World Coalition (TWC) (Hostetter, 2002, p. 581). AFSC's concern about South Africa predated the election of the National Party in 1948 and the implementation of Grand Apartheid. Moreover, throughout the 1950s and 1960s the Committee had facilitated visitation, dialogue, and interaction with southern Africa. In 1969, following years of discussion with Chase Manhattan Bank, AFSC closed its account to express its displeasure with the bank's loans to South Africa

(Hostetter, 2002, p. 576). In the 1970s AFSC went further and created the Southern Africa Representative Program as part of its International Division. In 1974 the Committee hired Bill Sutherland as director of that program, and in 1976, "the AFSC inaugurated the South Africa Program of the Peace Education Division as the domestic component of its antiapartheid work" (Hostetter, 2002, p. 578). The South Africa Program's (SAP) main focus was "the promotion of education and action in the United States based on deepening relationships with those opposing the status quo in southern Africa" (AFSC, [1976/77] SAP Prospectus, p. 1).

The implementation of the program came at a time when AFSC's opposition to American involvement in the Vietnam War had stimulated an internal evaluation of the Committee's goals and methods. Staffers and those who supported them were in solidarity with the Vietnamese people who suffered under the United States' aggressive campaign. They questioned the sufficiency of the continued emphasis on the alleviation of suffering and Quaker diplomacy. In 1972 Committee veteran, Jim Bristol, published an article titled "Nonviolence, Not First for Export" that provided an argument for what David Hostetter calls "liberation pacifism" (Hostetter, 2002, p. 578). AFSC reproduced and distributed the article as a pamphlet throughout the 1970s. Bristol urged "Americans, and pacifists in particular," to focus their efforts on "the removal of injustice, not the urging of nonviolence" (Lewy, 1988, p. 48). Bristol's counsel was clear: "We believe in nonviolence and in revolution and therefore in the possibility of nonviolent revolution. We understand that the oppressed do not share our faith in nonviolence. We have given them little reason to. Still we identify with the justice of their cause and urge all who are able in good conscience to do so to unite with them and support them in their revolution" (Lewy, 1988, pp. 48-49). Not everyone welcomed Bristol's suggestions (Hostetter, 2002, pp. 580-581).

AFSC, FWCC, and Southern African Friends were evaluating and re-evaluating pacifism, non-violence, Quaker diplomacy, and reconciliation in light of liberation struggles that might include armed resistance. Consider AFSC's SAP Study Tour "questions and dilemmas" outlined in its prospectus ([1976/77], p. 2-3):

- How should AFSC's commitment to nonviolence be expressed in relation to movements for self-determination which used armed force?
- How do we balance a concern to support movements for self-determination and a concern to seek nonviolent solutions to conflicts?
- How do we show a concern to understand the positions of the liberation movement and the key majority-ruled southern African

nations without appearing to show little concern to understand the fears and aspirations of minorities in southern Africa?

- How do we evaluate the involvement of great powers in southern Africa?
- How do we evaluate one state, nationalist, or liberation movement against others, and for what purposes might we want to make such evaluations?
- Can we effectively evaluate the policies of US businesses and governmental agencies without observing their impact first-hand?
- How do we balance contending challenges to our credibility from both black and white AFSC constituencies arising from the fact that we have visited certain countries and have failed to visit others?

These were the questions that on the minds of SA Quakers and Quaker-affiliated AFSC staffers when they encountered one another in Gaborone in August 1977.

The two groups did not intend to meet. The AFSC Study Tour Group, which had refused to travel to South Africa because of its opposition to the South African Government, was going to be in Gaborone between 10-13 August, and due to delays in the organization of the FWCC Non-Violence Seminar, there was a time of overlap. At the end of May 1977, David Sogge with AFSC's Africa Programs extended an invitation to SAYM for "several members of the Southern Africa Yearly Meeting to meet with members of an AFSC study tour" while both groups were in Gaborone (Sogge to Rory Short, 28 May 1977). Along with the invitation, Sogge included AFSC's lengthy prospectus for the SAP Study Tour. Rosemary Elliott, SAYM clerk, responded to Sogge that she was "not very happy that these two occasions almost coincide, both involving Friends in Africa, because although the Seminar is of different emphasis to the proposed Study Tour, it may very well be that Friends in Africa will have gained a new vision for the Quaker role in this situation, which your group will miss" (Elliott, to David Sogge, 14 June 1977). Nonetheless, Elliott endorsed the general principle of the group gaining "information and understanding" and included, in her response to AFSC, a paper that H.W. van der Merwe had presented to London Yearly Meeting and other Quaker groups. She then circulated AFSC's request to the "Yearly Meeting Committee and Others" (Elliott to David Sogge, 14 June 1977).

South African Friends lost little time in voicing their concerns about the AFSC Study Group. Olive Gibson, past clerk of SAYM, wrote a lengthy epistle to Sogge as her health prevented her from attending the Seminar: "I do feel a good many reservations about the approach outlined and implied in these documents: In particular by the great formulation and departmentalisation of the scheme and approach; the dividing and labelling of countries into 'majority-ruled' and 'minority-ruled,' and keeping of these rigidly apart in hygienically separated tours. (Do we need apartheid imported to Africa from AFSC?!)" she asked. Gibson pointed to her own participation in establishing "the Africa Section of FWCC to facilitate our cutting across all these boundaries." She chided AFSC's approach for its potential divisiveness and short-sightedness: "Many other bodies try at least to pursue unity and understanding and progress in a positive and normal way so far as is possible. If they are prevented and have to work within less ideal limits–that is one thing. But one tries not to set up barriers and obstructions to communication and understanding, oneself." As a South African, Gibson was particularly concerned that AFSC staff expressed a "commitment to non-violence" as a "dilemma" and had "at the outset decided to build relationships particularly with liberation movements which are by definition committed to use armed forces." "What body," Gibson wondered, "is addressing itself to helping the nonviolent movements, organisation and people within the countries concerned, which are still trying to find the non-armed solutions (which you say AFSC is seeking) which would, if those organisations and people could succeed, enable the armed movement to lay down their arms, at least sooner?" As for AFSC's question about the meaning of reconciliation, Gibson contended it could only be defined as "the achievement of justice, preferably voluntarily." But she insisted that the Study Group accept that injustice was not only a South African problem: "be it here or in Ethiopia, Uganda, UK or USA. We gain nothing by blinkering ourselves to this fact. Oppression is by no means confined to minority governments be they white, black, or yellow." (Gibson, to David Sogge, 16 June 1977, emphases in original).

Gibson was not the only concerned Friend. David Kikaya, Executive Secretary of FWCC/AS sternly reprimanded Sogge for his lack of communication regarding AFSC's tour to Africa. Kikaya claimed that he first learned of the Study Tour when Bill Sutherland arrived in Nairobi. Kikaya was frustrated that AFSC had not responded to more than one FWCC request for an AFSC representative to attend the non-violent seminar in Gaborone (Kikaya to David Sogge, 27 June 1977). Sogge hastily apologized for the miscommunication, which he was "at a loss to explain" (Sogge to David Kikaya, 11 July 1977). Both sides tried to patch their differences, but it is clear that disagreements between SA Friends and AFSC predated the Gaborone Seminar.

At Gaborone, the two groups came into direct conflict. AFSC staff reckoned H.W. van der Merwe, a relatively new member of the Religious Society of Friends, as "the most aggressive spokesperson of the Southern Africa Yearly Meeting" (Hostetter, 2002, p. 582). Certainly, van der Merwe's academic expertise and his comfort in presenting well-researched and carefully-argued papers made him a formidable obstacle in the path of AFSC's South African Program's staff, who seemed to have had a clear and certain view of what they could accomplish in South Africa through divestment. Van der Merwe had encountered the SAP and AFSC before the meeting in Gaborone. In 1974, while in Philadelphia at the World Congress of Sociology, he had been invited to comment on a draft of the program and had articulated concerns about what he considered a lack of Quaker orientation in the program. It did not oppose violence, it was not formulated in terms of a long-term future, and it involved itself with only one side of the conflict (van der Merwe, 1979a, p. 3). Van der Merwe saw divestment as a form of institutional violence that would harm the very people AFSC was striving to help. His thoughts on the program changed little through the years of conflict and, very closely, reflected the attitudes of other SA Friends. As he pointed out numerous times over the years, Quakers worldwide shared his concerns, including those in the United States (van der Merwe, to Louis Schneider and David Sogge, 15 June 1979, pp. 8-9). The work of South African Quakers, including van der Merwe, went a long way to bringing about the peaceful transition to democracy; as Hostetter (2002) notes, both the African National Congress (ANC) and Nelson Mandela especially affirmed van der Merwe's mediation efforts (p. 593). At the same time, AFSC maintained that apartheid would not have ended without the pressure of divestment and boycotts and the evolution of its antiapartheid activism to include the pursuit of justice through liberation pacifism (Hostetter, 2002, p. 593).

## Understanding the Conflict

Three factors help to explain the origins, nature, and extent of this conflict. First, SA Quakers considered AFSC approaches as American cultural imperialism, something they deeply opposed. Second, SA Quakers were deeply committed to the Quaker peace testimony; they could not countenance violence of any sort. And, third, strong individuals like H.W. van der Merwe, and those in AFSC who so deeply disliked van der Merwe, affected the tenor of the conflict.

## Cultural Imperialism

South African Friends were not inclined to accept commentary and interference from well-meaning, but ill-informed, Westerners who did not understand circumstances in South Africa. They viewed this as a form of cultural imperialism, something for which the United States was well known in the Cold War era. It may have been presented as a *kinder, gentler* and even *f/ Friendlier* sort,

242

but it was still cultural imperialism and South African Quakers were certain it did not align with Quaker principles and it needed to stop.

Concerns over cultural imperialism are apparent in the background papers prepared by attenders at the Gaborone Seminar. For instance, Ann Tweedie-Waggot claimed that "the building of true peace in Southern Africa, and revolutionary changes this will bring, will involve very sweeping changes in some other countries, particularly Britain." Moreover, "relations of true peace will not be neo-colonial relationships" (Tweedie-Waggot, 1977, p. 5). Fred Moorehouse explored the prospects for non-violence in southern Africa, lamenting the "'guilt complex' of the white communities in the USA and Britain in particular." In response to the rhetorical question, "Why have not Friends denounced South Africa's apartheid policies?" Moorehouse retorts, "Friends have—and Friends in South Africa have done so year in and year out. What is much more important, and the question to which Friends in Southern Africa, with all their weaknesses and imperfections admitted, have been and are addressing themselves, is how can we get rid of apartheid? It is easy to denounce, it is more difficult to change. But the latter is our responsibility" (Moorehouse, 1977, p. 3, emphasis added).

Following the Gaborone Seminar, African participants submitted comments on their interactions with Study Group members to both FWCC and AFSC. In that response, SA Friends expressed concerns about the SAP's American focus and offered the following observations:

1. It appears to be largely of a negative nature.
2. It shows little concern for the major requirements of building a stable society or the improvement of the quality of life.
3. It claims solidarity with a movement which, as we understand it, while relating largely to the exile groups and guerilla forces, makes little attempt to understand the people against whom they are working, and little attempt to relate to forces totally committed to non-violence.
4. It shows concern for the support given by Western powers to the South African economy and military establishment but none for the military intervention of Russian, Cuban, and other forces in Southern Africa.
5. It appears to be a one-sided program which does not nearly give expression to the wide diversity of Quaker approaches. We are disturbed to hear that some members of the group are not wholly committed to non-violence.
6. There seems to be more understanding sympathy among group members for the commitment of certain liberation groups to Marxist regimes in which no provision will be made for the free expression of

political views by the people of the Country (Response of Participants, 1977, p.2).

Van der Merwe also composed his own reaction to the meeting. Having been cautioned at the seminar "not to come to conclusions about the program without having obtained additional information," van der Merwe requested and received nine pieces of literature from Philadelphia.[3] After detailed assessments on each pamphlet or article, van der Merwe offered the following conclusion: "this Program is extremely biased. While it will obviously arouse public sympathy in the USA, I believe it will do much harm in the long run, because of its failure to clearly state its goals for Southern Africa and the means of achieving those goals, its negative orientation, its failure to support constructive, positive forces for change in Southern Africa, and its naïve belief that new governments established by violent armed rebellions and wars, supported by Soviet military forces, will be free and democratic" (van der Merwe, 1977a, p. 4). Van der Merwe reported similar findings to his own meeting in Cape Town, but noted additionally that lack of consultation between AFSC staff and South African residents, "especially with Quakers in South Africa, Rhodesia, Zambia, Kenya, and Tanzania" who "have complained in vain that they are unable to obtain clear information about the activities of the representative in Southern Africa. Also that their reservations about the programme were not seriously entertained by the senior staff members" (van der Merwe, 1977b, p. 6, emphasis in original). Clearly, SA Friends were troubled by more than AFSC's South Africa Program; they were also concerned about the attitude of AFSC staff.

Given the extent of disagreement between Southern Africans and Americans at Gaborone, Friends decided that reciprocal visits to one another's countries might help reduce, if not eliminate, conflict and mutual understanding. AFSC and FWCC jointly sponsored the visit of four Southern African Friends to the United States in June-July 1978–Raymond Cardoso, Rosemary Elliott, Jennifer Kinghorn, and H.W. van der Merwe (Elliott, to Herbert M. Hadley, 7 March 1978). At the end of the tour, these Friends submitted a joint report and recommendations to FWCC and AFSC, although AFSC did not initially receive its copy, straining relations further (Stever, to SA Friends who travelled to the USA, 5 February 1979). Moreover, since the group did not travel collectively the entire time they were in the US, Cardoso, Elliott, and van der Merwe submitted individual comments on their travel. A number of times these reports allude to the Southern Africans' feeling that AFSC was imposing expectations on South

---

[3] It is unclear whether this material came from AFSC offices in Philadelphia or from Friends in the city.

Africa that AFSC could not realize in the United States. Americans' divisive race issues were not lost on the SA visitors. Rosemary Elliott noted this irony: "I would understand the need of white and black Americans to find a common cause for which they can work, in view of the surprising lack of integration we noticed .... I would also see that, in focussing on the Southern Africa issues, this not only gives a common cause, but also an opportunity to tackle, at long distance (and therefore in a less immediately sensitive area), many problems still in existence in the United States." She noted, with hope that, "where there is a reason behind some of the AFSC programs, the understanding gained by examining the South African situation should be tested in United States' situations before being recommended as right or relevant in the South African situation" (Elliott, 1978, Report of Travel).

The Joint Report and Recommendations (1978) portrays the relationship between Southern African and American Friends very positively, stating that time spent with American Quakers was both "strengthening and illuminating," based as it was on "the customary spirit of enquiry, of openness and of concern" (p.1). The relationship with AFSC is cast in a less positive light. The Report notes that a spirit of openness or corporate seeking was missing due to an unrealistic commitment to a narrow understanding of South African conditions and means to change them. Plainly put, the South African visitors felt that AFSC staff was more committed to an idea of South Africa than to South Africans themselves: "We felt that AFSC in general ignored the very varied natures and responses and needs of the people of S Africa. They also underestimated the dignity and aspiration of the peoples of South Africa, their vitality, and their desire to discover the way of righteousness for themselves." The AFSC "seems committed to bringing down the S African government rather than to healing and restoring the people; it seemed more committed to the withdrawal of multinational companies than to the discovery by the S African people of a fair way of sharing the wealth and opportunities of the country" (p. 2). Van der Merwe, who did not draft the Report (van der Merwe, Letter to "Friends," 21 March 1979), declared he was "saddened and depressed" with the disagreements (van der Merwe, 1978b). He was frustrated with AFSC's attitude: "I felt we were getting nowhere. We were talking past each other. As Jennifer said on many earlier occasions about their audio-visual aids, we need not argue about the inaccuracies in their material. The basic disagreement is with their entire value-orientation, their approach, their interpretation of the South African and the world situation" (p. 8).

In their personal correspondence, SA Quakers also pointed out the ironies of American involvement in South African politics; they used these opportunities to remind Americans that they had first-hand knowledge of South African society. Raymond Cardoso corresponded with Ann Stever, former AFSC vice-Board chair. Stever had outlined for Cardoso her view that the difference between SA Friends and AFSC was one of emphasis. Cardoso responded, "the basic difference between us in this respect is that we (SA Friends) are far more physically involved in this problem than you. ... So, even though people are much the same, basically, different circumstances do show through, and I thought this was perfectly clear to you" (Cardoso, to Ann Stever, 20 March 1979). Cardoso softened his tone, but not his message, in subsequent correspondence: "Yes our difference in emphasis is significant. I, who live in the 'mess' and feel the unnatural curtains, and the fear it generates, address myself to racism foremost; whereas you, living in a country where racism is not embodied in law but where it persists in subtle or not so subtle ways, will be inclined to blame the political system." Citing his preference for evolutionary, rather than revolutionary, means to change, Cardoso stressed the importance of local over external forces for bringing about meaningful change: "the political system of a future South Africa would not matter as much as the fact that the whole nation arrived at it <u>together</u> in the fullest sense. And then morality in politics (and I do not mean to dig at you) is not quite the same as it is for individuals. Something to do with forcing other people to fit into one's vision of what is right" (Cardoso, to Ann Steever [sic], 12 April 1979).

South African Quakers wanted a just society. They also believed that South Africans, not Americans, were most-suitably equipped to create that society. When AFSC staff, especially the International Division Executive Committee (IDEC) reacted negatively to the Joint Report and Recommendations (Sogge, to South African Visiting Friends, 24 April 1979), H. W. van der Merwe, who had become clerk of South Africa General Meeting (SAGM), submitted an extensive reply to Louis Schneider and David Sogge at AFSC (van der Merwe, 15 June 1979). Van der Merwe, like other Friends, reiterated his commitment primarily to South Africa, "While I was convinced of the propaganda value of the programme in the States, I saw little or no evidence that it was contributing towards a better society in southern Africa. And that, to me, is the ultimate goal" (p. 5). After bemoaning "the false contrasts between American and South African Quakers" represented in the AFSC/IDEC position, van der Merwe reminded Schneider and Sogge that "The Gaborone Seminar had only three participants from South Africa [out of fifteen Africans] but we found ourselves in complete agreement with all participants, both white and black, from different parts of Africa. We reached consensus on the role of Quakers in bringing about justice in Southern Africa and I am confident that our resolutions are in agreement with the aims and aspirations of American Quakers" (p.8). He then contended that South African Quakers' disagreement was specifically with AFSC's South Africa Program "in its present form" (p. 10), not with AFSC generally, and certainly not with American Quakers, as AFSC claimed: "The fact that our concerns are shared by Quakers worldwide is evident from conversations I have had since 1974 with Quakers in England, Holland, Germany, Geneva, and in fact, all over the USA. ... For these reasons, I am at a complete loss to understand how this minute of the IDEC can treat our Joint Report as a surprise and as an indication of disagreements between South African and American Quakers" (p. 9, emphasis in original).

The reciprocal visit of American Friends to South Africa in 1979 supports van der Merwe's conclusions. Philadelphia Quaker Samuel Snipes wrote a lengthy and laudatory report for FWCC in which he outlined SA Quakers' extensive efforts to change their society. In evaluating the situation, Snipes's first observation is notable: "I sense a hunger among SAYM to be recognized by American and British Friends—as being as much opposed to the apartheid as the rest of Quakerdom. They have been made to feel guilty for continuing to live in South Africa, and participate in the apartheid economy" (Snipes, 1979, p. 4). Finally, no one was clearer than van der Merwe in 1984, who contended that as long as "American perspectives form the basis of a programme, all information on South Africa will be interpreted within that framework. There is a real danger of American imperialism" (van der Merwe, to Trish Swift, 12 September 1984, p. 8).

### Non-negotiable Non-violence

From a South African Quaker perspective, the peace testimony was not up for debate. American Quakers may have been divided over the peace testimony and the nature of pacifism; they may even have supported wars they considered "just," as they did when they supported the French over the Germans in World War One (Hamm, 2002; Valentine, 2013; Healey, 2016). Revolution, rather than evolution, as an approach to social change had indeed penetrated the American mindset in light of the American context of the Civil Rights Movement of the 1960s and 1970s and the anti-Vietnam War protests of the same period. Former AFSC vice-Board chair, Ann Stever, admitted to Raymond Cardoso that she found "the question of evolution/revolution [to be] a slippery one," and in the juxtaposition of the two, she "tend[ed] to come down on the side of revolution," although she clarified that, as a Friend, she favored nonviolent revolution (Stever, to Raymond Cardoso, 1 June 1979). Southern African Quakers viewed social change from within their own context. They were surrounded by destructive wars of liberation and lived in countries caught in the web of Cold War politics; exiled leaders were trained in guerilla tactics in East Germany and the USSR. South African Friends were not prepared to deviate from the *religious* basis of pacifism, or the belief in 'that of God in every person' so central to Quaker pacifism. They wanted to build a society that would work for all South Africans, regardless of their colour, rather than accepting a vision imposed from outside.

A number of the background papers for the Gaborone Seminar reflect on the importance of genuine nonviolence and the religious basis of Quaker pacifism (Acquah; Hoskins; Miller; Tweedie-Waggot). Moreover, in the Response of Participants in Seminar on Non-Violence at Gaborone to Discussions with AFSC Study Group ([South African Friends], 1977), SA Friends isolated significantly differing views on pacifism as being one of the significant sources of conflict:

> In discussing the South African situation, ultimate aims and means by which we want to achieve these aims, we found ourselves in disagreement with many, and usually the most vocal and forceful members of the group. We can give many examples, but perhaps the most fundamental difference was apparent in the emphasis by several members of the group on the need to destroy the South African economy and thereby the power of the white government, without any accompanying efforts to provide for constructive measures for the future. We fail to interpret this kind of approach as fully non-violent. In many respects it can be characterized as institutional violence which is bound to cause immense chaos increasing the suffering of people, both physically and mentally. As Quakers we find it difficult to associate ourselves with such an approach. We have wondered by and how such a program apparently out of line with acknowledged Quaker principles and approaches could have developed under Quaker auspices (p. 3).

When South African Friends invited American Quakers on a reciprocal visit and tour of South Africa in 1979, they agreed that those invited were to "be religiously oriented rather than activists" (van de Merwe, Confidential Memo, 27 March 1979). In addition, religious, not political, considerations were to govern the form of the tour. This needed clarification at the outset when American Friends indicated that, on political grounds, they were opposed to visiting Zimbabwe Rhodesia. The clerks of SAYM, SAGM, and Central Africa General Meeting (CAGM) responded that, "the invitation to the American team was sent on behalf of SAYM which includes Zimbabwe Rhodesia." "A restricted visit," they asserted, "will not only lead to a restricted understanding of Quakers in Southern Africa, but also a restricted understanding of the politico-economic problems and liberation struggles in the wider region of Southern Africa." Most explicitly, the clerks reminded the American team that "this is a visit BY Friends TO Friends, and we regard your visit as primarily concerned with pastoral care and not political strategy. We would therefore hope that you will be guided by moral rather than political considerations" (Elliott, Madenyika, and van der Merwe, to Lewis Hoskins, 8 July 1979). African Friends were pleased to have their position affirmed in Hoskins's positive response: "on principle, we feel that it is important to be able to travel in the Ministry freely anywhere, and not to be inhibited unduly by political considerations. We are particularly concerned to visit Quakers wherever they are living and working if they would welcome it" (Hoskins, to Rosemary Elliott, 10 July 1979).

Southern African Quakers who had visited the United States in 1978 expressed appreciation of AFSC's efforts to facilitate dialogue (Elliott, Report of Travel, 1978; van der Merwe, 1978a; Joint Report and Recommendations, 1978). Even so, SA Friends consistently remarked, "because of the theoretical rather than spiritual search corporately conducted by AFSC, it tended to oversimplify and depersonalise the S African situation, unrealistically" (Joint Report and Recommendations, 1978, p. 2). South African Quakers viewed the lack of a Quaker orientation in AFSC's Southern Africa Program as a serious problem. Van der Merwe was not the only South African Quaker to voice these concerns (see Elliott, 6 March 1979; Cardoso, 20 March 1979 and 12 April 1979). He was, however, the most consistently vocal, articulate, and tenacious in his opinions and attempts to change AFSC's SAP. As he wrote to "Friends" in March 1979, it was "not [his] nature" to "accept the situation [with AFSC] as beyond our control." Rather, "if something was wrong (and every single American, British, European, and African Quaker I talked to agreed that everything was *not* right!) something should be done about it." Nor was van der Merwe inclined to agree to disagree and withdraw from engagement with AFSC, given how "disturbed" he was "to learn how many Quaker groups, Yearly Meetings, etc., have withdrawn completely from AFSC and dissociate themselves from it" (van der Merwe, to "Friends," 21 March 1979).

### Personality Conflicts

Individuals had a profound impact on the way events unfolded in this conflict. Van der Merwe's tenacity and refusal to disengage may have prolonged the dispute with AFSC, but AFSC also has a responsibility in this conflict. AFSC staff viewed van der Merwe as an impediment to their South African Program;

some AFSC staff refused to believe that white South African Quakers, and H.W. van der Merwe specifically, could see beyond the privileges of their race (Hostetter, 2002, p. 589). Cultural differences and unwillingness on the part of AFSC staff to see beyond their own limited scope and perspective exacerbated this conflict. Certainly, van der Merwe's personality played a role, but the extensive collection of records suggest that AFSC as an organization was unprepared and unwilling to work alongside South African Friends led by van der Merwe's brand of nonviolent reconciliation. This caused serious challenges for Quakers around the world who were navigating their role in a Cold War world.[4]

Given the role van der Merwe played in this disagreement, it is important to understand him more clearly. Van der Merwe was born an Afrikaner; he was what South Africans call "a Boer," that is a rural Afrikaner farmer (van der Merwe, 2000, p. 13). Hendrik Willem (H.W.), born in 1929, was a ninth generation African. He grew up two hundred kilometres from Cape Town, but did not visit the city until he was sixteen years old (van der Merwe, 1978c). Van der Merwe's father, who was sixty years old when his son was born, fought against the English in the Boer War. He died the year before the National Party came to power in 1948, but H.W., like his father, was deeply supportive of the National Party's politics (van der Merwe, 2000, pp. 14-15). In 1948, two years after completing his matriculation, van der Merwe responded to a Dutch Reformed Church call for farmer missionaries to Mashonaland–in Southern Rhodesia, now Zimbabwe–what he referred to as "Dark Africa." Throughout his three years on the mission field he remained committed to the belief that "apartheid was the will of God" (van der Merwe, 2000, pp. 20-21). However, during H.W.'s years at University of Stellenbosch, where he completed a bachelor's and master's degree in sociology, a number of interactions through the Student Christian Association team and the university's Sociological Society (interacting with English-speaking counterparts at University of Cape Town which was more liberal and racially integrated) brought about a change of heart and mind. He remembered afterwards that a seminal moment in his change of heart was an interaction he had with his brother, Jaco, in 1950. Then, his brother had referred to a coloured woman with as *vrou*, an Afrikaans term reserved solely for white women, rather than *meid*, a derogatory term reserved for black and coloured women (van der Merwe, 2000 pp. 30-31). In 1957, H.W. married Marietjie Botha whose father, Hendrik Botha was a leading member of the secret Afrikaner Broederbond and whose mother had worked as a secretary for Dr

---

[4] Kenneth Boulding's and Chuck Fager's disagreements with AFSC suggest that van der Merwe was not the only Quaker at odds with the Committee (Ingle, 2016).

Hendrik Frensch Verwoerd, the grand architect of apartheid (van der Merwe, 2000, p. 28).

Throughout his time in his master's degree van der Merwe realized he needed to gain a stronger grasp of English. In his autobiography, van der Merwe states, "to reach out to the wider community and to the international academic world, I had to write in English." It was a time-consuming effort to write in this second language, but H.W. persevered and wrote his honours paper and his master's thesis in English. This set him on a course to pursue a PhD in the United States at UCLA (van der Merwe, 2000, p. 33). It was while he was at UCLA that H.W. was introduced to Quakers. He and Marietjie were appointed resident hosts at the Westwood International Student Center, founded and operated by the local Friends community. They only attended a single Quaker meeting in their years at UCLA. Nonetheless, they were influenced theologically by their time in the Methodist Church in the United States and the United Church of Canada, which they attended during a year's research stay in Esterhazy, Saskatchewan. The basis of van der Merwe's doctoral dissertation was his research on a dispute between an American multinational corporation that had opened a potash mine in Esterhazy and trade union leaders organizing inexperienced workers.

Van der Merwe's convincement to Quakerism–and it is important to understand the difference between conversion and convincement–was a process that took place over a number of years. He applied for membership in the Religious Society of Friends in 1976 (van der Merwe, 2000, p. 49). In 1977, then, at the Nonviolence Seminar in Gaborone, he was a relatively new Quaker. It is incorrect, however, to claim, as Hostetter (2002) does, that "the recently convinced Friend" applied "the zeal of a convert" to his interactions there (p. 582). He may have been a new member, but his convincement had taken place over many, many years (van der Merwe, 2000, p. 49). Becoming convinced of Quaker principles did have a dramatic impact on van der Merwe's career in South Africa. After five years at Rhodes University (1963-1968), he assumed the position of director of the Abe Bailey Institute of Inter-Racial Studies at the University of Cape Town; this subsequently became the Centre for Intergroup Studies. There van der Merwe specialized in mediation. He held this position until 1992, but maintained his association with the Centre until he retired in 1994. His position as an Afrikaner gave him an understanding of the fears of those in the ruling National Party as well as the even more right wing Conservative Party. As a sociologist he was trained to examine, observe, and analyse society. As director of the Centre for Intergroup Studies, he had a close relationship with Steve Biko early in the black consciousness movement. He was closely involved in mediation work with the ANC and Inkatha and, in 1984, he arranged the first meetings between the ANC-in-exile and government supporters, helping to break a deadlock which had lasted for twenty-four years. Rosemary Elliott certainly recognized, early on, the important role van der Merwe could play. In 1978, after her tour in the US, Elliott included a private note to Herbert Hadley along with her Travel Report:

> Of all the Friends in South Africa, HW has come the furthest in his thinking. He has also made greater sacrifices for what he feels to be right, and his position as an Afrikaner who has not only left his church and political affiliations, but actively seeks to bring understanding and reconciliation between all groups in the country, makes him more vulnerable. His commitment to Quaker principles and the nature of his own work at the Centre for Inter-group Studies, together with his knowledge and understanding of Afrikaner attitudes, especially those in top government positions, make him a potentially key figure in bringing new insights and initiatives to the South African situation. For these reasons I think it is important for American Friends to recognise there is a very positive Quaker presence inside South Africa, and one which can fruitfully be nourished and supported (Elliott, to Herbert Hadley, 19 August 1978).

From all accounts, van der Merwe was intensely bright; his proclivity, as an academic, to process through writing, and to keep records of everything, has produced an incredible personal archive, housed at the University of Cape Town.[5] AFSC staff accused him of opposing the Committee and of being a "conservative, racist Afrikaner" (van der Merwe, to Trish Swift, 12 September 1984). AFSC staff also thwarted van der Merwe's work with American Friends, intervening to prevent his appointment as a Friend in Residence in Pasadena, where he had developed positive relationships with AFSC (Young *et al.*, 31 August 1979). These attacks were deeply hurtful to van der Merwe. He maintained that "my stands and my actions (apart from the errors of judgement which I have made) are consistent with those of the wider body of Friends," even as he recognized that he was at the center of the unproductive tension between AFSC and Southern African Friends (van der Merwe, 12 September 1984).

---

[5] He was also responsible for the Quaker collection being at the University of Cape Town; this collection consists of meeting records and the extensive correspondence related to the Yearly Meeting.

Van der Merwe and the SAYM remained firm for the duration of this global conflict. In *Pursuing Justice and Peace in South Africa* (1989), van der Merwe outlined his approach to facilitation, mediation, and negotiation. The positions in his book echoed those he spearheaded with the Quaker Steering Committee on Mediation (QSCM) (van der Merwe, Proposal, 20 June 1988; van der Merwe, QSCM, Policies and Procedures, 28 September 1988; van der Merwe, Letter to Members of QSCM, 10 November 1988). His fellow South African Quakers admired his courage and commitment to Quaker nonviolence (Curle in van der Merwe, 1989, pp. xiii-xv). Nelson Mandela commended van der Merwe's unfaltering "vision of a free and democratic South Africa," and applauded him for "his courageous and dedicated service to this vision [that] contributed in no small way to the liberation of our country" (Mandela in van der Merwe, 2000, p. 7). And his colleagues recognized van der Merwe for "his remarkable contribution to the anti-apartheid struggle and the eventual resolving of the white-black conflict" as not being just "a structural one, however, but also an interrelated attitudinal one. His outreaching understanding and his courageous quest for justice and peace enabled him to bring adversaries together, and also to confront the unflinching guardians of apartheid." For his colleagues, van der Merwe's example was one "to emulate" (Malan, 2013, p. 21). By 1993, even FWCC openly questioned AFSC's approach in South Africa. Thomas Taylor, General Secretary of FWCC, responded to AFSC's 1992 Report on Violence in South Africa: "To us, the report read like the group had already written it before they went, and picked groups and people who would support their preconceived notions. I wondered why the names of prominent, very wise and sensible Friends like Duduzile Mtshazo, Jennifer Kinghorn, HW van der Merwe, Angus & Scotty Morton, Rosemary Elliott and others weren't on the list of people visited?" Thomas went on to ask, "After reading a report like that and experiencing what I have, how can I trust what AFSC puts out in the future?" He finally concluded, "I guess AFSC is that organization we all love and hate at the same time" (Taylor, to Corinne Johnson, 4 February 1993).

When apartheid ended, so, too, did the conflict between AFSC and South African Friends. In the years it lasted, South African Friends, including van der Merwe, worked consistently to end apartheid, a system they believed to be unjust and violent. They also refused to believe that violence, including violence they attributed to AFSC, would or could build a better, more just society. Van der Merwe and Southern African Quakers rested firmly on their commitment to the religious devotion to nonviolence and the belief that building the good, rather than destroying the bad, would result in more enduring peace and a just society.

# References

## Archival Sources

Acquah, D. (1977). "Friends and the Peace Testimony in Africa," Collection of Background Papers Presented at the Nonviolence Seminar." File K.2.2, Quaker Collection. University of Cape Town Manuscripts and Archives, Cape Town.

AFSC. (1993, January 21). Report on Violence in South Africa, 21 January 1993. BC 1148 Box 65 File A: H.W. van der Merwe Papers. University of Cape Town Manuscripts and Archives, Cape Town.

AFSC. [1976/77] AFSC Southern Africa Program Study Tour to the Key Majority-Ruled Countries of Southern Africa Prospectus, Appended to Letter David Sogge to Rory Short, 28 May 1977. File K.2.2, Quaker Collection. University of Cape Town Manuscripts and Archives, Cape Town.

Cardoso, R. (1979, March 20). Letter to Ann Stever, Visit of Southern Africa Friends to America Sponsored by AFSC/FWCC Jointly 1978. File K.2.2, Quaker Collection. University of Cape Town Manuscripts and Archives, Cape Town.

Cardoso, R. (1979, April 12). Letter to Ann Steever [Sic], Visit of Southern Africa Friends to America Sponsored by AFSC/FWCC Jointly 1978. File K.2.2, Quaker Collection. University of Cape Town Manuscripts and Archives, Cape Town.

De, S. K. (1977, April 4). To Friends World Committee for Consultation (Africa Section), Seminar on Non-Violence, April 4, 1977, Quaker Seminar on Non-Violence Held in Botswana 4th to 11th August 1977 under FWCC (Africa Section) Correspondence and Reports. File K.2.2, Quaker Collection. University of Cape Town Manuscripts and Archives, Cape Town.

Elliott, R. M. (1977, June 14). Rosemary M. Elliott, SAYM Clerk to David Sogge, AFSC, June 14, 1977, Quaker Seminar on Non-Violence Held in Botswana 4th to 11th August 1977 under FWCC (Africa Section) Correspondence and Reports. File K.2.2, Quaker Collection. University of Cape Town Manuscripts and Archives, Cape Town.

Elliott, R. M. (1978, March 7). "Letter Rosemary Elliott, Clerk SAYM to Herbert M. Hadley, Executive Secretary FWCC Section of the Americas, 7 March 1978, Visit of Southern Africa Friends to America Sponsored by AFSC/FWCC Jointly 1978." File K.2.2, Quaker Collection. University of Cape Town Manuscripts and Archives.

Elliott, R. M. (1978, August). Report of Travel in the USA in the Summer of 1978, Visit of Southern Africa Friends to America Sponsored by

AFSC/FWCC Jointly 1978. File K.2.2, Quaker Collection. University of Cape Town Manuscripts and Archives, Cape Town.

Elliott, R. M. (1978, August 19). Letter to Herbert Hadley, Visit of Southern Africa Friends to America Sponsored by AFSC/FWCC Jointly 1978. File K.2.2, Quaker Collection. University of Cape Town Manuscripts and Archives, Cape Town.

Elliott, R. M. (1979, March 6). Letter to Ann Stever. File K.2.2, Quaker Collection. University of Cape Town Manuscripts and Archives, Cape Town.

Elliott, R.M., Madenyika, E., and van der Merwe, H.W. (1979, July 8). Letter from SAYM, CAGM, and SAGM Clerks (Rosemary M. Elliott, SAYM; Ellison Madenyika, CAGM; H.W. van Der Merwe, SAGM) to Lewis Hoskins, Earlham College. File K.2.2, Quaker Collection. University of Cape Town Manuscripts and Archives, Cape Town.

Gibberd, T. (1977, May 15). Letter to Shelagh [Willet], Quaker Seminar on Non-Violence Held in Botswana 4th to 11th August 1977 under FWCC (Africa Section) Correspondence and Reports. File K.2.2, Quaker Collection. University of Cape Town Manuscripts and Archives, Cape Town.

Gibson, O. (1977, June 16). Olive Gibson to David Sogge, AFSC (Africa Programs), Quaker Seminar on Non-Violence Held in Botswana 4th to 11th August 1977 under FWCC (Africa Section) Correspondence and Reports. File K.2.2, Quaker Collection. University of Cape Town Manuscripts and Archives, Cape Town.

Hoskins, L. (1977). "Non-Violence in South Africa & the Quaker Response," Collection of Background Papers Presented at the Nonviolence Seminar. File K.2.2, Quaker Collection. University of Cape Town Manuscripts and Archives, Cape Town.

Hoskins, L. (1979, July 10). Letter to Rosemary Elliott" File K.2.2, Quaker Collection. University of Cape Town Manuscripts and Archives, Cape Town.

Kikaya, D. (1976, October 5). Circular Sent by FWCC Africa Section, Quaker Seminar on Non-Violence Held in Botswana 4th to 11th August 1977 under FWCC (Africa Section) Correspondence and Reports. File K.2.2, Quaker Collection. University of Cape Town Manuscripts and Archives, Cape Town.

Kikaya, D. (1977, June 27). David Kikaya (Executive Secretary, FWCC/AS) to David Sogge (AFSC), Quaker Seminar on Non-Violence Held in Botswana 4th to 11th August 1977 under FWCC (Africa Section) Correspondence and Reports. File K.2.2, Quaker Collection. University of Cape Town Manuscripts and Archives, Cape Town.

Miller, P. M. (1977). "Non-Violence: What Historic Peace Churches Can Do to Oppose the Violence of Apartheid," Collection of Background Papers Presented at the Nonviolence Seminar. File K.2.2, Quaker Collection. University of Cape Town Manuscripts and Archives, Cape Town.

Moorehouse, F. (1977). "Friends World Committee for Consultation Africa Section Seminar on Non-Violence Botswana August 4th -11th 1977 Paper," Collection of Background Papers Presented at the Nonviolence Seminar. File K.2.2, Quaker Collection. University of Cape Town Manuscripts and Archives, Cape Town.

Snipes, S. M. (1979). Report of Samuel M. Snipes on Trip to Southern African Yearly Meeting on Behalf of Friends World Committee - August - September 1979. File K.2.2, Quaker Collection. University of Cape Town Manuscripts and Archives, Cape Town.

Sogge, D. (1977, May 28). David Sogge (AFSC, Africa Programs) to Rory Short (Clerk, SAYM), Quaker Seminar on Non-Violence Held in Botswana 4th to 11th August 1977 under FWCC (Africa Section) Correspondence and Report. File K.2.2, Quaker Collection. University of Cape Town Manuscripts and Archives, Cape Town.

Sogge, D. (1977, July 11). Letter from David Sogge, AFSC, to David Kikaya, FWCC/AS, Quaker Seminar on Non-Violence Held in Botswana 4th to 11th August 1977 under FWCC (Africa Section) Correspondence and Reports. File K.2.2, Quaker Collection. University of Cape Town Manuscripts and Archives, Cape Town.

Sogge, D. (1979, April 24). Letter from Savid Sogge, Africa Programs AFSC to South African Visiting Friends, Visit of Southern Africa Friends to America Sponsored by AFSC/FWCC Jointly 1978. File K.2.2, Quaker Collection. University of Cape Town Manuscripts and Archives, Cape Town.

[South African Friends]. (1977). Response of Participants in Seminar on Non-Violence at Gaborone to Discussions with AFSC Study Group. File K.2.2, Quaker Collection. University of Cape Town Manuscripts and Archives, Cape Town.

[South African Visitors] (1978). Joint Report and Recommendations to FWCC, SAYM, and SAGM by Southern African Visitors, June, July 1978, [Presented at SAGM 1979], Visit of Southern Africa Friends to America Sponsored by AFSC/FWCC Jointly 1978. File K.2.2, Quaker Collection. University of Cape Town Manuscripts and Archives, Cape Town

Stever, A. (1979, February 5). Letter to South African Friends Who Travelled to USA, Visit of Southern Africa Friends to America Sponsored by AFSC/FWCC Jointly 1978. File K.2.2, Quaker Collection. University of Cape Town Manuscripts and Archives, Cape Town.

Stever, A. (1979, June 1). Letter to Raymond Cardoso, Visit of Southern Africa Friends to America Sponsored by AFSC/FWCC Jointly 1978. File K.2.2, Quaker Collection. University of Cape Town Manuscripts and Archives, Cape Town.

Taylor, T. F. (1993, Feburary 4). Letter from Thomas F. Taylor, General Secretary FWCC to Corinne Johnson, AFSC International Division, 4 February 1993. BC 1148 Box 65 File A: H.W. van der Merwe Papers. University of Cape Town Manuscripts and Archives, Cape Town.

Tweedie-Waggot, A. (1977). "Friends World Committee for Consultation Africa Section Seminar on Non-Violence Botswana August 4th -11th 1977 Paper," Collection of Background Papers Presented at the Nonviolence Seminar. File K.2.2, Quaker Collection. University of Cape Town Manuscripts and Archives, Cape Town.

Van der Merwe, H. W. (1977a). Follow-up on Report Back to CWMM on FWCC Seminar on Non-Violence, and Meeting with AFSC Study Group, 1977. File K.2.2, Quaker Collection. University of Cape Town Manuscripts and Archives, Cape Town.

Van der Merwe, H. W. (1977b). Report Back to Cape Town Monthly Meeting on Visit to England, FWCC Seminar on Non-Violence, and Meeting with AFSC Study Group in Gaborone, August 1977." File K.2.2, Quaker Collection. University of Cape Town Manuscripts and Archives, Cape Town.

Van der Merwe, H. W. (1978a). Brief Chronological Account of Visit to the USA. File K.2.2, Quaker Collection. University of Cape Town Manuscripts and Archives, Cape Town.

Van der Merwe, H. W. (1978b). Personal Confidential Report by H.W. van Der Merwe on Trip in 1978, Visit of Southern Africa Friends to America Sponsored by AFSC/FWCC Jointly 1978. File K.2.2, Quaker Collection. University of Cape Town Manuscripts and Archives, Cape Town.

Van der Merwe, H. W. (1978c). Afrikaner as African, Written for Quaker Esperanto Society. N.6 Personal: H.W. van der Merwe, 1974-1993. University of Cape Town Manuscripts and Archives, Cape Town.

Van der Merwe, H. W. (1979a). Comments on the Southern Africa Program of the AFSC, Report on a Visit to the USA–26 June to 6 August 1978, Submitted to SAYM, AFSC, and FWCC Section of the Americas. File K.2.2, Quaker Collection. University of Cape Town Manuscripts and Archives, Cape Town.

Van der Merwe, H. W. (1979, March 21). Letter to "Friends," Visit of Southern Africa Friends to America Sponsored by AFSC/FWCC Jointly 1978. File K.2.2, Quaker Collection. University of Cape Town Manuscripts and Archives, Cape Town.

Van der Merwe, H. W. (1979, March 27). Confidential Memo from Hendrik W. van Der Merwe to Rosemary Elliott, Jennifer Kinghorn, and Lewis Hoskins Re: Visit by American Quakers. File K.2.2, Quaker Collection. University of Cape Town Manuscripts and Archives, Cape Town.

Van der Merwe, H. W. (1979, June 15). Letter from HW van Der Merwe, Clerk SAGM, to Louis Schneider and David Sogge, AFSC, Visit of Southern Africa Friends to America Sponsored by AFSC/FWCC Jointly 1978. File K.2.2, Quaker Collection. University of Cape Town Manuscripts and Archives, Cape Town.

Van der Merwe, H. W. (1984). American Quaker Involvement in South Africa, 1984, Suggestions and Recommendations [after a Six-Week Lecture Tour in the USA]. N.6 Personal: HW van der Merwe, 1974-1993. University of Cape Town Manuscripts and Archives, Cape Town.

Van der Merwe, H. W. (1984, September 12). Letter to Trish Swift. N.6 Personal: HW van der Merwe, 1974-1993. University of Cape Town Manuscripts and Archives, Cape Town.

Van der Merwe, H. W. (1988, June 20) A Proposal for the Establishment of an Autonomous Mediation Body for Community and Political Conflict in South Africa. BC 1148 Box 64 File D: H.W. van der Merwe Papers. University of Cape Town Manuscripts and Archives, Cape Town.

Van der Merwe, H. W. (1988, September 28). Quaker Steering Committee on Mediation, Principles and Procedures. BC 1148 Box 64 File D: H.W. van der Merwe Papers. University of Cape Town Manuscripts and Archives, Cape Town.

Van der Merwe, H. W. (1988, November 10). Letter to the Members of Quaker Steering Committee on Mediation. BC 1148 Box 64 File D: H.W. van der Merwe Papers. University of Cape Town Manuscripts and Archives, Cape Town.

Young, R., Sogge, D., Hill, G. and Herman, J. (1979, August 31). Memorandum from Ron Young, David Sogge, Ginny Hill, and Jerry Herman to Lee Thornton Re: Consideration of Appointment of Hendrik van Der Merwe as Friend in Residence. N.6 Personal: HW van der Merwe, 1974-1993. University of Cape Town Manuscripts and Archives, Cape Town.

**Published Sources**

Austin, A. W. (2012). *Quaker Brotherhood: Interracial Activism and the American Friends Service Committee, 1917-1950.* Urbana: University of Illinois Press.

Chapman, S. (1979). "Shot from Guns." *The New Republic* 180 (23), 14-18.

Cromartie, M. (Ed.). (1990). *Peace Betrayed? Essays on Pacifism and Politics: Fifteen Responses to "Peace and Revolution" by Guenter Lewy*. Washington, D.C.: Ethics and Public Policy Center.

Crowe, A. and Dyckman W. V. (1990). *The Ministry of Presence: Without Agenda in South Africa*. Wallingford, PA: Pendle Hill Publications.

Fager, C. (Ed.). (1988). *Quaker Service at the Crossroads: American Friends, the American Friends Service Committee and Peace and Revolution*. Falls Church, VA: Kimo Press.

Frost, J. W. (1992). "'Our Deeds Carry Our Message': The Early History of the American Friends Serice Committee." *Quaker History* 81 (1), 1-51.

Hamm, T. D., Marconi, M., Salinas, G.K., and Whitman, B. (2002). "The Decline of Quaker Pacifism in the Twentieth Century: Indiana Yearly Meeting of Friends as a Case Study." *Indiana Magazine of History* 96 (1), 175-94.

Healey, R. R. (2016). "Quakers and World War One: Negotiating Individual Conscience and the Peace Testimony." In G. L. Health (Ed.) *American Churches and the First World War* (107-28). Eugene, OR: Wipf and Stock.

Hostetter, D. (2002). "Liberation in One Organization: Apartheid, Nonviolence, and the Politics of the AFSC." *Peace & Change* 27 (4), 572-99.

Ingle, H. L. (1998). "The American Friends Service Committee, 1947-49: The Cold War's Effect." *Peace & Change* 23 (1), 27-48.

Ingle, H. L. (2016). "'Truly Radical, Non-Violent, Friendly Approaches': Challenges to the American Friends Service Committee." *Quaker History* 105 (1), 1-21.

Lean, P. and Lean. (1981). *Quakers in South Africa: A Brief History*. Johannesburg: N.p.

Lewy, G. (1988). *Peace and Revolution: The Moral Crisis of American Pacifism*. Grand Rapids, MI: William Eerdmans Publishing.

Malan, J. (2013). "From Going between to Working Together: Learning from Structures and Attitudes in South Africa's Transition." *African Journal on Conflict Resolution* 13 (3), 21-43.

Smith, A. (1996). "The Renewal Movement: The Peace Testimony and Modern Quakerism." *Quaker History* 85 (2), 1-23.

Tonsing, B. K. (2002). *The Quakers in South Africa: A Social Witness*. Lewiston, NY: Edwin Mellen Press.

Valentine, L. (2013). "Quakers, War, and Peacemaking." In S. W. Angell and P. Dandelion (Eds.) *Oxford Handbook of Quaker Studies* (363-76). Oxford: Oxford University Press.

Van der Merwe, H. W. (2001). *Reconciling Opposites: Reflections on Peacemaking in South Africa*. Armadale North, Victoria: Australia Yearly Meeting of the Religious Society of Friends.

Van der Merwe, H. W. (2000). *Peacemaking in South Africa: A Life in Conflict Resolution*. Cape Town: Tafelberg.

Van der Merwe, H. W. (1989). *Pursuing Justice and Peace in South Africa*. London: Routledge.

Van der Merwe, H. W. (1981). *South Africa: Morality and Action: Quaker Efforts in a Difficult Environment*. Rondebosch, SA: Centre for Intergroup Studies, University of Cape Town.

Van der Merwe, H. W., Charton, N. C. J., Kotze, D. A., and Magnusson, A. (Eds.). (1978). *African Perspectives on South Africa: A Collection of Speeches, Articles, and Documents*. Stanford, CA: Hoover Institution Press.

# Discussion Questions

1. Benjamin Webb and Robert Dale Owen were sharply criticized by many Quakers in the 19th century. How would they be received among Quakers in the 21st century?

2. To what extent are Quakers critical of capitalism in the 21st century? To what extent are Quakers divided over this issue? Is there an alternative economic system embraced by a significant number of Quakers?

3. Healey describes a rift between South African Quakers and AFSC staff. Have there been similar disagreements between Quakers and other Quaker organizations? What can be done to address these conflicts?

4. How wide is the consensus on nonviolence within Quaker circles today? What issues have widespread agreement among Quakers?

# PART V
## *Contributions by Prominent Quakers*

# 12 | John Bellers and the Evolutionary Potential of Quakerism

**By Keith Helmuth**

### Introduction

When Kenneth Boulding gave the James Backhouse Lecture (1964) at Australia Yearly Meeting in 1964, he introduced a concept into Friends' lexicon that has become a Quaker meme[1]–*the evolutionary potential of Quakerism.*

Over the years, the story embedded in this phrase has become central to a fully rounded understanding of the Religious Society of Friends. Within the second generation of Friends, John Bellers (1654-1725) brought the evolutionary potential of Quakerism to an astonishing and prescient articulation. Many decades, indeed, centuries, would pass before much of what he envisioned would begin to emerge in the political and social economies of the modern world. Kenneth Boulding's concise phrase puts it all in perspective. His lecture looked mostly to the future with regard to the evolutionary potential of Quakerism. I will here be looking back to John Bellers who is a wellspring of its beginnings. But first, a quick review of how Boulding came to understand and articulate this Quaker meme.

---

[1] A meme is to cultural life as a gene is to biological life. A meme is a unit of self-replicating cultural information that spreads from imagination to imagination and from generation to generation. Memes encapsulate and transmit key features of cultural identity and provide narratives of cultural guidance.

The meme concept was introduced by Richard Dawkins (1976) in his book, *The Selfish Gene.* Susan Blackmore (2000) developed the concept further in her book, *The Meme Machine.* A particularly interesting application of the meme concept is found in Patrick Reinsborough and Doyle Canning's (2010) *Re–Imagining Change: How to Use Story–Based Strategy to Win Campaigns, Build Movements, and Change the World.*

263

Kenneth Boulding's genius was (at least) twofold: 1) As an economist, he was among the first to understand the biophysical basis of human adaptation as the flow-through of material and energy resources within the context of earth's ecosystems. 2) As a social scientist, he understood human cultural development within the dynamics of planetary evolution. In addition, he had a facility for using images that placed the human story within the scientific perspective of both biophysical economics and planetary evolution ("spaceship earth"). He was one of the founders (1956) of General Systems Theory.

In his Backhouse lecture, Kenneth Boulding (1964), employs a central scientific construct of evolutionary biology–mutation and selection–to illustrate the cultural position and significance of Quakerism in the history of Western civilization. He does not employ this construct as an analogy, but rather as an objective description of the way any system, biological or cultural, changes over time. In this context, he makes the following observation: "Each of the great religions can be seen as phylum stretching through time from its origins, growing or declining and branching with some branches possessing more evolutionary potential than others. Some branches come to an end, and some proliferate into the future" (p. 11). He comments further:

> Considered as a case of social evolution, the Society of Friends can be seen as a mutation from the Christian phylum. … The magnitude of the Quaker mutation alone makes it of an unusual historical interest. It represented a change from existing beliefs and practices in a considerable number of important religious cultural elements… (pp. 10, 13).

He then identifies two elements he considers central to the evolutionary potential of Quakerism: perfectionism and experimentalism. Quakers came early to experience the guidance of the inward light as not only revealing sin but as *a power that brought them out of it*. "They believed that life without sin could be lived on earth and they set about rather deliberately to organize a society to do this …" (p. 13).

Historically and theologically this cultural mutation has been called perfectionism, but I think this is misleading. The term perfectionism has a connotation of stasis, of reaching a state of perfection. This ethos can be at odds with experimentalism. Experimentalism is dynamic. I think it is more accurate to see the element of perfectionism as an ongoing quest for *right relationship*. Life is always relationship and relationship is inevitably dynamic. Aiming always for right relationship is an allegiance to what can be thought of as a dynamic of perfection, a perfection always in the making. This is a stance that can acknowledge mistakes, that allows for relationships that go wrong, but never loses its allegiance to the ethic of right relationship.

Experimentalism, the second element that added a powerful impetus to the Quaker mutation, was introduced when George Fox began speaking of the revelation that had come to him. He announced, "…Christ was come to teach people himself…" (Fox, 1998, p. 83). With that sense of continuing revelation, a whole new horizon of learning was opened within the Society of Friends. The message of continuing revelation that Fox and his compatriots launched into the culture of the time shifted the basis of spiritual life from a preoccupation with personal security after death to an engagement with the process of learning within an allegiance to right relationship.

Kenneth Boulding goes on in his Backhouse Lecture to unfold the effect this Quaker mutation has had on many aspects of human cultural development and then looks to the future and what Friends may yet contribute to human betterment. To understand how this evolutionary potential of Quakerism got started and persisted, we need to look carefully at John Bellers.

Although not well known in Quaker studies, John Bellers was amazingly prescient with regard to the evolutionary potential of Quakerism. The understanding of human betterment that emerged from his Quaker worldview is astonishing for the time in which he lived. His insight into the significance of universal education, vocational training, public healthcare, social fairness, political economy, finance and investment, governance, and international relations grew into an integral conception of human betterment the likes of which, I believe it is correct to say, had never been seen before. My project here is to show how, in all this, John Bellers foreshadows the evolutionary potential of Quakerism.

By the end of the 17th century, the initial growth of Quakerism was over and the Religious Society of Friends was settling into the forms and disciplines of an established dissenting sect. Quakerism was still regarded by many as heretical and a danger to society, but persecution had mostly ceased. Friends became increasingly successful in various business enterprises, and their place in society became ever more settled. Into this time comes John Bellers with a way of thinking that lifts the evolutionary potential of Quakerism into a fully rounded vision of human betterment and the common good.

From its earliest days, Quaker integrity transcended the distinction between sacred and secular. Integrity is integrity whether in spiritual ministry or in giving good value in the marketplace; the guide is always the same and is operational from one end of life's activities to the other. John Bellers applied this holistic

Quaker approach–one might say, this systems approach–to the economic and social realities of his time.

### John Bellers and the Quaker Ethos

John Bellers was a generation younger than George Fox. He was born in 1654, and died at age 71 in 1725. He was born into a Quaker family of some means and married into a Quaker family of even greater means. His business career prospered in the cloth trade, which allowed him time to study and analyze the contemporary religious, social, economic, and political situation. A few biographical details taken from George Clarke's book, *John Bellers: His Life, Times & Writings* (Bellers and Clarke, 1987) and from A. Ruth Fry's (1935) book, *John Bellers: Quaker, Economist and Social Reformer*, will provide a sense of this remarkable man.

Although nothing is known about his formative years, it is clear from his writings that he was well educated and widely read. He quoted or referred to Aristotle, Cato, Caesar, Cicero, Confucius, John Everard, Galen, Hippocrates, Plato, and Tauler. Like many Quakers at the time, he had a deep knowledge of the Bible from which he frequently quoted with great facility to support the reasoning of his observations and proposals.

Quakerism had won many converts in the city of London during this time and Bellers grew up immersed in a vibrant and sometimes contentious Quaker culture. He would have been in association with many strong-minded Friends, some from the Leveler and Digger movements, some who had been members of Cromwell's army, and some who had suffered severe persecution. He himself was twice arrested and fined for "riotous assembly"–which could be simply gathering with Friends at a time or place in which such gatherings had been legally prohibited. He became keenly aware of the terrible conditions in which the poor of London lived and died.

As a young adult, Bellers was actively involved in Quaker affairs. At the age of twenty-five, he was appointed treasurer of a Quaker fund for employing the poor. The fund was used to purchase flax for distribution to poor Friends in various meetings who would then spin it into yarn for making linen cloth. It seems likely this direct engagement with poverty, and with a supported employment program for its alleviation, started Bellers' thinking in a way that he eventually developed into his "Colledge of Industry" proposal.

In 1686 he married Frances Fettiplace. After Frances' father died, Bellers and his family–eventually totalling six children–moved into her family home, Coln St Aldwy in Gloucestershire, a manor house that was frequented by

Friends, including George Fox, William Penn, John Pennington and Thomas Ellwood.

The conditions for the poor in those times were utterly appalling. England had entered the early stages of the industrial and commercial transformation that was to produce the world's first "modern" society. A burgeoning empire built on military, naval, manufacturing, and commercial power offered the prospect of increased wealth to the already wealthy. Making money became the obsession of the times. Parliament was totally the instrument of landed Gentry and rising commercial interests. Yeoman, Commoners, and Peasants had no voice in government. Workers were viewed simply as raw material for industrial use and not as human beings with development potential. Workers were given only "starvation wages" and long hours in order that investment profits could be as high as possible. Rural families were being driven to the cities by the on going enclosures of common lands. Large numbers of people lived in continual insecurity, illness, conditions of violence, and exploitation. Abandoned children were commonplace, prostitution rampant, theft common. Education and healthcare for the poor were not even considered. The Parish workhouses were wretched places, often cruelly run.

Bellers looked on all this and set his mind to understanding the origin and cure of these conditions. It came to him that without poor labourers there would be no wealth for the rich. Gerard Winstanley (1652) sixty-three years earlier had written, "No man can be rich but he must be rich either by his own labours, or by the labours of other men." Bellers (Bellers and Clark, 1987), with a typical flourish, he put it like this: "The labours of the Poor are the Mines of the Rich" (p. 19).

In 1695 John Bellers began a campaign of writing and publishing that continued to the year he died. "Campaign" is the right word. Bellers did not write with literary ambition, although he was an accomplished writer. He did not aspire to philosophic stature, although he was mentally equipped in this regard. As a Quaker, he was blocked from a political career, although he would have been an excellent parliamentarian. He was, however, a Fellow of the Royal Society, which means he was recognized for his interest in "improving Natural Knowledge." An innovative way of thinking drew his talents and energy into a particular kind of focus, a focus that has little in the way of antecedents, a focus that begins to define a new way of thinking about the connections between social health and the economy. In Bellers, a talent for systematic assessment and analytic thinking are combined and applied to social and economic realities in a new way.

Where did this new angle of vision come from? He would not have thought as he did had he been raised an Anglican. He certainly would not have looked on the plight of the poor in the way he did had he been raised a Calvinist. It is clear in his writings that the root of his inspiration and the understandings that governed his thinking derived from his Quaker worldview.

In 1717 tragedy struck John Bellers. His wife, Frances, his daughter, Elizabeth, and his young son, Francis, all died, probably from smallpox, and he was suddenly alone. His older children were married or on their own. In these later years, even with failing health, John Bellers continued his study of social and economic conditions, matched them to the ethical demands of his faith, and renewed his call to Quakers and government to act effectively on behalf of the poor.

I have, in what follows, no dramatic discoveries or startling insights, but rather, I hope, a steady accumulation of evidence, a kind of intellectual and spiritual narrative that will build into a strong sense of the evolutionary potential of Quakerism as exemplified in the life and work of John Bellers.

## John Bellers: "A Phenomenon in the History of Political Economy" (Karl Marx)

In order to lay out the scope of John Bellers' contribution to the evolutionary potential of Quakerism, I will first list his twenty publications with comment. I will then document Bellers' historic significance and consider the deep narrative of the evolutionary potential of Quakerism and Bellers' place in this story (All quoted material in this section is from Clarke's edited text [Bellers and Clarke, 1987]).

The best way to begin is to give the full title page of his first published work: *Proposal for Raising a Colledge of Industry of All Useful Trades and Husbandry, with Profit for the Rich, A Plentiful Living for the Poor, A Good Education for Youth. Which will be Advantage to the Government, by Increase of the People, and their Riches* (Bellers and Clarke, 1987). At the bottom of the page is printed; "Motto, Industry Brings Plenty", followed by "The Sluggard shall be cloathed with Raggs. He that will not Work, shall not Eat."

Bellers first published this pamphlet in 1695. He immediately revised it, adding more statistics to his analysis, and answering the objections of his critics. This second edition carried the signed endorsement of 42 prominent Quakers including William Penn, Robert Barclay, Thomas Ellwood, and Leonard Fell. This *Proposal* became his signature work. He circulated to it Quakers, to Parliament, to the Archbishop, to the Anglican Clergy, to rich industrialists, and to wealthy landowners. He was not looking for charity. He was looking for investment. This proposal was a business enterprise.

In essence, Bellers' proposal for a "Colledge of Industry" described a cooperative community set up to provide basic education, vocational training, and the production of goods and services. In modern terms, it was closer to the concept of a "new town" than to an "intentional community." Although Bellers advanced the concept as an institution through which those in poverty could work themselves out of this condition, he calculated the investment return to funders in a way that would be attractive to those with surplus wealth. He further calculated that the education, training, and healthcare benefits would also be attractive to families of good means, creating a mix of participants that would help stabilize the projects.

At the same time, he published a letter entitled, *To the Children of Light, in Scorn called Quakers*. Many Friends by this time were doing well in business and accumulating surplus wealth. The letter explained why investing in the establishment of a "Colledge of Industry" would be fiscally prudent and morally excellent. He also addressed himself to the Government in a document titled, *To the Lords & Commons In Parliament Assembled*. In this publication, he argued for the welfare of the entire nation, saying that one example of a "Colledge of Industry" that was successful could spark a movement of duplication that would have a profoundly uplifting effect on the whole society.

In 1697 he published *An Epistle to Friends concerning the Education of Children* that linked the well-established concern among Quakers for education with the education component of his *Proposal*.

In 1699 Bellers published a major integration of his economic and religious perspective. Again, the full title will provided the scope; *Essays About the Poor, Manufactures, Trade, Plantations, & Immorality, and of the Excellency and Divinity of Inward Light, Demonstrated from the Attributes of God, and the Nature of Mans Soul, as well as from the Testimony of the Holy Scriptures*. This publication is addressed specifically "To the Lords and Commons in Parliament Assembled," with a subsidiary address "To the Intelligent and Thinking Reader." This latter address begins with the following sharp but tempered comment.

> Witty Men, who think but once upon a Subject, are able to make a Jest upon it; but Wise Men think twice, that will give the right judgment upon things: And these last are the Readers I address my self unto, who have the temper to receive a good Proposition, and Sense to disprove a bad or weak one, by Proposing a better: For that Physician that can advise nothing in a desparate Disease but contradicts others, will have no great Cure to boast of (p. 86).

The richness of this collection of short essays cannot easily be conveyed. Extensive quotation and comment would be required and I cannot do that here. Mainly, it provides historical, anthropological, behavioural, ethical, theological, and experiential evidence for the worldview from which he worked. The text is only twenty-two pages in Clarke's edition, but, in the power of its conception and execution, it dwarfs many of the lengthy and ponderous works of political economy that were to appear within the next century. Here is one sample of Bellers analysis:

> It is a certain Demonstration of the Illness of the Method the People are imployed in, if they cannot live by it: nothing being more plain, than that Men in proper Labour and Imployment are capable of Earning more than a Living; or else Mankind had been extinguished in the first Age of the World (p. 91).

This publication includes his most often noted pieces of economic and social analysis, "Of Money" and "Some Reasons against putting of Fellons to Death." The short essay on money is truly amazing. He fully understood money as a technology of social trust. He understood the labour theory of value, the dynamics and danger of inflation, and that money is only useful when it is "parted with." He was literally centuries ahead of his time in his understanding of money. Not even Marx quite escaped the mystification of money with as much clarity. Not until Irving Fisher (1922) developed his "quantity theory of money" and Silvio Gesell (1958) introduced the concept of demurrage, do we have a comparable lucidity on the subject. Likewise, his argument against the death penalty was without precedent. He was the first social thinker in history to reason his way to the abolition of this moral and legal custom. His argument was a seamless blend of social psychology, economics, and moral advancement.

He ended this collection with sections on "God," "Man's Soul," "Christian Virtue," and "Divine Worship," all cast in a mode of thought and expression that clearly illustrated the innovation in understanding that Quakerism was bringing to the times. For example, he writes: "And God being the most invisible Light, Spirit, and Life, he penetrates all Beings and Spirits, more thoroughly than the visible Light at Noon-day doth the Air" (p.104). In the section on Virtue he highlighted the cardinal transition of Quakerism that I earlier discussed:

> Reasons of State, Profit, Health, Reputation, or Danger of Punishment was part of the Motives given by the ancient Philosophers, to persuade Men from Vice; which, as it is the least, it is the first Step towards

Wisdom; Learning to do well, through Love to Virtue, being a degree higher, than ceasing to do evil for fear of Sufferings (p. 106).

In 1702 Bellers published a document that addressed what must have been a persistent problem within the Society of Friends. Although certainly aimed at Friends, it is, characteristically, framed in a way that made it universally applicable to all who might be concerned with its theme. Again, the full title: *A Caution Against All Perturbations of the Mind; But more particularly against (the Passion of) Anger, As An Enemy to the Soul, By making of it Unfit for The Presence of God, And Unable to Enter The Kingdom of Heaven.*

Quickness to anger and continuing grudges derived from conflicts must have been a persistent problem among Friends in those days; they were a diverse lot, pacifism was not yet a consistent view. Bellers took up his subject at the root. Here are a few choice lines:

> Anger is the parent of Murder ... as an Acorn is of an Oak. ...... Anger is the worst Temper of the Mind, it being the directest opposite to Love, which is the best, because God himself is Love; ... Love is the first Divine Impression the Soul of a Christian receives, and the last he loseth, ... No Man is Angry for God's sake, but it is for our Own Will; which not being Resigned to the Will of God as it should be, is that which gives the first motion to Anger; ... God is a God of Order, and the Glory of those Assemblies, where the Members have a Sense of Him upon their Souls. But it is also true, that any Disorder upon the Minds of Men will deprive their Souls of His Presence, and therefore such Perturbations must be Sin and Evil (p. 117-118).

In the last line of this essay, Bellers, in his gentle way, really put it to leaders, who, as we know, are often beset with outsize egos. He wrote as follows, using a reference for the evil power from the Book of Revelations: "But it's a Melancholy Consideration to think ... that the Dragons Tail should do more Mischief ... among the Stars of the Church, than his violence could do among the least of the Flock of Christ..." (p. 119).

The last section of this publication is titled: *Watch unto Prayer: or Considerations for All Who Profess They Believe in the Light, To see whether they walk in the Light, without which they cannot become the Children of It, nor be cleansed from their Sins.* In this essay, Bellers holds up the discipline of "watchfulness" in the same way Buddhist's hold up the practice of "mindfulness." Here is the way he started the essay:

271

> Watching is as needful to the soul as breathing is to the body; every quickening of the soul to God, gives a disposition to watchfulness, as much as the body, recovering out a swoon, is disposed to breath. ...As breathing whilst living, is inseparable from the body; so watching is inseparable from the soul, whilst it lives towards God. ...Watching is to be Spiritually minded, which is life and peace (p. 124).

Further on in the essay he wrote:

> Therefore he that governs his mind right, is the only sincere man; whereas he that keeps not a watch upon the thoughts of his heart, is much out of his way; for though he should imitate the best of forms, he is but of the outward court; it being impossible to worship God in the beauty of holiness, with an irregular mind. ... But he that watches in the Light it will bring him to the New Jerusalem (p. 125).

Although there is much Quaker literature I have not read, I have never before come across anything quite like this. Its resonance transcends culture. It leaps backwards and forwards over the centuries of spiritual discipline. Confucius would have understood this perfectly. Bodhidharma would have raised a hand in silent recognition. Thich Nhat Han would smile knowingly. Mary Oliver, the contemporary poet so loved by Friends and whose work is essentially a call to wakeup and pay attention, would surely salute a spiritual forerunner.

Bellers was primarily a pioneering political economist and a proto social ecologist, but you can see here that his work was founded on a depth of spiritual insight that Quakerism was advancing into the society of the time.

In the early 1700's the Protestant population of France's Rhemish Palatinate region had come under severe persecution and were fleeing in great numbers, over 400,000 in a few years. At least 15,000 came to England destitute and seeking refuge (Bellers and Clarke, 1987, p. 127). In 1709 John Bellers responded with a publication addressed *To the Lords and other Commissioners, appointed by the Queen to take Care of the Poor Palatines.*

With brevity and clarity he again offered his *Proposal for a Colledge of Industry* as a way of responding to the problem within a business investment framework. He saw this refugee immigrant population not as a burden on the Public Treasury, but as a prime opportunity to advance both human and economic development to the benefit of the folks in question and to the nation as a whole. No one, it seems, had the wit to understand the rationality of his project. The concept of combining financial investment with human uplift for the good of the nation was simply beyond the ken of economic thinking at the time. In many ways, Bellers' understanding of political economy had to wait until the 20th Century to be comprehended and implemented. Even now there are jurisdictions of special interest that do not want to advance the common good.

In 1710 Bellers unloaded a publication of stunning prescience into the teeth of the endless European wars. Modestly titled, *Some Reasons For an European State*, Bellers anticipated the League of Nations, the United Nations, and the European Union. This work undoubtedly grew from conversations with William Penn who, in 1693, had published *An Essay towards the Present and Future Peace of Europe.*

Bellers' publication is a strong logical advance over Penn's *Essay*; it introduced a sophisticated economic analysis with statistically backed arguments illustrating that European wars have greatly retarded the development of husbandry, manufacturing, industry, and trade. He argued that the Princes and Sovereigns who foment and extend these wars are foregoing the opportunity to advance economic development, increase the wealth of their jurisdictions, and so gain great favour with their subjects. He cautioned them to consider the placement of their responsibilities between God and society and how they could best fulfill the good of their people that God had entrusted to them.

As for a way out of these endless wars, he recommended the creation of a European parliament where conflicts can first come into open discussion, debate, and negotiation. He further proposed an agreement among those who come to this understanding that they combine, with armed force if necessary, against jurisdictions that violate with aggression the peace of the continent. This is international political thinking 250 years before the United Nations and its peacekeeping forces.

He then went one step further to the heart of the religious controversies that lay behind many of the conflicts that were erupting in persecutions, violence, and war. He asked the leaders of all the Christian denominations to come together in a great council for the end of the persecutions and violence that have so marred the Faith. He was a master of the gentle use of shame in this appeal.

He went further; he offered a technique of dialogue that, if sincerely employed, would enable Christian leaders to meet on common ground and advance a zone of understanding, tolerance, and peaceable relations that Europe so badly needed. He told them to focus on what they had in common, what they all shared at the heart of the Christian faith, and keep the things that created disagreement out of the room. This was precisely the practice of conflict resolution and decision making pioneered by Quakerism: in essentials unity, in non-essentials diversity, in all things charity. This was the evolutionary potential of Quakerism moving into ecumenism. Christian ecumenism, as first articulated by Bellers, is now a great force for good in the world.

We can't say that Bellers' proposals had much immediate effect on the wars of Europe, but it is clear he was exactly right about what was required for peace among nations, and especially with respect to conflict over religion. The European Union is now a reality, and though it is struggling, it is perhaps the most remarkable achievement of modern political life. And not only is Christian ecumenism a reality, but inter-faith ecumenism is also flowering.

In 1711, John Bellers followed his ecumenical intuition and published an open letter *To the Archbishop, Bishops and Clergy, of the Province of Canterbury Met in Convocation.* This letter powerfully challenged the Church of England to practice what it preached. His words were simple and direct, permitting no misunderstanding. Among other things, he asked the Church to urge the Queen to hold a Convention of all "religious persuasions in the British dominions", for the purpose of extending understanding and toleration. This is clearly associated with his similar plea to the Christian leaders of Europe. He probably thought that Britain should set the example for religious toleration.

Elections in England at this time were rife with influence peddling and corruption. Parliamentary government was up and running but there was little sense of fair contest in a democratic way. Class and moneyed interests readily bought members of Parliament. Political parties were all about gaining advantage for their members and supporters. Political debate and decision-making were rarely about the common good or the welfare of the nation. In 1712, in his typical targeted fashion, John Bellers published a proposal titled, *An Essay Towards the Ease of Elections of Members of Parliament.*

The main points of his proposal were to control excessive liquor sales around voting sites, institute severe fines for taking bribes, and make the qualification of electors (voters) more certain. Again, we see here the application of systems thinking to problem solving. This may seem like common sense to our ears, but it was a new way of thinking in those days.

In 1712, Bellers published another document titled *Some Consideration As an Essay toward Reconciling the Old and New Ministry.* This powerful, but strangely gentle, polemic was aimed foursquare at the political leadership of England. The "old and new ministry" referred to the political parties of the day that were locked in perpetual battle for partisan advantage, while the common good and public interest languished from neglect. It was an appeal for Parliamentarians to grow up into their potential for leadership and national guidance. It detailed in theory and by example what it means to be organized and operate in a politically mature way with regard to national wellbeing. Its political savvy is on par with

Machiavelli's *The Prince*, but it is the obverse; it described how to cooperate and collaborate in order to serve the wellbeing of the whole nation. Nothing, it seems, could discourage John Bellers in his quest for good order, best practice, and social wellbeing.

In 1714, Bellers published another major treatise; the title states the case, *An Essay Towards the Improvement of Physick. In Twelve Proposals. By which the Lives of many Thousands of the Rich, as well as of the Poor, may be Saved Yearly. With an Essay for Imploying the Able Poor; By which the Riches of the Kingdom may be greatly Increased; Humbly Dedicated to the Parliament of Great Britain.*

This was his plan for a national healthcare system, complete with new hospitals, specialty care, research and training institutes, and with focused attention on the poor. He argued that the National Treasury should fund this national system, and that its cost would be more than compensated for by the increase in national productivity due to a greatly improved health situation, especially among the poor. This was a detailed document of many parts that were integrated into an argument of economic logic and social ethics astonishingly modern in conception and reasoning. Indeed, many progressive jurisdictions in the world today have instituted virtually all the parts of Bellers' healthcare proposal.

In 1718 Bellers published *An Epistle to the Quarterly-Meeting of London and Middlesex* in which he appealed to their interest in the education and development of children and youth. He attached a restatement of his proposal for a "Colledge of Industry," emphasizing that charity is not enough, and that projects based on sound economics, educational opportunities, and the social uplift of self-provisioning would effect a much greater good for both individuals and society. He included "A Dialogue between a Learned Divine and a Beggar" in which the Beggar proves to have a superior understanding of both the material and spiritual worlds.

In 1723 Bellers redrafted his proposal for a "colledge of industry" into a briefer form and again presented it to Parliament. At the bottom of the now less elaborate title page he wrote the following: "If there were no Labourers, there would be no Lords. And if the Labourers did not raise more Food, and Manufactures than what did subsist themselves, every Gentlemen must be a Labourer, and idle Men must starve" (p. 238). This statement is yet another version of his aphorism, "The labours of the poor are the mines of the rich."

In the same year, he sent out essentially the same document addressed to *The Yearly, Quarterly, and Monthly Meetings of Great Britain, and Elsewhere.* By this time, his health was rapidly failing. He is trying one last time to reach out as widely as possible, especially among Friends, hoping for investment in his long nurtured dream of self-provisioning and wealth producing cooperative communities, where education, vocational training, and useful employment in husbandry, manufacture, and trades could provide the route to a secure and dignified life for many who were languishing in poverty.

In 1724 Bellers drew up and published *An Abstract of George Fox's Advice and Warning To the Magistrates of London in the Year 1657 Concerning the Poor*. It was essentially a warning against the ethic of social triage and a plea for the widest application of human solidarity. This kind of thinking and moral sensibility is here just emerging in modern thought.

In his last year, Bellers also wrote and sent out *An Epistle to Friends of the Yearly, Quarterly, and Monthly Meetings; Concerning the Prisoners, and Sick, in the Prisons, and Hospitals of Great Britain*. Attached to this was a separate letter *To the Criminals in Prison*. These short documents, in the form of broadsheets, were "unofficial" and it seems likely to George Clarke, a Bellers scholar, that the author delivered them himself to Friends and to the prisons. This final expression of his analysis and concern recommended that Friends act to provide vocational skills training for prisoners, and that prisoners be supplied with regular meals of baked beef. John Bellers, ever the systems thinker, knew that vocational skills training and a nutritionally upgraded diet would improve prisoners' chances for a better life when released.

This survey, although lengthy, just skims the riches that are found in the mind, heart, and writings of John Bellers. He is correct, one surface reading is not enough; but even in this survey, the evolutionary potential of Quakerism shines from the depths to the surface in the life and work of this spiritually grounded, beautifully rational, and ethically advanced Friend.

## The Persistence of the Quaker Ethos and the Perspective of the Long Haul

In the end, John Bellers was not successful in convincing Parliament to support any of his proposals. He did not get the investment support he sought to establish even one "Colledge of Industry." He did get forty-three prominent Friends to endorse his proposal for "raising a Colledge of Industry", but no investment support was forthcoming. Yet, he persisted. He never stopped promoting and republishing his proposals to which both compassion and reason compelled him to remain faithful. At the same time he served on the Board of the Quaker run Clerkenwell Workhouse, which sheltered, educated, and employed poor Quaker children and adults.

There is no evidence that Bellers was eccentric, obsessive, or strange in any way. He was successful in business and in family life and well placed socially.

From our standpoint, we can say he simply saw the reality of relationships in social and economic life in a way so different from the dominant worldview that the significance of his contribution was out of phase with what his compatriots were able to comprehend. His ability to identify and envision the kinds of changes that would set up a cascade of beneficial effects was far in advance of his time.

It is difficult to know whether his writings continued to be read after his death and what effect they might have had. George Clarke comments as follows:

> That he was ignored by the outside world is not surprising. His age was more concerned with the achievement of imperialist ambitions and the growth of trade than the human condition. There was infinitely more concern with the defence of private property than the welfare of ordinary people (Bellers and Clarke, 1987, p. 26).

With regard to the unresponsiveness of Friends, Clarke writes: "Perhaps, for the religiously minded, he dwelt too heavily upon economic considerations. … Truly the prophet is without honour among his own people" (p. 26).

By the end of 17th and into the early18th century, Quakers were settling successfully into the world of industry and commerce, and, in some cases accumulating considerable wealth. The thrust of Friends' pioneering social critique was being blunted by success and acceptance. John Bellers himself operated in this world, but for some extraordinary reason also transcended it with his vision of ethically based social investment on behalf of those in poverty, along with an economically based rationale for national healthcare, and a political solution for the peaceful and cooperative unification of Europe. He drew deeply on his Quaker faith and on its evolutionary potential for mapping out such prescient and practical social and geopolitical reforms.

## John Bellers Second Coming

There is, however, a second coming in the story of Bellers' work and influence–detailed again in Bellers and Clarke (1987). In 1817, Frances Place, a social reformer, discovered among his books and papers, a copy of the 1696 edition of Beller's *Proposal for a Colledge of Industry*. He was so impressed by the contents that he took it to his colleague, Robert Owen, one of the preeminent social reformers of the 19th century and, essentially, the founder of the Cooperative Movement. Owen, at that very time, was developing his "Villages of Co-operation."

Owen was so struck by Bellers' *Proposal*, that he had a thousand copies printed and distributed. He saw it as a direct and vital forerunner of his own social and economic views and his projects of reform. He then published a letter in *The Times*, on 25 July 1817, in which, as Clarke notes, he disclaimed personal credit for the principles on which his own Villages of Co-operation were founded. He wrote as follows:

> None, I believe, not one, of the principles [he means his own principles] has the least claim to originality: they have been repeatedly advocated and recommended by superior minds, from the earliest periods of history. I have no claim even to priority in regard to the combination of these principles in theory; this belongs, as far as I know, to John Bellers, who published them, and most ably recommended them to be adopted in practice in the year 1696. Without any aid from actual experience, he has distinctly shown how they might be applied to the improvement of society, according to the facts known to exist; thus evincing that his mind had the power to contemplate a point 120 years beyond his contemporaries. . . . Whatever merit can be due to an individual for the original discovery of a plan, that, in its consequences is calculated to affect some substantial and permanent benefit to Mankind than any yet perhaps contemplated by the human mind, it all belongs to John Bellers (Bellers and Clark, 1987, pp. 26-27).

There could hardly be a more ringing endorsement for the evolutionary potential of Quakerism. I think it likely that if Owen's accolade could be put to Bellers, he, too, would defer credit and tell us that his analysis and proposals logically flowed from the moral vision that had developed within Quakerism as the result of its openness to learning and the social ethic of human solidarity and human betterment.

Well, perhaps; but in addition, I think we can add that Bellers had a particular cast of mind moving toward what we now call "systems thinking." This approach to understanding social and economic reality, while informed by the Quaker ethos, also helped reform it in a new and evolutionarily significant way. It is not by chance that Kenneth Boulding was a founder of General Systems Theory.

Robert Owen was influenced not just by John Bellers, but by association with Quakers of his time. The Cooperative Movement, for which Owen's work was a catalyst, has become a major form of social and economic reality, and, in fact, a way of life in its higher reaches of development. Many Quakers have been drawn into or have grown up in the Cooperative Movement; this affinity has long been evident although many Friends may not know about the Quaker influence that was present from the beginning. The now worldwide Cooperative and Credit Union Movements stem from this tradition.

Karl Marx discovered Bellers while studying Owen and described Bellers in *Capital* in 1867 as "A veritable phenomenon in the history of Political Economy." (Bellers and Clarke, 1987, p. 27) In the 1880's Henry Meyer Hyndman, a London stockbroker read Marx and, through him, Bellers. He commented that Bellers displayed "a marvellous faculty for forecasting the future", and that "In his works will be found some of the most luminous thoughts on political economy ever met on paper" (Bellers and Clark, 1987, p. 28). Hyndman's books were widely read by social critics and activists at all levels, according to Clarke. Hyndman went on to play a major role in the founding of The Social Democratic Federation, a forerunner of the Labour Party.

In 1885, Joseph W. Corfield, a follower of Owen, a Christian Socialist, and a wealthy man erected an obelisk known as "Reformers' Memorial" in Kensal Green, London. The first name engraved on the monument is Robert Owen; the second is John Bellers. Seventy-two other names follow (Bellers and Clarke, 1987, p. 28). In 1898 German scholar, Eduard Bernstein, published *Cromwell and Communism*, a major study of 17th Century revolution and reform in England. He devoted an entire chapter to John Bellers. In 1919, with the publication of William Braithwaite's *The Second Period of Quakerism*, Quaker scholarship began to give Bellers his due. In 1935, A. Ruth Fry published, *John Bellers: Quaker, Economist, and Social Reformer*, which collected his major writings, along with a biographical essay. And finally, in 1987 George Clarke edited and published a complete collection of Bellers work, along with an extended introduction, notes, and commentary.[2]

## Clarity and Staying Power

As I come to the end of my story, I think of how every one of John Bellers' remarkable proposals has been recognized and implemented as sound and effective social, economic, and political policy by people who never heard his name and, in most cases, know little if anything about Quakers and their history. We might say all this would have happened anyway even if Bellers had never put pen to paper or Friends had not carried forward their passion for justice and fairness in social and economic life.

---

[2] Clarke's book is out of print, but used copies are available from online booksellers. Any good university library should have it or be able to get it through interlibrary loan. In addition, Bellers' publications are available online at universities that have access to primary historical document systems such as Quest.

I think such a claim highly dubious. Certainly, social change of various sorts would have occurred as the Western World evolved into modernity, and progressive reforms of various kinds would have been put in place. But if the Quaker mutation had not occurred in the Christian phylum there are practices of discernment, decision-making, learning, moral vision, ethical guidance, and cultural amplitude that would not have had the channel of development and transmission that Quakerism provided. Many of these Quaker practices are now widely taken for granted as best practices. The ways of thinking, feeling, and acting behind these practices did not come from nowhere. They came through a shift in worldview from hierarchal to egalitarian and through a shift in moral sensibility from insular to inclusive, both of which were carried forward from the 17th century, in large part, by the Religious Society of Friends.

There is a long underground tradition of human struggle against oppression that has emerged in various ways in various times. It emerged in the early 17th century in Gerard Winstanley and the Digger Movement with a particular singularity of consciousness. A generation later, George Fox and the early Friends picked it up. It was advanced and magnified in the Quaker movement and has never gone underground again. The movement is now worldwide and growing in many forms; Paul Hawken (2007) calls it "the blessed unrest."

I do not want to over-claim the significance of Quakerism in the unfolding of human betterment. But in tracing out the Quaker contribution to social equity and the common good, and, in particular, by bringing John Bellers into the picture, we can see that the evolutionary potential of Quakerism for advancing human betterment has an unusual clarity and staying power.

John Bellers observed and analyzed the relationships of power and the uses of wealth that were beginning to build toward the full flowering of a capitalist economy and a market society. He could clearly see the human costs imposed by single-minded wealth seeking. His proposals for reform addressed both mitigation and transformation. Unfortunately, he saw nothing of these reforms in his lifetime. *He was disappointed, but he was not wrong.* His faith in the power of spiritual insight and rational thinking was not misplaced. Circumstances of human betterment have accumulated over the long haul even though regressions have occurred.

We have now come to a time when another era of economic and social regression is ramping up. Wealth and privilege are clamping down on access to resources. Human betterment gains of the recent past are not secure; some have already been lost. And now, in addition to the social and economic distress of society, we are facing the ecological distress of disrupted and damaged ecosystems. As Kenneth Boulding (1965) put it, "This is no way to run a spaceship."[14]

The evolutionary potential of Quakerism must now combine social equity and an ecologically integrated economy into a single focus of wellbeing for human communities and Earth's whole commonwealth of life. There is clarity and staying power in the Quaker heritage that we can bring to this task. We can take heart from the way this clarity and staying power is exemplified in the life of John Bellers, and, like him, keep working for the long haul.

> He that doth not write whilst he is alive, can't Speak when he is Dead. And if a Man shall not be heard in the age, and the Country he lives in, if what he writes is for the general good of Mankind, he may be more minded in other Countries or in succeeding Generations.
>
> – John Bellers, 1699

## References

Bellers, J., & Clarke, G. (1987). *John Bellers: His life, times, and writings.* London: Routledge & K. Paul.

Bernstein, E. (1963). *Cromwell and communism: Socialism and democracy in the great English Revolution.* New York, NY: Schocken Books. (Original work published 1895.)

Blackmore, S. (2000). *The Meme Machine.* New York: NY: Oxford University Press.

Boulding, K. (1956). *General systems theory.* Retrieved from https://www.panarchy.org/boulding/systems.1956.html

Boulding, K. (1964). *The evolutionary potential of Quakerism.* Wallingford, PA: Pendle Hill Publications.

Boulding, K. (1965). Earth as a space ship. Presentation to the Washington State University Committee on Space Sciences. Retrieved from www.colorado.edu/econ/Kenneth.Boulding/spaceship-earth.html

Boulton, D. (1999). *Gerrard Winstanley and the republic of heaven.* Dent, Cumbria, UK: Dales Historical Monographs.

Braithwaite, W. C. (1919). *The second period of Quakerism.* London, UK: Macmillan.

Dawkins, R. (1976). The Selfish Gene. New York, NY: Oxford University Press.

Fisher, I. (1922). *The purchasing power of money.* Indianapolis, IN: Liberty Fund. (Original work published 1911.)

Fox, G. (1998). *Journal.* Nigel Smith (Ed.). London: Penguin Books. (Original work published 1694.)

Fry, A. R (1935). *John Bellers: Quaker, Economist and Social Reformer.* London UK: Cassell and Company.

Gesell, S. (1958). *The natural economic order.* London, UK: Peter Owen. (Original work published 1916.)

Hawken, P. (2007). *Blessed unrest: How the largest movement in the world came into being and why no one saw it coming.* New York, NY: Viking.

Penn, W. (2002). *The political writings of William Penn.* Andrew R. Murphy (Ed.). Indianapolis, IN: Liberty Fund. (Original work published 1693.)

Reinsborough, P., Canning, D. (2010). *Re-Imagining Change: How to Use Story-Based Strategy to Win Campaigns, Build Movements, and Change the World.* Oakland, CA: PM Press.

Winstanley, G. (1652). *The Law of Freedom in a Platform.* Retrieved from: http://www.bilderberg.org/land/lawofr

# 13 | John Woolman and Economics: "A Feeling Knowledge" of "the Connection of Things"

**By Mike Heller[1]**

"A nation that continues year after year to spend more money on military defense than on programs of social uplift is approaching spiritual death," Martin Luther King, Jr., prophetically declared in his 1967 speech "Beyond Vietnam" (p. 341). Much like King in his stand against the Vietnam War, John Woolman, the colonial American Quaker, would have been disturbed by our national priorities today. Many people today are uneasy about living in an economy based upon militarism, income inequality, continual economic growth, and consumerism. In 2016, the U.S. spent $611 billion on national defense, which is more than the next eight nations combined, that is more than the combined total of China, Russia, Saudi Arabia, India, France, the United Kingdom, Japan, and Germany (Peter G. Peterson Foundation, 2017). Regarding income inequality, in 2016, the CEOs of companies on the S&P 500 Index had an average annual compensation of 13.1 million dollars each (AFL-CIO), while the minimum wage for people at the other end of the earning spectrum fell below a livable income. Corporate and individual wealth seem to be dependent upon continual economic growth at the expense of the environment, including the pollution of the oceans and atmosphere, and loss of forests, wetlands, and animal habitats. Individuals and families dealing with serious illness are often forced into bankruptcy. How can we spend such money on the military and executive compensations, while at the same time not afford decent salary increases for

[1] My thanks to Ivan Brownotter, Charles M. Katz, Jon R. Kershner, and Edward Nik-Khah for their ideas and suggestions for this essay.

workers or universal health care? Isn't there something wrong with such a nation's priorities? I could also raise the issues of mass incarceration, structural poverty, race and gender-based discrimination, and refugee crises in the U.S. and worldwide. Our world is suffering from tremendous inequality.

Although much has changed since the mid-1700s, Woolman prophetically addressed related issues: the dangers of industrial pollution, the desire for luxuries that led to abuse of the poor, and the economic causes of war. Woolman warned his fellow Quakers that grasping for more wealth led to oppression and suffering. He argued for something that is almost alien to our culture today, that making as much money as possible and living in luxury can be harmful to oneself and one's children, as well as to those one employs or rents to. Although he wrote several essays on poverty and labor relations, Woolman's essay "A Plea for the Poor" especially appealed to succeeding generations, because of his call for the wealthy to attend to their inward faith and consider "the connection of things." Just over a hundred years after the publication of "A Plea for the Poor," the Fabian Society in England republished the essay. A comparison of Woolman's ideas and those of the Fabians can help us understand the economic implications of this eighteenth-century Quaker's writings.

## "A Plea for the Poor" and Its Reception

John Woolman (1720-1772) was born in Rancocas, New Jersey, grew up in a Quaker community and became deeply involved in the Philadelphia Yearly Meeting as well as his monthly and quarterly meetings. As a young man, he worked in and later owned a successful dry goods business, which no doubt gave him credibility when he addressed fellow Quaker business owners. His antislavery writings, his work with a like-minded group of reformers, and his travels in the ministry became a major factor in moving the Quakers, in the 1770s, to emancipate their slaves before any other large group in the American colonies. Woolman's *Journal*, first published in 1774, became known as one of the finest examples of Quaker spiritual autobiographies. Generations of readers have been impressed with how Woolman's faith and life were consistent, and how his writings and actions expressed the Quaker testimonies of equality, simplicity, peace, and community.

Woolman wrote several essays dealing with economic issues. One essay, "Conversations on the True Harmony of Mankind & How it May be Promoted," dated 1772, is in the form of two dialogues between a rich man and a laborer, and landholder and a laborer. His longer essay, "A Plea for the Poor," apparently written in 1763, was not published until 1793 in Ireland, and editors gave it the title "A Word of Remembrance and Caution to the Rich." I have not found an explanation either for why the essay was published nearly thirty years after Woolman's death or for why it was published in Ireland.

Some scholars in the early and mid-twentieth century wrote about Benjamin Franklin and Woolman side by side. Charles W. Eliot, the President of Harvard, devoted the first volume of the fifty-one volume *Harvard Classics*, first published in 1909, to Franklin's *Autobiography*, Woolman's *Journal*, and William Penn's *Fruits of Solitude*. Eliot's choice to begin this monumental collection with Franklin, Woolman, and Penn represents the esteem for Woolman held at the time. Joseph Dorfman (1946), the historian of economics, included a chapter on Franklin and Woolman in *The Economic Mind in American Civilization*. Dorfman described Franklin as a symbol of American success, of "industry and frugality," and as a cosmopolitan figure with inconsistencies, whose "religion sat lightly on him" (p. 195). In contrast, Woolman offered a "professed idealism." Woolman saw customs as a major obstacle to a right relation with God, a theme with which Woolman begins his first major antislavery essay, "Some Considerations on the Keeping of Negroes," published in 1754. In the opening paragraph, he described how "Customs generally approved and opinions received by youth from their superiors become like the natural produce of the soil" (p.198, all Woolman quotations are taken from Phillips Moulton's authoritative edition). Stating that "Woolman's starting point was the starting point of all the great Quakers and Puritans" (p. 198), Dorfman went on to say: "Worldly wisdom grows so insidiously into custom and convention that by the time it has completely overpowered righteousness, it is assumed to be the righteous way." (p. 198). "Conformity to customs" was harmful for the wealthy and the poor, a realization that revealed how Woolman understood systemic and structural injustice. In his opening paragraph of "A Plea for the Poor," Woolman wrote that wealth "for its own sake" is harmful to the rich, and "in the hands of selfish men" it causes the laboring class many problems: "Wealth desired for its own sake obstructs the increase of virtue, and large possessions in the hands of selfish men have a bad tendency" (p. 238). Such wealth serves only "the vain mind" (p. 238), it employs too small a number of people in useful work, and it forces them to work too hard while others cannot find employment. Woolman saw that adherence to custom, doing things as they had "always been done," led societies and individuals into extremely harmful practices. He focused his arguments most often on how the rich forced exorbitant rents on the poor. "Great traders" charged heavy interests in order to maintain their standard of living, and landowners needing to meet those interest charges passed them along to their tenants as crippling rents (Dorfman pp. 198-99).

The title of Frederick Tolles' (1948) study of colonial Philadelphia, *Meeting House and Counting House*, expressed the tension and growing opposition between those of wealth, identified as the city Quakers, and the reformers, identified as the country Quakers. By the mid-eighteenth century, "a spirit of compromise and concession" was believed by the reformers "to have overtaken Philadelphia Quakerism" (p. 234). The growth in wealth, and "political and economic dominion" threatened the Quakers' identity as "a peculiar people" (p. 230). Tolles wrote that Woolman was one of the leading reformers, and his "steadfast attention to the pure Light could wean the heart away from desires of outward greatness and open the way 'to cease from that Spirit that craves riches'" (p. 82). Because of their shared values, his trust that his listeners and readers could find their own right path made for tender yet forceful persuasion.

Douglas Gwyn's *The Covenant Crucified: Quakers and the Rise of Capitalism* (1995) and Hugh Barbour and J. William Frost's *The Quakers* (1988) described the growing conflict in eighteenth-century Pennsylvania between colonial exploitation and Quaker norms. Gwyn wrote that Woolman was "the most eloquent incisive interpreter of the Quaker dilemma" (p. 340), and that Woolman showed "that Friends' desire to bequeath ample lands and generous estates to their children inspired them to utilize the same exploitative measures rampant everywhere in the American colonies" (p. 341); he "saw the dire judgments of God contained in slaveholding, genocidal policies toward Native Americans, and the rapacious acceleration of capitalist exploitation, including its environmental hazards" (p. 348). Barbour and Frost elaborated on Woolman's ability to analyze this exploitation, using the example of frontier dwellers selling rum to the Indians. The renters took advantage of the Indians because of their own dire situation, caused by the oppressive practices of the wealthy (p. 134). Woolman understood that these dangers were linked like a chain. He asked his readers to "consider the connection of things" (p. 247). In the words of Thomas Slaughter (2008), who has written a biography of Woolman, "small injustices lead to larger ones, and this is true in racial, labor, and class relations" (p. 269).

## Woolman's Ideas about Wealth and Poverty

By 1763, when it is believed that Woolman finished "A Plea for the Poor," he had completed the four major journeys he would take in America. He had traveled twice in the southern colonies as far as North Carolina and twice into New England. In 1758, largely because of his efforts, the Philadelphia Yearly Meeting had established a committee to visit every slaveholding household in the Yearly Meeting. Woolman served on the committee, which took several years to complete its work. In 1761, despite apprehension about making himself stand out, or appear "singular," he reported in his *Journal* that he decided to wear only undyed clothing because he felt conflicted by the fact that dyes were made by slave labor (Woolman, 1971, pp. 119-20). In 1763, despite the on-going war with the Indians and the French, he traveled two hundred miles north in Pennsylvania to spend time with "the natives of this land who dwell far back in the wilderness" (p. 122). Woolman felt led by the inward spirit which was guiding his interactions with the wealthy, the slave owners, and the Indians.

As James Proud (2010) noted in his edition of Woolman's essays, these "formative encounters with the American rich as well as with the poor and dispossessed had so deeply settled into his spiritual being that his thoughts on the subject would have reached maturity and been ready for written expression" (p. 62). As the word "maturity" suggests, Woolman had thought for a long time about his experiences. His decision to avoid using dyed clothing was one in a series of decisions guided by conscience and developed over time. Woolman practiced self-denying actions much like Gandhi's "experiments with Truth": Woolman gave up his dry goods business to allow more time for what he felt the spirit calling him to do; he later refused to ride horses on his journeys in the ministry so that he might identify with enslaved people; he refused to travel in an ornate ship's cabin on his journey to England in 1772; in his last months, he refused to use the stagecoaches or to mail letters through the post because of abusive working conditions for the child workers and the horses; and he refused to use silverware because of abusive mining conditions. All of this wore on him. In his *Journal*'s final pages, he wrote about walking in the wet streets of northern England, where he tried to avoid filth and run-off from the use of dyes. At the same time, he was physically weak and fearful of smallpox: "where dirtiness under foot and the scent arising from filth ... more or less infects the air of all thick settled towns" (p. 190).

In "Answerable to the Design of our Creation," Paul Lacey (2003) described how, despite challenges in teaching "A Plea for the Poor" to first-year college students, he believed it had value for young people nevertheless. Lacey emphasized Woolman's message that oppression is "misapplied power" and arises from a lack of heart and sympathy. Woolman (1971) wrote that "a person who hath never felt the weight of misapplied power comes not to this knowledge but by an inward tenderness, in which the heart is prepared to sympathy with others" (p. 243, Lacey, p. 301). Wealth desired for its own sake created suffering because of its effects on workers (p. 238, Lacey, p. 297). The desire for luxuries created punishing working conditions that increased alcoholism, and alcoholism increased abusive relationships. If luxuries were reduced, Woolman argued, then rents and working hours could be reduced, and more people could be employed.

Woolman (1971) argued that the wealthy were insulated from knowing the experiences of the poor. They were removed from acquiring "a feeling knowledge" of the suffering of the poor. To illustrate this, he drew upon the Biblical call to treat "a stranger" with compassion:

> As many as this day who know not the heart of a stranger indulge themselves in ways of life which occasions more labour in the world than Infinite Goodness intends for man, and yet are compassionate toward such in distress who comes directly under their observation, were these to change circumstances a while with some who labour for them, were they to pass regularly through the means of *knowing the heart of a stranger* and come to *a feeling knowledge* of the straits and hardships which many poor, innocent people pass through in a hidden obscure life, ...I believe many of them would embrace a way of life less expensive and lighten the heavy burdens of some who now labour out of their sight to support them and pass through straits with which they are but little acquainted (pp. 243-44, italics added).

"A feeling knowledge" is a remarkable phrase, which suggests the importance of holistic knowing, based on both experiential and analytical understanding. Although "A Plea for the Poor" is aimed at a wide audience, his mode of addressing readers was based on an audience of fellow Quakers. Woolman had faith that his readers could be led by their own inward experience of "Infinite Goodness." This faith was not mere idealism but a realistic expectation of Quaker faith and worship, which was based on each individual turning to the inward Light. Woolman argued that if the wealthy could mentally trade places with those who labor to support them, they could experience an awakening compassion, which would lead in turn to reducing the ways of burdening their laborers.

He used his real-world observations not only to set forth a vision for the welfare of the landowner as well as the laborer, but also to call for consideration of what is best for succeeding generations. He composed an epistle for the Philadelphia Yearly Meeting of 1759, which would be signed by seven Friends, and which developed the argument for thinking of future generations. Toward the end of the epistle he asks readers to take seriously what they are leaving to posterity:

> Do we feel an affectionate regard to posterity and are we employed to promote their happiness? Do our minds in things outward look beyond

our own dissolution, and are we contriving for the posterity of our children after us? Let us then like wise builders lay the foundation deep, and by our constant, uniform regard to an inward piety and virtue, let them see that we really value it.

In our cares about worldly treasures, let us steadily bear in mind that riches possessed by children who do not truly serve God are likely to prove snares that may more grievously entangle them in that spirit of selfishness ... which stands in opposition to real peace and happiness (Woolman, 1971, p. 101).

This theme was picked up in "A Plea for the Poor" where Woolman (1971) emphasized that each generation must labor for "the necessaries of life," and do so "with a mind influenced by universal love:"

> The greater part of the necessaries of life are so far perishable that each generation hath occasion to labour for them; and when we look toward a succeeding age with a mind influenced by universal love, we endeavor not to exempt some from those cares which necessarily relate to this life, and give them power to oppress others, but desire they may all be the Lord's children (p. 250).

With "a mind influenced by universal love," he argued, "Our hearts [are] thus opened and enlarged, we feel content in a use of things as foreign to luxury and grandeur as that which our Redeemer laid down as a pattern" (p. 250). In an earlier section of "A Plea," he described how the tender mercies of God influence "our minds, so that we . . . feel a desire to take hold of every opportunity to lessen the distresses of the afflicted and increase the happiness of the creation" (p. 241). This assertion, about feeling the spirit move through creation and guide human behavior, leads to one of Woolman's most quoted sentences: "Here we have a prospect of one common interest from which our own is inseparable—that to turn all the treasures we possess into the channel of universal love becomes the business of our lives" (p. 241). In this statement, he turns upside down the idea that the primary purpose of business is to make money; rather his readers have the power to redirect "all the treasures we possess" into the moving stream of "universal love."

For Woolman, selfishness leads to all kinds of calamities; selfishness is at the root of cruelty, tyranny, economic oppression, and war. He wrote that "tyranny, as applied to a man, rises up and soon hath an end. But if we consider the numerous oppressions in many states and the calamities occasioned by nation contending with nation in various parts and ages of the world, and remember that selfishness hath been the original cause of them all . . . how terrible does this selfishness appear" (pp. 252-53). Making a convincing argument about the negative effects of selfishness would probably have been as difficult in the eighteenth century as it is today. In "A Plea for the Poor," Woolman wrote that

> [t]he way of carrying on wars, common in the world, is so far distinguishable from the purity of Christ's religion that many scruple to join in them.... Wealth is attended with power, by which bargains and proceedings contrary to universal righteousness are supported; and here oppression, carried on with worldly policy and order, *clothes itself* with the name of justice and becomes like *a seed of discord in the soil* (pp. 254-55, italics added).

He used the metaphor of "clothes itself" and the simile of "a seed of discord in the soil" to express how such wealth and power disrupted "worldly policy and order" and misled the individual in "the name of justice." A stand against war or exorbitant wealth required of the individual much self-examination:

> Oh, that we who declare against wars and acknowledge our trust to be in God only, may walk in the Light and therein examine our foundation and motives in holding great estates! May we look upon our treasures and the furniture of our houses and the garments in which we array ourselves and try whether the seeds of war have any nourishment in these our possessions or not (p. 255).

By linking even one's furniture and clothing to the seeds of war, Woolman tried to bring his readers to an understanding of privilege (to use today's terminology) that was as pervasive and subtle in his time as today.

For Woolman resistance to such entanglements is possible through the living presence of the spirit of Christ, which provides one with an example of humility and simplicity. Woolman wrote that if his readers

> remember the Prince of Peace, remember that we are his disciples, and remember that example of *humility* and *plainness* which he set for us, without feeling an earnest desire to be *disentangled* from everything connected with selfish customs in food, in raiment, in houses, and all things else; that being of Christ['s] family and *walking as he walked*, we may stand in that uprightness wherein man was first made, and have no

fellowship with those inventions which men in the fallen wisdom have sought out (p. 253, italics added).

Seeking unity with the spirit of Christ, so that one may "walk as he walked," is central to Woolman's economic proposals. The individual is thus experientially guided by a feeling knowledge of the spirit, which is perceived as the still small voice within. Seeking unity with God is a mystical goal that Gandhi sought as well. In his *Autobiography*, Gandhi (1983) said, "What I want to achieve,—what I have been striving and pining to achieve these thirty years,—is self-realization, to see God face to face, to attain *Moksha*" (p. viii). Woolman and Gandhi shared the mystical desire to find "face to face" unity with God. Woolman arrived at something of this unity, described in his *Journal*'s last chapter (pp. 185-86), when he had a nearly fatal illness, heard the words "*John Woolman is dead*" (p. 186), and felt deeply the words of Galatians 2:20.

Woolman encouraged his readers to feel the divine presence as servants and children who are thankful for the spiritual gifts of life: "As servants of God, what land or estate we hold, we hold under him as his gift.... Nor is this gift absolute, but conditional, for us to occupy as dutiful children" (p. 256). Here being "dutiful," arises from this relationship with the inward spirit. At the end of his 1754 essay against slavery, Woolman said, "Our duty and interest is inseparably united" (p. 208); "duty" and "interest" are linked in this statement by the singular verb "is." His use of the word "duty" also implies a sense of owing to God or fearing God's retribution. Jon Kershner, who has written extensively on Woolman's theology, argued that duty is "an irreducible part" of the individual Quaker's received revelation:

> God had delivered Quakers from persecution in England and from the apostasy of oppressive religious hierarchies, but God's beneficial providence was contingent on Quakers fulfilling their end of the bargain and being transformed accordingly in their inward lives and in their public witness. Quakers did not receive the Truth to possess it only but to embody it. Antislavery was a social message but by Woolman's day it was also *an irreducible part* of the content of the revelation they had received. To allow an antichristian habit like slavery to infiltrate the Quaker community was to ignore the purpose for their existence in salvation history and to endanger their corporate survival (personal communication, January 11, 2017, italics added).

Duty expressed the understanding that human beings are called to help bring about the Kingdom of God on earth, an understanding that also comes with contentment with what one is called to do. In "A Plea for the Poor," Woolman (1971) wrote in a section on education that "[w]hen we are thoroughly instructed in the kingdom of God, we are *content* with that use of things which his wisdom points out, both for ourselves and our children, and are not concerned to learn them the art of getting rich, but are careful that the love of God and a right regard for all their fellow creatures may possess their minds" (p. 263, italics added). Duty is inseparable from a loving divine relationship with the inward spirit: "Where divine love takes place in the hearts of any people, and they steadily act on a principle of universal righteousness, there the true intent of the Law is fulfilled" (p. 256). Woolman held the universalist belief that people of all faiths could experience God's love. He wrote that "divine love takes place in the hearts of any people" (p. 256). Similarly, in his *Journal*, he wrote that he "found no narrowness respecting sects and opinions, but believed that sincere, upright hearted people in every Society who truly loved God were accepted of him" (p. 28). He sought to reach his contemporaries not by condemning them but by appealing to their ability to respond to their own inward tenderness. For example, his first antislavery essay was focused not on the suffering of enslaved people but rather on how inheriting slaves was a terrible weight to lay upon one's children. He expected that slaveowners would respond to shared beliefs about the value of work and the danger that providing one's children a life of luxury would undercut their spiritual lives.

### Woolman and the Fabians

A brief history of the Fabian Society offers insight into how Woolman's example was important to later generations. The Fabians emerged in England in the last two decades of the nineteenth century. It was a time of tremendous social, industrial, and demographic change. The poor were streaming into overcrowded and polluted cities. In response, in the 1880s, socialist and cooperative movements were attracting followers. One such person was Edward R. Pease, who came from a well-to-do Quaker family, one of whom was the first Quaker elected to the House of Commons (MacKenzie and MacKenzie, 1977, p. 16). As a young man in London in 1881, Pease tried on for size the Society for Psychical Research, which was interested in spiritualism, séances, and hypnotism, but this did not fit him. Soon Pease turned his attention to questions of wealth, politics, and socialist ideals. He and a small group of friends, in January 1884, formed the Fabian Society.

The group's numbers and influence quickly grew, attracting George Bernard Shaw, Sydney and Beatrice Webb, and H. G. Wells–although Wells would later satirize the group. The Fabians asked questions, at least some of which would have resonated with Woolman. In their first tract, called "Why are the Many Poor?" published in 1884, the Fabians argued that poverty arose inevitably from the "competition for wages"; drawing upon the writings of J. S. Mill and Henry George, the Fabians believed that rent was "an income which was the unavoidable result of the special economic advantages ... appropriated by almost every social stratum above the level of subsistence wage-earners" (Callaghan, 1990, pp. 30-31). The Fabians looked to government to alleviate suffering. They asked not only why there was so much poverty but also why the government was so ineffective at dealing with it (MacKenzie and MacKenzie, pp. 308-309). *The Workers' Political Programme*, which the Fabians published in 1891, demanded adult suffrage, an eight-hour day, a national system of education, taxes on land and inheritance, and progressive income tax (Callaghan, p. 37).

Sydney and Beatrice Webb became major figures in the group. Their list of accomplishments is remarkable. A wealthy benefactor left half of his estate to the Fabians, naming Sidney to be the chairman of the trustees of the fund. The Webbs decided to use the money to found the London School of Economics (MacKenzie and MacKenzie, p. 214). The Webbs lobbied for minimum wage and supported labor unions; they coined the phrase "collective bargaining." Between 1905-1909, Beatrice led the group drafting the Minority Report, one of two reports published by the Royal Commission on the Poor Laws and Relief of Distress, 1905-1909, which was established by Parliament (the other report was the Majority Report). The Minority Report is considered one of the most important documents on social policy of the last hundred years. Beatrice argued for "'a national minimum of civilised life' and advocated that government–rather than charity–should be responsible for the well-being of citizens" and more than thirty years later Clement Attlee described "the Minority Report as '. . . the seed from which later blossomed the welfare state'" (Policy Press, 2017). (During the same years, the Quaker suffrage leader Alice Paul had the opportunity to learn from Beatrice while in London. This was during her time studying, in 1907-1909, at the Quaker study center at Woodbrooke [Zahniser and Fry, 2014]. Paul returned to the U.S. to earn a Ph.D. in sociology and lead the suffragette movement to its successful campaign for passage of the 19th Amendment.) In 1911, the Webbs advocated for universal health care. Sidney and Beatrice founded *The New Statesman* in 1913. Sydney rose to be a major advisor to the British Labor Party. Eventually he was elected to the House of Commons but did not prove to be happy or productive there. Under the MacDonald government in 1923, ten Fabians served in senior Cabinet posts, including Sydney as president of the Board of Trade and another Fabian, Sydney Olivier, as secretary of state for India (MacKenzie and MacKenzie, pp. 398, 400).

In 1897, the Fabians republished about half of Woolman's "A Plea for the Poor," using the title "A Word of Remembrance and Caution to the Rich." The Fabians published 192 tracts between 1884-1920. Of all these tracts, only six were on Christian Socialism, so it's significant that they chose Woolman's essay, which was tract No. 79. "What is more," according to A. M. McBriar (1966) in *Fabian Socialism and English Politics*, "these Tracts on Christian Socialism proved to be among the Tracts with the best and steadiest sale over a long period.... they were all intended to prove to Christians that Christianity and Socialism or Collectivism were compatible" (pp. 154-55). Woolman's essay quickly sold out, perhaps because it was bought up by members of the Society of Friends, but nevertheless it was sufficiently valued by the Fabians that they published three editions totaling over twenty thousand copies. McBriar also observed that, unlike some of their sister socialist organizations, the Fabians did not "attempt to persuade religious people to renounce their faith; it contented itself with persuading them to become Socialists, through the words of their co-religionists" (p. 155). In addition to his Christian perspective, Woolman's essay must have appealed to the Fabians because of his explanation of systemic inequality and oppression. The Fabian edition ended with this statement: "Thus oppression in the extreme appears terrible, but oppression in more refined appearances remains to be oppression, and where the small degree of it is cherished it grows stronger and more extensive" (p. 262). The Fabians would have been attracted to Woolman's understanding of how the wealthy in any society easily become blind to the harmful effects of privilege.

It must be added that by 1931, the Webbs were having doubts about what they could accomplish with Liberal and Conservative politicians. Beatrice particularly was looking for a new way forward. She and Sidney recognized the "fanatical brutality" of Soviet Russia, but they sided with the Soviet system rather than U.S. capitalism. As the McKenzies (1977) wrote, "[The Webbs] were abandoning capitalist individualism because of its failure to provide equal opportunity and a minimum wage" (p. 406); that same year Shaw and Lady Astor went to Russia and returned "declaring that the Stalin regime was nothing but applied Fabianism" (p. 406). The Webbs visited the Soviet Union in 1932 and were enthusiastic about what they saw, at the same time overlooking reports of famine and forced labor. They held to their admiration for Soviet collectivism and central planning, and set forth their position in their book *Soviet Communism: A New Civilization*, published in 1935 and revised in 1941, and in *The Truth About the Soviet Union*, in 1942. Of course, many intellectuals in the 1920s and 1930s had been attracted to communism, social evolution, and an intellectual justification for eugenics by way of sterilization. For adhering to these ideas to the end of their lives, the Webbs have been much criticized. In his critique of the Fabians, John Callaghan described how, in following Comte and Darwin, the Webbs embraced the writings of Herbert Spencer, believing they were taking a scientific approach to economic problems. Despite their working on behalf of laborers, there is some evidence that Shaw and the Webbs had condescending attitudes toward working men and women, as mere cogs in a "great social machine": "From the Society's earliest days," Callaghan (1990) wrote, "it had felt an undisguised contempt for the working class," the "average sensual man" (pp. 33, 35). But Beatrice was also repulsed by "the merely rich" (p. 35).

Despite the turn toward the Soviet Union by the Webbs and Shaw, the Fabians continued to influence Labor politics. By the end of World War II, the Fabians had over ten thousand members. Overall, they had a major influence in British Labor politics and early thinking about the welfare state. They had an important influence on the Labor Party throughout the twentieth century. Two Fabians became Prime Minister, Ramsey MacDonald and Clement Attlee. Their members had included Annie Besant, Emmeline Pankhurst, and Harold Laski, and they had a significant influence on Jawaharlal Nehru.

Nehru's example highlights the influence of the Fabians as well as problems with capitalism and socialism, admittedly from the unique perspective of Nehru's national leadership. In his biography of Nehru, Shashi Tharoor (2011) portrayed him as a truly remarkable man, but his vision for India and his distaste for imperialistic capitalism led to stifling economic stagnation:

> Nehruvian socialism was a curious amalgam of idealism (of a particularly English Fabian variety), a passionate if somewhat romanticized concern for the struggling masses (derived from his own increasingly imperial travels amid them), a Gandhian faith in self-reliance (learned at the spinning wheel and typified by the ostentatious wearing of khadi), a corollary distrust of Western capital (flowing from his elemental anticolonialism), and a "modern" belief in "scientific" methods like Planning (the capital letter is deliberate: Nehru elevated the technique to a dogma) (p. 175).

After Indian independence, Nehru carried with him a deep distrust of international capitalism, because of exploitation by the British empire but also because of the suffering caused by colonialism. Tharoor (2011) went on to say,

The ideas of Fabian Socialism captured an entire generation of English-educated Indians; Nehru was no exception. As a democrat, he saw the economic well-being of the poor as indispensable for their political empowerment, and he could not entrust its attainment to the rich.... Like many others of his generation, Nehru thought that central planning, state control of the "commanding heights" of the economy, and government-directed development were the "scientific" and "rational" means of creating social prosperity and ensuring its equitable distribution (p. 240).

Nehru "always put nationalism before ideology" (Tharoor, p. 175), and he put great value on "self-sufficiency" and "self-reliance" at the expense of economic progress:

the prospect of allowing a Western corporation into India to "exploit" its resources immediately revived memories of British oppression. (It is ironic that in the West, freedom is associated axiomatically with capitalism, whereas in the postcolonial world freedom was seen as freedom *from* the depredations of foreign capital.) "Self-reliance" thus became a slogan and a watch word: it guaranteed both political freedom and freedom from economic exploitation. The result was a state that ensured political freedom but presided over economic stagnation; that regulated entrepreneurial activity through a system of licenses, permits, and quotas that promoted both corruption and inefficiency but did little to promote growth; that enshrined bureaucratic power at the expense of individual enterprise. For most of the first five decades since independence, India pursued an economic policy of subsidizing unproductivity, regulating stagnation, and distributing poverty. Nehru called this socialism (pp. 240-41).

The example of Nehru and that of India in the second half of the twentieth century highlights, on the one hand, damage caused by colonialism and the exploitation of international capitalism, and, on the other hand, ways in which socialism can be ineffective.

### Comparing Woolman and the Fabians

The Fabians made use of Woolman's ideals to appeal to Christian socialists, and leaders like Sidney and Beatrice Webb introduced a concern for the poor that greatly influenced the welfare state which would emerge in Britain in the twentieth century. Unlike some Fabians, Woolman revealed no contempt for either the poor or the rich. He identified with slaves by walking rather than riding on horseback, and chose to sail in steerage with the sailors on his journey to England in 1772. Although the Fabians and Woolman shared deep concerns for improving the situation for the poor, the foundations of their ideas were very different. They would likely have agreed on the desirability of gradual change, but from completely different perspectives.

The Fabians, particularly the Webbs, looked to centralized government to provide economic solutions. They wanted their colleagues who had gotten into key roles throughout government to bring about slow but sure change; they adopted the term "permeation" as a political tactic of joining "all organizations where useful Socialist work could be done, and influence them" (McBriar, 1966, p. 95). Woolman (1971), with one exception, expressed little expectation that the government would alleviate social problems. In 1760, while attending the New England Yearly Meeting in Providence, Rhode Island, the legislature was in session in Providence. He wrote in his *Journal* that while there he wanted Friends to petition the legislature "to use their endeavours to discourage the future importation of them [slaves]" and he was prepared "to speak a few words" himself (p. 109). After a sleepless night of concern and wishing not to miss the yearly meeting sessions, he decided to share a brief essay he had written with several Friends who were appointed to speak with "men in authority" (p. 109). Aside from this one instance, Woolman probably saw government as an obstacle. He definitely could not support the government's military operations. He and twenty Friends refused to pay war taxes in 1755, and signed an epistle explaining their tax resistance (pp. 85-86).

The Webbs put the highest priority on a "scientific" focus and what could be accomplished through government programs. In contrast, Woolman was mystical and prophetic, centering upon not only the individual's relationship with the spirit of Christ within, but, as Jon Kershner (2015) has argued, the belief that "the government of Christ was impending": "Woolman's apocalypticism made claims on every aspect of British society and subverted them to a radical view of Christ's direct presence.... the revelation that Woolman felt he had received was not a religious opinion, but a universal law"; "He protested against the pollutions of industrialized society and the funneling of necessary resources into what he considered egregious displays of wealth and religiosity" (pp. 96-97). Kershner (2011) wrote that

> Woolman's fellow citizens struggled to understand the preacher who dressed in white, walked hundreds of miles, entered hostile lands, and

sailed in steerage when he could have had his own cabin. Woolman's presence was a stinging rebuke to the prosperity of the colonial ruling class. The aesthetics of Woolman's itinerant ministry, though, begin to come into focus when one considers Woolman's spiritual itinerary in which the divine "motion of love" revealed God's will for human affairs. Perfection was possible to the extent that one obeyed the workings of "divine love" (p. 33).

A "motion of love" was an especially memorable phrase in Woolman's (1971) writings, appearing in his *Journal*'s first sentence and in his explanation for why he made his journey in 1763 to visit the Indians (pp. 23, 127). Kershner (2011) went on to say,

> The redeemed society was to come about as faithful men and women looked to the inward Teacher, who would re-create the world according to God's Kingdom.... Sailing to England in 1772, on a long journey after many long journeys, Woolman anticipated the transformation of society because in union with God's love, he felt himself to be transformed: "... we can say that Jesus is the Lord, and the reformation in our souls, manifested in a full reformation of our lives, wherein all things are new and all things are of God." The radicalization of theological vision paralleled the radical austerity of the journey, itself. The prophetic embodiment of this theological vision created tensions and commotion. Woolman's example indicates that the intensity of the journey–whether spiritual, physical, or emotional–affects the experience of the journey (p. 33).

Woolman, like Gandhi, believed in the universality of his experience and universal law. Both men knew this Truth through mystical surrender, self-suffering, and unity with God. For Woolman, this universality was evidence of Divine created order.

Tom Head, a Quaker economist, wrote in "The Business of our Lives" (1996) that Woolman not only believed we live in a created order but that we have failed to attend to its requirements (p. 78). Our religion and the business of our lives are not separate realms (p. 80). He quoted from "A Plea for the Poor": "Our gracious Creator cares and provides for all his creatures. His tender mercies are over all his works; and so far as his love influences our minds, ... [we] feel a desire to take hold of every opportunity to lessen the distresses of the afflicted and increase the happiness of creation" (Woolman, 1971, p. 241). Bringing about the Kingdom of God on earth was Woolman's vision for decreasing the "distresses of the afflicted."

## A Bridge to Our Time

Woolman's ideas challenge readers to think about how they believe great social change can be accomplished. Sydney Webb wrote that "it is through the slow and gradual turning of the popular mind to new principles that social reorganization bit by bit comes" (McBriar, 1966, p. 62). Intervention was to be accomplished through gradual "organic change," and this was to be accomplished through "the unconscious permeation of all schools of thought" (Callaghan, pp. 32, 33). Woolman no doubt would have preferred gradual, peaceful change as well; time was needed for people to awaken to their own spiritual leadings. He was patient enough to expect change to come about through processes of Quaker worship, committee work, and ministry. But no doubt he passionately wanted to end the suffering of the poor as soon as possible.

The Quaker economist Kenneth Boulding (1953) wrote about questions of social change in numerous books. In an early book, *The Organizational Revolution*, he asked, "*how* wrongs are righted; what [organizational] machinery exists in the world for the correction of conditions which are perceived to need correction?" (pp. 67-68). Boulding answered the question by comparing the scientist, whose task is "to show us where we are," and the saint, whose task is "to show us where we ought to be" (p. 69). The scientist analyzes what is, while the saint proposes what should be, based upon revelation of the inward Light. His example of the saint was Woolman:

> The activities of [the scientist and the saint] frequently result in an increased awareness of divergence between the actual and ideal–the scientist because he dispels our illusions . . . and the saint because he gives us a new vision of the ideal. Thus, the impact of modern psychology and sociology upon family life has been to dispel certain romantic illusions and perhaps to create a sense of a wider gap between ideal and reality; the shadow that the ideal cast over the real has been dispelled. From the other end of the scale, prophetic figures like John Woolman opened men's eyes to the evil of slavery and created an acute sense of divergence between the actual and ideal, not by changing the perception of the actual, but by changing the perception of the ideal (p. 69).

Through this comparison Boulding showed the value of the scientist and the saint. The scientist, by dispelling illusions helps us to see what actually is, thus to know where we are. The saint, or prophet, not only changes "the perception of the ideal" but also "opened men's eyes."

Another Quaker economist, Gerald W. Sazama (2003), examined Woolman's essay "Conversations on the True Harmony of Mankind and How It May Be Promoted," which also focused on landowners and laborers. Sazama explored Woolman's ideas in contrast to Adam Smith's, whose *Wealth of Nations* was published in 1776 (pp. 198-204). However, I want to quote from Sazama's concluding section because it raises the difficulty that Woolman's thinking poses for us today:

> One temptation is to write off Woolman as economically naïve or as a creature of his times. A person might argue that Woolman's thinking may have been appropriate for a relatively simple colonial economy but not for a complex modern economy. Yet, many accept that the modern international economy has serious problems. We believe that it frequently leads to empty alienated lives, and to the oppression of others at home and in foreign lands…. As a result, we are again questioning where modern economics, as well as other contemporary social and moral forces, have led us and will lead us. Woolman presents a radically simple alternative: love of God and neighbor results in harmony with God, ourselves, others, and the globe. *But for me at least, it is an awesome, even frightening alternative because of the drastic changes it would require* (p. 204, italics added).

Sazama frankly stated Woolman's daunting, even frightening, challenge to his readers: "This means … the courage to die in our old ways, as Woolman did, so that we can be reborn in God's, Christ's love. This is not a utopian wish, but a condition of our physical, psychological, and spiritual health" (p. 205). But how does a person who shares this vision for social change come to terms with the sense that it is impractical in the face of stubborn realities?

One response can be found in the online article "Friends, Money, and the Earth" published by Quaker Earthcare Witness (2017), whose header reads, "Seeking emerging insights into right relationships with Earth and unity with nature." The writer(s) pose queries that echo Woolman's ideas and put them in today's terms: "Mindful earning, spending, giving, and investing can lower our ecological footprints and promote peace and social justice. But going beyond our personal relationship with money: Why is there enough money for war, but not for education or protecting the environment? Why is there enough money for real estate and financial market speculation but not for everyone to afford health care?" (para. 1). Like Woolman, these contemporary Quakers see the problems of inequity as systemic and structural: "the very structure of the nation's monetary system contributes to and reinforces inequitable distribution of wealth, as well as pressure to liquidate natural resources" (para. 6). They advise Friends to learn more about the monetary system and to work for a just and equitable world.

Another response can be found in Tom Cornell's (2017) "Christian Nonviolence," published in the *Catholic Worker*. Cornell writes that

> the basis of Christian nonviolence is the same premise that underlies all of the Church's social teaching: that every man, woman and child is created in the image and likeness of God. Persons are never a means to an end; they are ends in themselves and thus are not to be violated in any way, either in body, mind or spirit. Persons are not disconnected individuals in a war of all against all, as in the capitalist model; nor are they to be subsumed into a larger whole, as in the collectivist model. Instead, all are formed in, by and for community.... Wars can be fought only by stilling the voice of conscience. By contrast, nonviolence recognizes the humanity of the opponent and appeals to "that of God in everyone," as the Quakers put it—that which the Creator breathed into our first parents and which we all share, even the boss, the landlord, the racist, the oppressor, the warmonger (pp. 1, 4).

In saying that there is "that of God in everyone," Quakers believe that the inner life of every person matters. This belief goes back to their earliest beginnings. It is the basis of the Quaker testimonies of equality, simplicity, peace, and community. We don't want to take part in war because the inner life of every person matters. Woolman's warnings about the abuses of wealth and power point toward the failings of capitalism. The history of the Fabians and Nehru point to the failings of collectivism. We have yet to learn how to reject the worst in capitalism and retain the best of capitalism. The same can be said of socialism. We find capitalism and socialism to be deeply flawed because they do not respect the inner life of every person. Woolman called upon his readers to imagine a world where the inner life is valued. He called upon us to be consistent in our inward lives and our outward actions, but this is what Quakers have sought to do for centuries. Woolman's writings implicitly speak to our dependency upon economic growth at the expense and destruction of people's lives and the environment. He understood that wealth and poverty reflect how much a society embraces Jesus's teachings about the value of relationships and community.

## References

AFL-CIO (2017). "Highest paid CEOs." Retrieved from https://aflcio.org/paywatch/highest-paid-ceos

Barbour, H., Frost, J. W. (1994). *The Quakers*. Richmond, IN: Friends United Press. (Original work published 1988).

Boulding, K. E. (1953). *The organizational revolution: A study in the ethics of economic organization*. New York: Harper.

Callaghan, J. (1990). *Socialism in Britain since 1884*. Oxford: Basil Blackwell.

Cornell, T. (2017, December). Christian nonviolence. *The Catholic Worker*. pp. 1, 4.

Dorfman, J. (1946). *The economic mind in American civilization 1606-1865*. New York: Viking.

Eliot, C. W. (Ed.). (1991). *The Autobiography of Benjamin Franklin, the journal of John Woolman, fruits of solitude William Penn*. Danbury, CT: Grolier. (Original work published 1909).

Quaker Earthcare Witness. "Friends, money, and the earth." (n.d.). Retrieved from http://www.quakerearthcare.org/pamphlet/friends-money-and-earth

Gandhi, M. K. (1983). *Autobiography: The story of my experiments with truth*. NY: Dover. (Original work published 1927 and 1929).

Gwyn, D. (1995). *The covenant crucified: Quakers and the rise of capitalism*. Wallingford, PA: Pendle Hill.

Head, T. (1996). The business of our lives: Reflections on "a plea for the poor." In P. Anderson and H. Macy (Eds.), *Truth's bright embrace: Essays and poems in honor of Arthur O. Roberts* (pp. 75-80). Newberg, OR: George Fox University.

Kershner, J. R. (2011). "The (com)motion of love: Theological formation in John Woolman's itinerant ministry." *Quaker Religious Thought* 116(1), pp. 23-36.

Kershner, J. R. (2015). "'Come out of Babylon, my people': John Woolman's (1720-72) anti-slavery theology and the transatlantic economy." In Maurice Jackson and Susan Kozel (Eds.), *Quakers and Their Allies in the Abolitionist Cause, 1754-1808* (pp. 96-97). New York: Routledge.

King, M. L., Jr., (1998). "Beyond Vietnam." In Clayborne Carson (Ed.), *The autobiography of Martin Luther King, Jr.* (pp. 333-345). New York: Grand Central Publishing.

Lacey, P. (2003). Answerable to the design of our creation: Teaching "a plea for the poor." In Mike Heller (Ed.), *The tendering presence: Essays on John Woolman* (pp. 295-307). Wallingford, PA: Pendle Hill Publications.

MacKenzie, N., MacKenzie, J. (1977). *The Fabians.* NY: Simon and Schuster.

McBriar, A. M. (1966). *Fabian socialism and English politics, 1884-1918.* Cambridge: Cambridge University Press.

Proud, J. (2010). *John Woolman and the affairs of truth: The Journalist's Essays, Epistles, and Ephemera.* San Francisco: Inner Light Books.

Sazama, G. W. (2003). "On Woolman's 'conversations,' ethics, and economics." In Mike Heller (Ed.), *The tendering presence: Essays on John Woolman* (pp. 190-206). Wallingford, PA: Pendle Hill Publications.

Slaughter, T. P. (2008). *The beautiful soul of John Woolman, apostle of abolition.* New York: Hill and Wang.

Tharoor, S. (2011). *Nehru: The invention of India.* New York: Arcade Publishing. (Original work published 2003)

Tolles, F. (1948). *Meeting house and counting house: The Quaker merchants of colonial Philadelphia 1682-1763.* New York: Norton.

Peter G. Peterson Foundation. (2017, June 1). U.S. defense spending compared to other nations. Retrieved from http://www.pgpf.org/chart-archive/0053 _defense-comparison

Policy Press (2017) "What would Beatrice Webb say now?" (March 8, 2017). Retrieved from https://policypress.wordpress.com/2017/03/08/what-would-beatrice-webb-say-now/

Woolman, J. (1971). *The journal and major essays of John Woolman.* (P. Moulton, Ed.) Richmond, IN: Friends United Press.

Woolman, J. (1897). *A word of remembrance and caution to the rich. London: The Fabian Society, 1897.* (Original work published 1793).

Zahniser, J. D., Fry, A. R. (2014). *Alice Paul: Claiming power.* Oxford: Oxford University Press.

# 14 | John Woolman and Land

**By Geoffrey Plank**

Commentators and activists seeking lessons from the economic life of John Woolman generally concentrate on what he refused to do, and his warnings against harmful behavior.[1] Woolman assessed the local and international impact of the economic choices he made as a shopkeeper and consumer, because he did not want to promote or subsidize unjust, wasteful, damaging, or exploitative behavior. He refused to sell alcohol in his shop. He avoided slave-produced products, and toward the end of his life he renounced silverware to disassociate himself from the harsh labor conditions prevailing in the mines of Peru. He rejected frivolities and ostentation, and warned his neighbors that conspicuous displays of riches invited envy, discord, and theft. He wore clothes made from undyed cloth because colors were ostentatious and dishonest in the way they hid dirt, and dyes wastefully damaged cloth. He resolved not to ride in English carriages because the carriage drivers were cruel to their horses. We often, for good reason, associate Woolman with renunciation, boycotts, and morally informed austerity. But to fully understand his economic thinking, we need to think not only about the activities he opposed, but also those he pursued.

Woolman owned large tracts of land. He experimented with hog farming, kept an apple orchard, and rented pastureland to nearby farmers. Compared to most of the other inhabitants of Mount Holly, New Jersey, he was rich.

---

[1] Good overviews of Woolman's life and ministry can be found in Heller (2003), Kershner (2018), and Plank (2012).

Conscious of his patrimony, and deeply aware of the colonial history of New Jersey, he wrote emotionally about the origins of his title to land. He expressed gratitude toward the Native Americans who had made room for the first Quaker settlers. He associated landed wealth with responsibility, and he took it for granted that "men possessed of great estates" owed an obligation to those around them. Woolman thought that landowners set a moral example, for good or ill, for their neighbors. Land played a critical role in Woolman's economic life, his understanding of history, his social ideals, and his vision of the future. By examining his behavior as a landowner and his commentary on landownership, we can learn much about his social ideas and strategy for reform, and his specific aspirations regarding colonial expansion, gender relations, and the process of ending slavery.

In the early 1750s Woolman operated a busy, amply-stocked shop, selling a wide variety of products in Mount Holly, New Jersey. Then late in the autumn of 1754, he sold out of many things. First he ran out of coffee, molasses, tobacco, and snuff, and then by the end of 1755 he no longer had any indigo, rum, cordial, powder, or shot for sale. Woolman offered several explanations for dwindling his trade in this way. His only son died at the age of three months in September 1754, leaving John and his wife Sarah with one daughter. After the boy's death, John and Sarah knew, or resolved, that they would have no more children. With only a small family to support, John realized that he did not need to work so hard in his shop. He had always found the work distracting, and feared that "with an increase in wealth the desire of wealth increased" (Moulton, 1971, p. 35). He did not want his business to keep him from his religious vocation. Woolman was also concerned for the spiritual welfare of his customers. He had never liked selling things that "served chiefly to please the vain mind in people," and he was wary of promoting drunkenness (Moulton, 1971, p. 53). He had additional good reasons not to sell sugar and the products derived from it. Years later, he would explain his refusal to sell sugar, molasses, and rum as part of a comprehensive effort avoid the products of slave labor in the Caribbean (Moulton, 1971, pp. 156, 158).

Woolman's renunciations and boycotts fascinated his contemporaries, and they have caught the attention of politically concerned people in the centuries since his death. Within the antislavery movement, he became an inspirational figure for those later abolitionists, Quaker and non-Quaker alike, who renounced slave-produced sugar and cotton (Holcomb, 2016, pp. 27, 35). And his motivations and influence extended well beyond the problem of slavery. Woolman eventually came to view slavery one component in a comprehensively dehumanizing, exploitative, and destructive economic system. By the early 1770s, his critique of eighteenth-century consumer culture and Atlantic trade had become sweeping, rigorous, and detailed. He became extremely self-conscious, and opposed many common practices, as he strove to be good in all his economic dealings.

As Jon R. Kershner (2018) has explained, Woolman's social vision was animated by apocalyptic expectation. But his influence has spread far beyond the circle of those who shared his understanding of human history. By paying attention to the moral implications of his economic behavior, and trying ceaselessly to divorce himself from bad practice, he has inspired activists over several generations. Recently, contemplating the damaging impact of human-induced climate change, Kevin J. O'Brien was inspired by Woolman's example, and resolved to live without air conditioning. In his essay exploring what we can learn from Woolman, O'Brien (2017) demonstrates the twenty-first century resonance and possible applicability of Woolman's mode of thought and action (pp. 63, 84, 90). Historian Marcus Rediker has portrayed Woolman's message as a far-reaching protest, originally aimed at the societal structures of the eighteenth century, but clearly pertinent today. According to Rediker (2017), Woolman "criticized the destructive power of money, greed, and materialism, and he tried to dissociate himself from aspects of the growing international capitalist economy" (p. 138). Rediker argues that Woolman joined a struggle that was already underway and continues in the twenty-first century. He invites us to think long-term and broadly, to place Woolman in a global, world-historical context much larger and more enduring than eighteenth-century Mount Holly.

There is value in seeing Woolman in this way, but especially for historians, emphasizing the twenty-first century resonance of Woolman's thinking risks oversimplifying his life and message, flattening it, and making him indistinguishable from other protestors. Rediker's hero is the rebellious Quaker Benjamin Lay, and he argues that Woolman only continued what Lay began. "Many Quakers remarked on Woolman's 'singularities,' but as it happened, his practices were not singular at all. Benjamin [Lay] had pioneered every single one of them" (Rediker, 2017, p. 138). Woolman was far more original, and interesting, than this statement suggests.

It is true that as an opponent of slavery Woolman joined a campaign that had begun long before he was born and continues today. The first efforts to ban slavery in colonial America date from the 1640s (Donaghue, 2013, pp. 261-266). But Woolman's aims and tactics were distinctive. We can learn a great deal by examining how he differed from his predecessors and particularly from Lay. Both Woolman and Lay were animated by a vision of the end of human history, the final moment when God's judgment will be revealed, but when Lay imagined that climactic scene he focused on mortal conflict, enmity, and destruction. Woolman emphasized the enduring possibility of reconciliation and the restoration of peace. Lay devoted pages of his magnum opus, *All Slave-keepers that Keep the Innocent in Bondage, Apostates,* to analyzing the apocalyptic struggle recounted in Revelation, the "War in Heaven," which, he said, pitted the "true Church" against various "Anti-Christs" and devils including the red seven-headed dragon described in Revelation 12:3, which Lay described as a "furious beast" and a "bloody monster" (Lay, 1737, pp. 101-117). Woolman (1770) was more reticent in his treatment of Revelation. In his most extensive commentary on the text he concentrated on one message, "the language of the father of mercies is, my people, 'Come out of Babylon, my people!'" (p. 11). Like Lay, Woolman (1770) identified Babylon as a "city of business" inhabited by "the merchants of the Earth." (p. 10). Lay (1937) had similarly associated "Babilon's bastards" with "the worldly, covetous spirit" (p. 104). But while Woolman emphasized the possibility of redemption, Lay's focus was damnation.

We can see by comparing Woolman to Lay, even if we look only at their divergent treatments of Revelation, that by concentrating on the things Woolman opposed and rejected we risk overlooking his aspirations, and many features of his life and ministry that distinguished him from his contemporaries. Woolman's advice for the conduct of Quaker Meetings, the variety of persuasive strategies he adopted in the slavery debate, and his vision for the future of North America, reflected a positive vision founded on the promotion of social and spiritual harmony. His economic life reflected this vision and informed it. And the foundation of Woolman's economic life was property in land.

Woolman's four grandparents arrived in New Jersey in the seventeenth century with the first wave of Quaker colonists, and his grandfathers immediately laid claim to land. His father, in turn, followed the practice of his Quaker neighbors and made extraordinary efforts, buying land in several counties, to assure that John and his brothers would each be able to establish farms (Plank, 2012, p. 12). As the oldest son, and therefore the readiest to inherit, John was brought up in the expectation that he would take over his father's homestead. He learned farming skills, became "used to hard labor," and gained a strong sense of the moral responsibility and spiritual significance of raising livestock (Moulton, 1971, p. 118). Then, when he was twenty, Woolman made a break from the farming life. He bound himself as an apprentice to a shopkeeper in the small market town of Mount Holly, and began training as a tailor. In making this choice, he was following in the footsteps of his sainted older sister Elizabeth, who had moved away to take up tailoring two years earlier. He also believed, or hoped, that he was following God's leading in moving to town, but he also recognized immediately that his new occupation was morally dangerous. The apprenticeship exposed him to an array of potentially corrupting influences, including small crowds of idle boys, at least one frighteningly profane Scottish servant, and a master who asked him to perform the paperwork for the sale of a slave.

Woolman's work as an apprentice and his subsequent career after he opened his own shop exposed him to society. He served men and women of all ages including Quakers and non-Quakers, slaves and free blacks, iron workers, laundresses, farmers, and merchants. The work was challenging not only physically and intellectually, but also morally. To succeed as a shopkeeper Woolman had to please his customers. He sold goods on credit, and watched with dismay as men and women fell into debt purchasing "too costly apparel" and other things inconsistent with "universal righteousness" (Moulton, 1971, 54). Woolman was forced to confront what O'Brien (2017), citing the philosopher Brian Henning, calls "moral finitude" (p. 71). An array of social and pragmatic barriers prevented Woolman from living fully in accord with his ideals or setting a perfect example for others.

After he scaled back his retailing operations in 1754, Woolman experimented in an array of economic activities, presumably seeking a more righteous way of supporting his family. Surprisingly, perhaps, he began investing in hogs. By becoming a hog farmer, he followed the example of his neighbors. Pork was his county's leading export. Farmers from the countryside around Mount Holly sent salted meat to Philadelphia, where merchants like Thomas Clifford amassed shipments for resale in the Caribbean. Clifford purchased eighty barrels of gammon and salted pork from Woolman in 1757 (Plank, 2012, pp. 14, 86-87).

We know two things about Woolman's career as a hog farmer. The first is that it did not last long. Woolman found it difficult to negotiate contracts long-distance and arrange deliveries, and by the winter of 1758 he had given up the business. This experience may have contributed to the objections he raised later against overseas commerce generally. Woolman had always been alert to the implicit moral messages and lessons embedded in commercial dealings. When working in the pork trade he had been unable to see his ultimate customers face to face. He worked instead through agents who stood in for him, and by the end of his life Woolman was convinced that most men involved in export trades behaved badly. He argued against maritime trade citing the words of Timothy: "Be not partaker in another man's sins. Keep thyself pure" (Gummere 1922, 507). He did not want to associate with merchants, ship captains and sailors, and he may have also disliked supplying pork to plantations in the Caribbean because of their reliance on slavery.

We can only speculate about Woolman's reasons for abandoning hog raising, because the second thing we know with certainty about this stage in his career is that he never wrote about it publicly. He did not mention it in any drafts of his essays, epistles, pamphlets, or journal. This omission reminds us that Woolman's public account of his life was filtered. It was crafted with instructive purposes in mind. He did not aim to hide all his mistakes. On the contrary, he confessed to many misdeeds, especially in his journal, but the episodes of bad behavior that he recounted had lessons attached to them and functioned as parables. Perhaps hog raising was too complicated, and implicated too many issues at once for Woolman to use it to draw an intelligible moral lesson. Another possibility is that he was reticent for political reasons, as he was, for example, in Virginia in 1757 when he accepted the local Yearly Meeting's compromise on the issue of slaveholding (Moulton, 1971, pp. 66-67). Hog raising was pervasive among the farmers surrounding Mount Holly. Woolman may not have felt moved to condemn everyone around him and so chose not to cite his experience as a hog farmer as a cautionary tale.

After he had left hog-raising, Woolman engaged in a variety of money-raising activities which sustained him and often gave him an opportunity to minister and advance his moral teachings. He continued to run his shop, but with an intensified resolve to sell only "things really useful" (Moulton, 1971, p. 53). He kept working as a tailor, though he had great qualms about his customers' tastes. By the mid-1760s he was campaigning against cloth dyes, and sought to set an example to others by wearing only undyed clothing (Plank, 2009). As far as we know, none of Woolman's customers wanted a full set of clothes of the type he recommended. He also worked as a scribe and executor, an occupation that led to some of his most dramatic confrontations with those he intended to serve. Through the 1740s and early 1750s he became increasingly adamant that he would not participate in the transfer of slaves as property. By the 1770s, it appears, he declined work on estates bequeathing silver ornaments and other decorative items to the next generation (Plank, 2012, p. 186).

Woolman's various chosen careers provided him many opportunities to caution, admonish, and correct the behavior of his customers. He also found ways to encourage good behavior. Perhaps this is most evident in Woolman's work as a schoolteacher. His primers and lessons combined reading, writing, spelling, and grammar with implicit and explicit spiritual lessons. He promoted Christian ethics and the pastoral ideal. His *First Book for Children* began with this lesson:

The Sun is up my Boy,
Get out of thy Bed,
Go thy way for the Cow,
Let her eat the Hay.
Now the Sun is set,
And the Cow is put up,
The Boy may go to his Bed.
Go not in the Way of a bad Man;
Do not tell a Lie my Son (Woolman, 1769).

These lines contain hints of Woolman's upbringing and the lessons his father gave him. *A First Book for Children* conveys his vision of the good life, a prescription he promoted not only in the primer, but also in his pamphlets, journal, and public ministry. Following his maxim that "conduct is more convincing than language," he also pointed his way to a better life in his chosen economic activities (Moulton, 1971, p. 60).

Woolman owned more land than he could cultivate on his own. He observed, "By the agreements and contracts of our fathers and predecessors, and by doings and proceedings of our own, some claim a much greater share of this world than others; and whilst those possessions are faithfully improved to the good of the whole, it consists with equity" (Moulton, 1971, 239). In 1755, he began planting an apple orchard, and it expanded over the rest of the decade. Within a few years, he was selling apples and pears, and he eventually began selling trees. On other plots he grew grain and raised cattle, and he rented pastureland to his neighbors (Plank, 2012, 88). He hired laborers to help him, particularly for the harvest; but when he did so he made a point of working alongside his crew, in keeping with his general belief that landlords and employers should take "every opportunity of being acquainted with the hardships and fatigues of those who labor for their living" (Moulton, 1971, 242; Cox, n.d., p. 1). He argued that landlords, employers and masters should be constantly charitable towards their laborers, and this was more likely to occur if those in possession of "great estates" experienced "hard labor" themselves. Landlords who knew how strenuously their tenants and laborers worked would "regulate their demands agreeable to universal love." Those who demanded "greater toil or application to business than is consistent with pure love" violated their laborers' "rights as inhabitants of that world of which a good and gracious God is proprietor" (Moulton, 1971, pp. 239-240).

These comments appeared in an essay entitled "A Plea for the Poor," which was not published until after Woolman's death. Woolman made similar arguments in essays he saw printed, but in those he used slightly different language. In *Considerations on the True Harmony of Mankind*, a widely-distributed essay published in 1770, he described all humanity as one family. He quoted the words of Jesus, "Ye cannot serve God and mammon," but proceeded to argue that the rich could be good. "A person in outward prosperity may have the power of obtaining riches, but the same mind being in him which is in Christ Jesus, he may feel a tenderness of heart toward those of low degree, and instead of setting himself above them, may look upon it as an unmerited favor that his way through life is more easy than the way of many others." A good wealthy man "may improve every opportunity of leading forth out of those customs which have entangled the family [of mankind], employ his time in looking into the wants of the poor members, and hold forth such a perfect example of humiliation, that the pure witness may be reached in many minds, and the way opened for a harmonious walking together" (Woolman, 1770, pp. 13-14).

In his effort to live in a way that promoted this vision of social harmony, Woolman differed greatly from Lay. Despite Rediker's assertions to the contrary, both men were rich, compared to their neighbours (Rediker, 2017, p. 147). We know much less about Lay than Woolman, but we do know that during his lifetime and for many years after he was celebrated as a recluse who lived in a cave and produced his own food. There may be reason to doubt whether Lay actually lived in a cave, but nothing in his writing or behaviour suggests that he espoused or practiced the kind of benevolence that Woolman pursued (Rather, 2002, pp. 826-828). Lay did not aspire to become a good landlord.

The contrast between Lay and Woolman has implications far beyond our appreciation of these two men. Woolman's conception of how society worked, and how it should work, was grounded in agriculture. In one of his last essays, he looked forward to the day when the "inhabitants of cities will be less in number. Those who have much lands would become fathers to the poor. More people would be employed in the sweet employment of husbandry, and in the path of pure wisdom, labour would be an agreeable, healthful employment" (Gummere, 1922, pp. 505-556). These ideals helped shape Woolman's economic dealings, his relations with his neighbours, much of his ministry in Quaker meetings, and his engagement with many of the troubling controversies of his day. Not all Quakers shared Woolman's vision of the ideal society. By closely examining Woolman's views on land, we can gain a clearer sense of the difference in outlook separating him from others like Lay. On many issues, Woolman's views prevailed. For historians, Woolman's views on land help illuminate eighteenth-century Quakerism in general, the antislavery struggle, and the Quakers' relations with their non-Quaker neighbours. More specifically, Woolman's views tell us much about Quaker understandings of colonization, gender relations, and the right process for emancipating slaves.

The land that Woolman's grandparents and parents occupied, and all the land that he himself possessed in his lifetime, had belonged to American Indians before the Quakers arrived in the 1680s. As Woolman observed in his first anti-slavery essay, "The wilderness and solitary deserts in which our fathers passed the days of their pilgrimage are now turned into pleasant fields. The natives are gone from before us, and we establish peaceably in the possession of the land, enjoying our civil and religious liberties" (Moulton, 1971, p. 207). Woolman revered the first Quaker settlers in New Jersey. He loved the newly planted "pleasant fields" that surrounded his home, and in his journal he also wrote that he felt love in his heart "toward the natives of this land who dwell far back in the wilderness, whose ancestors were the owners and possessors of the land where we dwell, and who for a very small consideration assigned their inheritance to us" (Moulton, 1971, p. 122). In a private letter he went further, declaring, "I often think on the fruitfulness of the soil where we live. The care that hath been taken to agree with the former owners the natives, and the conveniences this land affords for our use." These thoughts reminded him to make good use of the advantages he had received, to "take care that my cravings may be bounded, and that no wandering desire may lead me to so strengthen the hands of the wicked as to partake of their sins" (Woolman, 1831, pp. 6-7).

Woolman did not regret colonization. On the contrary, he viewed the Quakers' arrival in the Delaware Valley as part of a divine plan, but it was one that placed heavy responsibility on the people who cleared, occupied, and cultivated hillsides, plains, and valleys that had formerly belonged to Native Americans. During the Seven Years' War, many American Indians took up arms against the English colonies, and the Quakers in New Jersey and Pennsylvania believed that they were facing an existential test. In the midst of that conflict, Woolman became a founding member of a Quaker benevolent society called the New Jersey Association for Helping the Indians. The group's charter began with a declaration of gratitude toward the original people of the Delaware Valley. The founders observed that it was "a truth fresh in the memory of several yet living" that "the native Indians of New Jersey were remarkably kind" to the first Quakers to arrive in the region. They had been cooperative "at a time when there were many hundreds of them to one white, and had they been disposed to have crushed the growing settlement, according to the natural appearance of things, nothing would have been easier." Nonetheless the "native Indians" had sold the

Quakers land, allowed them to "sit down and improve their possessions quietly," and helped them in times of distress. Recognizing this history, the Association gave thanks "to the natural and original proprietors of the soil whereon we reside, who treated our predecessors with such a distinguished regard" (New Jersey Association, 1757, pp. 1-2).

The New Jersey Association for Helping the Indians hoped to acquire land in the Pine Barrens for Native Americans, to establish a refuge where they could hunt, fish, cultivate crops, and build their own communities peacefully, unmolested by land-hungry settlers. Their charter made it clear that the Association's board would retain title to the land. The Quakers would finance the construction of houses, barns, and fences. Eventually, it was hoped, Friends would also establish a reservation school. Like Woolman's short career in hog-farming, the Association does not appear in Woolman's journal or other published writings. The group failed to establish a reservation, because Presbyterians seized the initiative in framing New Jersey's policies toward Native Americans. Nonetheless, its proposals foreshadowed others that Woolman would later advance more publicly and vigorously.

In 1761 Woolman became engaged in a widely publicized effort to establish peace with Native Americans after he met with the Munsee preacher Papunhank in Philadelphia. At that meeting, Papunhank told Woolman that they should "look upon all mankind as one and so become as one family" (Woolman, 1761, n.p.). That message fascinated Woolman, and inspired him quietly over the next two years. He eventually decided to see the community where Papunhank lived. In 1763, riding over "barren hills" in wartime to visit Papunhank in his village, Woolman ruminated on "the alternation of the circumstances of the natives of this land since the coming of the English. The lands near the sea are conveniently situated for fishing. The lands near the rivers, where the tides flow, and some above, are in many places fertile and not mountainous, which the running of the tides makes passing up and down easy with any kind of traffic. Those natives have in some places, for trifling considerations, sold their inheritance...." Reaching the top of a hill, Woolman had a vision encompassing the whole of eastern North America. "I had a prospect of the English along the coast for upward of nine hundred miles where I have traveled. And the favorable situation of the English and the difficulties attending the natives in many places, and the Negroes, were open before me. And a weighty and heavenly care came over my mind, and love filled my heart toward all mankind" (Moulton, 1971, p. 128).

Land lay at the heart of Woolman's understanding of the plight of Native Americans, and at the center of his prescription for their future. In September 1763, with Woolman in attendance, Philadelphia Yearly Meeting resolved that

"Friends should not purchase nor remove to settle such lands as have not been fairly and openly first purchased from the Indians by those persons who are or may be fully authorized by the government to make such purchases" (Philadelphia Yearly Meeting, 1744-1779, p. 183). Later that autumn, with the authority of the Yearly Meeting, Woolman and John Pemberton wrote an epistle to the Quakers on Long Island. They relayed their meeting's stance against the unauthorized private purchase of Native American land, and added an extra warning directed to Quakers "who have plenty of this world's goods." Implicitly including themselves among those with "plenty," Woolman and Pemberton declared that well-off Quakers should "apply our treasures to charitable and benevolent purposes, that we may truly honor God with our substance, and that those in low circumstances amongst us, being treated with tenderness, may have less temptation to seek settlements on lands which have not been properly purchased of the natives." (Philadelphia Yearly Meeting, 1748-1762, p. 14; Philadelphia Yearly Meeting, 1744-1779, p. 180). In this analysis of the Quakers' relations with American Indians, as on other occasions, Woolman associated wealth with responsibility. Wealthy landowning Quakers owed a debt to Native Americans, and rich Quakers generally had an obligation to reduce the incentives among the poor to squat or illicitly bargain for the American Indians' land. The aim was not to halt the westward migration of colonists and secure Native American land in perpetuity. Instead, Philadelphia Yearly Meeting supported the regulation of land distribution, to make sure that the process of colonial expansion was lawful, consensual, and peaceful. And to facilitate that process, Woolman and Pemberton believed that wealthy Quakers should provide a guiding hand.

Land, wealth, and social hierarchy preoccupied Woolman for most of his adult life, and his writings on these subjects expose the complexity of his historical circumstances and the years in which he lived. He had confidence in the power of benevolence. In his descriptions of a better world, wealthy landlords always assumed custodial care over their poor neighbors. But when he discussed his contemporary circumstances, his critique of some existing social hierarchies was scathing. We remember these objections because his analysis of social injustice often seems to anticipate twentieth- and twenty-first century commentary, especially in his discussion of the cumulative, hereditary impact of haughtiness, violence, and exploitation. In his first anti-slavery essay, for example, he described the effect of slaveholding on the children of bad masters, employing a logic that might easily be applied to any children raised in unrighteous affluence. "It appears by experience that where children are educated in fullness, ease, and idleness, evil habits are more prevalent than is common amongst such who are prudently employed in the necessary affairs of life. And if children are not only educated in the way of so great temptation, but have also the opportunity of lording it over their fellow creatures and being masters of men in their childhood, how can we hope otherwise than that their tender minds will be possessed with thoughts too high for them?" (Moulton, 1971, pp. 205-256). In a similar vein, during his travels through the south he was reminded of "the warlike disposition of many of the first settlers in those provinces, and of their numerous engagements with the natives in which much blood was shed" (Moulton, 1971, p. 147). Those early colonists had set an example for their children and grandchildren, and the legacy of that violence lasted for generations. Woolman saw the legacies of that original violence all around him.

Understandably, most commentators today emphasize the modernity of Woolman, and celebrate him and other like-minded Quakers for their rejection of warlike imperialism and permanent racial hierarchy. But Woolman's analysis of social relations and the reform strategies he adopted, with their emphasis on intergenerational legacies, sometimes had the effect of reinforcing long-standing social hierarchies. During his journey to Papunhank's village, Woolman responded to Native American violence in much the same way he did to the ancestral violence of white southerners. He saw pictographs on the sides of trees which he interpreted as "representations of men going to and returning from the wars, and of some killed in battle." Interpreting these images as "Indian histories," he lamented "the innumerable afflictions which the proud, fierce spirit produceth in the world" and "the hatred which mutually grows up in the minds of the children of those nations engaged in war with each other" (Moulton, 1971, p. 126). Woolman's implicit solution to this problem was a future in which all men, including Native American men, would no longer be drawn "far from home." His vision of social peace assumed that people should be sedentary and rooted in a righteous community. They should cease wandering. This was the future the New Jersey Association hoped to secure for Native Americans, and like Woolman, the group assumed that reforming the lives of American Indians would require a long process of intergenerational cultural change.

Not just in his commentary on Native Americans, but more generally in his reform proposals, Woolman stressed the importance of landholding, and he attributed great power to benevolent landlords. The significance he placed on land affected his assumptions about many things, including the role of women in society and the appropriate process for emancipating slaves.

Since their founding in the seventeenth century, the Quakers had granted unusual respect and authority to women. Like many of his fellow Quaker schoolteachers and ministers, Woolman worked closely with women, and he often deferred to them. When he became a tailor he was emulating his sister, and in the last months of his life he gave the revered reformer Sophia Hume authority to edit his journal. Woolman's behavior reflected a shared Quaker respect for female authority, but if we look at his analysis of landed wealth, the limits of his egalitarianism are clear. His vision was patriarchal, and his disposition of his own real estate reinforced and maintained masculine authority over several generations. His father's testamentary arrangements had drawn a sharp distinction between sons and daughters, assuring that only men would hold title to land. Woolman took elaborate steps of his own to make sure that the pattern continued. Before leaving on his final trip to England in 1772, he deeded his house and land to his son-in-law's father, to hold the land in trust for the benefit of Sarah during her lifetime (Woolman, 1772). For the next fifteen years Sarah profited from the estate, which continued to generate income as it had in John's lifetime. Though she did not have title or control of the land, Sarah received profits. Her will, and the financial accounts of her grandchildren, provide the most specific measure available of the family's wealth, even though they do not mention the underlying value of the real estate itself. In her will, Sarah left equal shares of money to her five grandchildren (all boys) to be paid when they reached the age of 21 (Gummere, 1922, pp. 606-607). Each of them eventually received $387.27 (Comfort Family, n.d.). $1,936.35 was a large sum of money at a time when laborers earned between 40 cents and 70 cents a day (Simler, 1990, p. 182). New Jersey land was a good investment in the eighteenth century. But for the Woolman family, it provided more than financial security. Land was the foundation of a moral social order. Sarah endorsed this view. Though she never received title to any land, she was passionately devoted to the farming life, so much so that in 1777 she protested vigorously when she learned that a neighboring boy had been encouraged to become a doctor. "[I]f he should choose to be a farmer," Sarah asked, "would it not be best and his mind more at liberty and serene in meditation on divinity and the divine being?" As a farmer, Sarah insisted, he would "have time to read good books and seek after humility of heart and find acquaintance and acceptance with his creator" (Gummere, 1922, 40-41).

Sarah and John agreed that good farming was godly, and that farmers should exert a positive moral influence on their neighbors. Nonetheless, the redistribution of colonized land played no role in any of John's reform plans, not for the benefit of the poor, not for dispossessed Native Americans, not for slaves. He believed that there might be land securely available for Native Americans in the Pine Barrens of New Jersey, for example, or west of the

Appalachian Mountains. But freed slaves, by contrast, were almost universally landless, and Woolman advanced no large-scale proposals to secure real estate for them. Still, his comments on their misfortunes suggest that he believed that they should aspire to the same kind of righteous patriarchy that he sought to embody in his own life. Talking to a colonel of the militia in Virginia in 1757, Woolman observed that "free men whose minds were properly on their business found a satisfaction in improving, cultivating, and providing for their families, but Negroes, laboring to support others who claim them as their property and expecting nothing but slavery during life, had not the like inducement to be industrious" (Moulton, 1971, p. 61). Slavery deprived fathers of the chance to support families and leave an inheritance to their children. It also deprived enslaved children of the full legacy that a patriarch might bequeath them. In a famous passage in *A Plea for the Poor*, Woolman suggested that masters who profited unjustly from slave labor owed a debt not only to the laborer, but also to that person's heirs, with compound interest accruing at 3% a year (Moulton, 1971, p. 268).

For years, commentators emphasizing the modernity of Woolman have pointed out that *A Plea for the Poor* anticipated postcolonial appeals for reparations for the descendants of slaves (Moulton, 1971, p. 197). Woolman's analysis continues to resonate, but to understand his contemporary circumstances and his position in eighteenth-century slavery debates, it is good to pay attention to the context in which he made this proposal. Woolman was engaged in a very specific debate about the process of emancipation. The principal question he was addressing was the age at which a person held in slavery should be freed. Woolman believed that the age of emancipation should be 21, and he was arguing against holding people as slaves until they reached 30. The "reparations" Woolman was discussing did not cover all the slave labor a person had performed since birth, but only the work done between the ages of 22 and 30. In his journal, Woolman recounted his personal struggle with this issue in connection with an enslaved man named Jem, who worshipped with Woolman at the Mount Holly Meeting. In 1751, when Jem was six years old, Woolman had helped draft a will for Jem's master, a wealthy Quaker named Thomas Shinn. The will stipulated that Jem would be freed at the age of thirty. Woolman later regretted facilitating these arrangements. "With abasement of heart I may now say that sometimes I have sat in a meeting with my heart exercised toward that awful Being who respecteth not persons or colours, and have looked upon this lad, and I have felt that all was not clear in my mind respecting him" (Moulton, 1971, 153). In a gesture toward making amends he decided to pay a half-share of the wages that Jem would have earned as a free laborer between the ages of 22 and 30. It is noteworthy that Woolman did not suggest that Jem should have been paid for the work he performed before the age of 21. Nor did he express any remorse for having originally helped to negotiate an arrangement that had assigned custodial authority over Jem during his childhood to Shinn, and in effect abrogated the parental authority of Jem's father, who was almost certainly an indigent man named Tabby who had been enslaved in the Shinn household (Plank, 2012, pp. 102, 172-173). This episode starkly illustrates the contrast between Woolman's antislavery actions and those of Benjamin Lay. Lay is reported to have kidnapped the six-year-old son of a Quaker slaveholder so that that man and his wife could share the experience of losing a loved one to captivity (Vaux, 1815, pp. 25-29).

Almost from the moment the Quakers began debating the morality of slavery in the 1660s, a divide emerged. Quaker leaders including George Fox and William Edmundson began by insisting that masters should treat their slaves well, live virtuously, and set a good example. This message, promoting benevolent slaveholding, evolved steadily through the first half of the eighteenth century, and eventually it became an essential component of one strand of Quaker abolitionism–the Quaker project of ending slavery gradually, after a peaceful, transitional stage during which slave owners prepared their slaves for freedom by educating them, introducing them to the Gospel, and instilling virtue within them. Enslaved children became special targets of Quaker benevolence. Woolman's readiness to accept that enslaved children would be kept in bondage until they had reached the age of majority was later codified as a general policy, affecting Quakers and non-Quakers alike, in gradual emancipation statutes drafted and supported by Quaker abolitionists like Anthony Benezet (Sassi, 2011).

But there was a dissenting Quaker view. Since the seventeenth century, a number of Quakers dissidents had objected to the hierarchical assumptions informing the Society of Friends' evolving pacifist, benevolent, gradualist solution to the problem of slavery. They cited the Quakers' professed belief that all people, regardless of gender, education, race, or social standing, could receive immediate inspiration from God. The egalitarian implications of this conviction led them to challenge a wide range of social conventions and hierarchies, occasionally to the point of questioning the privileged status of Christians among the peoples of the earth. The men and women who followed this line of thinking generally shared an iconoclastic, confrontational style and a tendency toward eccentricity that almost invited censure from Quaker authorities (Plank, 2016). Benjamin Lay was one of these.

In contrast with Lay, Woolman was careful in every part of his ministry to proceed with support from his Quaker meetings. This impulse made his work both institutional and intimate. He spent many days attending meetings, participating in committee work, and traveling and visiting slaveholders throughout the Delaware Valley and up and down the coast from Rhode Island to North Carolina. In keeping with his understanding of Quaker practice and the ultimate goals of the Friends' mission, he always aimed to promote and maintain harmony. He saw this both as a tactical necessity and a long term goal. Lay may have been more "fearless," as Rediker describes him, and Benezet may have had closer attachments to individual Africans and African Americans, but Woolman spent more time speaking persuasively to other Quakers.

While Woolman was tireless, his persuasive powers sometimes failed, and often on those occasions he deferred to authority. We can see this pattern of behavior in his first antislavery statement. After he found the courage to voice his opposition to slavery, he acquiesced to those around him and helped them draft a slave's bill of sale. In that instance Woolman was excessively timid, and he came to regret his action. On other occasions, he deferred to others pragmatically, after assessing the limits of his own powers of persuasion and choosing not to engage in a futile argument. But overall, Woolman respected authority because he believed in it.

Unique circumstances shaped Woolman's understanding of social hierarchy. He was born at an important historical moment, in a peculiar place, to a distinctive family. As a grandchild of the founding generation of Quaker migrants to the Delaware Valley, his understanding of the region's history was both grand and specific. He revered the accomplishments of his grandparents and their peers. His childhood intimacy with them deepened his appreciation of their pervasive impact on the landscape, and this, in turn, led him to think carefully about what they had taken from Native Americans. His reverence for his parents and grandparents, combined with his deep respect for the indigenous people who had ceded them land, led Woolman to associate land ownership with social responsibility. From his childhood, Woolman had expected to inherit land. His father raised him to be a farmer, and though Woolman decided later to seek other employment, his father's lessons stayed with him. Even as he worked as a tailor, shopkeeper, scribe, and teacher, he continued to praise farming and exalt the rural life. And he assumed that within rural communities, landowners would lead. No other Quaker reformer was quite like Woolman. To understand him we need to acknowledge the peculiarities of his circumstances, his family's history, and the burdens it placed on him. But it is equally important to recognize that Woolman's ideas resonated with other Quakers. His desire to make good use of the property that had been bequeathed to him, and his intuitive sense that the rich will always set a moral example for the poor, was typical of many Quaker leaders in his and subsequent generations. This sensibility helped inspire much Quaker benevolence, and many of the specific programs Woolman championed, including Quaker–led Indian reservations and an emancipation program that released slaves at the age of 21, would be pursued widely by Quakers later in the eighteenth and nineteenth centuries. We misunderstand Woolman and his entire reform legacy if we describe him as poor. He considered himself materially rich in the best possible way. Woolman hoped that in the future, "Those who have much lands would become fathers to the poor." Men with great landed estates would live and work face-to-face with their poorer and younger neighbors, and they would set an example for them. They would work hard, trade only locally, and live off the produce of the land.

## References

Comfort Family. (n.d.). Receipt Book. Quaker and Special Collections, Haverford College Library, Haverford, Pennsylvania.

Cox, J. (n.d.). Sketches and Reminiscences of Prominent Friends and Historic Facts. Dyllwyn Parrish Recollections and Sketches. Historical Society of Pennsylvania, Philadelphia.

Donaghue, J. (2013). *Fire Under the Ashes: An Atlantic History of the English Revolution.* Chicago: University of Chicago Press.

Gummere, A.M. (Ed.). (1922). *The Journal and Essays of John Woolman.* New York: Macmillan.

Heller, M. (Ed.). (2003). *The Tendering Presence: Essays on John Woolman.* Wallingford, Penn.: Pendle Hill Publications.

Holcolmb, J.L. (2016). *Moral Commerce: Quakers and the Transatlantic Boycott of the Slave Labor Economy.* Ithaca, N.Y.: Cornell University Press.

Kershner, J.R. (2018). *John Woolman and the Government of Christ.* Oxford: Oxford University Press.

Lay, B. (1737). *All Slave-keepers that Keep the Innocent in Bondage, Apostates.* Philadelphia.

Moulton, P.P. (Ed.). (1971). *The Journal and Major Essays of John Woolman.* Richmond, Ind.: Friends United Press.

New Jersey Association for Helping the Indians (1757). Articles. Quaker and Special Collections, 975B, Haverford College Library, Haverford, Pennsylvania.

O'Brien, K.J. (2017). *The Violence of Climate Change: Lessons of Resistance from Nonviolent Activists.* Washington, D.C.: Georgetown University Press.

Philadelphia Yearly Meeting (1744-1779). Minutes. Quaker and Special Collections, Haverford College Library, Haverford, Pennsylvania.

Philadelphia Yearly Meeting (1748-1762) Miscellaneous Papers. Friends Historical Library, Swarthmore College, Swarthmore, Pennsylvania.

Plank, G. (2009). "The First Person in Antislavery Literature: John Woolman, his Clothes and his Journal." *Slavery and Abolition* 30, 67 91.

Plank, G. (2012). *John Woolman's Path to the Peaceable Kingdom: A Quaker in the British Empire*. Philadelphia: University of Pennsylvania Press.

Plank, G. (2016). Discipline and Divinity: Colonial Quakerism, Christianity, and 'Heathenism' in the Seventeenth Century. *Church History* 85, 502-528.

Rather, S. (2002). Benjamin West's Professional Endgame and the Historical Conundrum of William Williams. *William and Mary Quarterly* 3d. Ser., 59, 821-864.

Rediker, M. (2017). *The Fearless Benjamin Lay: The Quaker Dwarf Who Became the First Revolutionary Abolitionist*. London: Verso.

Sassi, J. (2011). With a Little Help from the Friends: The Quaker and Tactical Contexts of Anthony Benezet's Abolitionist Publishing. *Pennsylvania Magazine of History and Biography* 135, 33-71.

Simler, L. (1990). The Landless Worker: An Index of Economic and Social Change in Chester County, Pennsylvania, 1750-1820. *Pennsylvania Magazine of History and Biography* 114, 163-199.

Vaux, R. (1815). *Memoirs of the Lives of Benjamin Lay and Ralph Sandiford*. Philadelphia: Conrad.

Woolman, J. (1761). The substance of some conversation with Paponahoal the Indian Chief at AB in presence of Jo. W-n AB Etc. Pemberton Papers, 13:23, Historical Society of Pennsylvania, Philadelphia.

Woolman, J. (1769). *A First Book for Children*. Philadelphia.

Woolman, J. (1770). *Considerations on the True Harmony of Mankind*. Philadelphia.

Woolman, J. (1772). Deed of trust to Stephen Comfort, April 27, 1772. Woolman Collection, Box 1, 11, Historical Society of Pennsylvania, Philadelphia.

Woolman, J. (1831). John Woolman's Letters to a Friend. *Friends Miscellany* 1, 5-12.

# 15 | Lucretia Coffin Mott: A Rebel for Social Change

**By Jean Mulhern and Cathy Pitzer**

Lucretia Coffin Mott was a nineteenth century Quaker minister, social reformer, abolitionist, feminist, suffragette, and pacifist, all aspects of a principled lifelong pursuit of universal equality and social justice. When she died in 1880, at the age of 88, *The New York Times* called her the woman "whose name was probably as widely known as any other public woman in this or the preceding generation" (*New York Times*, 1880). Social commentators said she "was widely judged by her contemporaries...as the greatest American woman of the nineteenth century" (Jacoby, 2005, p. 95). Although her political activism and strategic public challenges of social norms came a century ahead of the American civil rights and feminist eras, Lucretia Mott's early contributions to these national movements have been largely forgotten, reduced to a footnote in the "women's history" of voting rights. The following overview integrates insights from Mott's personal correspondence with the perspectives of twenty-first century biographers, social scientists, and historians to reestablish Lucretia Mott's role as a pivotal figure in American social reform history.

### Early Life

Born in Nantucket, Massachusetts in 1793, Lucretia Mott was the daughter of Quakers Thomas Coffin and Anne Folger (Bacon, 1980). Nantucket, an island off the shore of Massachusetts, was populated at that time by descendants of island owners who had arrived in the 1660s, fleeing religious persecution in England and then awakened to Quakerism in the early 1700s. Nantucket was the center of the whaling industry in America, a business enterprise sometimes so profitable that in 1790 it was one of the wealthiest communities in early America

(Philbrick, 2015). During wartime such as during the War of 1812, the people of Nantucket were isolated 30 miles offshore, vulnerable to attack, with no access to income or supplies.

The ever present dangers of whaling meant that Nantucket was home to numerous suddenly independent wives, widows, and orphaned children (Philbrick, 2015). Lucretia's father invested in the *Trial*, a whaling ship, and led his diverse crew out to sea for months at a time. As a result, Lucretia's mother Anna, like many women on the island, conducted the daily business, headed the social structure, and exerted more independence than was typical of mainland women of that era (Bacon, 1980). Young Lucretia saw firsthand how skillfully women could manage the island economy. In fact, the main shopping street on Nantucket had so many shops run by local women that it was nicknamed "Petticoat Row" (Finger, 2014). Nantucket's married women also enjoyed another perk of independence. While their men were at sea, they were awarded legal household and business authority under the Mariner's Power of Attorney, in effect between 1774 and 1847 (Finger, 2014).

Lucretia credited much of her success in life to the role models provided by these "liberated" Nantucket Quaker women, who were merchants, manufacturers, preachers, community leaders, and equal partners with their husbands (Kovach, 2015; Palmer, 2002). As a birthright Quaker she also saw how women had an equal right to speak during meeting, could be elders with religious authority, and could travel alone and publish under their own names, as demonstrated by Quaker preacher Elizabeth Coggeshall (Bacon, 1980).

In 1804 Thomas Coffin moved his family to Boston, leaving whaling for the safer and more stable occupation of a merchant. Lucretia attended public school, which her father felt would familiarize her with democratic principles and avoid "class pride" (Bacon, 1980, p. 20). At age thirteen she was sent to Nine Partners Boarding School in Dutchess County, New York. Nine Partners had been established by the New York Yearly Meeting, founding members of which included Elias Hicks and James Mott Sr., the grandfather of Lucretia's future husband James. Both sexes studied substantially the same rigorous curriculum of reading, writing, mathematics, accounts, grammar, and poetry (Bacon, 1980). Quaker girls at such schools were among the first females in the United States to receive higher education, enabling them to challenge gender bias as professionals and as community leaders. At Nine Partners, Lucretia continued her habit of reading widely, mastered the *Bible*, and completed the school's curriculum at age sixteen (Bacon, 1980; Isenberg, 2003). She then became an assistant teacher to Deborah Rogers, head female teacher at Nine Partners, which was among the first schools to employ women as teachers. Always sensitive to any kind of injustice, Lucretia found to her dismay that

> the charge for the education of girls was the same as that for boys, but that when they became teachers, women received but half as much as men for their services, the injustice was so apparent that I early resolved to claim for my sex all that an impartial Creator had bestowed (Bacon, 2013, p. 33).

### Early Married Life for Lucretia and James

In 1811, at age 19, Lucretia made what was probably the most propitious decision of her life, marrying James Mott who was not just the love of her life but her strongest supporter in all of the causes she actively embraced. James was a teacher at Nine Partners but after marriage became a partner in Lucretia's father's cut nail and wholesale merchandise businesses in Philadelphia, later becoming a textile merchant. Together they had six children, five of whom survived to adulthood. During the early years of marriage, their extended household struggled financially, especially after the death of Lucretia's father. She continued to teach school until the birth of her third child, James took on work as a bookkeeper (Faulkner, 2011), and Lucretia's mother, who lived with them, opened a store. Eventually James became a successful textile merchant.

Lucretia herself looked to her experiences on Nantucket and at the Nine Partners School as preparing her well for her adult private and public life as an activist in seeking justice for all (Bacon, 1980; Faulkner, 2011; Kovach, 2015; Palmer, 2002). Both Quaker religious practices and the Nine Partners School curriculum had equipped Lucretia with leadership skills. She had argued during mock trials, honing her extemporaneous public speaking and critical reasoning skills. These debates hardened her opposition to disownment (expulsion) for marrying a non-Quaker, an unjust practice in her eyes. She had heard Nine Partners co-founder Elias Hicks preach against a growing hierarchical orthodoxy, openly criticizing the Quaker elders. Hicks was fiery in his denunciation of slavery and advocated for immediate abolition. He opposed an unjust market economy that disadvantaged the poor who could not pay high prices. He favored the free produce movement as a way to actively protest slavery. Finally, Hicks opposed efforts to make Sunday the legal day of worship and rest, saying that it violated the Constitutional right to free conscience (Faulkner, 2011).

Lucretia learned of progressive child discipline from Superintendent Mott (1816), author of *Observations on the Education of Children; and Hints to Young People on the Duties of Civil Life*. He espoused patience, high expectations, and gentle role modeling by adults to educate children, a philosophy she and James employed with their own children. He also advocated mindful action, productive use of time, and respect for all persons. Lucretia wrote the venerable Mott after her marriage that she was rereading his book and aspired to adhere to his advice (Palmer, 2002). While rocking her babies, she read the complete works of William Penn and was deeply moved by Mary Wollstonecraft's *Vindication of the Rights of Women* (1792), "a pet book" she kept at hand throughout her life (Faulkner, 2011; Isenberg, 2003).

After 1811, the Motts lived most of their lives in or near Philadelphia. Pre-Civil War Philadelphia and its surrounding area had the largest number of members of the Society of Friends in the country. Philadelphia Quakers established a prosperous international trading economy and controlled the counting houses as well. Their religious beliefs inspired a strong antislavery movement and support for the local community of freedmen and women (Faulkner, 2011).

### Lucretia as a Quaker Minister

After the death of her first son in 1817, Lucretia, at age 26, spoke out in her Quaker meeting about her reflections on the Testimonies, appealing for strength to resist worldly temptations and to be protected from evil (Faulkner, 2011). She was accepted as a recorded minister of the Twelfth Street Monthly Meeting in 1821 with a letter to travel and preach. As was the custom, she expected to speak to groups of women, primarily at Quaker women's business meetings. Her reputation as a powerful preacher soon drew larger audiences, including men who had heard about her inspiring messages. Thus, beyond her control, Lucretia found herself out of order among Quakers for speaking publicly with men in the audience. Contemporary reports of her speeches marveled that such a tiny woman, only four foot ten inches and 95 pounds, could draw repeatedly such large mixed gender audiences (Faulkner, 2011).

James financed her ministry because the Society viewed accepting payment for preaching a sin. He often traveled with her, helped with logistics, and chaired meetings when asked. Her social issue topics, often informational, included abolition of slavery, free produce, the rights of women in marriage and in society, the importance of education, and the status of Native Americans. Concerning matters of faith, she spoke about the Inner Light, peace, church hierarchy, non-resistance, quietism (peaceful acceptance of social norms), the role of the *Bible*, and women's responsibilities. She argued that reason and science were gifts from God, intended to help address society's ills. Her sermons were extemporaneous, guided by hours of deep reflection as she read extensively and as she sewed rag carpets and mended clothes for her family. She demonstrated her "commitment to the inner light, or individual conscience, above all other forms of religious or temporal authority" (Faulkner, 2011, p. 17).

Although a prodigious letter writer, Lucretia had only a few published works under her own name (*A Sermon to the Medical Students*, 1849 and *Discourse on Woman*, 1850) and possibly a few newspaper comments under a pseudonym. Lucretia almost never wrote out her speeches; however, others in her audience took notes and reported her speeches in Quaker publications or newspapers. These secondary sources were edited by Dana Green in 1980 and much more thoroughly in 2017 (Mott). She also expanded on her preferred topics in her personal correspondence, collected and edited in 1884 (Hallowell) and more comprehensively in 2002 (Palmer). It is through her letters and the reports of her speeches that scholars finally have been able to document her life's work.

Her speaking style has been variously described in second hand sources. Faulkner (2011) concluded that she was witty, outgoing, overly modest, critical, and stubborn. She loved a good debate and was an ideologue, a moral purist who refused the compromises often required in politics. She stood her ground against men or women on the tactics of the anti-slavery movement, opposing the purchase of individual slaves out of slavery (Faulkner, 2011). Instead, influenced by William Lloyd Garrison, she favored the outright and immediate abolition of slavery with no compensation to slaveholders. All types of audiences reported her presentations to be logical, rational, factual, eloquent, and feminine, in a "sweet and melodious voice" (Faulkner, 2011, p. 41) with a "...hopeful vision of human progress, from sin, tradition, and slavery to personal morality, equality, and freedom" (Faulkner, 2011, p. 6). She believed that she had a duty to raise the issue of slavery before slaveholders and for that purpose she made a tour in late 1842 of Delaware, Maryland, Virginia, and Washington, D.C. She spoke before an audience gathered by a slaveholder and also in a Washington Unitarian Church before at least thirty legislators. Her best known speech was made in 1849 before an audience of medical students and faculty in Philadelphia at the Cherry Street Meeting. There she spoke out against the evil of slavery and emphasized the importance of education for all people. Some of the students from the South left mid-speech; however, Lucretia persisted, making her plea that those in her audience "be willing to receive that which conflicts with their education, their prejudices and preconceived opinions" (Mott, 1849).

Lucretia spoke courageously before thousands of people during her lifetime. Her messages were usually received respectfully but they were sometimes met with disdain and occasionally with violence. Even the women in her own Quaker meeting voiced "passionate opposition to Mott's sermons over the course of her ministry" (Faulkner, 2011, p. 41), but still respected her loyalty to the Quaker faith and her ability to quote Biblical scripture to counter other Biblical points. She called herself obnoxious and a heretic. She admitted that she was fully conscious of how audiences rejected her messages as unrealistic in terms of her vision of everyone *standing up* for racial and sexual equality, marital equality, religious tolerance, and nonviolence. Through it all, her strategy was individual conscious-raising through repetitive and persistent appeals to reason and morality, thereby preparing her audiences to accept and even promote the societal changes she anticipated were forthcoming and necessary (Faulkner, 2011).

When the Quaker Orthodox and Hicksite factions separated in 1827, Lucretia and James joined with the Hicksites, moving from the Twelfth Street to the Cherry Street meeting. Orthodox meetings emphasized Biblical authority and a stronger power for church hierarchy while Hicksite meetings chose to focus on the Inner Light to guide the individual. While theologically aligned with Hicksites, the decision was nonetheless a difficult one for her as many of her friends and relatives, including her mother-in-law, remained Orthodox. The Orthodox meeting houses became closed to her as a preacher. Unquestionably, the disownment of her sister and other relatives for marrying non-Quakers was a factor in her decision, as was her distaste for the heavy handedness of the Orthodox Quaker elders in enforcing their rules. Lucretia's willingness to speak persuasively on unjust social practices led to her emergence as a leader in her meeting and earned her the esteem of others as a person of integrity and great faith. She was elected year after year in the 1830s as clerk of the Philadelphia Women's Yearly Meeting. Throughout their lives Lucretia and James Mott maintained membership in their Hicksite Quaker meeting although none of their children remained Quakers as adults (Faulkner, 2011).

Eventually, Lucretia's advocacy of women's legal rights and the abolition of slavery and her "promiscuous" practice of traveling without a male escort and speaking to audiences that included men, resulted in accusations of heresy, even by the liberal Hicksites (Faulkner, 2011). Mott's acceptance of other religions also placed her at odds with the Society of Friends. She spoke frequently before other denominations and most of the black congregations in Philadelphia. She believed Native American religions to be adequate for their culture and not inferior to the Quaker faith. "It was far from me to say," she wrote in a letter after visiting the Seneca American Indians in 1848, "that our silent voiceless worship was better adapted to their condition, or that even the Missionary, Baptism, or Sabbath and organ are so much higher evidence of a civilized, spiritual, and Christian state" (Parker, 2002, p. 166). She also observed Seneca women in leadership roles, affirming her belief in natural gender equality (Wagner, 2011).

In her later years Lucretia encouraged those leading the Progressive and Congregational Quaker movements that attracted some Quakers and others (Faulkner, 2011). She helped to establish the Free Religious Association, a group of radicals of all religious persuasions, Quakers, Unitarians, even agnostics, most notably Ralph Waldo Emerson (American Unitarian Conference, 2004). In her 1867 speech before the Free Religionists she said, "I am here, as some say, 'on my own hook,'" representing neither the Hicksite nor Orthodox Quakers, as "a kind of outlaw in my own society." She continued to say that she was "much attached" to her Meeting and devoted to the Society of Friends despite occasional calls for her disownment (Greene, 1980, pp. 291-297).

## Lucretia as an Abolitionist

It is widely known that Quakers in England and America were some of the earliest opponents of slavery although prior to 1740 many Quakers in America owned slaves. Some Quakers were outspoken in their opposition to slavery, most notably John Woolman who published "Some Contradictions on the Keeping of Negroes" in 1754 (Mueller, 2008). In 1758 Philadelphia Yearly Meeting became the first to exclude members who owned or traded slaves, and while meetings throughout the country followed, most were nonetheless not welcoming to freed slaves. Those meetings which permitted freed men and women to attend usually relegated them to a separate seating section. In 1844, Sarah Mapps Douglass, the noted African American educator, complained that "for several years we were squeezed into a little box under the stairs at Arch Street meeting," being told that it was "set aside for colored people" (Moore, 2017).

Many Quakers, while nominally against slavery, profited from the existence of slavery through their business dealings. Elias Hicks and John Woolman led the consumer boycott of all goods produced by slaves, a strategy difficult to implement as the slave economy produced most of the nation's available cotton, sugar, molasses, rice, tobacco, and even indigo ink (Glickman, 2004). Lucretia's husband James changed from selling cotton to selling wool to avoid this dilemma. Interestingly, when Lucretia spoke before the Philadelphia Free Produce Society in 1827, it was the first time most men in attendance had heard a woman lecture in public on any topic (Bacon, 1980).

Lucretia sought the abolition of slavery as an "execrable system…and its ever-attendant prejudice which have so sunk and degraded its victims" (Parker, 2002, p. 165). While Quakers opposed slavery, there were wide divisions of opinion as to how to end it. Some believed in a gradual approach while others favored immediate emancipation. In 1840 one of the visitors to the Mott home was William Lloyd Garrison, who later became editor of the influential abolitionist newspaper *The Liberator*. Garrison argued that slaves had no interest in returning to Africa and the only answer was immediate emancipation. Lucretia and James took up the Garrisonian tactics of non-violent moral suasion to end slavery. The Mott home became a gathering spot for abolitionists and fugitive slaves, as many as 50 of whom often stayed at her home at one time (Bacon, 1980).

Abolition of slavery was promoted through petitions, publications, conventions, organizations, lectures, and speeches. Formed in 1784, the Philadelphia Anti-Slavery Society was, like other similar groups that followed, open to white men only. As a result, Garrison, James Mott, and others, black and white, founded the American Anti-Slavery Society (AASS). Lucretia helped edit the AASS "Declaration of Sentiments" during the 1833 convention. Lucretia and other women then formed a parallel organization, the Philadelphia Female Anti-Slavery Society (PFASS), which would become the longest lasting anti-slavery organization in the country (1833-1870). The group was unusual in that it was integrated racially, economically, and socially. PFASS founders Harriett Forten Purvis and Sarah Mapps Douglass, prominent free African-Americans, visited Lucretia's home frequently. This shocked Lucretia's mother Anna, who believed in integration in theory but not practice (Faulkner, 2011).

The Quaker practice of holding separate male and female religious meetings permitted women to choose and lead their own initiatives. Quaker women provided a number of social services including schools for former slaves, resources to Native Americans, particularly in western New York, and donations of clothing and tools to former slaves in Canada (Faulkner, 2011; Palmer, 2002). As a middle-class educated Quaker woman, Lucretia shared household duties with her mother, her adult daughters, and at least two Irish household employees (United States, *Federal Census*, 1860, 1870, 1880). She had sufficient household help and resources to work actively in public to raise funds, publish and distribute pamphlets, and organize informational meetings on behalf of social initiatives (Hewitt, 1986). Lucretia further prioritized her use of time by minimizing all "excess duties" such as fancy needlework (Hewitt, 1986, p. 30).

Taking their lead from Lucretia, a number of women of that period became popular orators, most notably the Grimke sisters and Abby Kelley. Other women galvanized the anti-slavery movement through their writings, particularly Harriett Beecher Stowe and Lydia Child. In fact the book with the most copies sold in the nineteenth century, excepting the *Bible*, was Stowe's (1852) antislavery novel *Uncle Tom's Cabin*. Some women such as Harriett Tubman and Mary Ann Shadd

(Cary) were active in the Underground Railroad movement that extended into Canada (Rhodes, 1998). Women conducted petition campaigns and lobbied Congress. They operated free produce stores and had fundraising fairs that provided much of the financing for abolitionist publications. It is estimated the yearly fairs of PFASS raised almost $900,000 (in today's dollars) that was used for publications, schools for African American children, and petition drives (Faulkner, 2011).

Political opposition to the anti-slavery movement became increasingly violent on the East coast in the 1830s and 1840s, with unruly mobs, race riots, and church burnings. Abolitionist presses were attacked as far west as Illinois. In 1838, Pennsylvania Hall, a large meeting place constructed by and for abolitionists, was burned to the ground only three days after it was completed. The same mob damaged Mother Bethel African Methodist Episcopal (AME) Church, targeted a "colored orphanage," and threatened the home of the Motts before it was diverted (Faulker, 2011). Concerns about violence led to criticism of Lucretia in the Quaker community. In 1842 Philadelphia Quakers refused to give her permission to travel as a minister and British Quakers refused to recognize her as a member of the Society of Friends (Faulkner, 2011). The abolitionist movement, in frustration after a half-century of activism, was becoming fragmented over whether moral suasion was sufficient, whether violence should be met with violence, whether issues of women's rights were impeding efforts to end slavery, and even whether women should be involved in abolitionism at all.

In 1840 the Motts traveled to London to attend the World Anti-Slavery Convention, the objective of which was to better coordinate global abolitionist movements. Originally attending as delegates, Lucretia and other women found themselves excluded by men, who required them to sit behind a screen as silent observers. A few of the male delegates sat with the women in protest, most notably William Lloyd Garrison and Boston orator Wendell Phillips. Another woman forced to sit in the female section was Elizabeth Cady Stanton, a young activist from upstate New York who attended with her husband on their honeymoon. The two women briefly discussed organizing a convention in America to promote the rights of women. It would be eight years before this convention came to pass (Bacon, 1980). Often overlooked was that, despite the Convention snub, Lucretia used her time constructively in Great Britain, making numerous public speeches in London and in Ireland and forming a network of useful Quaker and abolitionist contacts that she maintained the rest of her life (Palmer, 2002).

Lucretia continued her anti-slavery activities during the decade of the 1840s, addressing state legislatures, delivering public speeches and sermons, and even meeting with President John Tyler, a slave owner himself. While she never addressed Congress, over 40 members of Congress came to hear her when she spoke in the District of Columbia. The Motts traveled to the South, upstate New York, the Midwest, and even to Canada, sometimes being greeted warmly by Quakers but just as often receiving a hostile reception. Her speeches encompassed not only abolition of slavery but also women's rights, temperance, prison reform, and Indian rights.

In 1847 they traveled 2,800 miles over two months and attended 71 meetings in Ohio and Indiana. After a quietist Quaker doctor in Indiana refused to treat her chills, fever, and sudden back pain because of her "rebellious spirit," she leveled harsh criticism at the Indiana Yearly Meeting, saying they "ought to have gone with the Orthodox, at the Separation" (Faulkner, 2011, p. 124). The Indiana YM had disowned *en masse* many members of the Green Plain (Ohio) meeting for their abolition activism. It was also in Indiana that Lucretia and James were forced to defend themselves from false accusations of being paid speakers for the AASS. Lucretia's spirits understandably were low in that trying decade due to the death of her mother in 1844 and her frequent bouts of dyspepsia (Faulkner, 2011).

Passage of the Fugitive Slave Act in 1850, violence in Kansas, the Dred Scott decision, and John Brown's Harpers Ferry insurrection all served to reinvigorate the abolitionist movement in the 1850s. Lucretia and James helped hide many slaves escaping on the Underground Railroad, including "Box" Brown, who shipped himself to Philadelphia (Faulkner, 2011). Later in the 1850s Lucretia and James moved to an old stone house north of Philadelphia called "Roadside." James retired and while the couple occasionally drove their carriage into Philadelphia, they immersed themselves in farm and family life. Lucretia's trips throughout the country to speak and preach had largely ended.

Lucretia regarded the Civil War with mixed feelings as she was a pacifist and had always hoped slavery would be eliminated because the Inner Light would lead people to realize for themselves that it was morally wrong. Many abolitionists and Quakers had joined the Union Army, including her son-in-law (Fager, 2004; Faulkner, 2011). Women in PFASS sewed for soldiers and kept active in Freedmen's Aid Societies. They also fought to end segregation on the Philadelphia railway system (Bacon, 1980).

### Lucretia as a Feminist and Woman Suffragist

For Lucretia, the independence of women was a natural right, based upon their humanity (Hewett, 1968). Her earliest social concern was with the rights of women, especially equal pay, those property rights lost when a woman married, and equitable and just divorce proceedings. She believed that the Quaker practice of disownment for premarital sex and for marrying non-Quakers excluded otherwise faithful Quakers. She had internalized the injustice experienced by a Nantucket woman beaten in public for disobedience to her husband as well as the unequal pay experienced by female teachers. Throughout her life she preached about equality of the sexes before God and the importance of both women and men seeking guidance from God directly through the Inner Light.

Not until 1848 did Lucretia become associated with the woman suffrage movement, as it was called at that time, and even then, not willingly. She believed emphasis upon voting rights for women detracted from and divided the abolitionist movement. She and James were in western New York observing Quaker projects with a Seneca American Indian tribe and with freedmen in Canada. She also was preparing to speak to the Auburn State Prison and at a Universalist Church. She attended an informal tea at the Auburn, New York home of Quaker Jane Hunt where Elizabeth Cady Stanton was present. This social gathering in July 1848 was the first time that Lucretia and Stanton had met since their brief time together eight years before at the anti-slavery convention in London. At this reunion tea the women discussed the issues of the day and at Stanton's urging, agreed to draft a *Declaration of Sentiments* and call a women's rights convention at Seneca Falls (Tetrault, 2014).

Non-Quaker Stanton and others, not Lucretia, drafted the *Declaration of Sentiments*, with its decidedly political theme of electoral politics and voting rights for women (Tetrault, 2014). To the contrary, Lucretia's views focused on "liberty, justice, and humanity" and on the "social, civil, and religious condition of women" (Faulkner, 2011, p. 139). Her position also reflected the fact that Quakers generally rejected participation in electoral politics. Lucretia did not view the vote as an important goal for women at a time when there were so many threats to individual liberty from "mindless tradition and savage greed" (Faulkner, 2011, p. 140). The Emancipation Proclamation was still almost fifteen years in the future and voting rights for former slave men were not specifically secured until passage of the Fifteenth Amendment to the U.S. Constitution in 1870.

The Seneca Falls convention started on July 19, 1848 and the follow-up convention in Rochester, New York, began on August 19. That convention considered openly the rights of women and featured a series of debates in which

Lucretia, among others, effectively countered arguments against rights for women. She used the platform to argue that they work for all of those oppressed, again placing the lack of woman suffrage within the broader framework of societal injustice. She called for women to "rise, when she shall occupy her appropriate position in society" (Faulkner, 2011, p. 143). The next year, Lucretia modified her stance to encourage women to claim their rights but to make an individual choice about whether to exercise their right to vote or participate in politics, staying true to the Quaker principle against participation in electoral politics. In 1850 she published her *Discourse on Woman* and distributed it in lieu of a speech in Salem, Ohio. She added in a letter that the "great political and social evils that curse and desolate the land will not be eradicated as long as women's rights are so unacknowledged and not demanded" (Palmer, 2002, p. 203). She signed this letter to the Convention of the Women of Ohio, "Yours for woman's redemption and consequent elevation" (Palmer, 2002, p. 203).

In 1855, she wrote to Stanton: "I have never liked the undeserved praise in the Report of that Meeting's Proceedings, of being 'the moving spirit of that occasion,' when to thyself belongs the honor" (Palmer, 2002, p. 236). Stanton dismissed Lucretia's rebuke as an expression of modesty, not acknowledging the bitter feud between factions of the woman suffrage movement that surfaced early on, beginning with Lucretia's ignored request that the Convention schedule time for speeches about what she considered to be more pressing social issues such as abolition of slavery (Faulkner, 2011; Tetrault, 2014).

Stanton and Susan B. Anthony broke with Lucretia after the Civil War when they began active opposition to ratification of the Fourteenth and Fifteenth Amendments on the grounds that black men should not obtain the right to vote before women, specifically white women. Despite the racist tone of their activism, Stanton and Anthony advocated for "all or nothing," voting rights, for men and women, black and white. They believed that if woman suffrage and additional women's rights were not achieved along with those of black men, women might not achieve the right to vote for many decades, if at all (which proved to be the case) (Tetrault, 2014). The woman suffrage movement split between those seeking universal suffrage and expanded women's rights and those seeking to delay woman suffrage in favor of accomplishing black male suffrage first. Lucretia, in addition to her demanding schedule of speaking appearances, began a years-long struggle to broker peace in the woman suffrage movement, to bridge the schism that threatened to stymie efforts to win more rights for women. She spoke at the conventions of each faction, made personal visits and corresponded with the leaders of the two groups to no avail during her lifetime (Palmer, 2002; Tetrault, 2014). In 1890 the two factions united, forming the National American Woman Suffrage Association (NAWSA) yet women were not granted the federal right to vote until 1920 with passage of the Nineteenth Amendment (Tetrault, 2014).

When Stanton and Anthony began producing the eight-volume *History of Woman Suffrage* in 1881, they intentionally co-opted Lucretia, who had died in 1880, as the *mother* of their political movement to win the vote for white women. Lucretia, for her part, had made little of the London convention exclusion and barely mentioned the Auburn tea and Seneca Falls and Rochester conventions in her letters and notes (Tetrault, 2014). Extending many rights to women, not only the vote, was her broad agenda.

### Lucretia as a Social Reformer

Beginning in the 1830s Lucretia made public speeches throughout the Atlantic mid-states region and the Midwest on all aspects of social justice. She often attracted upwards of 5,000 persons to hear her speeches. While some believed the peace testimony of Friends meant quiet acceptance of social norms (quietism) and even of slaveholding by non-Quakers, Mott saw her role as publicly defying social and religious injustices. "The early Friends were agitators," she told an audience of abolitionists, "disturbers of the Peace" (Faulkner, 2011, 13). In 1860 before the Pennsylvania Anti-Slavery Society, Lucretia declared:

> Robert Purvis has said that I was "the most belligerent Non-Resistant he ever saw." I accept the character he gives me; and I glory in it. I have no idea, because I am a Non-Resistant, of submitting tamely to injustice inflicted either on me or on the slave. I will oppose it with all the moral powers with which I am endowed (Greene, 1980, p. 262).

Quakers were particularly interested in the plights of Southern slaves and of Native Americans; Lucretia had a more expansive view. Her activism for social change integrated the specific instances of societal injustice and oppression, whether to slaves, American Indians, women, children, prisoners, or believers in the variety of religious faiths. She pressed for effective action against the root causes of injustice, including racism, poverty, and militarism.

The examples of how Lucretia acted on her principles to address the root causes of injustice are many. By teaching, giving, speaking, organizing, and *showing up*, she supported education at all levels from community centers in Philadelphia to a manual labor school for the Seneca people to helping found Swarthmore College. By her own example, she encouraged extensive reading of books and newspapers, questioning others, attending lectures on many topics, and sharing her knowledge through preaching. She valued empowering others to help themselves. Thus she donated personally and continued her appeals for material and financial assistance for former slaves before and after the Civil War. She visited and praised the former slaves at Dawn in Canada West as they learned to be independent farmers and sent them boxes of clothing and tools (Palmer, 2002, p. 429).

In 1851 she sat in the Pennsylvania State House courtroom in solidarity with 30 white and black men in the Christiana case that tested the Fugitive Slave Law. The defendants were charged with treason for a riot related to the killing of an owner chasing down a runaway slave. At one point Lucretia was called out from the bench as a "vagrant lecturer" who was tainting the proceedings by her presence (Reid-Maroney, 2013, p. 25). She was said to have been knitting red, white, and blue scarves for the defendants to wear; she also provided assistance to their families (Reid-Maroney, 2013).

Lucretia abhorred organizational conflict as a distraction from higher purposes. She embraced the believers in many religious traditions and, through her own example, welcomed them into her home. Such associations were not approved Quaker practice. Her letters show how she pressed onward despite the slights and rebuffs experienced by women in the abolitionist movement. When marginalized by the Philadelphia Anti-Slavery Society (PASS), she co-founded the Philadelphia Female Anti-Slavery Society (PFASS) so that black and white women could implement their activities without male interference even while she continued to serve on committees in the PASS. She also was dismayed by the strident competition between factions of the woman suffrage movement, divided by racist innuendo and conflicting agendas. Lucretia attended meetings on all sides in the abolition and suffrage movements and among the Quaker factions. She worked tirelessly to refocus flagging efforts, broker agreements, mend frayed friendships, and strengthen networks, all toward ending injustice in its variety of forms (Palmer, 2002).

### The Later Years

After the Civil War, Lucretia, like many Quakers, transferred her attention from abolitionism to American Indian affairs and rights. Mott, along with Philadelphia's Radical Club (a group promoting secularization in public affairs), pressured President Ulysses S. Grant to prevent the Army from exterminating the Modoc Indians in California. Eight of the Modocs had been sentenced to death after the conclusion of the last California Indian war. On one memorable evening, according to historian Boyd Cothran, Mott interrupted Grant's dinner party, demanding that he commute the sentences of the two youngest defendants. He did (Cothran, 2014; Madley, 2016).

In 1868 James Mott passed away from pneumonia. After his death Lucretia withdrew for a time from most public activity and missed him terribly: "Scarcely a day passes that I do not think, of course for an instant only, that I will consult him about this or that…We have loved each other," she wrote, "with perfect love" (Haines, 2013). Despite her mourning and chronic illness, Lucretia never ceased advocating for positive change in her multifaceted struggle against injustice. As a widow, she appeared at numerous conventions organized on behalf of woman suffrage, freedom of religion, and peace and wrote numerous letters of critique and encouragement to those active in her causes. She helped found the Free Religion Society and the Pennsylvania Peace Society, and served as an officer of the Universal Peace Union (UPU). In 1870, when asked for a donation to the UPU related to the Franco-Prussian war, Lucretia responded: "Even the woman question, as far as voting goes, does not take hold of my every feeling as does War" (Faulkner, 2011, p. 199).

On November 11, 1880 Lucretia Mott passed away and was buried next to her husband at Fair Hill Cemetery in Philadelphia (Faulkner, 2011). Obituaries testifying to her national stature appeared not only in Quaker publications but also in *The New York Times* and the *Philadelphia Inquirer*. The *Fort Wayne (IN) Weekly Sentinel* printed: "Every man and woman who was ever a slave ought to have a tear to drop upon Lucretia Mott's coffin; every friend of freedom should have a flower to plant upon her grave" (Mott, 1880, p. 4).

### Recent Academic Scholarship

Few recognize the name Lucretia Mott today and even fewer can name her significant contributions to improved conditions in the lives of slaves, freedmen, Native Americans, women, and children. Victorian historians depicted Lucretia as a soft-spoken, domestically-inclined woman suffragist. To oppose that myth and the traditional histories of "great men in great wars," Margaret Hope Bacon (1980), Quaker historian, worked to elevate Lucretia's story through multiple articles and her biography *Valiant Friend, The Life of Lucretia Mott*. Ironically, Bacon's publisher muted her central argument for a feisty, confrontational Lucretia with the book cover tag, "The Gentle Quaker."

Nancy Isenberg (2003) detailed the "ultra reformer" Lucretia's voracious reading habit as a radical act that she shared through correspondence and book exchanges with other emerging feminists of the era (Palmer, 2002). Lucretia as a feminist bemoaned through metaphor the strictures placed on women by society in a letter to Nathaniel Barney in 1852: "Convents we have yet, with high walls, whose inmates having taken the veil, dare not give range to their free-born spirit, now so miserably cramped, & shrouded" (Isenberg 2003, p. 7). Through extensive reading, Lucretia found personal freedom and liberty.

The feminist scholar Lisa P. Vetter (2015) took a deep dive into Lucretia's contributions to the abolition and woman's suffrage movements. She asserts that Lucretia did the hard work and deserves to be included in the leadership rosters of those movements. Furthermore Vetter elevates Lucretia's original thinking as her most interesting contribution to modern studies of political power, oppression, and feminism. She describes how Lucretia recognized that the inherent causes of inequality were embedded deep in the American psyche and that legislation and changes to the Constitution would not be the ultimate fix. Hence, Lucretia had focused on moral suasion grounded in rational argument to move people to just actions, through changed hearts and minds. Pertinent to this discussion, Vetter finds parallels between Gandhi's and Lucretia's understanding of nonviolent resistance to oppression and injustice. She describes Lucretia's vision of an inclusive society, recognizing and respecting the value and humanity in every individual, acting for the betterment of each other rather than depending on some higher authority. Martin Luther King, Jr. describes his similar vision as "The Beloved Community" (King, 1963). Vetter concludes:

> Anti-dogmatic yet principled, radical yet moderate, idealistic yet pragmatic, the "belligerent Non-Resistant" Lucretia Mott offers vital contributions to our understanding of the early women's rights movement. ...As Mott continually reminds her audience, the task of challenging assumptions about the nature of political power and oppression, the meaning of autonomy, and the requirements of justice is never complete. By advocating a more active, participatory society, Mott urges current and future generations to continue the struggle for greater equality and freedom and a more just political order (2015, p. 623).

Chuck Fager (2004) highlighted Lucretia's impact on Quaker faith practices, an aspect of her legacy often overlooked. Fager argued that Lucretia "is the veritable God-Mother of modern liberal Quaker theology, at least in the United States" (pp. 1-2). She had preached against select meetings, the recording of ministers, and the concept of Quakers as a chosen people. She had multiple objections to the practice of religious disownment. For her the Light Within each individual was central to her faith and the *Bible* was a document among many. According to Fager, "a review of Lucretia's letters turns up efforts to have her silenced or disowned in 1842, 1847, 1848, and 1850, and in at least two of those years there were multiple attempts (Palmer, 2002; Hallowell, 1884; Fager, 2004). She prevailed in her right to speak and became highly respected within her own meeting. Fager (2004) concluded: "Lucretia Mott was a central figure in the theological revolution which forged liberal American Quakerism in the twentieth century. ...If Lucretia had been a man, publishing her work in books, and thus allowed into the 'official' theological discourse, this conclusion would have been obvious long ago. Nevertheless, it is clear" (p. 4).

*Lucretia Mott's Heresy* (2011), a biography by Carol Faulkner, was the first full-length book about Lucretia Mott published since Bacon's groundbreaking work. Faulkner drew upon 21st century archival preservation activities and scholarship. *Selected Letters of Lucretia Coffin Mott* (2002), edited by Beverly Wilson Palmer, was essential in Faulkner's assessment of Lucretia's place in history. A companion volume followed recently: *Lucretia Mott Speaks: The Essential Speeches and Sermons* (Densmore, et al., 2017). These two significant works culminated a monumental and expensive collaborative project funded by multiple sources including the National Historical Publications and Records Commission. The project made available letters and reports scattered among 73 Quaker, public, and academic repositories.

## The Legacy of Lucretia Mott

Lucretia Mott, as established in recent academic scholarship, was a self-described "heretic," a "radical non-resistant," a bookish subversive, who sought to open entrapped minds. She worked to effect change and to help others raise their expectations for a just society and envision change in all aspects of American life. She was, in the words of Faulkner (2011), "an amazing woman whose work and ideas inspired the transformation of American society" (inside cover flap).

Although variously labeled as an abolitionist or a woman suffragist, Lucretia from her early years into old age acted on one overarching principle, to publicly confront injustice and achieve basic human rights for all through nonviolent change. Lucretia achieved clarity on how to lead the changes she sought by integrating the testimonies of her Quaker faith, her mother's example of strong Nantucket Quaker womanhood, her progressive Quaker education, and intellectual curiosity. She embodied a social change process that combined nonviolence and her belief in the fundamental equality of all persons with Garrisonian moral suasion and determined persistence.

Today we recognize that how Lucretia Coffin Mott lived her life and organized opposition to injustice can be called *nonviolent social change leadership*

(King Center, 2014). Based on her principled philosophy of nonviolent social change, Lucretia employed activist strategies to right the injustices in nineteenth century American society. In the twentieth century we saw similar strategies articulated by the Rev. Dr. Martin Luther King, Jr. in his "Letter from Birmingham Jail" (1963).

Despite the recent academic reevaluation of Lucretia's legacy, the expansion of her historical reputation has not yet gone mainstream. For example, the Freedom Center in Cincinnati barely mentions Lucretia's name in its display about women abolitionists. In her early *Discourse on Woman* (1850), Mott decried the position of woman as a "cipher" in history, invisible and overlooked. Yet she herself did not engage in the kind of self-promotion employed by feminists Elizabeth Cady Stanton or Susan B. Anthony. Susan McMillan (2009) posits Mott's lack of public recognition today may be because the two great reform movements of the Nineteenth century in which she was involved, abolition and woman suffrage, now, out of context, may seem to be "no brainers" to new generations.

To be fair, Lucretia has received some public recognition, almost all related to her lowest priority issue, woman suffrage. A commissioned statue of Mott, Stanton, and Anthony, sculpted by Adelaide Johnson, was dedicated in the U.S. Capitol in 1921. Sadly it ended up in a basement closet in that building for 75 years, only to be put back on display in 1996. The modernist sculpture acquired the derogatory nickname of "three women in a bathtub" because the women and their unformed companion appear to be emerging from an uncut block of marble (Brooke, 1996; Boissoneault, 2017). Mott's portrait shared a three cent stamp with Stanton and Carrie Chapman Catt, entitled "100 Years of Progress of Women: 1848-1948." More recently, she was inducted into the National Women's Hall of Fame in Seneca Falls, New York (National Women's Hall of Fame, 2017) and the National Abolition Hall of Fame and Museum (National Abolition Hall of Fame and Museum, 2017) in Peterboro, New York. In 2016 the Barack Obama administration scheduled a tiny portrait of Lucretia and four others to appear on the back of the $10 bill (Alexander Hamilton remaining on the front) sometime after 2020 (Helsel, 2016).

One suspects, however, that the lack of general public recognition today would not matter to Lucretia Mott. She once avoided a suffrage reception in her honor, writing in a letter to her family, "I will *not* be lionized when I can avoid it" (Palmer, 2002, p. 411). Her objective was always to align the moral compass of the country against injustice, a long-term project.

Two hundred years ago Lucretia stood up and spoke out for the first time. One hundred years ago came the 19th Amendment to the Constitution, guaranteeing women the vote and completing the struggle for basic civic equality for all Americans. Perhaps now our society is ready for a new generation of selfless social reform leaders equipped with education, moral authority, and national visibility to continue the efforts to create the peaceful, inclusive, just society envisioned by Lucretia C. Mott, Quaker outlaw and societal rebel.

## References

Bacon, M.H. (1980). *Valiant friend.* New York, NY: Walker and Company.

Bacon, M.H. (2013). *Lucretia Mott Speaking;* Pendle Hill: Pamphlet 234. Kindle Version. Retrieved from Amazon.com.

Boissoneault, L. (2017, May 12). The suffragist statue trapped in a broom closet for 75 years. Retrieved from http://www.smithsonianmag.com /history/suffragist-statue-trapped-broom-closet-75-years-180963274/

Brooke, J. (1996, Sept. 27). 3 suffragists (in marble) to move up in the Capitol. *The New York Times.* Retrieved from http://www.nytimes.com /1996/09/27/us/3-suffragists-in-marble-to-move-up-in-the-capitol.html ?mcubz=0

Cothran, B. (2014). *Remembering the Modoc war: Redemption, violence, and the making of American innocence.* Chapel Hill: University of North Carolina Press.

Densmore, C., Faulkner, C., Hewitt, N., & Palmer, B.W. (Eds.). (2017). *Lucretia Mott speaks: The essential speeches and sermons.* Champaign, IL: University of Illinois Press.

Fager, C. (2004). Lucretia Mott, liberal Quaker theologian. *Quaker Theology #10.* (Spring/Summer). Retrieved from http://quakertheology.org/issue-10-mott-CEF-01.htm

Faulkner. C. (2011). *Lucretia Mott's heresy: Abolition and women's rights in nineteenth-century America.* Philadelphia: University of Pennsylvania Press.

Finger, J. L. (2014, Sept. 10). These ladies weren't flouncy: Nantucket's Petticoat Row." *Nantucket Chronicle.* Retrieved from https://www.nantucket chronicle.com/nation-nantucket/2014/these-ladies-werent-flouncy-nantuckets-petticoat-row

Glickman, L. B. (2004). 'Buy for the sake of the slave': Abolitionism and the origins of American consumer activism." *American Quarterly*, 56 (4), 889-912. Project MUSE, doi:10.1353/aq.2004.0056 Sept.

Greene, D. (1980). *Lucretia Mott: Her complete speeches and sermons.* NY: Edwin Mellen Press.

Haines, P. (2013 Sept.). Lucretia and James: Living in perfect love. *Friends Journal.* Retrieved from https://www.friendsjournal.org/lucretia-james-living-perfect-love/

Hallowell, A. D., ed. (1884). *James and Lucretia Mott: Life and letters.* NY: Houghton Mifflin.

Helsel, P. (2016). Anthony, Mott, Truth, Stanton and Paul: Meet the Women on the new $10 bill. *NBC News* online (April 26). Retrieved from https://www.nbcnews.com/news/us-news/anthony-mott-truth-stanton-paul-meet-women-new-10-bill-n559476

Hewitt, N. A. (1986, Spring). Feminist Friends: Agrarian Quakers and the emergence of woman's rights in America. *Feminist Studies 12* (1), 27-49.

Isenberg, N. (2003). To stand out in heresy: Lucretia Mott, liberty, and the hysterical woman. *Pennsylvania Magazine of History and Biography 127 (1),* 7-34.

Jacoby, S. (2005). *Freethinkers: A history of American secularism.* New York: Metropolitan/Owl.

The King Center. (2014). The King philosophy. Retrieved from http://www.thekingcenter.org/king-philosophy

King, M. L. Jr. (1963). Letter from Birmingham jail. In *Why we can't wait.* New York: Penguin Books.

Kovach, J. D. (2015). *Nantucket women: Public authority and education in the eighteenth century Nantucket Quaker Women's Meeting and the foundation for female activism* (Doctoral dissertation). Retrieved from http://scholarworks.umass.edu/dissertations_2/374

Lucretia Mott tribute. (1880, Nov. 17). *Fort Wayne (IN) Sentinel,* p. 4. Reprint from the *Philadelphia Chronicle Herald.* Retrieved from Newspaper Archive online.

Macy, H. R. (2004). Intersections between Martin Luther King Jr. and the Quakers. *Quaker Religious Thought 103* (1/2). Retrieved from http://digitalcommons.georgefox.edu/qrt/vol103/iss1/2

Madley, B. (2016). *An American genocide: The United States and the California Indian catastrophe.* New Haven. Yale University Press.

McMillen, S. (2009). *Seneca Falls and the origins of the women's rights movement.* NY: Oxford University Press.

Moore, P. (2017, Oct. 17). Quakers and slavery–history tour, Old City., Philadelphia. Retrieved from http://www.archstreetfriends.org/tour/

Mott, J. Sr. (1816). *Observations on the education of children; and hints to young people on the duties of civil life.* New York: Samuel Wood & Sons. Google Books for various editions.

Mott, L. C. (1849). *A sermon to the medical students*. Philadelphia, Penn. Retrieved from http://archives.dickinson.edu/digitized-resources/sermon-medical-students-delivered-lucretia-mott-cherry-street-meeting-house

Mott, L. C. (1850). *Discourse on woman*. Philadelphia, PA: T. B. Peterson. Retrieved from https://cdn.loc.gov/service/rbc/rbnawsa/n2748/n2748.pdf

Mueller, A. M. (2008). Some considerations on the keeping of Negroes. In *Quakers and slavery: John Woolman* [digital archive]. Retrieved from http://web.tricolib.brynmawr.edu/speccoll/quakersandslavery/commentary/people/woolman.php

National Abolition Hall of Fame and Museum. (2017). Lucretia Mott. Retrieved from http://www.nationalabolitionhalloffameandmuseum.org/lmott.html

National Women's Hall of Fame. (2017). Discover the women of the Hall. Retrieved from https://www.womenofthehall.org/women-of-the-hall/?keyword=lucretia+mott&view=photos

New York Times (1880). Obituary: Lucretia Mott. (Nov. 12). Retrieved from http://www.nytimes.com/learning/general/onthisday/bday/0103.html?mcubz=3.

Palmer, B. W, (Ed.). (2002). *Selected letters of Lucretia Coffin Mott*. Urbana, IL: University of Illinois Press.

Philbrick, N. (2015, Dec.). How Nantucket came to be the whaling capital of the world. *Smithsonian Magazine*. Retrieved from http://www.smithsonianmag.com/history/nantucket-came-to-be-whaling-capital-of-world-180957198/

Reid-Maroney, N. (2013). *The Reverend Jennie Johnson and African Canadian history, 1868-1967*. Rochester, NY: University Rochester Press.

Rhodes, J. (1998). *Mary Ann Shadd Cary: The Black press and protest in the nineteenth century*. Bloomington: Indiana University Press.

Stanton, E. C. (1881-1922). *History of woman suffrage*. 8 vol. E. C. Stanton, S. B. Anthony, and M. J. Gage (Eds.). New York: Fowler & Wells.

Stow, H. B. (1852). *Uncle Tom's cabin; or, life among the lowly*. Boston: John P. Jewett.

Tetrault, L. (2014). *The myth of Seneca Falls: Memory and the women's suffrage movement, 1848-1898*. Chapel Hill: University of North Carolina Press.

United States. (1860, 1870, 1880). *Federal Census*. Retrieved from Ancestry.com.

Vetter, L. P. (2015). The most belligerent non-resistant. *Political Theory 43*(5), 600-630. DOI 10.1177/0090591714522043

Wagner, S. R. (2011). *Sisters in Spirit: Haudenosaunee (Iroquois) influence on early American feminists*. Summertown TN: Native Voices Books.

Wollstonecraft, M. (1792). *Vindication of the rights of women.* Project Gutenberg online edition. Retrieved from http://www.gutenberg.org/ebooks/3420

# 16| Kenneth and Elise Boulding: The Quaker Foundations of their Contributions to the Social Sciences

## By Robert H. Scott, III and J. Russell Boulding

The twentieth century produced a handful of married couples who made outstanding contributions to the social sciences—for example, Alva (1902-1986) and Gunnar (1898-1987) Myrdal, Margaret Mead (1901-1978) and Gregory Bateson (1904-1980), and the subject of this chapter, Kenneth (1910-1993) and Elise (1920-2010) Boulding. A common characteristic of these couples was that their scholarly contributions spanned multiple disciplines and were not confined to the ivory towers of academia but extended into the realms of sociopolitical activism. A distinctive aspect of Kenneth's and Elise's work is the extent to which it was grounded in the values they held as members of the Religious Society of Friends. They each made tremendous contributions to their academic fields and to Quakerism and Quaker scholarship. Both Kenneth and Elise were nominated for the Nobel Peace Prize (at different times) due to work resulting from their strong pacifist beliefs. However, to date, there exists no research that examines the many important linkages between their work as social scientists, and perhaps most interesting, how their views differed. In this chapter we identify the areas where Kenneth and Elise made significant contributions to the social sciences and explore the Quaker foundations of their work.

### A Biographical Overview of Kenneth and Elise Boulding

Kenneth has been the subject of two biographies, *Creative Tension: The Life and Thought of Kenneth Boulding* (Kerman, 1974), published when he was 64 years old, and *Kenneth Boulding: A Voice Crying in the Wilderness* (Scott, 2015).[1] His most important autobiographical writing provides a statistical analysis of the 1019 publications written between 1932 and 1988 (Boulding, K., 1989).

Elise has been the subject of one full-length biography, *Elise Boulding: A Life in the Cause of Peace* (Morrison, 2005) published when she was 85 years old. In Quaker circles her Pendle Hill Pamphlet, *Born Remembering* (Boulding, E., 1975) is considered a classic in spiritual autobiography, and her book *One Small Plot of Heaven: Reflections on Family Life by a Quaker Sociologist* (Boulding, E., 1989) provides the best picture of the ways in which her values as a Quaker influenced her scholarship. More recently, writings about and by Elise have been published (Boulding, J.R., 2017a-d). These volumes include new biographical material, the first complete bibliography of her publications (2017a) and selections from her unpublished journals and letters (2017d).

## Kenneth: Early Life and Influences

Kenneth Ewart Boulding was born on January 18, 1910 in Liverpool, England. He was the only child of William and Elizabeth Boulding. William Boulding was a plumber who owned his own small shop. Elizabeth took care of the family and wrote poetry. The Bouldings were devout Methodists. William was a lay preacher at his church, where he spent considerable time teaching young people and mentoring them. William had a difficult upbringing, but rather than letting it cause him to become resentful and angry, he remained benevolent and gentle. Elizabeth provided Kenneth a creative atmosphere and is no doubt the reason he began writing poetry and would continue to do so throughout his life–he was particularly fond of writing sonnets.

Early in his life, Kenneth decided to be a Christian and his experiences as a child during World War I (1914-1918) contributed to his becoming a pacifist six years later at age 14 (Wright, 1988). It was the experience of seeing his Uncle Bert, psychologically traumatized by trench warfare, that most impressed upon him the vulgarity of war. He wrote that he was very fond of Uncle Bert and that when he returned from the war he had "an expression in his eyes I can still see" (Boulding, K., 1989, p. 367). Further, Boulding wrote that his closest friend and playmate, who lived next door, had an older brother who was killed in the war. Upon learning of his death, his mother came over in hysterics. Soon after, Boulding writes, "I even recall being horrified at a toy I got, with wounded soldiers in little stretchers" (p. 367). There were many other injuries and deaths of close friends and relatives. So deeply affected was Boulding that it was around

---

[1] Kenneth was also one of three scientists profiled in *Three Scientists and Their Gods* (Wright, 1988).

this time he developed a life-long stutter. So common is stuttering (or stammering as it was called at the time) among English boys that it became known as the mark of the English gentleman. It is a hereditary trait, yet no known person in Boulding's family had a stutter (Kerman, 1974). Boulding's stutter became a trait endearing him to people.

Boulding's pacifism was resolute. In high school, he read John William Graham's "Conscription and Conscience" (1922)–a study of conscientious objectors from World War I and their struggle to live their faith during wartime. He was impressed by arguments in the book and came to respect the Quakers for their commitment to pacifism. This knowledge led him to talk with his friend Robin Wall (a Quaker) about Friends and their spiritual practices (Kerman, 1974). Wall took Boulding to some Quaker meetings, and Boulding felt an immediate spiritual connection with the Quaker method of worship–especially the silence from which spoken ministry arose. Boulding started regularly attending the Liverpool Friends Meeting and continued while he attended Oxford University. While remaining an active Methodist during much of this time, he finally became a convinced Friend in 1931 (Kerman, 1974). Being a Quaker comprised his primary social circle during the rest of his life–and had a profound effect on his professional life.

Serving as a Quaker delegate at the 1937 Friends World Conference in Philadelphia, Kenneth received a call from a friend about a job at Colgate University in Hamilton, New York. He interviewed immediately and after some negotiating took the job. His two years at Colgate were largely spent writing a textbook, *Economic Analysis* (1941). It was an immediate success that furthered his reputation and acceptance among economists, and he argued later it was a primary reason he won the John Bates Clark Medal in 1949 since it was "as pure as the driven snow" (Mott, 1992, p. 356). The medal is awarded by the American Economic Association to an American under the age of forty who is judged to have made the most significant contribution to economic thought and knowledge.

The atrocities of Nazism in Europe tested Kenneth's pacifism to almost the breaking point when in May 1940 he felt almost overwhelmed by hate. As a young man, Kenneth's son Russell, remembers Kenneth recounting the experience. While taking a bath Kenneth says he was filled with a feeling of unbearable hatred, then as if a plug was pulled from a water-filled bathtub it drained away. According to Kerman (1974): "Something broke in on him, an experiencing, almost a vision, of the suffering that Christ had taken on himself for people no better than the Germans, no better than the Bouldings" (119).

He described the experience in a poem, titled "Out of Blackness," published in 1940 in *The American Friend* (Boulding, K., 1975):

> I feel hate rising in my throat.
> Nay—on a flood of hate I float.
> My mooring lost, my anchor gone,
> I cannot steer by star or sun.
> . . .
> Black are the fountains of my soul
> And red the slime on which they roll.
> . . .
> I hate! I hate! I hate! I hate!
> I hate this thrice-accursed State,
> I'll smash each bloodshot German face
> That travesties the human race!
>
> Hatred and sorrow murder me.
> But out of blackness, bright I see
> Our Blessed Lord upon his cross.
> His mouth moves wanly, wry with loss
> Of blood and being, pity-drained.
> Between the thieves alone he reigned:
> (Was this one I, and that one you?)
> "If I forgive, will ye not too?"
>
> The vial of wrath breaks suddenly,
> And fear and hate drain from me dry.
> There is a glory in this place:
> My Lord! I see thee face to face (p. 38).

For the rest of Kenneth's life his pacifism only grew stronger as threats such as nuclear war and modern warfare provided further evidence that his convictions were correct—war was never a solution.

### Elise: Early Life and Influences

Elise Biorn-Hansen was born July 6, 1920 in Oslo, Norway. Her parents emigrated to the United States when Elise was three years old, and she grew up in a closely-knit Norwegian immigrant community in the New Jersey-Long Island area. Her mother Birgit was an ardent pacifist and imbued Elise with a strong concern for social justice. Writing about major milestones in her life in *Friendly Women* she explained her first major pacifist realization as an adult in April 1940, a month before Kenneth's spiritual epiphany:

> I am 19, a senior in college, and Norway has just been invaded, shattering my safe world. As a child I was terrified by war stories from World War I, and always comforted myself that should there be another war I would somehow get back to Norway (a country we left when I was three), because this would be a safe place. Working through pain and disbelief, I finally confront the old childhood fantasy and realize it must be rejected. There can be no place to hide. If I want a safe world I am going to have to help make it so. God can't do it for me (Boulding, E., 1994a; p. 6).

Elise graduated from New Jersey College for Women (now Douglas College) with a degree in English and "no other scholarly ambitions...than to teach English at a local high school" (Morrison, 2005, p. 36). After graduating, Elise worked at several publishing houses in New York City. During this time, she came in contact with the great Unitarian pacifist preacher John Haynes Holmes, co-founder of the NAACP and ACLU, and "the Baroness" Catherine de Hueck, a Russian émigré who directed a Catholic Worker house in Harlem. Elise recounted:

> The impact that these persons made on my life was out of all proportion to my contact with them. I did not stay in New York more than five months in all. The contrast between the moral stature of the Baroness and Holmes and my own life was too great (Boulding, E., 1975, p. 11).

Elise had first discovered the Religious Society of Friends while in college, through several Quaker musicians with whom she played as a cellist. She was impressed by their spiritual commitment combined with a deep commitment to activism and attended Friends Meetings irregularly during her "atheist" period in college (Morrison, 2005, p. 38). Elise left New York City for Syracuse where her parents and younger sisters lived and began attending with some regularity the Syracuse Friends Meeting, which was known for its activism.

### Kenneth and Elise Together

Kenneth Boulding (31) and Elise Bjorn-Hansen (21) met one another on May 4, 1941 while attending a Quarterly Meeting (a gathering of Friends from a collection of local Meetings) in Syracuse. After an 18-day whirlwind courtship they announced their engagement, and within three months they were married. Kenneth was already well known in Quaker circles.

> For Elise, her marriage and her entrance into the Society of Friends, both occurring at the same time in 1941, were two experiences that were to transform her and ground all of her future work. Spiritual issues played pivotal roles both in bringing her deeply together with Kenneth and, later at times, driving them painfully apart (Morrison, 2005, p. 42).

Over the next 52 years Kenneth and Elise were active in the Religious Society of Friends at all levels, with the local Friends Meeting usually the primary focus. It is difficult to summarize the activities of two such prolifically active people.[2] The following chronology identifies selected Friends-related and academic activities in the places they lived together:

- 1941-1942, Princeton, NJ. Kenneth works at League of Nations Economic and Financial Section. K&E are active in Princeton Friends Meeting. K&E send out an epistle titled "A Call to Disarm" (July 1942).
- 1942-1943, Nashville, TN. Kenneth teaches at Fisk University. K&E are active in Nashville Friends Meeting, Elise starts a newsletter for South Central Friends Yearly Meeting.
- 1943-1949, Ames, IA. Kenneth teaches at Iowa State University. Their son, Russell, is born in 1947. Elise receives a Master's in sociology (1949). K&E found Friends Student Colony based in their home and are active in Bear Creek Monthly Meeting.
- 1949-1967, Ann Arbor, MI. Kenneth teaches at University of Michigan, helps found the Center for Research on Conflict Resolution (1959), and helps organize the first Teach-In opposing the war in Vietnam (March 1964). Elise focuses mainly on family life as more children are born: Mark (1949), Christie (1951), Philip (1953), and William (1955). K&E are active in Ann Arbor Friends Meeting.
- 1967-1993, Boulder, CO. Kenneth works as a professor of Economics at University of Colorado (1967-1980). Elise works as a professor of Sociology (1967-1978) and receives a PhD in sociology in 1969. K&E are active in Boulder Friends Meeting.

---

[2] Kenneth's archives fill more than 250 boxes, 47 at the Bentley Historical Collection at the University of Michigan (up to 1967) and 216 at the University of Colorado Archives. Elise's archives at the University of Colorado fill 138 boxes.

- 1978-1985, Hanover, NH. Elise works as a professor and becomes the chair of the Sociology Department at Dartmouth College. K&E maintain a commuter marriage while Kenneth remains based in Boulder.

### Elise: Life after Kenneth

Kenneth died peacefully of prostate cancer on March 18, 1993 with Elise at his side in their Pearl Street apartment in Boulder. As the rest of his body gradually shut down, his strong heart beat firmly until the end. His last words were "I love the world." Writing in 1994, Elise described this closing milestone of their life together:

> 1993: One is never ready. We receive the warning that Kenneth's prostate cancer, earlier operated on, is now slowly going out of control. We have nine precious months together, knowing it is our special time. He is very weak, but writing beautiful sonnets almost to the very end.[3] Now we are ready, and he must go, after the gentle joy of holding our sixteenth just-born grandchild in his frail arms. Then blackness. An empty hole. And then, wonder of wonders, Kenneth is with me! He is with me now as I write these words. I know that I am what is left of us, and God is helping me carry on (Boulding, E. 1994a, p. 7).

Elise never stopped missing Kenneth in the 17 years she lived after his death–3 in Boulder, 4 in Wayland, MA, in an apartment built by her daughter Christie and son-in-law Greg attached to their house, and 10 at North Hill retirement community in Needham, MA. Her activism (Boulding, E., 2001) and scholarship continued almost unabated until she was diagnosed with Alzheimer's in 2007. Even after the Alzheimer's set in, Elise continued to serve as an inspiration to those who knew her up until she died in 2010 (Benson, 2012, Boulding, J.R., 2017d).

### Kenneth Boulding: A Pioneer in Economics, General Systems, Peace & Conflict Resolution, and Human Betterment

Kenneth's contributions to the social sciences are astonishing in their breadth, depth, and amount. In the introduction to a bibliography of his publications from 1932 to 1984 he wrote: "I am a compulsive writer (I once almost thought of forming a Writers' Anonymous for people like myself) and at

---

[3] These sonnets were published posthumously (Boulding, K. 1994).

the age of seventy-five I seem to be aging quite slowly, so I cannot guarantee that this volume is final" (Wilson, 1985).

In a statistical analysis of his articles, books, book reviews, monographs, and pamphlets written between 1932 and 1988, a table showing the number of publications by decade in 31 topical categories totals 1019 (Boulding, K., 1989). His collected works published in six volumes by the University of Colorado total more than 3,300 pages (Boulding, K., 1975-1985). More recently a wide-ranging collection of Kenneth's writings with commentaries by other scholars was published as *Interdisciplinary Economics: Kenneth E. Boulding's Engagement in the Sciences* (Dolfsma and Kesting, 2013).

Kenneth's creativity knew no bounds with poetry being his preferred artistic medium, though he sculpted, drew, painted, and composed music. Published proceedings of conferences that he attended commonly included verse that captured the spirit of the meetings. His published poetry includes some 350 sonnets in *There Is a Spirit, The Naylor Sonnets* (Boulding, K., 1945a), a classic in Quaker poetry, *Sonnets from the Interior Life and Other Autobiographical Verse* (Boulding, K., 1975), *Sonnets on Courtship, Marriage and Family* (Boulding, 1990a) and *Sonnets from Later Life* (Boulding, 1994). Kenneth was well known for his wit and sense of humor as a teacher and speaker, and in his writing he had a knack for expressing ideas in unexpected ways. *Beasts, Ballads, and Bouldingisms* (Beilock, 1980) collects many of his unconventional turns of phrase and humorous drawings and verse into a single volume.

One measure of a scholar's influence is how frequently he or she is cited by other scholars. By this measure Kenneth was exceptionally influential. A Google Scholar search yields the following as his ten most cited publications (in descending order of number of citations)[4]:

1. *The Image* (1956a–3765 citations) was written at the end of an academic year as a Fellow at the Center for Advanced Studies in the Behavioral Sciences at Stanford University (1954-55). His experience interacting with some three-dozen social and biological scientists cemented a shift from being a conventional economist to an interdisciplinary scholar, which began in 1950 with interdisciplinary faculty seminars at the University of Michigan.

---

[4] Google Scholar search on August 7, 2017: https://scholar.google.com/scholar?start=0& q=Kenneth+Boulding&hl=en&as_sdt=1,15. Other publications with more than 100 citations are identified in the text when they are first cited. Note that Google Scholar may list citations with the variants of the same title. Numbers shown are totals where multiple listings were found.

2.  *"General Systems Theory–The Skeleton of Science"* (1956b–3473 citations). Another outgrowth of Boulding's year at the Center for Advanced Studies was the co-founding of the Society for General Systems Research in 1954 with three other Fellows at the Center. In the years that followed, Kenneth's publications focused increasingly on interdisciplinary topics. In addition to items 4, 5, 6, 8, and 9 below, additional examples include: *The Impact of the Social Sciences* (1966a–191 citations), *Beyond Economics* (1968–530 citations), *A Primer on Social Dynamics* (1970a–246 citations), and *The World as a Total System* (1985s–432 citations).

3.  *"The Economics of the Coming Spaceship Earth"* (1966b–2790 citations). Though not Kenneth's foundational contribution to the field of ecological economics, it is his most widely known. His book *A Reconstruction of Economics* (1950–524 citations) laid early foundations for the field. In 1994 the International Society for Ecological Economics established the biennial Kenneth Boulding Memorial Award.

4.  *Conflict and Defense* (1962a–2771 citations). Though not Kenneth's first publication related to peace and conflict (see, for example, *The Economics of Peace*, 1945b–94 citations), this book established him as one of the foremost scholars in the newly emerging field of peace research. *Stable Peace* (1977a–448 citations) is another one of Kenneth's significant contributions to the field.

5.  *Ecodynamics* (1978–1063 citations) presents a multidisciplinary examination of universal patterns in physical and cultural evolution.

6.  *The Three Faces of Power* (1990b–868 citations). An early product of Kenneth's interest in integrative power (the power to create relationships based on love, respect, friendship and legitimacy) was the field of grants economics–the economics of one-way transfers. See, for example, *Notes on a Theory of Philanthropy* (1962b–121 citations), *The Economy of Love and Fear* (1973–519 citations), and *A Preface to Grants Economics* (1981a–147 citations).

7.  *Evolutionary Economics* (1981b–708 citations), represented Kenneth's challenge to the approach that mainstream economics has taken to evolutionary economics.[5]

8.  *"National Images and International Systems"* (1959–744 citations).

---

[5] Some quirk in Google Scholar cites Kenneth's book by this title as published in 1983 in *Journal of Business Ethics 2 (2):160-162*. A check of citations in Wilson (1985) reveals no article by this title, only the book published in 1978.

9. *The Meaning of the Twentieth Century: The Great Transition* (1964a–672 citations).

10. "Economics as a Moral Science" (1969–596 citations). Kenneth's December 1968 presidential address to the American Economic Association reflects his lifetime commitment to challenging the profession to give the discipline an ethical grounding. See also *The Organizational Revolution* (Boulding, K., 1953–588 citations).

Kenneth was one of the great interdisciplinary thinkers of the twentieth century, yet he always considered himself to be first and foremost an economist. In *Economics as a Science* he devoted chapters to economics as a social, ecological, behavioral, political, mathematical, and moral science (1970b–448 citations). Toward the end of his life, Russell remembers hearing him express on more than one occasion his disappointment that his chosen discipline did not pay more attention to him. *Economic Analysis* (1941–474 citations), the work that earned him the John Bates Clark Award, does not appear in the list of his top-ten most cited publications. He never stopped encouraging his fellow economists to broaden their horizons (Boulding, K., 1986a). His last book, *Structure of a Modern Economy*, represented something of a return to mainstream economics (Boulding, K., 1993–29 citations) and went largely unnoticed.

Kenneth established the idea of human betterment as a legitimate avenue for inquiry by social scientists beginning in the 1960s (Boulding, K, 1965) and it remained a focus for the rest of his life (Boulding, K., 1984, 1985b).[6] According to author Robert Wright (1988): "Once he told me that he has spent his professional life studying two questions: First, what does it mean to say that things have gone from bad to better rather than from bad to worse? Second, how do we get better?" (p. 295). Wright goes on to note that Kenneth's "devotion to human betterment represents a link between his religious convictions and his work" (p. 295). Certainly his concern for human betterment had an impact on the Religious Society of Friends. In the last decade of his life he convened a project on "Quaker Studies on Human Betterment" which in turn led to the founding of the Quaker Institute for the Future in 2003.[7] Kenneth also inspired

---

[6] Kenneth does not seem to have been aware that the idea of human betterment also has an unfortunate association with the eugenics movement in the United States from the 1920s to the 1940s. Using human betterment as key words with three different search engines (Google, Firefox, and Microsoft Edge), most of the links on the first page were related to eugenics. Fortunately, Kenneth's publications also appeared as a way to direct those interested toward his work in this area.

[7] QIF's Heritage and Goals: http://www.quakerinstitute.org/?page_id=3. See also Keith Helmuth's "Friends Testimonies and Ecological Understanding"

a long-running conversation within the Friends Association for Higher Education around the theme of human betterment (Boulding, 1988). Twenty-four years after his death, Kenneth remains a voice crying in the wilderness as far as mainstream economics is concerned. In a review of Kenneth's book *Human Betterment* (1985), economist Martin Bronfenbrenner noted (1988): "It has been economics' loss that he has largely strayed off our little reservation into the wider world of ethics, conflict resolution, sociology, and versification. (We may not have taken sufficiently to heart this 1949 effort to reconstruct us from the ground up)" (p. 834).

Nevertheless, his voice continues to be heard at the edges of the field (Dorfsma and Kesting, 2013).[8] Robert Garnett (2007) notes that "After [Adam] Smith we still need Boulding" (27). He encourages economists across the ideological spectrum who argue for a "broader vision of economic life," as well as a new generation of Smith scholars seeking to reinvigorate economics as a moral philosophy to consider their "intellectual debts to Boulding" and to "take up where Boulding left off" (pp. 22, 23, 28).

## Elise Boulding: A Pioneer in Peace Research, Peacemaking, Feminism, Future Studies, and the Family

Elise left her own remarkable legacy to the social sciences as a scholar and practitioner. Considering that her contributions as a scholar were in addition to roles as a homemaker for a household with five children and a husband engaged in his own prodigious scholarly work[9], an activist, a community builder, and a networker, the extent of her published work is impressive. Her publications included 42 books, monographs, pamphlets, and edited volumes and more than 330 articles, book chapters, and other shorter works (Boulding, J.R., 2017a). As noted below, Google Scholar provides a more limited measure of her impact, yet a listing of her most cited books provides a glimpse of the areas where she made foundational contributions to the social sciences:[10]

---

(http://www.quakerinstitute.org/?page_id=489) as an example of how the "evolutionary heritage of Quakerism" has led to new perspectives on the testimonies.

[8] This volume includes commentary by a dozen economists on seminal papers by Kenneth on topics such as ecological economics, grants economics, evolutionary economics, and institutional economics.

[9] The idea of more or less equal sharing of home and child-rearing was in its infancy with Kenneth's family involvement mainly during times of family holidays and vacations when the children were growing up. Childcare responsibilities for Elise were also eased by live-in students and a closely-knit community of Quaker parents with children around the same ages.

[10] Citation numbers from Google Scholar search on August 8, 2017.

1. *Building a Global Civic Culture* (1988a–702 citations). Elise was one of the first to recognize the importance of transnational nongovernmental organizations (NGOs) in promoting peace and human rights.

2. *The Image of the Future* (1973–645 citations). During the year in Palo Alto while Kenneth was a Fellow at the Center for Advanced Studies, another Fellow, the Dutch futurist Fred Polak, lived with the family. Elise taught herself Dutch in order to translate his opus into English (the unabridged two-volume version was published in 1961). Elise went on to make her own original contributions to the fledgling field of future studies (1970, 1978a & 1978b).

3. *Cultures of Peace: The Hidden Side of History* (2000–539 citations). Elise was one of the matriarchs of the twentieth century peace movement (Morrison, 2017) and this book was the culmination of a lifetime devoted to peace research and activism. She is acknowledged as one of the founders of the field of peace education (Morrison and Harris, 2012), which Elise called the "stepchild of the peace research and peace action communities" (Boulding, E., 1987b).

4. *The Underside of History: A View of Women through Time* (1976a and 1992–416 citations) is Elise's best known work that offers a feminist perspective. Other examples include 1981a, 1994b, and 1995.

5. *Women in the Twentieth Century World* (1977–185 citations) was a ground-breaking book on the importance of women's roles in international development and peace and the ways in which policy makers systematically ignore the contributions that women make.

6. *The Future: Images and Process* (Boulding, E. & Boulding, K., 1995–107 citations).

7. *Children's Rights and the Wheel of Life* (1979–60 citations). The relative lack of attention that this book has received is an indication of the extent to which the rights of children remain a blind spot in the academic community. Other examples of her work in this area include 1976b and 1978c.

8. *One Small Plot of Heaven: Reflections on Family Life by a Quaker Sociologist* (1989–30 citations). Elise was not as iconoclastic as Kenneth in her relationship to her chosen discipline of sociology as she wrote about the family as an agent of social change (1972), a small society (1982), and maker of the future (1983).

Beyond her major writings, Elise had a global reach within and outside of academia:

Elise had the rare combination of an incisive intellect and an empathetic heart. She had a knack for seeing the unconscious cultural blind spots of peace and other academic researchers and in herself. As a feminist, Elise drew a circle around and spoke for all who were marginalized by the dominant culture, as a result of their race, ethnicity, indigenous culture, religion, sexual orientation, age, or economic status (Boulding, E., 1987a, 1993, 1994b, 1996, 2003a). Elise challenged the dominance of the powerful in the writing of history by looking at the underside (Boulding, E., 1976a, 1992), and combined her sense of the broad sweep of human history and recognition of the importance of a positive view of the future in the now-moment of the 200-year present (Boulding, E., 1988a, pp. 3-7). Elise's workshops on imagining a nonviolent world inspired thousands to renew their commitment to creating the potentials for a more peaceful world (Boulding, E., 1988b, 2002). Above all, Elise was a consummate networker. Before the Internet she functioned as a one-person LinkedIn, making connections between researchers and activists all over the world who shared common interests, but didn't know one another (Boulding, J.R., *et al.*, 2016).

## Kenneth and Elise Boulding as Partners, Collaborators, and Adversaries

In a letter to a friend written in 2005 in response to a question how Kenneth and Elise "survived the war" as pacifists, Elise responded:

> I was still 20 when we met at Quaker Meeting in Syracuse, love at first sight for us both, engaged in 18 days, married the end of that summer, I then 21. Both deeply moved by war, both ardent pacifists, but Kenneth 10 years older & had a much richer, more complex understanding of the world than I. What an incredible mind he had, such profound analysis of a torn-apart, in-process-of-re-creation world, somehow drawing on the pure poetry of reality while showing scientifically how that reality, including so much violence and suffering, could be reconstructed into a world at peace. I was his student from the day we met, and still am, though he is no longer with me as a physical presence.
>
> Becoming his wife, I could not simply remain his student, or continually hover at the edge of his crowds of admirers, as I found myself doing for the first couple of years of our marriage. I had to create my own role, my skills in organizing groups & creating networks, developing community-based practical peacemaking. Those were skills

Kenneth didn't have. So we developed a working partnership (Boulding, J.R., 2017d, p. 45).

Early in their marriage Kenneth and Elise found solidarity in their shared pacifism. In the spring of 1942, in response to the Japanese bombing of Pearl Harbor they drafted a statement, "A Call to Disarm." When they brought it to the monthly meeting of the Princeton Friends Meeting it was considered seditious, and they were strongly advised not to send it out (Kerman, 1974, p. 121). Kenneth was informed by his supervisor at the League of Nations that he would be fired if he released it. In July 1942 Kenneth resigned and they jointly sent the epistle out signed under their names. After moving to Nashville, Tennessee, they published another (similar) statement that argued people should ignore their country-based allegiances and instead honor the universal Kingdom of Truth, which did not ask them to "hate, kill, maim, burn and destroy" (Kerman, 1974, p. 121).

After the move to Ames, Iowa, in late 1944 and then to Ann Arbor, Michigan, in 1949, Elise focused on her own academic studies, and on homemaking as the family grew. The formation of the Center for Conflict Resolution at the University of Michigan in 1959 created the opportunity for Kenneth and Elise to work together, Kenneth as one of the key academic players, and Elise as a secretary.

> While working as a secretary at the Center for Conflict Resolution, it was Elise's idea to retrieve from the wastebasket letters from peace scholars and related newsletters that the Center had received. She clipped relevant passages, pasted them, added her own comments and then sent them out as a compiled newsletter, initiating what would soon become the IPRA newsletter (Morrison, 2005, pp.86-87).

The newsletter predated by two years the formal founding of the International Peace Research Association (IPRA) in 1965, and Elise soon established herself as a scholar in her own right (Boulding, E., 1963, 1967). As Elise continued to establish her own academic identity, the only major collaborative work she did with Kenneth was a jointly taught introductory freshman course titled "The Social System of the Planet Earth" (Boulding, K., Boulding, E. & Burgess, G., 1980).[11] Most of Elise's work was on peace and the role of households (a micro view), while Kenneth thought more in terms of systems and institutions (a macro

---

[11] Elise was the sole author of 96% of her non-book publications. For Kenneth the percentage probably exceeds 98%.

view). *The Future: Images and Processes*, a collection of their writings about the future, illustrates the way in which their work complemented each other (Boulding, E. & Boulding, K., 1995).

As far as we know Kenneth's inner spiritual life was not again assailed by doubts after his bathtub epiphany. He had made a peace of sorts with the fallen world and in the later years of his life that peace emerged as a growing conservatism: "In America, Boulding, who was for some time a Democrat, broke with the Democrats over Vietnam, became a defiant nonvoter, and in 1970, though with some sense of anomaly, registered as Republican" (Kerman, 1974, pp.106-107).

In the early 1960s he served as faculty advisor for the fledgling Students for Democratic Society. At the University of Colorado he became faculty advisor for the Young Republicans.

> A move like this may startle some observers who are accustomed to thinking of Boulding as a radical heretic. He is a heretic, even among radicals. On the radical-conservative continuum he has always, since his Oxford days, had one foot in each side of the line (sometimes he stands on one foot, sometimes on the other) (Kerman, 1974, p. 107).

Kenneth left the Republican Party in response to Ronald Reagan's economic and military policies (Boulding, K., 1981c), yet his conservative streak gained ascendancy during the later years of his life.

Elise felt a lifelong tension between her yearning for a quiet inner spiritual life and the outward demands of family, community, and profession as she sought, with God's guidance, to lay the foundations for a more peaceful and just world (Boulding, E., 1975). Even those who knew her well saw only glimpses of the inner turbulence of her spiritual life: "These tensions and challenges are evident in her journals throughout the 1970s, 1980s, and 1990s. I had not anticipated in reading her journals how tumultuous her inner spiritual life was during these years" (Boulding, J.R., 2017d, p. xii).

Elise wrote in a journal entry on March 19, 2002:

> On my early morning walks I frequently find myself reaching out to a sense of the far-far future; & experiencing earth as one of many planets linked to un-numbered stars–as a way of dealing with inner despair about the state of the world…In a sense it's the daily *New York Times*

against my sense of a universe moved by grace & love (Boulding, J.R., 2017d, p. 152).

All too often the *New York Times* gained the upper hand. As Kenneth's conservatism became more pronounced (Boulding, K., 1977b), Elise's continuing awareness of the brokenness of the world accentuated her differences with Kenneth on matters of social policy related to racial justice and economic disparities between the wealthy and the poor. When these differences were aired in public on panels at conferences and professional meetings, the result was entertaining and thought-provoking for the audiences. Kenneth thrived on such differences.[12] For Elise they were painful. To say that their differences were adversarial is perhaps too strong a word. Their relationship was always grounded in a deep love for each other[13] and their commitment to pacifism and nonviolence. The next section examines how these differences were expressed in the ways they related to the Friends' testimonies.

### The Quaker Foundations of the Bouldings' Scholarly Work

In a century when academia became increasingly secular (Marsden, 1992) Kenneth and Elise were unapologetic about their faith as Quakers. As the umbrella of the Religious Society of Friends came to include non-Christian universalists, they remained Christocentric. While active in unprogrammed meetings wherever they lived, they maintained close ties with programmed and evangelical Friends. In Iowa they became members of Bear Creek Meeting in Iowa Conservative Yearly Meeting. They held such affection for Conservative Friends that they did not transfer their membership to Ann Arbor Meeting until the early 1960s. Their relationship with the Religious Society of Friends was a two-way street. Their perspective as Quakers informed their work as social scientists (Boulding, E., 1989, Boulding, K., 1986b). Their work enriched the Religious Society of Friends through spiritual insights (Boulding, E., 1956,

---

[12] As a Commonwealth Fellow at the University of Chicago Kenneth attended classes taught by the well-known economist Frank Knight and found them "enormously stimulating, though...rather disorganized" (Boulding, 1989, p. 371). He and Knight would have heated discussions about economic theory (and no doubt many other topics). When Kenneth arrived in Chicago he printed a copy of his only published paper (on displacement costs) and sent it to Knight, to which Knight wrote back to him "Professor Knight thanks Mr. Boulding for his paper, which he thinks is as wrong and confused as it is possible to be" (Boulding, 1992, p. 72). Kenneth felt "that got our relationship off on a very good level and I became very fond of him. I am sure my thinking has been much influenced by his teachings" (p. 72).
[13] Russell keeps on his writing desk a small plastic card that he found in Elise's desk after she died. It says "Some things never change with time...my love for you." The back of the card has Kenneth's faded signature.

Boulding, K., 1945a, 2004), and by sharing how their work could be applied in a Quaker context, such as family life for gays and lesbians (Boulding, E., 1987a), children and social action (Boulding, E.,1996), economics (Boulding, K., 1951), peace (Boulding, K., 1954), and the evolutionary potential of Quakerism (Boulding, K., 1964b).

Lasersohn (2010) has discussed problematic aspects of the use of the word *testimony* in the twentieth century:

> What is new is the use of the word *testimony* for just this specific set of four or five principles, rather than the full range of truths to which Friends testify, and the conception of Quakerism as organized around a small number of highly abstract, maximally general ethical concepts – almost as though it were an academic system of moral philosophy, compactly axiomatized so that all other aspects of Quaker practice and individual conduct can be shown to follow.

Modern usage of the "social testimonies" can be traced to Howard Brinton's *Guide to Quaker Practice* (Brinton, 1943). Brinton was clear that the categorization of the testimonies was an "over-simplification" of the more fundamental principle that the outward individual and collective expression of Quaker practice arose from the inward experience of the Inner Light/Christ Within. Certainly, as a young convinced Friend and mother, Elise understood Brinton's usage when she broke new ground by applying four testimonies to family life as "useful categories in checking out the state of our family witness" (Boulding, E., 1952) and when she discussed the same four testimonies in the First Day School text she wrote for children (Boulding, E., 1958; first edition 1953). The four testimonies referred to in these two publications were peace,[14] equality, community, and simplicity. These four are a useful framework for examining how Kenneth's and Elise's lives and work were grounded in Quaker faith and practice.[15]

---

[14] In the context of family life Elise called this the testimony of harmony.

[15] Elise did not refer to the testimony of integrity–speaking truth and seeking consistency of life with beliefs– from which the other testimonies might be considered to follow. Whatever their differences, Kenneth and Elise lived lives of utmost integrity. Kenneth's most comprehensive treatment of this testimony (though not framed in that context) was his 1970 Swarthmore lecture, *The Prospering of Truth*. The closing paragraph is worth quoting:
Yet in spite of everything; of the temptations of worldly success, of my commitment to mechanism as far as it will go (and I once had a very angry letter from a young man who accused me of being a sophisticated mechanist), my faith in the necessity for a scientific method of sampling and testing, especially in social systems, yet I must almost testify that out of my own experience I know what George Fox means when he says 'The Lord's power rose

**The Peaceable Kingdom and the Peace Testimony.** The image of the peaceable kingdom (Isaiah 11:1-9) captures at a macro level the Quaker focus on creating heaven on earth rather than the afterlife.[16] The image of the family life as "one small plot of heaven" in Kenneth's 1944 "Sonnet for a Quaker Wedding" (1990, p. 69) captures the peace testimony at a micro level:

> Put off the garb of woe, let mourning cease;
> Today we celebrate with solemn mirth,
> The planting in the ravaged waste of earth
> One small plot of heaven, a Home of peace,
> Where love unfeigned shall rule, and bring increase,
> And pure eternal joy shall come to birth
> And grow, and flow, that neither drought nor dearth
> Shall wither, 'til the Reaper brings release.

Kenneth and Elise both brought a predisposition to pacifism to the Religious Society of Friends when they joined as young adults. The history and practice of Quakerism provided fertile ground that solidified their pacifist convictions. Cynthia Kerman's biography of Kenneth includes an entire chapter titled "Nonviolence: The Deep Root" (Kerman, 1974, pp.111-135; see also, "Pacifist Born" in Scott, 2015, pp.18-21). Early in their married life they made joint public pacifist statements at a time when it took courage to do so (noted earlier). Their shared concern for creating a more peaceful world is the dominant theme in their respective manifold contributions to the social sciences. Kenneth published more about peace and conflict than any other topic (152 publications) followed by the economics of peace and war (147–Boulding, K., 1988). The two categories combined make up 29.3% of his published work. A comparable keyword search in the titles of Elise's publications yields a higher percentage of 43%, and when additional words such as non-violence and violence are added the total is about 47%.

**Testimony of equality.** The idea of equality in the early practices of Friends was more implicit than explicit. The spiritual egalitarianism of the early Quakers arose from the understanding that women had the same access to the leadings of the Spirit in ministry and social concerns. Social action arising from leadings of the Spirit tended to be expressed individually rather than corporately. John

---

over all', and the Lord's power is the power of truth, both in the head and in the heart. (Boulding, K., 1970c, p. 51).
[16]The image by Quaker artist Edward Hicks' paintings titled" Peaceable Kingdom" graces the cover of Elise's last major book, *Cultures of Peace* (2000).

Woolman's concern for the injustice of Friends owning slaves in the eighteenth century led to Quakers becoming leaders in the anti-slavery movement of the nineteenth century. Quaker women provided prominent leadership in the women's suffrage movement in the nineteenth century. Similarly, the nineteenth century saw individual Quakers provide leadership in the humane treatment of those with mental health needs and those who were imprisoned.

The articulation of the testimony of equality in the twentieth century in the United States has gone hand-in-hand with the civil rights and gay liberation movements. Elise was an early supporter of LGBTQ rights within the Religious Society of Friends (Boulding, E., 1987a) and Kenneth was a sympathetic bystander. The differences between Kenneth and Elise were most pronounced when it came to matters of injustices related to race, ethnicity, and economic status.[17] Kenneth was not overtly racist. Kenneth and Elise were "eldered very severely" by Princeton Friends when they had a black couple over for dinner (Kerman, 1974, p. 146), and when Kenneth taught at Fisk University his students were mainly African American. Nevertheless, Kenneth tended to turn a blind eye to the deep racial and economic injustices in his adopted country. Cynthia Kerman (1974) provides part of the explanation for this:

> His love affair with America was partly youthful idealism about a new, fresh world, partly a breaking out of the British class system (in America, "nobody asked us who our grandfathers had been, they accepted us as people"), and partly a rejection of narrow British nationalism, "to become larger than English….In a sense I became an American because this is as close as you could get to being human" (p. 106).

What Kenneth did not seem to see was the extent to which the freedom he felt in coming to America was the result of being white and male. Elise, on the other hand, had first-hand experience facing gender inequalities as a woman in academia.[18] Also, her work as a sociologist documenting the unrecognized importance of women's economic contributions in developing nations (Boulding, E., 1977), and the various ways in which women experienced violence (Boulding, E. 1981b), gave her a global perspective on injustices of all sorts. Perhaps if Kenneth had stayed in Britain and continued to experience the

---

[17] The discussion that follows reflects the understanding that Russell has come to about the basis for the real differences between Kenneth and Elise on social justice issues. This understanding has only come since they both died and continues to develop.

[18] Kenneth actively supported the American Economic Association's Committee for Women's Status in the Profession (Pfaff, 1976, p. 4). That he considered it important can be attributed to both his perspective as a Quaker and observation of Elise's experience in academia.

strictures of its class system he would have been more sympathetic to fellow peace researcher Johan Galtung's ideas of structural violence and negative peace as policy issues that needed to be addressed along with the threats of nuclear weapons at the international level (Boulding, K., 1977b).[19] The idea of structural violence was integral to Elise's work as an academic and activist.

**Testimony of community.** Elise wrote: "The testimony of community was an expression of the Quaker belief that the whole world was part of God's family" (Boulding, E., 1958, p. 16). She built community wherever she and Kenneth lived and traveled, with Kenneth for the most part being a willing participant. Early in their marriage, the community building was fully collaborative as they traveled in the ministry, organizing regional Young Friends conferences that cut across Quaker doctrinal differences–conservative, liberal, pastoral, and fundamentalist–and when they established the Friends Student Colony in their home in Ames, Iowa in the mid-1940s (Kerman, 1974). Kenneth's one notable foray into the process of community building were the interdisciplinary faculty seminars that he organized at the University of Michigan starting in spring of 1950 (Kerman, 1974). Beyond that he tended not to have the patience required for individuals to work through differences that naturally arise when creating community.[20] As noted earlier, it was Elise who was a driving force in the creation of the International Peace Research Association in the 1960s from the "wastebasket" at the Center for Conflict Resolution (she later served as secretary for the organizing committee of the Consortium on Peace Research Education and Development–now the Peace and Justice Studies Association). In the early 1960s Elise and Kenneth together were instrumental in organizing the Friends Lake Cooperative Community in Michigan, a Quaker recreational and residential community. Elise was a driving force in the formation of the 624 Pearl Street Residences Community for retired scholars in Boulder, Colorado, where she and Kenneth lived in a modest four-room apartment from 1985 until he died in 1993 (Kenneth's initial resistance to the idea was fierce, but after the move he gracefully acknowledged that it was a very good idea). Toward the end of her life Elise articulated a multidimensional model of citizenship that encompassed one's local community, nation, and the United Nations (Boulding, E., 2003b).[21]

**Testimony of simplicity.** Though not directly relatable to their work as social scientists, at a personal level the testimony of simplicity provides a window

---

[19] Ten years later, Johan Galtung distilled his differences with Kenneth to only one quarrel, the idea of structural violence (Galtung, 1987).
[20] Russell remembers him saying more than once "The price of community is palaver."
[21] An unpublished journal entry dated January 6, 2002 adds two more levels: Gaia–beloved community of life on the planet, and Creation–the cosmos, the all-encompassing spiritual wholeness of all creation (Boulding, J.R., 2017d, p. 156).

for examining the area of greatest tension in the marriage of two equally strong-willed individuals. Kenneth and Elise were generous in sharing the fruits of the prosperity that came from successful careers as academics and authors with the local Friends Meetings they were involved in, other Friends organizations, and numerous other worthy causes.[22] Kenworthy (1987) notes that there is more than a grain of truth to the aphorism "Friends came to America to do good–and ended up doing well," and that grain of truth applied to Kenneth as well. Though never extravagant, he took delight in the large house on Willowbrook Road in Boulder with its spectacular view of the Flatirons that they bought in 1967. In January 1971, Elise experienced an "upside-down turning" while staying in the unheated apartment of the director of the Gandhi Museum and his wife in India and a "call" to strip herself of what she did not need. Elise found upon returning to Boulder ("suburbia") that "words could convey neither the outward experience nor inward state" to Kenneth or to most of her children and friends/Friends, of her view of the "domestic comforts that sealed us all off from the living God" (Boulding, E., 1975, pp. 14-16). With varying degrees of intensity, Elise lived for the rest of her life with a tension between the inward call for a simpler life and the challenges of practicing that calling when most around her accommodated themselves to the materialism of the dominant culture. A journal entry written on her 55th birthday describes beautifully how the unbreakable bond of love that united Elise and Kenneth kept them together:

> Hermitage, July 6, 1975. Writing the date reminds me that this is my birthday. What can I offer you, Lord, on my birthday?...I am indeed of lowly estate, and have nothing to offer...If I have nothing to give myself, I can at least use well what is given to me.
>
> Watching Kenneth scrubbing the rocks around the waterfall yesterday while I was emptying sand from the rock pool, I was struck with the symbolism of his activities and mine, as presenting the two ways of being for humans. Kenneth lovingly brings new order to nature. He works for hours rearranging rocks, raking sand, creating beauty according to his human vision. No one is better fed or cared for by this activity–it has no economic consequences whatever–it is a pure expression of joy in creation. The mode of expression is an *elaboration*

---

[22] In 1980 with a joint adjusted income of $101,319, their tax deductible contributions total $14,669 (14.5%), with approximately equal amounts listed as Kenneth's and Elise's contributions. The respective percentages of church and other contributions gives a rough indication of their relative priorities at the time: Kenneth– church (69.3%) and other (30.7%), Elise–church (14.2%) and other (85.8%). The large majority of church contributions went to Friends organizations (Kenneth–98.3%; Elise–74.7%).

of what has been given us. In our home we are surrounded by elaborations, which go naturally with many purchases, casually made.

By contrast I sit in the hermitage trying to strip down, to limit, to simplify. Beauty and goodness lie in the bare unelaborated essence of creation. Creaturely activity in stimulating new wants, focusing on variety in food and style in clothing, in forever complexifying our homes and our communities, lead to oppression and greed. True joy lies in stripping all this away.

God gives to his human children both impulses: the impulse to create and adorn, and the impulse to strip and simplify. In Kenneth and me, he yoked the two together (Boulding, J.R., 2017d, p.73-74).

## Conclusion

Kenneth Boulding and Elise Boulding were influential social scientists who produced important research, engaged in activism and had a successful marriage that lasted over fifty years. Quakerism brought them together and served as a source of inspiration for their work on peace, human betterment, and many other topics. Individually they produced hundreds of articles and many dozens of books. While they were both social scientists, they approached problems from different angles. Elise was focused on individual behavior influencing communities and society. Her work on families and the role they play in peace and well-being is still influential today. She was a feminist who viewed the role of women as critical in creating a healthy society. Kenneth viewed problems more broadly. His view of society was one built on systems and institutions. When he thought of promoting peace his focus was on nations and global cooperation. Elise, too, believed this was important. As a leading scholar on the positive influence of non-governmental agencies promoting human rights and peace, her views were not constrained by the value she placed on families and community building. As devout Quakers, the Bouldings lived up to the faith's testimonies and applied them in their everyday lives. The testimonies of peace, equality, community, and simplicity flow into and out of the work of both Kenneth and Elise. While they did not agree on all issues and sometimes viewed the world very differently, their Quaker beliefs and mutual respect resulted in significant personal and professional successes. While neither are alive today, much of their work is accessible and will remain relevant until the world achieves complete peace and prosperity.

# References

Beilock, R P. (Ed.) (1980). *Beasts, ballads and Bouldingisms A collection of writing by Kenneth E. Boulding.* New Brunswick, NJ: Transaction Books.

Benson, V. (2012). Remembering Elise. *Journal of Peace Education 9(2),* 185-189.

Boulding, E. (1952). *Friends testimonies in the home.* Philadelphia: Friends General Conference. Updated version published in Boulding, E. (1989, pp. 83-108).

Boulding, E. (1956). The joy that is set before us. *Friends Journal, 2(15),* 228-229. Reprinted in Boulding, J.R. (2017c, Chapter 11).

Boulding, E. (1958). *My part in the Quaker adventure, new edition.* (Philadelphia: Religious Education Committee of Friends General Conference). First edition published in 1953.

Boulding, E. (1963). Peace research: the new intellectual frontier. *Women Speaking,* January. Reprinted in Boulding, J.R. (2017a, Chapter 4).

Boulding, E. (1967). Summary and challenges for future research. *The Journal of Social Issues (special issue on Conflict and Community in the International System), XII(1),* 144-158. Reprinted in Boulding, J.R. (2017b, Chapter 11).

Boulding, E. (1970). Futurology and the imaging capacity of the west. *World Futures Society Bulletin, III(12),* 1-21. Reprinted in Boulding, J.R. (2017c, Chapter 11)

Boulding, E. (1972). The family as an agent of social change. *The Futurist, 6(5),* 363-378. Reprinted in Boulding, J.R. (2017a, Chapter 9).

Boulding, E., Translator (1973). *The image of the future.* San Francisco: Jossey-Bass. One volume abridgement of 1961 two-volume translation from the Dutch of *De toekomst is verledan tyd,* by Fred Polak; W. De Haan N.W., 1953

Boulding, E. (1975). Born remembering. *Pamphlet 200.* Wallingford, PA: Pendle Hill Press. Updated version published in Boulding, E. (1989, pp. 45-73) and Boulding, J.R. (2017c, Chapter 1).

Boulding, E. (1976a). *The underside of history: A view of women through time.* Boulder, CO: Westview Press.

Boulding, E. (1976b). *The personhood of children: Nonviolence and children in the technological society.* Philadelphia: Religious Education Committee of the Friends General Conference. Reprinted in Boulding, E., (1989, pp. 32-44) with title "Personhood of children and the flight from relationship".

Boulding, E. (1977). Women in the twentieth century world. New York: Sage.

Boulding, E. (1978a). The dynamics of imaging futures. *World Future Society Bulletin, XII(5),* 1-8. Reprinted in Boulding, J.R. (2017c, Chapter 12).

Boulding, E. (1978b). The family as a way into the future. *Pamphlet 222*. Wallingford, PA: Pendle Hill Publications. Reprinted in Boulding, J.R. (2017c, Chapter 5).

Boulding, E. (1978c). The child and nonviolent social change. In I. Charny (Ed.), *Strategies against violence: Design for nonviolent change* (pp. 68-99). Boulder, CO: Westview Press. Reprinted in Boulding, J.R. (2017b, Chapter 6).

Boulding, E. (1979). *Children's rights and the wheel of life*. New Brunswick, NJ: Transaction Press.

Boulding, E. (1981a). Perspectives of women researchers on disarmament, national security and world order. *Women's Studies International Quarterly, 4(1)*, 27-40. Reprinted in Boulding, J.R. (2017b, Chapter 3).

Boulding, E. (1981b). Women and social violence. In: Alain Joxe, (Ed.), *Violence and its causes: Theoretical and methodological aspects of recent research on violence* (pp. 239-251) Paris: UNESCO.. Reprinted in Boulding, J.R. (2017c, Chapter 2).

Boulding, E. (1982). *The family as a small society*. Great Barrington, MA: E.F. Schumacher Society. Reprinted in Boulding, J.R. (2017c, Chapter 6).

Boulding, E. (1983). Familia faber: The family as maker of the future. *Journal of Marriage and the Family, 45(2)*, 257-266. Reprinted in Boulding, J.R. (2017c, Chapter 7).

Boulding, E. (1987a). The challenge of nonconformity: Reweaving the web of family life for gays and lesbians. *Friends Journal, 33(13)*, 16-18. Reprinted in Boulding, J.R. (2017c. Chapter 8).

Boulding, E. (1987b). Peace education as peace development. *Transnational Associations, 6*, 321-326. Reprinted in Boulding, J.R. (2017b, Chapter 5).

Boulding, E. (1988a). *Building a global civic culture: Education for an interdependent world*. New York: Columbia University Teachers College Press.

Boulding, E. (1988b). Image and action in peace building. *Journal of Social Issues, 44(2)*, 17-37. Reprinted in Boulding, J.R. (2017b, Chapter 7.

Boulding, E. (1989). *One small plot of heaven: Reflections on family life by a Quaker sociologist*. Wallingford, PA: Pendle Hill Press.

Boulding, E. (1992). *The underside of history: A view of women through time* (Revised Edition, 2 vols.). Newbury Park, CA: Sage.

Boulding, E. (1993). Ethnicity and the new constitutive orders. In J. Brecher, J. Brown Childs, & J. Cutler (Eds.), *Global visions beyond the new world order*. Boston: South End Press, pp. 213-231. Reprinted in Boulding, J.R. (2017c, Chapter 3).

Boulding, E. (1994a). Milestones. *Friendly Woman 11(7)*, 6-7. Reprinted in Boulding, J.R. (2017d, Chapter 2).

Boulding, E. (1994b). Women's movements for social change: Social feminism and equity feminism. Paper presented at session on Gender and Social Transformation at International Sociological Association Symposium No.3 on Old and New Forms of Solidarity and Identify, Bielefeld, Germany, July 1994. [Reprinted in Boulding, J.R. 2017c: Chapter 4]

Boulding, E. (1995). Feminist inventions in the art of peacemaking. *Peace and Change 20(4)*, 408-438. [Reprinted in Boulding, J.R. 2017a: Chapter 6]

Boulding, E. (1996). Our children, our partners: A new vision for social action in the 21st century. Brisbane: Australia Yearly Meeting of the Religious Society of Friends. Reprinted in Boulding, J.R. (2017c, Chapter 10).

Boulding, E. (2000). *Cultures of peace: The hidden side of history*. Syracuse, NY: Syracuse University Press.

Boulding, E. (2001). Reflections on activism in one's eighties. *Fellowship, 67(9-10)*, 8-9. Reprinted in Boulding, J.R. (2017a, Chapter 8).

Boulding, E. (2002). A journey into the future: Imagining a nonviolent world. *Peace and Conflict Studies, 9(1)*, 51-54. Reprinted in Boulding, J.R. (2017b, Chapter 13).

Boulding, E. (2003a). Witness to Islam's creativity: A scholar's reflections on the Islamic contribution to peace dialogue among faiths. *Islamic Horizons, January-February*, 60-61. Reprinted in Boulding, J.R. (2017b, Chapter 10).

Boulding, E. (2003b). New understandings of citizenship: Path to a peaceful future? In D. Krieger (Ed.), *Hope in dark times* (pp. 119-132). Santa Barbara, CA: Capra Press,. Reprinted in Boulding, J.R. (2017b, Chapter 8).

Boulding, E., & Boulding, Kenneth (1995). *The future: Images and processes*. Thousand Oaks, CA: Sage.

Boulding, J.R. (Ed.) (2017a). *Elise Boulding: A pioneer in peace research, peacemaking, feminism, future studies, and the family from a Quaker perspective*. Pioneers in Arts, Humanities, Science, Engineering Practice (PAHSEP) V.6. New York: Springer.

Boulding, J.R. (Ed.) (2017b). *Elise Boulding: Writings on peace research, peacemaking and the future*. PAHSEP V.7. New York: Springer.

Boulding, J.R. (Ed.) (2017c). *Elise Boulding: Writings on feminism, the family and Quakerism*. PAHSEP V.8. New York: Springer.

Boulding, J.R. (Ed.) (2017d). *Elise Boulding: Autobiographical writings and selections from unpublished journals and letters*. PAHSEP V.9. New York: Springer.

Boulding, J.R., Clements, K., Morrison, M.L. and Strimling Yodsampa, A. (2016). Elise Boulding's legacy to the twenty-first century: Reflections on her contributions to understanding conflict and peace. *Negotiation and Conflict Management Research 9(4)*, 274-291.

Boulding, K. (1940). Out of blackness. *The American Friend*, June 6, 1940.

Boulding, K. (1941). *Economic analysis*. New York: Harper & Row. Later editions published in 1948, 1955 and 1966.

Boulding, K. (1945a). *There is a spirit: The Naylor sonnets*. New York: Fellowship Press. Republished in 1998 as Pendle Hill Pamphlet 337.

Boulding, K. (1945b). *The economics of peace*. New York, Prentice-Hall.

Boulding, K. (1950). *A reconstruction of economics*. New York, NY: John Wiley and Sons.

Boulding, K. (1951). What about Christian economics? *American Friend 39(23)*, 361.

Boulding, K. (1953). *The organizational revolution: A study in the ethics of economic organization*. New York: Harper & Brothers.

Boulding, K. (1954). Twenty-five theses on peace and trade. *Friend* 127, 23-27.

Boulding, K. (1956a). *The image: Knowledge in life and society*. Ann Arbor, MI: University of Michigan Press.

Boulding, K. (1956b), General systems theory–The skeleton of science. *Management Science 2(3)*, 197-208.

Boulding, K. (1959). National images and international systems. *Journal of Conflict Resolution 3(2)*, 120-131.

Boulding, K. (1962a). *Conflict and defense: A general theory*. New York: Harper.

Boulding, K. (1962b). Notes on a theory of philanthropy. In F.G. Dickinson (Ed.), *Philanthropy and public policy* (pp.57-71). New York: Bureau of Economic Research.

Boulding, K. (1964a). *The meaning of the twentieth century: The great transition*. New York: Harper & Row.

Boulding, K. (1964b). The evolutionary potential of Quakerism. *Pamphlet 136*. Wallingford, PA: Pendle Hill Publications.

Boulding, K. (1965). The difficult art of doing good. *Colorado Quarterly, 13(3)*, 197-211.

Boulding, K. (1966a). *The impact of the social sciences*. New Brunswick, NJ: Rutgers University Press.

Boulding, K. (1966b). The economics of the coming spaceship earth. In H. Jarrett (Ed.), *Environmental quality in a growing economy, essays for the sixth RFF forum* (pp. 3-14). Baltimore, MD: Johns Hopkins Press, for Resources for the Future.

Boulding, K. 1968. *Beyond economics: essays on society, religion and ethics.* Ann Arbor, MI: University of Michigan Press.

Boulding, K. (1969). Economics as a moral science. *American Economic Review, 59(1),*1-12.

Boulding, K. (1970a). *A primer on social dynamics: History as dialectics and development.* New York: The Free Press/Macmillan.

Boulding, K. (1970b). *Economics as a science.* New York: McGraw-Hill.

Boulding, K. (1970c). *The prospering of truth: Swarthmore lecture 1970.* London: Friends

Home Service Committee.

Boulding, K. (1971-1985). *Collected papers. Vol. I Economics (1971, 492 p.), Vol. II Economics (1971, 510 p.), Vol. III Political economy (1973, 614 p.), Vol. IV Toward a general social science (1974, 623 p.), Vol. V International systems: Peace, conflict resolution, and politics (1975, 428 p.), Vol. VI Toward the twenty-first century: Political economy, social systems and world peace (1985, 695 p.).* Boulder, CO: Colorado Associated University Press. First two volumes edited by F.R. Glahe, and last four by L.D. Singel.

Boulding, K. (1973). *The economy of love and fear: A preface to grants economics.* Belmont, CA: Wadsworth.

Boulding, K. (1975). *Sonnets from the interior life and other autobiographical verse.* Boulder, CO: Associated University Press. [Collects poetry written between 1930 and 1974].

Boulding, K. (1977a). *Stable peace.* Austin: University of Texas Press

Boulding, K. (1977b). Twelve friendly quarrels with Johan Galtung. *Journal of Peace Research, 14(1),* 75-86.

Boulding, K. (1978). *Ecodynamics: A new theory of societal evolution.* Beverley Hills, CA: Sage.

Boulding, K. (1981a). *A preface to grants economics: The economy of love and fear.* New York: Praeger.

Boulding, K. (1981b). *Evolutionary economics.* Beverley Hills, CA: Sage.

Boulding, K. (1981c). Defending whom from what? *Technology Review, 83(7),* 6-7.

Boulding, K. (Ed.) (1984). *The economics of human betterment.* London: Macmillan

Boulding, K. (1985a). *The world as a total system,* Newbury Park, CA, Sage Publications.

Boulding, K. (1985b). *Human betterment*. Beverley Hills, CA: Sage.

Boulding, K. (1986a). What went wrong with economics? *The American Economist*, *30 (1)*, 5-12.

Boulding, K. (1986b). Mending the world: Quaker insights on the social order. *Pamphlet 266*. Wallingford, PA: Pendle Hill Publications.

Boulding, K. (1988). On power. In J. Nichols (Ed.), *Conference on Quaker Studies on Human Betterment*. Swarthmore, PA: Swarthmore College, pp. 117-129.

Boulding, K. (1989). A biographical autobiography. *Banca Nazionale del Lavoro*, 171, 365-393.

Boulding, K. (1990a). *Sonnets on courtship, marriage and family*, 2nd Edition. Bloomington, IN: Peaceable Press.

Boulding, K. (1990b). *The three faces of power*. Newbury Park, CA: Sage.

Boulding, K. (1992). From chemistry to economics and beyond. In M. Szenberg (Ed.), *Eminent economists: Their life philosophies*. Cambridge: Cambridge University Press, pp. 69-83.

Boulding, K. (1993). *The structure of a modern economy: The United States, 1929-1989*. New York: New York University Press.

Boulding, K. (1994). *Sonnets from Later Life 1981-1993*. Wallingford, PA: Pendle Hill Press.

Boulding, K. 2004. The Practice of the love of God. *Pamphlet 374*. Wallingford, PA: Pendle Hill Publications. [Republication of Kenneth's 1942 William Penn Lecture].

Boulding, K., Boulding, Elise, and Burgess, Guy (1980). *The social system of the planet earth*. Reading, MA: Addison-Wesley.

Brinton, H. 1943. Guide to Quaker practice. *Pamphlet 20*. Wallingford, PA: Pendle Hill Publications.

Bronfenbrenner, M. 1988. Review of *Human betterment* by Kenneth E. Boulding. *Economic Development and Cultural Change, 36(4)*, 834-835.

Dolfsma, W. & S. Kesting (Eds.) (2013). *Interdisciplinary economics: Kenneth E. Boulding's engagement in the sciences*. New York: Routledge.

Galtung, J. (1987). Review essay: Only one quarrel with Kenneth Boulding. *Journal of Peace Research, 24(2)*, 199-203.

Garnet, Jr., R. F. (2007). Philanthropy, economy and human betterment: A conversation with Kenneth Boulding. *Conversations in Philanthropy, IV*, 13-35.

Graham, J. W. (1922). *Conscription and conscience: A history, 1916-1919*. G. Allen & Unwin.

Kenworthy, L.S. (1987). *Friends face the world: Some continuing and current Quaker concerns.* Philadelphia: Friends General Conference.

Kerman, C. (1974). *Creative tension: The life and thought of Kenneth Boulding.* Ann Arbor, MI: University of Michigan Press.

Lasersohn, P. (2010). Four or five testimonies. *Quaker Historical Lexicon*, 20th of 3rd Mo. A blog on historical changes in distinctive Quaker vocabulary, accessed on August 8, 2017: https://quakerlexicon.wordpress.com/2010/03/20/four-or-five-testimonies/

Marsden, G.M. (Ed.) (1992). *The secularization of the academy.* New York: Oxford University Press.

Morrison, M.L. (2005). *Elise Boulding: A life in the cause of peace.* Jefferson, NC: McFarland & Co.

Morrison, M.L. (2017). Elise Boulding: A life in the cause of peace. In Boulding, J.R. (2017a, pp. 3-7).

Morrison, M.L. and I. Harris (Eds.) (2012). Special Issue: Elise Boulding: Her life and work. *Journal of Peace Education. 9(2)*, 111-200.

Mott, T. (1992). Kenneth Boulding interviewed by Tracy Mott 28-29 March 1991. *Review of Political Economy*, 4(3), 341-374.

Pfaff, M. (1976). A tribute to Kenneth E. Boulding: A personal dedication. In: M. Pfaff (Ed.), *Frontiers in social thought: Essays in honor of Kenneth E. Boulding* (pp. 3-11). New York: North-Holland Publishing.

Scott, R. (2015). *Kenneth Boulding: A voice crying in the wilderness.* London, UK: Palgrave Macmillan.

Wilson, V.L. (Compiler). (1985). *Bibliography of published works by Kenneth E. Boulding.* Boulder, CO: Colorado Associated University Press.

Wright, R.. (1988). *Three scientists and their gods: Looking for meaning in an age of information.* New York: Harper & Row.

# Discussion Questions

1. In his Backhouse Lecture, Boulding defined evolutionary potential as the power of mutation (whether through natural selection or human intervention) to overcome the entropy of the status quo. How does the "quest for right relationship" and "continuing revelation" combine to create what Boulding described as the evolutionary potential of Quakerism? In what ways was that potential made manifest in the writings of Bellers, Woolman, Mott and Kenneth and Elise Boulding?

2. Do you agree with Bellers that wars—even those fought over fundamental controversies—fail to pass a social cost-benefit test? His vision for a European State called for members of the proposed European parliament to focus on their common commitment to the Christian faith. Create a list of contemporary, universally-held principles that could be the basis for resolving conflicts in international bodies such as the United Nations.

3. Many of Bellers' proposals widely adopted today—such as national healthcare systems, vocational training for prisoners, and organizations for international cooperation—were seen as total fantasy by the conventional wisdom of the day. What contemporary utopian visions do you expect to become concrete reality over the next couple of centuries?

4. What do you see as universal in the prophetic visions offered by Bellers, Woolman, Mott and the Bouldings? To what extent were those visions determined by circumstances of vocation, family, and community?

5. Pick one or two of the causes championed by one of the Quakers featured in this section of the book and discuss how their advocacy was based on the goal to align the moral compass of the polity against injustice.

6. Pick one of the Friends featured in this section and identify an inconsistency between their grand vision and individual life choices. What are we to make of that inconsistency?

7. Refer back to Gray Cox's discussion of the application of Quaker approaches to scholarly research. Link that discussion to the ways the Quakers featured in this section practiced the scholarship that led to their public advocacy.

# Index

## A

| | |
|---|---|
| Abolitionist | 305, 318, 322, 328-335, 338-339 |
| African National Congress | 235, 242 |
| American Civil Liberties Union (ACLU) | 128, 348 |
| American Friends Service Committee (AFSC) | 3-5, 28, 32, 67, 120-121, 123-129, 131-139, 146, 164, 170, 173, 177, 180, 235-250, 252-253, 260 |
| Anthony, Susan B. | 333-334, 339 |
| Anti-personnel Mine Ban Treaty | 171, 174 |
| Apartheid | 5, 235-239, 241-243, 247, 250-251, 253 |
| Arthurdale | 130-136 |
| Augustine, Saint | 37, 42-43, 45-46, 49 |

## B

| | |
|---|---|
| Bailey, Lloyd | 203 |
| Barclay Bank | 17, 24, 92 |
| Barclay, Robert | 268 |
| Barritt, Denis | 192, 201 |
| Barton, William E. | 193 |
| Bellers, John | 5-7, 19-20, 25, 28, 34, 51, 107, 263, 265-281, 373 |
| Birchard, Bruce | 203 |
| Birmingham, Maisie | 189-191, 193 |
| Birmingham, Walter | 189-191, 193 |
| Blatchly, Cornelius C. | 214, 219-227 |
| Booth, Charles | 26-27 |
| Boulding, Elise | 5, 7, 344-350, 354-365, 373 |
| Boulding, Kenneth | 5, 6-7, 30-31, 34, 71, 250, 263-265, 278, 281, 299-300, 344-354, 356-365, 373 |
| Boulding, Russell | 7, 346, 349, 353, 359, 362, 363 |
| Bretton Woods Institutions | 180-181 |
| Brinton, Howard | 360 |
| Brueggemann, Walter | 208 |
| Buber, Martin | 86 |
| Business in the Community | 105, 110 |

## C

| | |
|---|---|
| Cadbury, Adrian | 100 |
| Cadbury Chocolate | 24, 100 |
| Cadbury Families | 97 |

Cadbury, Richard — 97
Cardoso, Raymond — 244, 246-247
Chalmers, Thomas — 21
China — 18, 3, 65, 74, 283,
Church of England — 12, 14, 274
Churchill, Winston — 26-27
Clapp, Elsie Ripley — 121, 132-133, 135-136
Clinton, Bill — 163-165
Coffin, Thomas — 322-323
Commission to End All forms
    of Discrimination Against Women — 171
Cope, Alfred Haines — 202

# D

Davis, Alice O. — 121, 127, 129, 133, 137
Denmark — 2, 55, 56, 64, 66-67, 185
Dreiser Committee — 128

# E

Earlham College — 126-127, 190, 206
Earth Quaker Action Team (EQAT) — 32, 68
Edmundson, William — 318
Elliot, Rosemary — 240, 244-245, 249, 252-253
Engels, Friedrich — 19-20
Evers, Medgar — 148, 158

# F

Fabians (Society) — 282, 284, 292-297, 301
Faulkner, Carol — 338
Ferris, Benjamin — 215-216, 226-227
Fourth World Conference of Friends
    (Guilford; 1967) — 29, 189, 191, 197, 201, 204-205, 208
Fox, George — 85, 93-94, 265-267, 276, 280, 318, 360
Franklin, Benjamin — 285
Friends Committee on National
    Legislation (FCNL) — 3-4, 28, 37-38, 144-151, 153-166, 194, 196, 212
Friends General Conference — 194, 214
Friends World Conference,
    (Philadelphia; 1920) — 346
Friends World Committee on Consultation — 3, 29, 169-170, 189-194, 196-205, 235, 237-241, 243-244, 247, 253
Fry, Joseph — 18

# G

Gandhi, Mahatma (Gandhian)       72-74, 76-77, 80, 82-87, 287, 291, 295, 298, 337

Garrison, William Lloyd (Garrisonian)    326, 328-330, 338

Geneva Declaration on Armed Violence
    and Development       178

Geneva Forum       175

Gibbons, William       215-217, 224, 226-228

Gingrich, Newt       163-164

Goslee, Cindi       206

Grundtvig, Bishop N.F.S.       57

Guilford College       29, 154, 189

Gurney Bank       17

Gurney, Joseph John       14, 21

# H

Haines, Jennifer       199, 203

Hamer, Fannie Lou       148

Hanh, Thich Nhat       47-49

Haughton, Joseph       193

Height, Dorothy       148

Helmuth, Keith       5-6, 71

Hicks, Edward       362

Hicks, Elias       215-216, 218-222, 323-324, 328

Hicksite (Friends)       4, 23, 32, 214-221, 223-228, 327-328

Hilles, Eli       227

Hobbs, Mary Mendenhall       122

Hoover, Herbert       30-31, 124, 128

# I

Iceland       2, 55-56, 58-59, 65

International Action Network on
    Small Arms (IANSA)       175

International Monetary Fund (IMF)       59, 180-181

International Women's Conferences       171

# J

Jackman, David       173-176

Johnson, Lyndon B.       26

Johnson, Phebe       225-228

Jones, Rufus       24, 122, 124

# K

Kelly, Thomas                           2, 37-43, 45-46, 49, 123
Kennedy, John F.                        158
Kennedy, Robert F.                      148, 158
King, Jr., Martin Luther                39-40, 51, 92-93, 144, 148, 158, 283, 337, 339
Kreager, Roland                         200, 203, 205-207
Kurz, Demie                             203

# L

Lacey, Paul                             287
Lakey, George                           2, 31-32, 54, 65, 67
Lamb's War                              11-12
Lay, Benjamin                           306-307, 311, 318-319
League of Nations                       273, 349, 356
Lewis, John                             148
Lloyds Bank                             92, 117
London Yearly Meeting                   19, 23, 32, 124, 193, 203, 220, 240

# M

Malcolm X                               148, 158
Malthus, Thomas Robert                  21-22
Manchester Conference                   23, 25
Mandela, Nelson                         235, 242, 253
Marx, Karl (Marxist)                    19-20, 57, 123-124, 243, 268, 270, 279
McAteer, Davitt                         138
Mill, John Stuart                       21, 214, 293
Mohonk Mountain House                   183
Monterrey Consensus (on Financing for
    Development)                        179-180, 184-185
Morris, Homer                           121, 123, 126-128, 130-133
Mott, James                             323-324, 327, 329, 336
Mott, Lucretia                          5, 7, 68, 228, 322-327, 329-331, 334-340, 373
Mott, Lydia                             228
Mount Holly                             225, 305-309, 317
Movement for Black Lives                67, 69
Muste, A. J.                            30, 51
Myrdal, Gunnar                          57, 63, 66, 344

# N

National Industrial Recovery Act        130, 134, 137
Nehru, Jawaharlal                       295-296, 301

| | |
|---|---|
| Nixon, Richard | 19, 158, 163, 164 |
| Non-violence | 39, 77, 173, 235, 237-241, 243, 247-248, 361 |
| Nonviolence | 54, 77-78, 237-239, 248, 251, 253, 261, 301, 327, 338, 359, 361 |
| Nonviolent Peaceforce | 78 |
| Norway | 2, 55-58, 60, 63-66, 347-348 |

## O

| | |
|---|---|
| Obama, Barack | 54, 339 |
| Orshansky, Mollie | 26 |
| Orthodox (Friends) | 23, 32, 57, 135, 215-216, 218, 224-226, 327-328, 331 |
| Owen, Robert | 107, 216-218, 221-225, 227-228, 261, 277-280 |

## P

| | |
|---|---|
| Papunhank | 313, 315 |
| Parks, Rosa | 148 |
| Peckham, Errol | 123, 129 |
| Pendle Hill | 30, 71, 130, 154, 344 |
| Penn, William | 19, 67, 267-268, 273, 285, 325 |
| Pentagon | 161 |
| Philadelphia Female Anti-Slavery Society (PFASS) | 329, 335 |
| Philadelphia Yearly Meeting | 23, 198, 216, 226, 284, 286, 288, 314, 328 |
| Pickett, Clarence | 120-121, 123-125, 127-134, 136, 138 |
| Powelson, Jack | 31 |
| Puritan | 13, 285 |
| Purdy, Alexander | 123 |

## Q

| | |
|---|---|
| Quaker Council for European Affairs | 170 |
| Quaker Earthcare Witness | 300 |
| Quaker Hill | 154 |
| Quaker Institute for the Future (QIF) | 2, 28, 29-30, 71-72, 353 |
| Quaker Knoll Camp | 205 |
| Quaker United Nations Office (QUNO) | 3-4, 28, 168, 169-186, 196, 212 |

## R

| | |
|---|---|
| Ransome, Robert | 18 |
| Rauschenbush, Walter | 123 |
| Reagan, Ronald | 78, 155, 158, 161, 163 |

Richardson, Betty                                   201
Richmond Conference                                 23, 25
Richmond Declaration                                23
Right Sharing for World Resources (RSWR)            4, 29, 189-190, 198-206, 212
Roosevelt, Eleanor                                  121, 129-130, 132-133, 135-136
Roosevelt, Franklin D.                              30, 125, 130, 135
Ross, David                                         59
Rowntree Families                                   97
Rowntree, Joseph                                    97
Rowntree, Seebohm                                   19, 25-28, 34, 208
Russell, Elbert                                     122
Rustin, Bayard                                      68, 148

## S

Satyagraha                                          72-76-79, 80-82, 85
Scotts Run                                          126, 129, 131-132, 136
Sein, Heberto                                       201
Seneca Falls Convention                             332, 334
Sexton, John                                        194, 198-199
Small Arms Survey                                   177
Snarr, Michael                                      37
Snarr, Neil                                         37
Stanton, Elizabeth Cady                             330, 332-334, 339
Steere, Douglas                                     37, 48-49, 190, 192
Stillwell, Jacqueline                               207
South Africa                                        5, 77, 171, 235-253, 261
Subsistence Homestead Division                      130
Sweden                                              2, 55-58, 64-66, 197, 199

## T

Testimonies (Friends)                              2, 4, 42, 54, 69, 72, 95, 110, 146, 170, 180,
                                                   186, 195, 203, 284, 301, 325, 338, 353,
                                                   354, 359-360, 365
Thomas, Norman                                      123-124
Toleration Act                                      14, 27

## U

United Nations                                      3-4, 105, 147, 168-177, 181-186, 196, 199,
                                                   202, 273, 363, 373
United Nations Development Programme
    (UNDP)                                          178
United Nations Earth Summit                         185
United Nations General Assembly                     3, 170, 173, 181, 184
United Nations Global Compact                       105, 110, 184

United Nations Sustainable Development
   Goals                     171

# V

Van der Merwe           236, 240-242, 244-253
Vietnam                31, 33, 191-192, 236, 239, 247, 283,
                           349, 358

# W

Wallace, Henry         132
Warner, Bernard A.     127
Webb, Beatrice         293, 296
Webb, Benjamin       214-217, 224-228, 261
Webb, Sydney         293, 296, 299
Webbs (The)           293-295, 297
Weber, Max             15
Wencke, Winifred Waye  127
White, Gilbert          202
William Penn House    194
Willoughby, George     203
Wilmington College     37
Wilmington (Delaware) Friends  215-216, 224, 226-228
Wilson, Milburn L.    130, 132
Wilson, Rick           138
Wilson, Roger         41-43, 49, 51
Woman Sufferage      332-339
Woolman, John        5-6, 20, 25, 44-45, 47, 49, 51, 94, 122, 180,
                         283-294, 296-301, 304-320, 328, 362, 373
Woolman, Sarah        305, 316
Workingmen's movement  214, 216-218, 222, 224
World Conference of Friends
    (London; 1920)      124
World Trade Organization   171
World War I           27, 120-121, 126, 345-346, 348
World War II          32, 129, 131, 133-134, 136, 147, 152, 295
Wright, Frances "Fanny"   216-218, 224-226, 228

89530367R00238

Made in the USA
Lexington, KY
31 May 2018